HOLOCAUST THEOLOGY: A READER

HOLOCAUST THEOLOGY
A READER

compiled and edited by

Dan Cohn-Sherbok

NEW YORK UNIVERSITY PRESS

Washington Square, New York

First published in the U.S.A. in 2002 by
NEW YORK UNIVERSITY PRESS
Washington Square
New York, NY 10003

Library of Congress Cataloging-in-Publication Data
Holocaust theology : a reader / compiled and edited by Dan Cohn-Sherbok.
    p. cm.
Includes bibliographical references and index.
ISBN 0-8147-1619-9 (alk. paper) -- ISBN 0-8147-1620-2 (pbk. : alk. paper)
1. Holocaust (Jewish theology) 2. Holocaust (Christian theology) I. Cohn-Sherbok,
Dan.

BM645.H6 H69 2002   2001052103
296.3'1174--dc21

Typeset in Monotype Bembo by XL Publishing Services, Tiverton
Printed and bound in Great Britain by Antony Rowe Ltd, Chippenham

For Lavinia

Contents

Chapter Outline	ix
Glossary	xiv
Introduction	1
The Holocaust: Historical Background	26

THE READINGS

Part I: The Challenge **39**

1 The Religious Challenge of the Holocaust 41

Part II: Faith in the Death Camps **71**

2 Religious Faith 73
3 The Holocaust and Divine Providence 93
4 The Holocaust and Mystery 106
5 Faithfulness and Suffering 112

Part III: Wrestling with the Holocaust **123**

6 The Suffering of God 127
7 Human Free Will 153
8 The Holocaust and Christian Faith 170
9 The Holocaust and the Kingdom 178
10 The Holocaust and Covenant 186
11 The Holocaust and Human Evil 192
12 The Holocaust and Jewish Survival 216
13 Reconstructing Judaism 237

Part IV: Jews, Christians and the Holocaust   **271**

14 The Holocaust and Christian Responsibility   273
15 Re-evaluating Christian Theology   313
16 Jewish-Christian Dialogue   355

Epilogue: The Future of Holocaust Theology   383

Bibliography   389
Acknowledgements   399
Index of Authors   401
General Index   405

Chapter Outline

Introduction	**1**
The Holocaust: Historical Background	**26**

PART I: THE CHALLENGE

CHAPTER 1 The Religious Challenge of the Holocaust	**41**
Richard Rubenstein: The Death of God	41
Elie Wiesel: The Holocaust and Religious Protest	43
David H. Hirsch: The Holocaust and Camp Songs	47
Alexander Donat: The Holocaust and Human Perplexity	50
Sherwin Wine: The Rejection of God	52
Michael Oppenheim: The Holocaust and Religious Langauge	55
Steven T. Katz: The Uniqueness of the Holocaust	58
Jakob Jocz: Judaism after the Holocaust	61
Harry James Cargas: The Holocaust and Christian Responsibility	64
John Roth: The Holocaust and Religious Perplexity	67

PART II: FAITH IN THE DEATH CAMPS

CHAPTER 2 Religious Faith	**73**
Yaffa Eliach: Faith among the Hasidim	73
Pesach Schindler: Hasidim and the Holocaust	75
Zvi Kolitz: Faith in the Ghetto	78
Leo Baeck: The Holocaust and Faithfulness	80
Nissim Nadav: The Holocaust and Jewish Heroism	83
Dror Schwartz: The Holocaust and Sanctification of Life	86
Irving Greenberg: The Dialectic of Faith	89

CHAPTER 3   The Holocaust and Divine Providence   **93**
Bernard Maza: The Holocaust and the Torah   93
Ignaz Maybaum: The Holocaust and Modernity   96
Sha'ar Yashuv Cohen: The Holocaust and the Messiah   98
Hayyim Kanfo: The Holocaust and Redemption   101
Yosef Roth: The Holocaust and Providence   103

CHAPTER 4   The Holocaust and Mystery   **106**
David Ariel: Divine Mystery   106
Neil Gillman: The Holocaust and Transcendence   109

CHAPTER 5   Faithfulness and Suffering   **112**
Irving Rosenbaum: The Holocaust and Law   112
Norman Solomon: The Holocaust and the Jewish Tradition   115
David Patterson: The Holocaust and Recovery   117
Ulrich Simon: The Holocaust and Sacrifice   120

PART III: WRESTLING WITH THE HOLOCAUST

CHAPTER 6   The Suffering of God   **127**
Paul Fiddes: The Holocaust and Divine Suffering   127
Dorothee Sölle: Divine Pain   129
Marcus Braybrooke: Suffering Love   132
Colin Eimer: Jewish and Christian Suffering   135
Hans Jonas: God after Auschwitz   138
Franklin Sherman: Theodicy and Suffering   140
Marcel Jacques Dubois: The Holocaust and the Cross   144
David Tracy: Theology of Suspicion   147
Kalonymus Kalman Shapira: The Holocaust and
   Divine Suffering   150

CHAPTER 7   Human Free Will   **153**
Eliezer Berkovits: The Holocaust and Human Free Will   153
Jonathan Sacks: Evil, Free Will and Jewish History   157
André Neher: The Holocaust and Human Free Will   160
David Birnbaum: The Holocaust and Freedom   162
Didier Pollefyt: The Holocaust and Evil   166

CHAPTER 8   The Holocaust and Christian Faith   **170**
Graham Keith: The Holocaust and Jewish Christianity   170
Hugh Montefiore: The Holocaust and the Cross   173
David Stern: The Holocaust and Evangelism   176

CHAPTER 9   The Holocaust and the Kingdom   **178**
Richard Harries: The Holocaust and the Kingdom of God   178
Seymour Siegel: The Holocaust and Messianism   180
Dan Cohn-Sherbok: The Holocaust and the Hereafter   183

CHAPTER 10   The Holocaust and Covenant   **186**
Eugene Borowitz: Covenant and Holocaust   186
David Weiss: Holocaust and Covenant   189

CHAPTER 11   The Holocaust and Human Evil   **192**
Alan T. Davies: Overcoming Nihilism   192
Paul van Buren: Auschwitz and Moral Responsibility   195
Immanuel Jakobovits: The Holocaust and Human Responsibility 198
Jack Bemporad: The Holocaust and Human Nature   199
Abraham Joshua Heschel: The Holocaust and Sin   202
Allan R. Brockway: Religion and Faith   204
Nicholas de Lange: The Holocaust and Human Sin   206
Julio de Santa Ana: The Holocaust and Liberation   209
Marc Ellis: The Holocaust and Atrocity   212

CHAPTER 12   The Holocaust and Jewish Survival   **216**
Robert Weltsch: Zionism and Jewish Survival   216
Emil Fackenheim: The Holocaust and the Commanding Voice   218
Lionel Rubinoff: The Holocaust and God's Presence   221
Byron Sherwin: Jewish Survival and the Holocaust   223
Michael Goldberg: The Holocaust and Survival   225
Roberta Strauss Feuerlicht: The Holocaust and Israel   229
Primo Levi: The Holocaust, the Doomed and the Saved   232
Jacob Neusner: The Holocaust and Redemption   234

CHAPTER 13   Reconstructing Judaism   **237**
Oliver Leaman: The Holocaust and Evil   237
David Blumenthal: Theology and Protest   240

Arthur A. Cohen: A Detached God   242
Melissa Raphael: The Holocaust and Jewish Feminism   245
Susan Shapiro: The Holocaust and Negation   248
Harold Schulweis: The Holocaust and Evil   251
Zachary Braiterman: Jewish Thought after Auschwitz   254
Steven Jacobs: The Holocaust and Jewish Faith   256
Edward Feld: The Holocaust and Spirituality   260
Eliezer Schweid: The Holocaust and Jewish Thought   263
Robert Reeve Brenner: Holocaust Survivors and Religious
    Belief   265

PART IV: JEWS, CHRISTIANS AND THE HOLOCAUST

CHAPTER 14   The Holocaust and Christian Responsibility

**CHAPTER 14   The Holocaust and Christian
    Responsibility**   **273**
David A. Rausch: The Holocaust and the Church   273
Rolf Hochhuth: The Holocaust and Christian Indifference   276
Susannah Heschel: The Holocaust and German Theology   280
Michael D. Ryan: The Theology of Adolf Hitler   282
Ben Zion Bokser: Christianity and the Nazis   286
Eberhard Bethge: The Church Struggle   288
Leonore Siegele-Wenschkewitz: The Holocaust and Christian
    Anti-Judaism   291
Edward Flannery: The Holocaust and Christian Anti-Semitism   294
Gordon C. Zahn: Catholic Resistance   297
Michael Marrus: The Holocaust and Catholicism   300
Hyam Maccoby: The Holocaust and Anti-Semitism   303
Franklin H. Littell: The Holocaust and Church Struggle   306
Stephen T. Davis: The Holocaust and Christian Evangelicals   309

CHAPTER 15   Re-evaluating Christian Theology   **313**
Rosemary Radford Ruether: Reinterpreting Christology   313
John Pawlikowski: The Holocaust and Christology   316
Gregory Baum: Reinterpreting Christianity   319
Mary Knutsen: The Holocaust and Truth   322
Michael McGarry: The Holocaust and Christology   326
Paul Tillich: Jewish History and the Holocaust   329

Stephen R. Haynes: Post-Holocaust Christian Theology 332
Alice Eckardt: Theology of the Holocaust 335
Roy Eckardt: The Holocaust and Christian Spirituality 338
Clark Williamson: Christian Theology and the Shoah 341
James F. Moore: Christianity after Auschwitz 344
Yosef Hayim Yerushalmi: Christianity and Nazi Anti-Semitism 347
Thomas J.J. Altizer: The Holocaust and God's Absence 350
William Hamilton: The Holocaust and Radical Theology 352

CHAPTER 16   Jewish–Christian Dialogue **355**
Edward Kessler: The Holocaust and Jewish–Christian Dialogue 355
Katharine T. Hargrove: Contemporary Holocaust Theology 358
Isabel Wollaston: Christian Theology and the Holocaust 362
Randall Falk: The Holocaust, Jews and Christians 364
Walter Harrelson: The Holocaust and the Modern World 367
Johann Baptist Metz: Jews and Christians after the Holocaust 369
Frank Longford: The Holocaust and Forgiveness 372
Albert Friedlander: The Holocaust and Jewish–Christian
    Dialogue 376
Eugene Fisher: Catholics and Jews 379

Epilogue: The Future of Holocaust Theology **383**

Glossary

Adversus Judaeos	Anti-Jewish
Amoraim	Jewish scholars of the third to sixth century CE
Ani Maamin	Prayer of Affirmation of Belief
Bat Kol	Voice From Heaven
Bet Din	Rabbinic Court
Bimah	Platform for the Reading Desk
Chalutzim	Pioneers in Israel
Churban	Act of destruction
Conservative Judaism	Modernist, non-Orthodox traditional approach to Judaism
Devekut	Cleaving to God
Einsatzgrüppen	Mobile killing squads
El Mistater	The Hiding of God
En Sof	Infinite
Eretz Yisrael	Land of Israel
Galut	Diaspora
Gestapo	Secret Police
Haggadah	Passover Prayer Book
Halakhah	Jewish law
Hanukkah	Festival of Light
Hasidism	Pietistic religious movement founded by the Baal Shem Tov
Haskalah	Jewish Enlightenment
Hester Panim	Hiding of God's Presence
Hillul ha-Shem	Desecration of the Divine Name

Humanistic Judaism	Non-theistic branch of Judaism
Humash	Five Books of Moses
Huppah	Marriage Canopy
Kabbalah	Jewish Mysticism
Kaddish	Prayer for the Dead
Kelal Yisrael	Community of Israel
Kiddush ha-Hayyim	Sanctification of Life
Kiddush ha-Shem	Martyrdom
Kinot	Elegiac Prayers
Kittel	White Robe
Kol Nidre	Evening Service of Yom Kippur
Kristallnacht	Night of Broken Glass
Messianic Judaism	Jews who subscribe to a belief in Jesus and wish to observe Judaism
Midrash	Commentary on Scripture
Minyan	Ten Men
Mishnah	Early Rabbinic Collection of Law
Mitzvot	Commandments
Mussulmaner	Living Dead
Orthodox Judaism	Traditionalist form of Judaism
Passover	Festival Commemorating the Exodus
Purim	Feast of Esther
Rebbe	Leader of hasidic sect
Reform Judaism	Modern progressive movement
Rosh Hashanah	New Year's Day
Seder	Passover evening meal
Shekhinah	Divine Presence
Shoah	Holocaust
Shofar	Ram's Horn
Siddur	Prayer Book
Simhat Torah	Rejoicing of the Law
Tahanun	Supplication
Tallit	Prayer Shawl

Talmud	Records of discussions of Jewish law from the second to the fifth century
Tefillin	Phylacteries
Tehilim	Psalms
Teshuvah	Repentance
Tikkun	Divine Repair
Tishah B'Av	Ninth of Av
Torah	Five Books of Moses
Yeshivah	Rabbinical Academy
Yom ha-Atzmaut	Israel Independence Day
Yom ha-Shoah	Holocaust Day
Yom Kippur	Day of Atonement
Yom Yerushalayim	Jerusalem Day
Zaddik	Righteous individual; also *Rebbe*

Introduction

Several years ago I wrote a study of contemporary Jewish Holocaust thinkers entitled *Holocaust Theology*. This work discussed the views of eight major thinkers who in different ways have wrestled with the religious problems presented by the Holocaust: Bernard Maza, Ignaz Maybaum, Emil Fackenheim, Eliezer Berkovits, Arthur A. Cohen, Richard Rubenstein, Elie Wiesel and Marc Ellis. Throughout this book I attempted to demonstrate that all these attempts to come to terms with the Holocaust suffer from numerous defects. In the bibliography I listed the major works published by these writers as well as other books and articles dealing with the Holocaust. Subsequently, this study was republished as *God and the Holocaust*, and the bibliography was expanded to include important works by a range of Christian thinkers.

Increasingly I came to see that there is a need for a more comprehensive introduction to both Jewish and Christian writers who have discussed the religious issues connected with the Nazi onslaught against the Jews. Although there is a wide range of single works as well as collections of essays dealing with this subject, there is no single volume which contains readings which survey these varieties of responses. This book is thus designed to provide a panoramic survey of Holocaust theology—throughout I have selected representative passages from over one hundred important Jewish and Christian thinkers. While this study is not exhaustive, it nonetheless aims to offer a representative sample of material drawn from over fifty years of religious reflection. After each reading I have included several questions to stimulate discussion and debate.

The Challenge

The book begins in Part I with an exploration of the religious challenge posed by the Holocaust. The first reading is from *After Auschwitz*

1

published in the 1960s by the Jewish scholar Richard Rubenstein. In this controversial work he argues that the most important issue for the Jewish community arises out of the question of God and the destruction of six million Jews at the hands of the Nazis. According to Rubenstein, it is no longer possible to believe in a supernatural Deity who acts in history. Rather, the Holocaust has demonstrated that such a belief has no foundation. Jews today, he contends, live in the time of the death of God.

Such disenchantment permeates the writings of the Jewish novelist Elie Wiesel. In his autobiographical novel *Night*, Wiesel describes his despair in the camps. As he explains, religious doubt set in as he experienced the horrors of the Nazi regime. Describing scenes of terror, he portrays the evolution of his religious protest. Such rebellion was heightened during the High Holy Days. Unable to pray, Wiesel became the accuser. On the Day of Atonement, he refused to fast. He no longer accepted God's silence in the face of suffering and murder.

In the camps themselves, Jews were frequently overwhelmed with despair. In 'Camp Music and Camp Songs', the Jewish scholar David H. Hirsch discusses the collection of songs recorded by Aleksander Kulisiewicz. In a song composed anonymously, Birkenau is compared to Hell. It is an evil kingdom without God. There crematoria consume human carcasses; it is the journey's end. All will become ashes. An accursed place devoid of God's presence, Birkenau is a thorny path where millions of victims are buried in a common grave.

Such despair is reflected by the survivor Alexander Donat in 'The Holocaust Kingdom'. Here Donat describes the terrors of the siege of the Warsaw ghetto. As news of the deportations spread, the inhabitants of the ghetto became aware of their eventual destination. Amidst suffering and death, they questioned why they had been abandoned by both God and fellow human beings. Why had they been singled out to die in the most grotesque way? They waited for deliverance, but to no end.

In *Judaism Beyond God*, the founder of Humanistic Judaism Sherwin Wine argues that Jews today must abandon their belief in a supernatural Deity. In his opinion, all theistic interpretations of God's involvement in history should be replaced by a naturalistic perspective. The world of reason has revealed that it has been a mistake for Jews to expect God to save them from diaster. Hence, there can be no adequate theological solution to the problem of human suffering.

According to the Jewish scholar Michael Oppenheim, it is still possible to use religious language in a post-Holocaust world. Such a recognition of a transcendent dimension to Jewish life is recognized by both Jewish thinkers and the community as a whole. Such religious commemorations as *Yom Ha-Shoah* (Holocaust Day), *Yom Ha-Atzmaut* (Israel Independence Day) and *Yom Yerushalayim* (Jerusalem Day) symbolically express such commitment. Yet in Oppenheim's view, Jews must grapple with the religious perplexities raised by the horrors of the Nazi era.

The Jewish scholar Steven T. Katz similarly stresses the importance of further theological exploration of the Holocaust. In his view, the Nazi assault against the Jewish nation was a unique event in human history. Killing Jews, he argues, is not a new phenomenon; however, the Nazi quest to eliminate Jews was singularly different from any previous form of evil. Reviewing the theologies of a number of major Holocaust theologians, Katz stresses that the events of the Nazi era are amenable to a variety of interpretations. However, this does not mean that such theological investigations are pointless; rather, there remains enormous scope for future study.

In a similar vein the Christian writer Jakob Jocz stresses that a number of Jewish theologians are currently wrestling with some of the most vexing dilemmas posed by the Holocaust. Regarding religious belief after Auschwitz, he points out that Jewish thinkers from across the religious spectrum have struggled to make sense of God's seeming absence during the Nazi era. In addition, they have been compelled to ask fundamental questions about the nature of humanity in light of the events of the Holocaust.

In *Shadows of Auschwitz: A Christian Response to the Holocaust*, the Christian scholar Harry James Cargas emphasizes that the *Shoah* (Holocaust) raises important questions for Christians. Given the legacy of Christian anti-Semitism, Christians today must acknowledge the atrocities they have unleashed upon the Jewish population. Not only should anti-Jewish attitudes be eliminated from the Christian community: Christians are obliged to reconsider some of the central tenets of their faith which have brought about Jewish suffering in the past. What is now required is a reassessment of a number of central religious beliefs.

Describing his development as a Christian thinker, John Roth stresses that theological reflection must be related to real events. In his view, if one is to understand the Holocaust, it is necessary to study the details of the Nazi era. Reckoning with particularity is not generally what philosophers do. Yet, the big questions cannot be answered without such immersion in the history of the Third Reich. This is an urgent task for both Jewish and Christian theologians.

Religious Faith

These readings set the stage for a variety of affirmations of faith in Part II. Here the Jewish scholar Yaffa Eliach in her anthology of Hasidic tales of the Holocaust witnesses to the piety of believers who faced death with confidence. As she explains, Hasidim expressed courage in ghettos, hiding places and camps. According to Eliach, religious faith sustained these individuals, providing the inner strength necessary to endure the horrors of the Nazi era. In her view, these tales of heroism can offer solace to those whose faith has been undermined by the murder of millions of innocent victims.

An example of such religious conviction is found in the Jewish scholar Pesach Schindler's study of Hasidic responses to the Holocaust. In this work Schindler depicts the faith of Hasidic Jews as they faced persecution and suffering in the concentration camps. According to Schindler, the tragedy of the Nazi onslaught gave rise to a range of reactions. Some Hasidim attempted to justify God's providential plan for the chosen people. Other thinkers related the Holocaust to the suffering prior to the coming of the Messiah. Another response focused on the sanctification of God in life in defiance of the Nazi aim to exterminate the Jewish people.

Another example of such religious conviction is expressed in the Jewish writer Zvi Kolitz's description of Yassel Rakover's last moments in the Warsaw ghetto. This fictional account symbolizes the faith of those who were confronted by death. Despite his despair over the fate of the Jewish people, Yassel Rakover remains convinced of the promise of eternal life. As the Nazis surround the ghetto, he writes his final testimony: God, he believes, will reunite him with his loved ones for all eternity.

A parallel response to the Holocaust was recorded in the Reform Jewish leader Leo Baeck's prayer which he composed during the Nazi era. Determined to stand firm against the German assault on the Jewish people, Baeck turned to God on the Day of Atonement. 'In this hour', he writes, 'all Israel stands before God, the judge and the forgiver. In his presence let us examine our ways, our deeds, and what we have failed to do. . . God has led our fathers from generation to generation.

He will guide us and our children through these days.' According to Baeck, God's ways are ultimately incomprehensible.

In 'The Lights of Faith and Heroism in the Darkness of the Holocaust', the Jewish writer Nissim Nadav acknowledges the religious challenge of the Holocaust. Nonetheless, he stresses that the faith of Jews in the camps illustrates the power of belief to overcome all obstacles. In his view, it is not possible to explain why the Holocaust occurred; the pious must simply accept the inscrutability of God's direction of the history of the Jewish nation. Unquestioning accepting of God's providence, however, does not exempt one from learning from the facts of the Holocaust. What was apparent during the Nazi era was that numerous Jews remained faithful to the tradition despite their suffering.

Such heroism is further demonstrated by the Jewish writer Dror Schwartz in 'The Heroism of Masada and the Martyrs of the Holocaust'. As he explains, Jews in the ghettos and the concentration camps were determined to survive in order to defeat the Nazis' plan of exterminating the Jewish nation. Stressing the concept of *Kiddush ha-Hayyim* (sanctification of life), he explains how the belief that one should live rather than die as a martyr became a central feature of Jewish existence. Here he cites the example of Rabbi Yitzhak Nissenbaum, who encouraged the faithful to overcome Hitler's evil designs.

In 'Cloud of Smoke, Pillar of Fire: Judaism, Christianity and Modernity after the Holocaust', the Jewish theologian Irving Greenberg emphasizes that Jews must re-examine their faith in the light of the Holocaust. Yet, he stresses that the image of Job is of central importance in attempting to make sense of this tragedy. Modern Jews, he argues, should attempt to model themselves on Job's example. Like Job, they should recognize that there are no easy pieties which explain away the perplexities posed by the Holocaust. What is important about the biblical account is that Job demonstrates that God's presence is manifest in the whirlwind and that contact with God can be restored despite suffering and death.

The Holocaust and Divine Providence

For these writers religious faith is of fundamental importance: no attempt is made to offer a theological explanation for the events of the Nazi regime. Other thinkers, however, have sought to formulate a wide range of theodicies. In the view of some theologians, the

Holocaust should be understood as part of God's providential plan for his people. In *With Fury Poured Out*, the Jewish writer Bernard Maza contends that God brought about the Holocaust in order to revive Jewish life in a post-Enlightenment world.

An alternative approach is outlined in *The Face of God after Auschwitz* by the Jewish theologian Ignaz Maybaum. In his view, the Holocaust was part of God's providential plan. According to Maybaum, it served as a means whereby the medieval institutions of Jewish life were eliminated in the Nazi onslaught against European Jewry. Hitler thus served as a divine instrument for the reconstruction of Jewish existence in the twentieth century. Jewish progress, therefore, is the direct result of this modern catastrophe.

Arguing along different lines, a number of Orthodox thinkers have attempted to make sense of the Holocaust in terms of God's aim for the Jewish nation. In '*Hester Panim* in the Holocaust versus the Manifest Miracles in our Generation', Sha'ar Yashuv Cohen maintains that it is a mistake to believe that the Holocaust is a punishment for sin. Rather, the murder of millions of Jews in the camps should be understood as part of God's plan. The suffering of Jewry, he argues, should be seen as the last phase of the birth pangs of the Messiah. Those who walked to the gas chambers singing 'I believe with perfect faith in the coming of the Messiah' were aware that they were living in the last days prior to divine deliverance.

In a similar vein Hayyim Kanfo contends in 'Manifestation of Divine Providence in the Gloom of the Holocaust' that God was present in the death camps. The horrors of the Nazi era were part of a divine process of redemption. The function of the Holocaust was to prepare the way for God's deliverance of the Jewish nation. In his opinion, the Holocaust constitutes the darkness before salvation. Out of agony and travail a new birth will take place. The Jewish people will go from destruction to national revival, from exile to redemption.

Again, Yosef Roth states in 'The Jewish Fate and the Holocaust' that the events of the Nazi period should be understood as part of the unfolding of God's providential plan for the Jewish people. Understandably a significant portion of the Jewish community were deeply troubled by the Holocaust: how, they asked, could the God of Israel allow six million victims to die in the most tragic conditions? This searching question, however, cannot be answered. God's direction of the world is unfathomable. Nonetheless, faithful Jews believe that within the hidden there are manifestations of the divine scheme.

The Holocaust and Mystery

This mysterious aspect of the Holocaust is central for other thinkers who have wrestled with the implications of the murder of millions of Jews under the Nazis. In *What Do Jews Believe?*, the Jewish writer David Ariel maintains that there is simply no way that the Holocaust can be explained. God's will is unfathomable. In this regard he refers to God's response to Job. Although we can empathize with Job's suffering, it is impossible to understand God's will. The mystery how God could have permitted the murder of millions of innocent victims remains inexplicable. Nonetheless, we must acknowledge the depth of evil perpetrated by the Nazis and ensure that such atrocities are prevented in the future.

Arguing along similar lines, the Jewish theologian Neil Gillman writes that all theodicies proposed by Jewish scholars fail to answer the problem posed by the events of the Nazi regime. After surveying a range of solutions, he affirms that there can be no resolution of the religious perplexities posed by the onslaught against European Jewry. Today we should stop trying to explain what is beyond comprehension.

Faithfulness and Suffering

Other writers, however, stress that some sense can be made of the events of the Nazi era. In the view of the Jewish scholar Irving Rosenbaum, the halakhic tradition enabled many Jews to face death in the camps. In *The Holocaust and Halakhah*, he notes that hundreds of thousands of Jews caught up in the Holocaust observed the *mitzvot*. This commitment to the legal tradition, he insists, enabled pious Jews to remain loyal to God. By observing the commandments, these individuals were able to bring some semblance of meaning and sanctity into their lives. In his estimation, the *halakhah* provided a means whereby Jews could transcend the chaos of their lives.

A parallel account of the importance of the Jewish tradition in sustaining faith is found in *Judaism and World Religion* by the Jewish scholar Norman Solomon. In his opinion, there is no need for a new Jewish theology to confront the horrors of the Nazi era. Suffering, he points out, has been a central feature of Jewish existence through the centuries. Despite persecution and murder Jews have been able to survive. Today, it is still possible to have confidence in a God who acts in history. What is required is dedication to God and his commandments.

Arguing along similar lines, the Jewish scholar David Patterson asserts in *Sun Turned to Darkness* that Jewish recovery is dependent on faithfulness to God. In a survey of Holocaust memoirs, he points out that the recovery of the Divine can sanctify human life even in the face of terror and tragedy. It is the promise of God and the divine covenant that makes recovery possible. The desire for God is without end even when God reveals himself as absence rather than presence.

Such religious dedication is echoed in the Christian theologian Ulrich Simon's discussion of the Holocaust. In *A Theology of Auschwitz*, he contends that the Holocaust was a sacrifice to God. In the light of Christ's death, the murder of millions of Jews should be perceived as an act of sacrificial offering. Many of those who died never doubted the providential nature of the Nazi onslaught. Such a heroic vision was exemplified by those martyrs who substituted themselves for others. The cross and Auschwitz thus serve as a framework for making sense of human degradation and misery.

The Suffering of God

Drawing on the theme of human suffering, other theologians have focused on the nature of divine suffering in the Holocaust. In *The Creative Suffering of God*, the Christian theologian Paul Fiddes states that the key to understanding the events of the Nazi period is to accept that God suffers with humanity. Here he presents a conception of a suffering God who empathizes with those who are victimized. In discussing the existence of evil, Fiddes contends that God freely chooses to limit himself, endure change, and experience death while remaining the living God.

Such divine pain is the topic of the Christian theologian Dorothee Sölle's treatment of the Nazi era. In 'God's Pain and Our Pain', she argues that the traditional doctrine of a benevolent and omnipotent Deity must be modified in the light of the Holocaust. In her view, it is no longer possible to accept that God possesses such attributes. Instead, we must acknowledge that God is all-loving, but not omnipotent. Hence, he suffers along with those who are victimized. God experiences our pain, and thereby consoles the afflicted.

In 'The Power of Suffering Love', the Christian theologian Marcus Braybrooke similarly affirms that the religious dilemmas posed by the

Holocaust can be resolved solely by appealing to the concept of suffering love. In his view, only a suffering God is credible in the light of the events of the Nazi era. Here the image of Jesus dying on the cross serves as the basis for understanding God's presence in the concentration camps. The cross, he maintains, discloses the nature of God and the way to life.

For the Reform Jewish writer Colin Eimer, the image of divine suffering is of similar significance. Although he is unable to accept the doctrine of the incarnation, he alleges that the Jewish tradition speaks of a God who suffers with his chosen people. As a hidden God, he suffers in silence when innocent human beings are victimized. Jewish theology therefore parallels the emphasis on divine suffering in Christian sources.

The Jewish philosopher Hans Jonas argues along similar lines in 'The Concept of God after Auschwitz'. In his opinion, the traditional concept of divine impassibility should be set aside in the post-Holocaust period. Today it should be acknowledged that God is not omnipotent. Rather, he is limited and suffers when human beings are overwhelmed by evil. In Jonas's view, God was present in the camps and suffered along with those who endured pain and death. It is a mistake to think that he was detached from the tragedies that took place during the Nazi reign of terror.

Again, the Christian theologian Franklin Sherman contends that the various solutions to the religious perplexities of the Holocaust are flawed in various ways. The Holocaust was not God's judgment upon the Jews, nor did the suffering in the camps serve some purpose. Further, it is insufficient to regard the events of the Nazi era as a mystery. Rather, it must be accepted that God participates in human suffering. Within the Christian tradition, the symbol of the agonizing God is the cross of Christ.

The same outlook is found in the Christian theologian Marcel Jacques Dubois's 'Christian Reflection on the Holocaust'. Here he discusses the piety of religious Jews in the camps. In his estimation these individuals were sustained by a belief in God's abiding presence. In the very abyss of anguish, he writes, believers turned to God in hope. Rather than being overwhelmed by despair, they found in their faith the strength to cry out to God. According to Dubois, Jews and Christians can be united in accepting the mystery of divine suffering. If we believe in Christ's victory over death, then there is hope for all. The cross of Christ is a sacrament that permeates all human existence.

For the Christian theologian David Tracy, God must be understood as the suffering Lord of history. In 'Religious Values after the Holocaust: A Catholic View', he asserts that in a post-Holocaust age Catholic theologians must be suspicious of traditional religious assumptions about God's nature and activity. In his view, God is none other than pure, unbounded love. It is human beings who inflict evil on one another—the suffering of the six million who died in the camps should thus be understood as the voice of the suffering of God.

Echoing such sentiments, the Hasidic writer Kalonymus Kalman Shapira in *The Holy Fire* maintains that God suffers on behalf of his chosen people. Jewish sacred literature, he states, affirms that when a Jew is afflicted, God suffers much more than the person concerned. God, he continues, is to be found in his inner chambers weeping; when one comes close to him, one weeps as well. Through this encounter, an individual is strengthened so that he or she can study and worship. This understanding serves as a framework for coming to terms with the horrors of the Nazi regime.

Human Free Will

An alternative approach to the Holocaust has been forged by a range of thinkers who contend that religious perplexities posed by Auschwitz can be solved by appealing to the free will argument. *In Faith after the Holocaust*, the Jewish theologian Eliezer Berkovits asserts that if God did not respect human freedom, then men and women would cease to be human. Freedom and responsibility are the preconditions of human life. Hence, the Holocaust should be understood as a manifestation of evil, a tragedy inflicted by the Germans on the Jewish people. God did not intervene because he had bestowed free will on human beings at the time of creation.

For the Jewish scholar Jonathan Sacks, the questions raised by the tragedy of the Holocaust must be faced by contemporary Jewish writers. Drawing on the writings of Eliezer Berkovits, he similarly argues that the Holocaust was the result of free choice. In his opinion, the murder of six million innocent victims illustrates that human beings are capable of the most horrendous acts. It is a mistake to blame God for this tragedy. Because human beings have been given the freedom to choose to be good, they are free also to choose evil. God does not intervene to curtail such freedom. Even though he is all-powerful, he exercises self-restraint so as not to undermine the freedom he bestowed at creation.

In 'The Exile of the Word: From the Silence of the Bible to the Silence of Auschwitz', the Jewish scholar André Neher maintains that after Auschwitz there can only be silence. The Holocaust cannot be explained. Nonetheless, the death camps illustrate the importance of human freedom. By creating human beings free, God introduced into the universe a degree of uncertainty—both angelic and bestial actions became a possibility. In this light, it is a mistake to blame God for the existence of human suffering.

Echoing this position, the Jewish scholar David Birnbaum insists in *God and Evil* that Jews must transcend their dependence on God; they must acknowledge that God allows the exercise of personal freedom. According to Birnbaum, God has granted human beings the freedom to achieve ascending levels of spiritual maturity. The Nazis, however, chose the path of radical evil.

According to the theologian Didier Pollefyt in 'Auschwitz or How Good People Can Do Evil', extraordinary conditions can drive people to hideous actions. Surveying the human suffering caused by Nazi perpetrators, he concludes that a number of factors led these individuals to commit acts of incredible barbarism. The evil of the Nazi regime can thus be explained in purely human terms.

The Holocaust and Christian Faith

In the view of other theologians, the Holocaust can be understood in terms of traditional Christian teaching. In *Hated Without a Cause*, Graham Keith argues that anti-Semitic attacks on Jews were instigated by Satan. What is now required is a concerted effort to combat demonic forces and draw the Jewish people to Christ. The Jewish people, he asserts, must be led away from unbelief to an acceptance of Jesus as the Saviour of humanity.

An alternative approach is advocated by the Christian writer Hugh Montefiore, who highlights the unique character of the Holocaust. In the past Jews were used to violence, but invariably this had a religious cause. The Nazis, however, embarked on a policy of genocide based on racial theory. In attempting to come to terms with the Nazi regime, he suggests that the pattern of life through death, which Jesus reluctantly accepted, can serve as a basis for spiritual renewal.

A similar stance is proposed by the Messianic Jewish writer David Stern in *Messianic Jewish Manifesto*. According to Stern, the Holocaust has not ruled out the need for Jews to come to Christ. Jesus, he states, is the Messianic redeemer. As such, he is the fulfilment of biblical prophecy. Only God, he continues, can make restitution for the lives that were lost in death camps. In a miraculous way, God can bring about healing through Christ. Without Christ, he claims, the Jewish people have no hope.

The Holocaust and the Kingdom

Other thinkers express their faith in God despite the events of the Holocaust in a different manner. In the view of the Christian theologian Richard Harries, there is hope beyond the grave. Such a vision, he contends, is central to Christian teaching. Only by accepting God's kingdom can one hope to make sense of the tragedies of the period of Nazi rule. If there is a loving God, he states, then his purposes cannot be limited to this life: there must be fulfilment in a future world.

In 'Response to Emil Fackenheim', the Jewish scholar Seymour Siegel connects the Holocaust to Messianic redemption. In his view, Zionism has brought about a fundamental change in Messianic belief. No longer should Jews expect the Messiah to bring about a miraculous transformation of history. In his opinion, the creation of the Jewish state should be seen as a prelude to the coming of the Messianic kingdom. The establishment of a Jewish homeland is one step in the long road toward the redemption of the world.

In *Holocaust Theology*, the Jewish theologian Dan Cohn-Sherbok connects the Holocaust to the afterlife. In his view, the belief in the hereafter offers the only solution to the religious perplexities posed by the Holocaust. In the past the Jewish people were sustained by their belief in reward in the hereafter as they faced persecution and death. Today this traditional belief should again sustain the Jewish nation as they contemplate the horrors of the Nazi era.

The Holocaust and Covenant

Adopting a different approach, other Jewish thinkers believe the Holocaust should be interpreted in terms of God's covenant with the Jewish people. In *Choices in Modern Jewish Thought*, Eugene Borowitz argues that the Jewish people stand in a covenantal relationship to God. In his view, the problem of evil can only be solved within this context. Such a view, he contends, can resolve the religious dilemmas posed by the Holocaust. Despite the murder of millions of Jews in the camps,

Jewry can be assured of God's abiding presence despite his seeming absence.

In a similar fashion, the Jewish scholar David Weiss in 'The Holocaust and the New Covenant' states that the Holocaust was not a unique event. On the contrary, it was simply a modern manifestation of anti-Semitism. In a post-Holocaust world, God's covenant with his chosen people remains intact despite the horrors of the Nazi era. In contemporary society, Jews must struggle to come to terms with the horrors of the last century through an adherence to God's commandments.

The Holocaust and Human Evil

In the writings of both Jewish and Christian theologians, an alternative model of overcoming the horrors of the Nazi period has been formulated which focuses on human evil. In 'Response to Irving Greenberg', the Christian theologian Alan T. Davies argues that history plays a different role in Judaism and Christianity. For the Christian, the cross and Jesus's resurrection are of pivotal importance. As a consequence, Christians can find ultimate meaning beyond history. This provides a basis for coming to terms with the horrors of the *Shoah*.

For the Christian theologian Paul van Buren, the Holocaust raises fundamental questions about the nature of God. In *Discerning the Way: A Theology of the Jewish-Christian Reality*, he states that Christian theology must be reconstructed. Using the image of the way, he contends that the Gentile Church has been called by God to join the Jewish nation in cooperating to build God's kingdom. Redemption of the world thus entails human action in creating a society which is free from the evils of the Nazi regime.

Responding to the question: where was God at Auschwitz?, the former Chief Rabbi of Great Britain Immanuel Jakobovits states that the most important issue of the Holocaust was: where was man? Where was human morality amidst the horrors of the Nazi regime? Even though Auschwitz has been liberated from Nazi barbarians, neo-fascists are still prevalent in Western and Eastern Europe. Fifty years on, the legacy of Auschwitz continues.

In the view of the Reform rabbi Jack Bemporad, human beings are neither inherently good nor evil. Rather, men and women are capable of acting ethically or behaving in the most immoral manner. The Holocaust has demonstrated that human beings are capable of murdering others; nonetheless, it has not shown that human beings are by nature evil. Instead the events of the Nazi era have illustrated the potentialities of each person to sin. According to Bemporad, we must seek to preserve the human potentiality for good and foster those personal and social elements that make for personal integration.

In 'The Meaning of this Hour', the Jewish theologian Abraham Joshua Heschel points out that the world was plunged into darkness during the Nazi regime. What is now required is for men and women to assume responsibility for their actions. God, he contends, will return to us when we shall let him in through righteous endeavours. Such a vision animated the prophets and rabbis who dreamed of a society free from ignorance and sin, and it must serve as a hope for the future.

In 'Religious Values after the Holocaust: A Protestant View', the Christian theologian Allan R. Brockway draws a distinction between religion and faith. According to Brockway, the Holocaust occurred because the Nazis misused religious values during the Third Reich. Faith, however, protects the rights of all human beings. In contemporary society, men and women must learn from the tragedy of the Holocaust and insure that faith guides us in our dealings with one another.

The Jewish scholar Nicholas de Lange argues in 'Jesus Christ and Auschwitz' that Jews and Christians need to acknowledge the different ways in which their sinfulness was responsible for the Nazi period. In confronting the question: where was Jesus at Auschwitz?, we must recognize the complexity of this question and listen attentively to Jesus who says: 'forgive our sins'. It was our failure that makes the tragedy of the Holocaust possible.

Continuing this theme, the Protestant theologian Julio de Santa Ana challenges contemporary theologians to examine the policies of the State of Israel. In 'The Holocaust and Liberation', he stresses that the theology of the Holocaust should be replaced by a theology of solidarity with all people who are afflicted. The Jewish people who suffered at the hands of Nazi aggressors must acknowledge that they are currently oppressing the Palestinian population in their midst.

According to the Jewish theologian Marc Ellis, Israel is guilty of committing crimes against humanity. Now that the Jewish people are empowered in their own country, they are capable of suppressing the rights of the Palestinian population in their midst just as Jews were oppressed by the Nazis. Jews in Israel and the diaspora must acknowledge this paradoxical reversal of events and strive to liberate the Palestinian people from their suffering.

The Holocaust and Jewish Survival

For many Jews who faced the rise of Nazism, the quest for Jewish survival was of central importance. In 'Wear the Yellow Badge with Pride', the German Zionist Robert Weltsch perceived the onslaught against German Jewry as a challenge for German Jews to reassess their future. In his opinion, the only solution to the problem of anti-Semitism was for Jews to settle in Palestine. In his view, God would not intervene to save his people from the Nazis. Instead, the Jewish people would have to save themselves.

In contemporary society, a number of Jewish theologians have stressed the theme of Jewish survival in their reflections on the Holocaust. Emil Fackenheim, for example, argues that God issued the 614th commandment out of the ashes of Auschwitz: thou shalt not grant Hitler a posthumous victory. In his view, Jews are commanded to survive as Jews lest the Jewish people perish. They are obliged as well to remember the victims of Auschwitz lest their memory perish. In addition, they are forbidden to despair of humanity and the world, lest they cooperate in delivering the world over to the forces of Auschwitz.

Drawing on the writings of Emil Fackenheim, the Jewish writer Lionel Rubinoff outlines what he believes to be an authentic response to the Nazi era. In his view, Jews must remain loyal to the tradition, and thereby insure that Judaism continues in the future. How, he asks, can a Jew respond Jewishly to an event like Auschwitz? Jews can only respond by dedicating themselves to survival in the age of the death camps. Jews today, he insists, must confront the demons of Auschwitz and prevail against them. Given that there is no solution to the theological problems raised by the Holocaust, one must simply remain faithful to the tradition.

In *Toward a Jewish Theology*, the Jewish scholar Byron Sherwin contends that American and Israeli Jews have focused on acts of resistance under Nazi rule rather than martyrdom. Yet this shift in emphasis is problematic since it can lead to the abandonment of spiritual ideals. According to Sherwin, the primary values of Judaism are embodied in its religious message, ethical lifestyle and theological beliefs. Jewish survival is not an end in itself.

Echoing this view, the Jewish scholar Michael Goldberg explores the ways in which the Holocaust has influenced contemporary Jewish life. In *Why Should Jews Survive?*, he observes that Jews in contemporary society fervently proclaim the message of Jewish survival. Yet, in doing so, they have overlooked the reason for such survival: the belief that God will redeem humanity. The *kaddish* (Jewish prayer for the dead), he states, gives voice to why Jews should survive—they constitute the hope of the world.

In *The Fate of the Jews*, the Jewish writer Roberta Strauss Feuerlicht points out that in modern society Jews have come to perceive Israel as a necessary safe-haven for Jewry in persecuted lands. The concept of vicarious suffering and redemption is not part of the Jewish tradition; nonetheless, following the assault against Jews during the Holocaust, the Jewish people have gratefully welcomed what appears to be the renaissance of Jewish existence. The State of Israel has thereby become a new religion for American Jews.

Survival is also a theme of the writings of the Jewish novelist Primo Levi. In *If This is a Man*, he describes those who were unable to resist the Nazi onslaught. These individuals were the damned, unable to cope in the camps. As *mussulmaner* (living dead), they were doomed. However, there were others who were able to rise above such despair. These figures fought against the forces of evil despite exhaustion, hunger and cold.

In *Introduction to American Judaism*, the Jewish scholar Jacob Neusner describes the role of the Holocaust in modern American life as an animating force for Jewish survival. Alongside the religious tradition, he contends, there is another type of Judaism—the Judaism of the Holocaust which is animated by this-worldly concerns. Unlike Torah Judaism, the Judaism of the Holocaust seeks to transform civic and public affairs. It commemorates the catastrophe of European Jewry from 1933 to 1945, and redemption in this new context is perceived as the creation of the State of Israel.

Reconstructing Judaism

For a number of Jewish scholars, Judaism must be reconstructed in the light of the murder of millions of Jews at the hands of the Nazis. In *Evil and Suffering in Jewish Philosophy*, the Jewish philosopher Oliver Leaman argues that the Holocaust calls for a recognition of the distance between God and the world. Surveying a range of Jewish responses, Leaman points out that various Holocaust theologians insist that a new theology is now required to deal with the horrors of the Holocaust.

In 'Despair and Hope in Post-*Shoah* Jewish Life', the Jewish scholar David Blumenthal argues along similar lines. In his view the *Shoah* raises fundamental questions about the nature of the Divine. God, he contends, is partly responsible for the events of the Nazi era. He was capable of tolerating or even bringing about evil. Nonetheless, he is capable of great good. What is required therefore is the formulation of a new theology which takes account of the terrors of the Nazi period.

One of the most prominent Jewish Holocaust theologians, Arthur A. Cohen, insists that Jews must now re-evaluate the traditional understanding of God's providential concern for his people. In *Tremendum* he states that God is not an interruptive agent. Instead, Jews should conceive of the Deity as transcendent. If God were to act in the world, the created order would simply be an extension of his will rather than an independent domain in which human beings would be able to act freely. Hence it is a mistake to blame God for the terrible events of the Nazi regime.

An alternative understanding of God's nature is found in 'When God Beheld God' by the Jewish feminist theologian Melissa Raphael. In her view, the patriarchal models of God must now be set aside. Instead, the experiences of women during the Holocaust should serve as a framework for understanding God's presence at Auschwitz. In this context Jewish mysticism provides a basis for developing a feminist theology in relation to the horrors of the Nazi regime.

According to the Jewish writer Susan Shapiro, the Holocaust requires the recognition of negation. In 'Hearing the Testimony of Radical Negation', she states that our assumptions about the world and God have been thrown into question by the events of modern times. How, she asks, can we imagine or conceive of a God who did not deliver the Jewish people from death and destruction? What is needed is for both Jews and Christians to hear the testimony of radical negation.

The Jewish theologian Harold Schulweis offers a different approach. In *Evil and the Morality of God*, he proposes a predicative theology to deal with the religious perplexities of the *Shoah*. Rejecting what he refers to as a 'subject theology', he argues that the Divine should be understood in terms of predicates. These predicates do not refer to pre-existent hypostatized entities which are part of the subject, but to actions themselves.

In *(God) After Auschwitz*, the Jewish scholar Zachary Braiterman explores the writings of various Holocaust theologians. In his opinion, the Holocaust and its memory have recast the theodic and antitheodic contours of Jewish theology. What is now required is a post-modernist approach to the dilemmas posed by the Holocaust.

In *Rethinking Jewish Faith*, the Jewish scholar Steven Jacobs argues that traditional Jewish theology is inadequate to solve the problems presented by the events of the Nazi era. What is now needed is a thorough re-evaluation of the religious tenets of the Jewish faith. In his view, it is no longer possible to believe in a God who intervenes in the world. This concept must be replaced by the notion of a God who is compatible with the reality of radical evil which admits of human freedom for good or evil. Such a revision of Jewish theology has important implications for worship and religious practice.

In a similar vein, the writer Edward Feld rejects the traditional understanding of the Deity. In *The Spirit of Renewal: Finding Faith after the Holocaust*, he states that it is now necessary to reformulate religious belief in order to take account of God's presence in human life. Traditional theodicy, he writes, can make no sense of the theological issues posed by the Nazi onslaught against the Jews. The traditional understanding of God's nature and action in the world is mistaken. Today we must reformulate our belief in God as spiritual presence.

The Jewish theologian Eliezer Schweid offers an alternative approach in *Wrestling Until Day-Break*. Here he posits a critical evaluation of various responses to the Holocaust from both Orthodox and radical theologians. All of these theodicies, he states, fail to provide an adequate response to the religious problem of the Holocaust. There can be no overarching solution to this dilemma. Today, he argues, Jews must take responsibility for the enigma of the Jewish believer's loneliness before a hiding God.

In a study of Holocaust survivors, the Jewish scholar Robert Reeve Brenner surveys the various responses of those who lived through the horrors of the camps. Very few were sustained by a belief in the hereafter, or sought to escape from the dilemmas raised by the Holocaust by denying the reality of evil. Some survivors resolved the problem of God's seeming absence by contending that he had nothing to do with the murder of Jewry. Others believed that God should be held responsible for these events. Arguably these responses are important in evaluating the viability of a coherent Holocaust theology.

The Holocaust and Christian Responsibility

A central issue which has emerged in the writings of both Jewish and Christian thinkers has been the responsibility of the Christian community for the devastation of the war years. Over the last decades there has been considerable debate about the role of Christian teaching in fuelling the flames of anti-Semitism. The third part of this volume thus begins with an outline of various responses to this problem. In *A Legacy of Hatred*, the Christian theologian David A. Rausch discusses the Church's failure to protest against Nazism. With few exceptions, Christian leaders refused to denounce Hitler and the politics of the Third Reich.

In *The Deputy*, the German Christian playwright Rolf Hochhuth depicts the Catholic Church as morally deficient in the face of Nazi aggression. In this play a young Catholic priest seeks to persuade church authorities to act on behalf of the Jewish community. Later he confronts a camp doctor who challenges his beliefs. The priest accuses the doctor of the most heinous crimes against those who were deported to the camps; in reply the doctor taunts him for his foolishness.

In her research into the role of the German theologians during the Second World War, the Jewish scholar Susannah Heschel illustrates that the German church attempted to create a niche for itself within the Nazi regime. The Institute for the Study of Jewish Influence on German Religious Life became a vehicle to disseminate propaganda in support of persecution of the Jews. In her view, this Institute should be seen in the context of the German tradition of Protestant New Testament scholarship that presented Jesus in opposition to the faith of his day.

Extending this analysis of the anti-Semitic climate of Nazi Germany, the Christian theologian Michael D. Ryan explores the religious underpinning of *Mein Kampf*. In 'Hitler's Challenge to the Churches: A Theological Political Analysis of *Mein Kampf*', he maintains that Hitler subscribed to a world-view in which eternal struggle was a central feature. This ideology, he argues, is akin to a religious faith which condones brutality as a means to an end. Such a conception, he contends, has important implications for the modern world.

Continuing this theme, the Jewish scholar Ben Zion Bokser argues that Christianity had desensitized the German population from appreciating the heinous character of Nazi propaganda. Such a process silenced the Christian conscience, enabling some Germans to accept the crimes of the Nazi Party. However, the ethical failure of the Church has been exposed by a number of Christians in the post-war period; as a result, both religious and lay leaders have insisted that Christians must play a role in correcting the problems of the social order.

In 'Troubled Self-Interpretation and Uncertain Reception in the

Church Struggle', the German theologian Eberhard Bethge discusses the evolution of the German Church Struggle. According to Bethge, this phenomenon has been largely misrepresented. In his view, those who engaged in the Church Struggle were not political resisters, and their opposition to the Nazi state was based on other concerns.

According to the Christian theologian Leonore Siegele-Wenschkewitz, the Confessing Church was not free of anti-Semitism during the war years. It is now apparent how great the failure of the Confessing Church had been in relation to the Jewish community. Anti-Jewish ways of thought permeated Christian theology, and prevented members of the Confessing Church from speaking out and acting without compromise on the Jewish question. Continuing this discussion, she also depicts the collaboration that took place between professors of theology and Nazism: their aim, she states, was to de-Judaize the theology of the Church and separate the Christian faith from its Jewish roots.

In *The Anguish of the Jews*, the Christian writer Edward Flannery surveys the history of Christian hatred of Jewry. In his view, there are significant differences between such antipathy and the Nazi assault against Jewry. While Christians condemned the Jews for not accepting Christ, they were not racists. Christian anti-Semitism was religious in character. Nazi anti-Semitism, however, was racial. Unlike previous centuries, there was no way for Jews living under Nazi rule to escape from their identity as members of a perfidious race.

Turning to the subject of Catholic resistance to the Nazi regime, the sociologist Gordon C. Zahn contends that it is now possible to evaluate Catholic resistance against the Third Reich. In his view, there was simply no uniformity in policy amongst Church leaders. Instead, there was acquiescence as well as the determination to expose the moral degeneracy of Hitler and his cohorts.

For the Jewish historian Michael Marrus, the Pope and others were at fault during the Nazi period for failing to criticize the Catholic hierarchy. In his opinion, they were motivated by political consider-ations, rather than humanitarian concerns. During the first few years of persecution, there were few ripples at the Vatican, and little sympathy was expressed for the plight of German Jewry. When mass killing occurred, the Vatican was well informed but little resistance was voiced by communal leaders.

In *A Pariah People*, the Jewish writer Hyam Maccoby accuses the Church of laying the foundations for Nazi persecution of the Jewish nation. In his view, Church teaching laid the foundation for later suffering. Hitler's decision to exterminate Jewry should thus be seen as the outcome of centuries of hostility to the Jewish people. The Holocaust was thus not a mystery, but a tragic event which could have been foreseen.

For the Christian writer Franklin H. Littell, the actions of the Confessing Church are of critical importance in understanding the Christian message in opposition to the teachings of the Third Reich. In his view, National Socialism represents a distortion of the true faith of the Church. The Holocaust, he argues, challenges Jews and Christians to reflect on the potential barbarism of modern society.

Again, in 'Evangelical Christians and Holocaust Theology', the Christian theologian Stephen T. Davis contends that despite the horrors of the Holocaust, evangelical Christians continue to subscribe to traditional teachings of the Church. Christians, he declares, were not all responsible for the events of the Nazi period. A distinction must be made between cultural Christians as opposed to committed Christians. According to Davis, the actions of the Nazis cannot be reconciled with true Christian teaching.

Re-evaluating Christian Theology

Reflecting on the role of Christians in the Third Reich, a number of Christian theologians have sought to formulate a new conception of theology for the modern world. In 'Anti-Semitism and Christian Theology', Rosemary Radford Ruether maintains that traditional Christology must be re-evaluated in the light of the events of the Nazi era. In her view, the doctrine of the Incarnation implies that Judaism must be set aside in the light of Jesus's crucifixion. The Church must repudiate its traditional conviction that Christianity is the only true path to salvation.

In 'The Holocaust and Contemporary Christology', the Catholic theologian John Pawlikowski similarly argues that Christians should forge a new conception of the relationship between God and human beings in the light of the Holocaust. In his view, the initial act of creation constituted the liberation of humankind from its total encasement in the Godhead. For Pawlikowski, Christianity must now provide an understanding and experience of the God–human relationship which can guide humanity in its newly discovered power and freedom.

According to the Catholic theologian Gregory Baum, the Church must divest itself of religious triumphalism. Rather than claiming their superiority to Judaism, Christians need to engage in positive dialogue with Jews. In the light of the events of the Nazi period, Christian theology should be reinterpreted so that the Church's eschatological views can be recovered. In *Christian Theology after Auschwitz*, he proposes a new vision of Christian theology which confronts the horrors of the death camps.

In 'The Holocaust in Theology and Philosophy', the Christian writer Mary Knutsen similarly emphasizes the challenge to Christian theology and philosophy posed by the events of the Nazi reign of terror. According to Knutsen, Christians must reformulate their understanding of human suffering and God's providence. In her opinion, no viable Christian theology, teaching or symbol can have the effect of systematically devaluing the authenticity of others.

For the Catholic theologian Michael McGarry, the Christian community must now reinterpret previous Christian doctrines regarding the Jewish faith. In a post-Holocaust age, Christians must rethink their previous conceptions of Jewry. In his view, the multiplicity of faiths should encourage Christians to formulate a *logos*-Christology which recognizes the validity of other religions. Karl Rahner, he points out, was a pioneer of such theological reconstruction. A theological pluralism fleshed out by a *logos*-Christology, he argues, would account for a Christ who is Messiah for Christians and for the abiding validity of the Jewish tradition for Jews.

In 'A Final Conversation with Paul Tillich', the Jewish theologian Albert Friedlander depicts a conversation he had with Paul Tillich. In discussing God's role in the Holocaust, Tillich maintains that it is a mistake to think that God would have intervened at Auschwitz. Contemporary Church thinking, Tillich notes, tends to depict God as a super-human figure who is able to do everything. In Tillich's view, this is a mistake; instead, God is the ground of all being. But human beings are free to choose evil actions.

In *Prospects for Post-Holocaust Theology*, the Christian theologian Stephen R. Haynes contends that post-Holocaust theology needs to be thoroughly revised. Influenced by Paul van Buren and Jürgen Moltmann, he outlines a new vision of the relationship between the Christian community and the Jewish people. In his opinion, the Holocaust teaches that theology which is wrong about the Jews may lead to overwhelming evil. Post-Holocaust theology must not ignore the Jewish community either as they exist in contemporary society.

Arguing along similar lines the Christian theologian Alice Eckardt stresses that Christian theology must undergo radical change in the modern world. In 'The *Shoah*-Road to a Revised/Revived Christianity', she argues that Christian teaching of contempt for Judaism should be overcome. Today Christians should accept that suffering is not part of God's will or wish for creation. God cares for all creation, but has left the future in the hands of human beings. God is thus subject to human action.

For the Christian theologian Roy Eckardt, the Holocaust should be understood in the context of the history of Christian anti-Semitism. What is required today is a new spirituality which takes into account the condition in which God and humanity, having been one in their crimes, may become one in forgiveness.

In *A Guest in the House of Israel: Post-Holocaust Theology*, the Christian theologian Clark Williamson maintains that Christian theology must now take account of the events of the Nazi era. According to Williamson, Christians must recognize the anti-Jewish legacy of the Church and seek to overcome such teachings by formulating a new theology for the modern age. Such a post-*Shoah* theology would seek to liberate the Church's witness and theology from its inherited *adversus Judaeos* ideology.

In a similar vein, the Christian theologian James F. Moore in 'A Spectrum of Views: Traditional Christian Responses to the Holocaust' contends that the task of reformulating Christian theology is an urgent requirement. Surveying the views of various Christian thinkers, Moore insists that Christian theology must undergo major revisions in the light of the events of the Nazi period.

Adopting a different approach, the Jewish scholar Yosef Hayim Yerushalmi disputes the view of Ruether and others that Christian doctrine must undergo radical revision. According to Yerushalmi, Nazi anti-Semitism was simply a modern form of discrimination against Judaism and the Jewish people. In the past the Church sought to convert Jews to the true faith. Unlike the Nazis, Christians did not adopt a policy of genocide. Thus, Christian theologians do not need to repudiate the fundamental tenets of the faith.

Yerushalmi's position, however, is challenged by other Christian thinkers. In 'The Holocaust and the Theology of the Death of God', the Christian theologian Thomas J.J. Altizer contends that there must be a transformation of Christian theology in modern society. The

Holocaust, he argues, was an apocalyptic event which calls for an apocalyptic theology. Given the horrific nature of the *Shoah*, what is now required is a theology which distances itself from everything that Christian history has known and affirmed as God.

In 'Genocide and the Death of God', William Hamilton argues along similar lines. In his view, radical theology has an immeasurably important task in the light of the events of the Nazi period. Christians must renounce all triumphalist attitudes. The bridge between monotheism and killing, he writes, is long and twisting. The danger is that those who differ in their theological opinions will be viewed as enemies who deserve to be slain in the name of the God of Christianity.

Jewish–Christian Dialogue

Turning to the subject of Jewish–Christian dialogue, a number of Jewish and Christian writers have emphasized the need for both communities to explore their common features. In 'The Future of Jewish–Christian Relations', the Jewish writer Edward Kessler explores the question of whether the Holocaust can serve as a basis for a Jewish–Christian encounter. In his view, neither the murder of six million Jews under the Nazis nor the establishment of a Jewish state can serve as the foundation for fruitful discussion.

Following a different line, the Christian theologian Katharine T. Hargrove contends that the contemporary Christian community must take seriously the conclusions reached by Jewish Holocaust theologians. These writings, she states, can serve as a framework for positive Jewish–Christian debate.

In 'Responses to Anti-Judaism and Anti-Semitism in Contemporary Christian-Jewish Relations', the Christian theologian Isabel Wollaston discusses a variety of Christian responses to the *Shoah*. For Wollaston there are serious dangers confronting those theologians who are overcome with guilt concerning the Christian involvement in the Nazi onslaught against the Jews. The danger is that such attitudes can stifle legitimate criticisms of the Jewish state.

For the Jewish theologian Randall Falk, the Nazi period raises serious questions about the nature of modern Christianity. How, he asks, could leading Christians have been oblivious to the evil of the Nazi executioners? Jews, he states, cannot forget the role of the Catholic Church during the war. Nonetheless, he points out that decisive steps have been taken in Jewish–Christian relations in recent years. In his view, both Christians and Jews cannot afford to be complacent about the need for establishing positive relationships in modern society.

In the view of the Christian theologian Walter Harrelson, it is vital that the Holocaust be remembered by both the Jewish and Christian communities. Hatred, he points out, has led to violence throughout history, yet never before has there been such systematic barbarism. Yet despite the tragedy of the Nazi era, the creation of the State of Israel has provided a bulwark against future aggression. Further, statements produced by Church bodies have sought to counter the anti-Judaic elements of Church teaching.

According to the Catholic theologian Johann Baptist Metz, the death camps serve as a turning point in Jewish–Christian relationships. In his view, the relations between Christians and Jews ultimately depend on the attitude Christians adopt toward the Nazi period. Auschwitz cannot be comprehended, but the way is now open to fruitful dialogue rather than missionizing.

For the Christian writer Frank Longford, the Holocaust raises serious questions about the differences between the Jewish and Christian understanding of forgiveness. For the Christian, forgiveness is demanded regardless of the attitudes of the offender. Jewish theology, however, teaches that forgiveness is required only if the offender repents of his or her sin and seeks to be pardoned. In considering the issue of whether Jews should forgive the Nazis for their brutality, this difference of approach should not be ignored.

In 'The *Shoah* and Contemporary Religious Thinking', the Jewish theologian Albert Friedlander argues that Christians must now re-evaluate their relationship to the Jewish people. According to Friedlander, there can be no adequate theological explanation for God's seeming inactivity. Thus, rather than engage in such speculation, Friedlander insists that Jews and Christians should engage in acts of worship commemorative of the *Shoah*.

Arguing along different lines, the Catholic theologian Eugene Fisher contends that it is a mistake to believe that Christian antipathy to Judaism led to the Holocaust. While it is true that Christians persecuted the Jewish people, the Nazi onslaught against the Jews was based on racial rather than religious ideology. Nonetheless, Christians must be sensitive to past conflict between Christianity and Judaism.

The Holocaust
Historical Background

Prelude to Catastrophe

During the last days of the First World War, the assembly at Weimar drafted a new constitution which transformed Germany into a federal republic. Immediately this new regime faced opposition from the extreme right and left. During 1922–3 there was massive inflation, but during the next five years there was greater stability as well as important intellectual and cultural developments. This period of prosperity was followed by the Great Depression—over six million were unemployed between 1930 and 1933. As a consequence the Communists and the Nazis gained considerable support. To cope with this crisis, the government began to rule by presidential decree. After several ineffective conservative coalitions, Field Marshall Paul von Hindenburg appointed Adolf Hitler Chancellor of Germany on 30 January 1933.

Hitler was born and raised in Austria. As a frustrated and unsuccessful artist he spent several years in Vienna and subsequently moved to Munich in 1913. Volunteering for the German army, he fought on the Western Front and returned to Munich in 1919 where he joined the National Socialist German Workers' Party, later becoming its leader. Between 1919 and 1924 he combined German nationalism, anti-capitalism and anti-Semitism into a political ideology.

According to Hitler, the Jews were parasites and degenerates. Germany, he believed, lost the war because of treachery by Jewish socialists, liberals and pacifists. Further, he argued that the Bolshevik revolution was part of a world-wide Jewish plot. Such a fusion of anti-Jewish sentiment and anti-communism provided a justification for the belief that the Germans were entitled to greater living space in Eastern Europe: the Jews had taken control over the Slavs and therefore the struggle against communism (defined as Jewish Bolshevism) was synonymous with the attack on Jewry itself. Hitler saw himself as the leader (*Führer*) of a heroic battle against a malignant part of Europe: an Aryan victory would provide Germany with control of an empire (*Reich*) which it rightly deserved.

During the 1920s Hitler's party was a minor force in Germany. In November 1923 the Nazis attempted a coup in Munich which failed. But the Depression gained Hitler the support of several sectors of society: German industrialists who feared communism; those who were insecure about their social positions; and boisterous youth. In 1928 the Nazis achieved 810,000 votes in the Reichstag elections; in 1930 6,380,000; and in 1932 14,000,000. On 5 March 1933 the Nazis won 44 per cent of the vote.

When the Nazis gained power, they dissolved a number of social institutions and absorbed others. In the spring and summer of 1933 all political parties were eliminated, strikes were outlawed and trade unions were replaced by a government- and employer-controlled labour front. In May 1933 book burnings took place and scientists, scholars and artists were arrested. In June 1934 a purge of the SA (Stormtroops) eliminated the party's social radicals and made way for the expansion of the SS (Protection Squad). Under Heinrich Himmler, the SS troops took over many of the functions of the police, including the Gestapo (Secret Police), as well as the running of the concentration camps.

After Hindenburg's death in August 1934, Hitler became the party chief and head of state. In September 1935 all sexual liaisons between Jews and non-Jews were described as crimes against the state. In 1938 Jewish communal bodies were put under the control of the Gestapo, and Jews were forced to register their property. Later in the year the Nazi party organized an onslaught against the Jewish population. This event, known as *Kristallnacht*, 'night of the broken glass', was a prelude to the terrors of the death camps.

The first stage of the Nazi's plan for European Jewry began with the invasion of Poland in September 1939. In every conquered town and village the Germans forced Jews to clear rubble, carry heavy loads, hand over jewellery, and scrub floors and lavatories with their prayer shawls. In addition, the Germans cut off religious Jews' beards and sidelocks with scissors or tore them from their faces. When the Jewish population was forced into what Hitler referred to as a huge Polish labour camp, a massive work programme was initiated.

The next stage in the plan of extermination began with the invasion of Russia in 1941. This was designed to destroy what was described by the Nazis as the 'Jewish Bolshevik conspiracy'. At first mobile killing battalions of 500–900 men (the *Einsatzgrüppen*) under the supervision of Reinhard Heydrich began the slaughter of Russian Jewry. Of the 4,500,000 Jews who resided in Soviet territory, more than half fled before the German invasion; those who remained were concentrated in large cities making it easier for Heydrich's troops to carry out their task. Throughout the country the *Einsatzgrüppen* moved into Russian towns, sought out the rabbis or Jewish council and obtained a list of all Jewish inhabitants. The Jews were then rounded up in market places, crowded into trains, buses and trucks and taken to woods where mass graves had been dug. They were then machine-gunned to death.

The Death Camps

Other methods were also employed by the Nazis. Mobile gas vans were sent to each battalion of the *Einsatzgrüppen*. Meanwhile the mobile killing operations were being supplemented by the use of fixed centres, the death camps. Six of these were at Chelmno and Auschwitz in the Polish territories, and at Treblinka, Sobibor, Majdanek and Belzec in the Polish 'General Government'. Construction of this mass murder industry began in 1941. Two civilians from Hamburg went to Auschwitz to teach the staff how to use Zyklon-B gas. In September 1941 the first gassing took place in Auschwitz Block II; then work began at Birkenau, the central killing centre in Auschwitz. The first death camp to be completed was Chelmno near Lodz, which started functioning in December 1941. Subsequently Belzec became operational and the building of Sobibor began in March 1942. At the same time Majdanek and Treblinka were transformed into death centres.

The horrors of the rounding up of Jews and the journey and arrival at the camps have been depicted in numerous accounts. According to a Polish pharmacist who witnessed the Jews of Cracow being gathered together in the Cracow ghetto:

> Old people, women and children pass by the pharmacy window like ghosts. I see an old woman of around seventy years, her hair loose, walking alone, a few steps away from a larger group of deportees. Her eyes have a glazed look; immobile, wide-open, filled with horror, they stare straight ahead. She walks slowly, quietly, only in her dress and slippers, without even a bundle, or handbag. She holds in her hands something small, something black, which she caresses fondly and keeps

close to her old breast. It is a small puppy—her most precious possession, all that she saved and would not leave behind. Laughing, inarticulately gesturing with her hands, walks a young deranged girl of about fourteen, so familiar to all inhabitants of the ghetto. She walks barefoot, in a crumpled nightgown. One shuddered watching the girl laughing, having a good time. Old and young pass by, some dressed, some only in their underwear, hauled out of their beds and driven out.[1]

Crowded together, Jews travelled to their deaths as the pace of murder accelerated. As a local Pole later recalled, the trains carrying these victims were horrifying:

The small windows were covered with planks or lots of barbed wire, and in some places planks were missing from the walls, which was proof of desperate struggles taking place inside. Through the cracks in the planks and through the wired-up windows peered scared human faces. Sometimes we could tell that a train was approaching, although it was still far off because of the shouting of the guards; they were standing on the buffers of the wagons and shooting those who tried to escape. When such a train stopped at Zwierzyniec station in order to allow another train to pass through, screams, laments and cries could be heard from all the wagons, 'Water, water!' The Jews were holding out bottles and money fastened to sticks or broken parts of planks—but no-one was allowed to approach the wagons. The Germans were shooting without warning all those who begged for water, as well as those who tried to give it to them. Soldiers were marching along the train breaking the bottles with sticks and pocketing the money. Women were throwing rings, ear-rings and jewellery through the windows and cracks, begging for a glass of water for their children who were dying of thirst.[2]

One of the survivors of a convoy of Jews who travelled from Paris to Auschwitz later recounted the terrors of this journey:

Piled up in freight cars, unable to bend or to budge, sticking one to another, breathless, crushed by one's neighbour's every move, this was already hell. During the day, a torrid heat, with a pestilential smell. After several days and several nights, the doors were opened. We arrived worn out, dehydrated, with many ills. A newborn baby, snatched from its mother's arms, was thrown against a column. The mother, crazed from pain, began to scream. The SS man struck her violently with the butt end of his weapon over the head. Her eyes haggard, with fearful screams, her beautiful hair became tinted with her own blood. She was struck down by a bullet in her head.[3]

On arrival at the camps, Jews were ordered out of the train and separated into groups. According to a survivor of Treblinka, women and children were sent to the left, men to the right:

The women all went into the barracks on the left, and as we later learned, they were told at once to strip naked and were driven out of the barracks through another door. From there, they entered a narrow path lined on either side with barbed wire. This path led through a small grove to the building that housed the gas-chamber. Only a few minutes later we could hear their terrible screams, but we could not see anything, because the trees of the grove blocked our view.[4]

At Treblinka the women on arrival were shaved to the skin; their hair was later packed up for dispatch to Germany. At the Nuremberg Tribunal one of those who survived gave an account of this procedure:

Because little children at their mother's breasts were a great nuisance during the shaving procedure, later the system was modified and babies were taken from their mothers as soon as they got off the train. The children were taken to an enormous ditch; when a large number of them were gathered together they were killed by firearms and thrown into the fire.

Here, too, no one bothered to see whether all the children were really dead. Sometimes one could hear infants wailing in the fire. When mothers succeeded in keeping their babies with them and this fact interfered with the shaving, a German guard took the baby by its legs and smashed it against the wall of the barracks until only a bloody mass remained in his hands. The unfortunate mother had to take this mass with her to the 'bath'.[5]

The most horrible of all horrors were the gas chambers. An eyewitness to the killings at Belzec later recounted a typical occurrence:

A little before seven, there was an announcement: 'The first train will arrive in ten minutes!' A few minutes later a train arrived from

Lemberg: forty-five carriages with more than six thousand people; two hundred Ukrainian assigned to this work flung open the doors and drove the Jews out of the cars with leather whips. A loudspeaker gave instructions: 'Strip, even artificial limbs and glasses. Hand all money and valuables in at the "valuables" window. Women and girls are to have their hair cut in the "barber's" hut.' Then the march began. Barbed wire on both sides, in the rear two dozen Ukrainians with rifles. . .

Stark naked men, women, children and cripples passed by. . . SS men pushed the men into the chambers. . . Seven to eight hundred people in ninety-three square metres. The doors closed. Twenty five minutes passed. You could see through the windows that many were already dead, for an electric light illuminated the interior of the room.

All were dead after thirty-two minutes. Jewish workers on the other side opened the wooden doors. They had been promised their lives in return for doing this horrible work, plus a small percentage of the money and valuables collected.

The people were still standing like columns of stone, with no room to fall or lean. Even in death you could tell the families, all holding hands. It was difficult to separate them while emptying the room for the next batch. The bodies were tossed out, blue, wet with sweat and urine, the legs smeared with excrement and menstrual blood. Two dozen workers were busy checking mouths they opened with iron hooks. . . Dentists knocked out gold teeth, bridges and crowns with hammers.[6]

Jewish Resistance

By September 1942 German troops had conquered most of Europe. Yet as the murder of Jews continued, resistance spread. On 24 September the Jews of the White Russian town of Korzec set the ghetto on fire and a number of Jews established a partisan band. On 25 September in Kaluszyn near Warsaw, the chairman of the Jewish Council in Lukow near Lublin collected money from Jews assembled in the main square in the expectation that he could use the funds to ransom the Jewish community. When he discovered the deportation would take place, he shouted: 'Here is your payment for your trip, you bloody tyrant.' Tearing the money into shreds, he slapped the German supervisor in the face and was shot on the spot by the Ukrainian guards. In the same month a former Jewish soldier in the Polish army who was being held with several hundred other prisoners in a prison camp in Lublin escaped with seventeen Jews, forming a small partisan group.

In the Warsaw ghetto, the Jewish Fighting Organization prepared itself for action. On 29 October a member of the Organization killed the commander of the Jewish police in the ghetto. In the Bialystok ghetto resistance was also taking place with the assistance of German soldiers from whom they obtained weapons. Near Cracow six members of the Jewish Fighting Organization set off for the forests armed with pistols and a knife, but were betrayed by local peasants. The next month the Jewish Fighting Organization in Cracow sabotaged railway lines, raided a German clothing store, and killed several Germans. In Marcinkance the chairman of the Jewish Council called out to the Jews who had been brought to the railway station: 'Fellow Jews, everybody run for his life. Everything is lost!' As the Jews ran towards the ghetto fence, attacking the guards with their fists, over a hundred were shot.

In November Polish Jews who had escaped the deportation to Treblinka organized a small group to protect those Jews who were in hiding. The news of executions in the labour camps in December stimulated plans for resistance in Warsaw. An eyewitness wrote: 'The community wants the enemy to pay dearly. They will attack them with knives, sticks, carbolic acid; they will not allow themselves to be seized in the streets, because now they know that labour camps these days mean death.'[7]

In the labour camp at Kruszyna near Radom Jews decided to resist with knives and fists in December. When they were ordered to assemble, they attacked the guards. Three weeks later 400 Jews imprisoned in the Kopernik camp in Minsk Mazowiecki barricaded themselves into the building and resisted with sticks, stones and bricks. On 22 December in Cracow the Jewish Fighting Organization attacked a café frequented by the SS and the Gestapo. In Czestochowa on 4 January members of the Jewish Fighting Organization wounded the German commander.

On 18 January 1943 the Germans entered the Warsaw ghetto determined to deport Jews to Treblinka. They did not expect any resistance, but preparations had been made in the ghetto for months. Pistols and grenades were obtained; those who had no weapons armed themselves with sticks, bottles and lengths of pipe. As Jews were being deported along the street, a small group began to throw grenades at the Germans. In the words of one of those who observed these events:

The fighters set up a barricade in a little house of Niska street and held it against the German reinforcements which soon arrived. The Germans found it impossible to enter the house, so they set it afire. The fighters inside continued firing until the last bullet. . . though the unit was destroyed the battle on Niska street encouraged us. For the first time since the occupation we saw Germans clinging to the walls, crawling on the ground; running for cover, hesitating before making a step in the fear of being hit by a Jewish bullet. The cries of the wounded caused us joy, and increased our thirst for battle.[8]

Several months later the Jews in Warsaw learned that the ghetto was to be destroyed. In response the Jewish community was determined to fight for its survival. The commander of the Jewish resistance group, Mordecai Anielewicz, declared: 'He who has arms will fight. He who has no arms—women and children—will go down into the bunkers.' As the Germans entered the Warsaw ghetto on 19 April, the Jews attacked. As one of the resistance fighters recounted:

All of a sudden they started entering the ghetto, thousands armed. . . And we, some twenty men and women, young. And what were our arms? The arms we had—we had a revolver, a grenade, and a whole group had two guns, and some bombs, home-made, prepared in a very primitive way. . . When the Germans came to our posts and marched by us we threw those hand grenades and bombs and saw blood pouring over the streets of Warsaw. . . There was rejoicing.[9]

The next day German soldiers shelled buildings and burned apartment blocks. Yet the Jewish fighters continued their battle. By the end of the first week of May the last stage of Jewish resistance was a bunker in which 120 fighters were assembled. For two hours the entrance was bombarded and then the Germans used gas against the Jews. Street by street the ghetto had been eliminated. In the fighting 7,000 Jews lost their lives, and 30,000 were deported to Treblinka.

The Final Stage of Terror

Reports of resistance in Warsaw spread throughout Europe, but pressure against the Jews continued. The advance of the Red Army on the Eastern Front since early 1943 led to the decision to dig up the corpses of Jews and burn them. On 15 June at the Janowska death pits in Lvov hundreds of Jewish labourers were forced to dig up those who had been murdered and extract gold teeth and rings from the fingers of the dead. As a witness recounted:

> The fire crackles and sizzles. Some of the bodies in the fire have had their hands extended. It looks as if they are pleading to be taken out. Many bodies are lying around with open mouths. Could they be trying to say: 'We are your own mothers, fathers, who raised you and took care of you. Now you are burning us.' If they could have spoken, maybe they would have said this, but they are forbidden to talk too— they are guarded. Maybe they would forgive us. They know that we are being forced to do this by the same murderers that killed them. We are under their whips and machine guns.[10]

The pace of killing was unchanging. On 4 October Himmler addressed his SS officers; the Jewish race was being eliminated, he explained:

> Most of you know what it means when one hundred corpses are lying side by side, or five hundred, or one thousand. To have stuck it out and at the same time—apart from exceptional cases of human weakness—to have remained decent fellows, that is what has made us hard. This is a page of glory in our history which has never to be written. . . we had the moral right, we had the duty to world peace, to destroy this people which wished to destroy us.[11]

Several days later a number of Jews who were imprisoned in Warsaw in Pawiak prison attempted to celebrate the Day of Atonement. One of the inmates later stated:

> In a cell in the Pawiak prisons, ruled by barbarians bent on exterminating world Jewry, stood a group of Jews deep in prayer. Atlasowicz was standing by a greenish-brown prison table which served as a makeshift lectern. His broad back swayed reverently in a constant motion as he recited the ancient prayer. Atlasowicz intoned the Psalm in a muffled voice, not quite his own.
>
> > 'Light will shine on the righteous.'
> > 'And joy upon the upright of heart.'
>
> For a moment he was silent. Then he turned to the others, and in

a hushed voice, as though talking to himself, he continued 'Our *Kol Nidre* in this place is unique and symbolic. It is our continuation. Here we take up the golden tradition of sanctity handed down to us by generations of Jews before us. We are human beings and will not yield our souls to the barbarians; we defy our enemies by remaining true to our people and traditions.'[12]

During the winter of 1943 the murder of Jews continued without pause. At Birkenau on Christmas Day Jewish women who had been starved were brought from the barracks. Trucks drove up to the block where they were assembled, and women were piled into them. The victims knew they were going to the gas chambers and tried to escape and were massacred. According to an account of this incident, when the lorry motors started, a terrible noise arose—the death cry of thousands of young women. As they tried to break out, a rabbi's son cried out: 'God show them your power—this is against you.' When nothing happened, the boy cried out: 'There is no God.'

As the months passed, Jews continued to be subjected to equally terrible events. In Kovno several thousand children were rounded up, driven off in trucks and murdered. As an observer of this action related: I saw shattered scenes. It was near the hospital. I saw automobiles which from time to time would approach mothers with children, or children who were on their own. In the back of them, two Germans with rifles would be going as if they were escorting criminals. They would toss the children in the automobile. I saw mothers screaming. A mother whose three children had been taken away—she went up to this automobile and shouted at the German, 'Give me the children', and he said, 'You may have one'. And she went up into that automobile, and all three children looked at her and stretched out their hands. Of course, all of them wanted to go with their mother, and the mother didn't know which child to select and she went down alone, and she left the car.[13]

By the summer of 1944 the last deportations took place. More than 67,000 were deported from the Lodz ghetto to Birkenau. Most were selected for the gas chamber, but some were chosen for medical experimentation. According to an account:

When the convoys arrive, Dr. Mengele espied, among those lined up for selection, a hunchbacked man about fifty years old. He was not alone; standing beside him was a tall handsome boy of fifteen or sixteen. The latter, however, had a deformed right foot. . . Father and son— their faces wan from their miserable years in the Lodz ghetto. . . I first examined the father in detail, omitting nothing. . . Before proceeding to the examination of the boy I conversed with him at some length. He had a pleasant face, an intelligent look, but his morale was badly shaken. . . Scarcely half an hour later SS Quartermaster Sergeant Mussfeld appeared with four *Sonderkommando* men. They took the two prisoners into the furnace room and had them undress. Then the Ober's revolver cracked twice.[14]

At Birkenau the Day of Atonement was celebrated on 1 October with a note of religious exaltation despite the horror of the camp:

The moon shone through the window. Its light was dazzling that night and gave the pale wasted faces of the prisoners a ghostly appearance. It was as if all the life had ebbed out of them. I shuddered with dread, for it suddenly occurred to me that I was the only living man among corpses. All at once the oppressive silence was broken by a mournful tune. It was the plaintive tones of the ancient *Kol Nidre* prayer. . . When at last he was silent, there was exaltation among us, an exaltation which men can experience only when they have fallen as low as we had fallen and then, through the mystic power of a deathless prayer, have awakened once more to the world of the spirit.[15]

Other Jews in Dachau on this Day of Atonement also prayed. But the experiences these faced had shaken their faith in God:

We gather closer to the cantor, a young Hungarian lad. Lips murmur after him—quiet muffled words hardly manage to pass, remain sticking in the throat. Here stands Warsaw's last rabbi, his face yellow, hairless, wrinkled, his aged body bent; his hands are rocking like reeds in the wind; only the eyes, sparkling stars, look out towards the cold sky above, and his lips, half open, murmur softly.

What does he say now, how does he pray, this last of the rabbis of Warsaw? Does he lovingly accept the pain and suffering, or does he, through the medium of his prayer, conduct a dispute with the Almighty? asking him the ancient question: 'Is this the reward for faith?' Huddling to the cantor stands Alter der Klinger, the Kovno cab driver. His broad shoulders lean against a young tree and his mouth emits staccato sounds as if they were hummed out of his inside. No, he does not beg; he does not pray; he demands! He demands his rights. He calls for justice. Why were his children burned by the Nazis? Why was his wife reduced to ashes?[16]

References

1. Testimony of Tadeusz Pankiewicz in Eisenberg, *Witness to the Holocaust* in Martin Gilbert, *The Holocaust*, London, 1987, 356–357
2. Testimony of Stanislaw Bohdanowicz of Zwierzyniec, 'Tregenza Collection', in Gilbert, op. cit., 413
3. Convoy 25, 28 August 1942 in Gilbert, op. cit., 437
4. Testimony of Abraham Krzepicki in Gilbert, op. cit., 458
5. Testimony of Samuel Rujzman: 'Punishment of War Criminals', in Gilbert, op. cit., 457
6. Kurt Gerstein, Statement of 6 May 1945, Tübingen: International Military Tribunal, Nuremberg document PS-2170
7. Rhingelblum Notes, 5 December 1942 in Gilbert, op. cit., 503
8. Siemiatycze Memorial Book in Gilbert, op. cit., 523–524
9. Testimony of Zivia Liubetkin, 2 May 1961, Eichmann Trial, Session 25
10. Leon Weliczker Well, *The Janowska Road*, New York, 1970, 141–142
11. Himmler Speech, 4 October 1943: International Military Tribunal, Nuremberg document PS-1919
12. Julien Hirshaut, *Jewish Martyrs of Pawiak*, New York, 1982, 164–165
13. Testimony of Dr Aharon Peretz, 4 May 1961, Eichmann Trial, Session 28
14. Miklos Nyiszli, 'Auschwitz' in Gilbert, op. cit., 719–720
15. Leon Szalet, *Experiment 'E'*, New York, 1945, 70–71
16. Levi Shalit, *Beyond Dachau*, Johannesburg, 1980, 104–105

PART I

The Challenge

Chapter 1: The Religious Challenge of the Holocaust   41

Richard Rubenstein: The Death of God   41

Elie Wiesel: The Holocaust and Religious Protest   43

David H. Hirsch: The Holocaust and Camp Songs   47

Alexander Donat: The Holocaust and Human Perplexity   50

Sherwin Wine: The Rejection of God   52

Michael Oppenheim: The Holocaust and Religious Language   55

Steven T. Katz: The Uniqueness of the Holocaust   58

Jakob Jocz: Judaism after the Holocaust   61

Harry James Cargas: The Holocaust and Chrisitan Responsibility   64

John Roth: The Holocaust and Religious Perplexity   67

CHAPTER ONE

The Religious Challenge of the Holocaust

Richard Rubenstein: The Death of God

An American-born Conservative rabbi, Richard Rubenstein served as Robert O. Lawton Distinguished Professor of Religion at the University of Florida and as President of the University of Bridgeport, Connecticut. In After Auschwitz, *he argues that it is no longer possible to sustain a belief in a supernatural Deity after the events of the Nazi era. Given God's seeming absence in the death camps, Jews should abandon the traditional belief in the Lord of history. In a later controversial work,* Approaches to Auschwitz, *Rubenstein explains the origin of his disbelief, and elaborates his conception of God as Divine Nothingness.*

Rejecting God

I believe the greatest single challenge to modern Judaism arises out of the question of God and the death camps. I am amazed at the silence of contemporary Jewish theologians on this most crucial and agonizing of all Jewish issues. How can Jews believe in an omnipotent, beneficent God after Auschwitz? Traditional Jewish theology maintains that God is the ultimate, omnipotent actor in historical drama. It has interpreted every major catastrophe in Jewish history as God's punishment of a sinful Israel. I fail to see how this position can be maintained without regarding Hitler and the SS as instruments of God's will. The agony of European Jewry cannot be likened to the testing of Job. To see any purpose in the death camps, the traditional believer is forced to regard the most demonic, anti-human explosion of all history as a meaningful expression of God's purposes. The idea is simply too obscene for me to accept. I do not think that the full impact of Auschwitz has yet been felt in Jewish theology or Jewish life. Great religious revolutions have their own period of gestation. No man knows when the full impact of

41

Auschwitz can be felt, but no religious community can endure so hideous a wounding without undergoing vast inner disorders.

(Richard Rubenstein, *After Auschwitz*, Indianapolis, Bobbs Merrill, 1966, 153)

The Death of God

No man can really say that God is dead. How can we know that? Nevertheless, I am compelled to say that we live in the time of the 'death of God.' This is more a statement about man and his culture than about God. The death of God is a cultural fact. Buber felt this. He spoke of the eclipse of God. I can understand his reluctance to use the more explicitly Christian terminology. I am compelled to utilize it because of my conviction that the time when Nietzsche's madman said was too far off has come upon us. There is no way around Nietzsche. Had I lived in another time or another culture, I might have found some other vocabulary to express my meanings. I am, however, a religious existentialist after Nietzsche and after Auschwitz. When I say we live in the time of the death of God, I mean that the thread uniting God and man, heaven and earth, has been broken. We stand in a cold, silent, unfeeling cosmos, unaided by any purposeful power beyond our own resources. After Auschwitz, what else can a Jew say about God?

(Richard Rubenstein, *After Auschwitz*, Indianapolis, Bobbs Merrill, 1966, 151–152)

Nothingness and God

I believe there is a conception of God. . . which remains meaningful after the death of the God-who-acts-in-history. It is a very old conception of God with deep roots in both Western and Oriental mysticism. According to this conception, God is spoken of as the Holy Nothingness. When God is thus designated, he is conceived of as the ground and source of all existence. To speak of God as the Holy Nothingness is not to suggest that he is a void. On the contrary, he is an indivisible *plenum* so rich that all existence derives from his very essence. God as the Nothing is not absence of being but superfluity of being.

Why then use the term Nothingness? Use of the term rests in part upon a very ancient observation that all definition of finite entities involves negation. The infinite God is nothing. At times, mystics also spoke of God in similar terms as the *Urgrund*, the primary ground, the dark unnameable abyss out of which the empirical world has come.

At first glance, these ideas might seem little more than word play. Nevertheless, wise men of all the major religious traditions have expressed themselves in almost identical images when they have attempted to communicate the mystery of divinity. It is also helpful to note that whoever believes God is the source or ground of being usually believes that human personality is coterminous with the life of the human body. Death may be entrance into eternal life, the perfect life of God; death may also end pain, craving, and suffering, but it involves the dissolution and disappearance of individual identity. . .

Perhaps the best available metaphor for the conception of God as the Holy Nothingness is that God is the ocean and we are the waves. In some sense each wave has its moment in which it is distinguishable as a somewhat separate entity. Nevertheless, no wave is entirely distinct from the ocean which is its substantial ground.

(Richard Rubenstein, *Approaches to Auschwitz*, London, SCM, 1987, 315–316)

Discussion

1. Is it possible for Judaism to exist without a Deity?
2. Does Rubenstein's conception of God as the Holy Nothingness make sense?

Elie Wiesel: The Holocaust and Religious Protest

A Romanian Nobel Peace Prize winner and novelist, Elie Wiesel served as Chairman of the US Presidential Commission on the Holocaust and as Andrew Mellon Professor of Humanities at Boston University. In the novel Night, *he portrays the evolution of his despair. In this work, he depicts his initial transition from youthful belief to disillusionment. At the beginning of the novel, Wiesel describes himself as a young boy fascinated with God's mystery, studying* Talmud *and* Kabbalah *in the Transylvanian town of Sighet. After being transported to Auschwitz, the erosion of his faith began. Shortly after his arrival he questioned God. Later, he ceased to pray.*

Religious Doubt

One day when we came back from work, we saw three gallows rearing up in the assembly place, three black crows. Roll call. SS all round us, machine guns trained: the traditional ceremony. Three victims in chains—and one of them, the little servant, the sad-eyed angel.

The SS seemed more preoccupied, more disturbed than usual. To hang a young boy in front of thousands of spectators was no light matter. The head of the camp read the verdict. All eyes were on the child. He was lividly pale, almost calm, biting his lips. The gallows threw its shadow over him. . . .

'Where is God? Where is He?' someone behind me asked.

At a sign from the head of the camp the three chairs tipped over.

Total silence throughout the camp. On the horizon, the sun was setting. . . .

Then the march past began. The two adults were no longer alive. Their tongues hung swollen, blue-tinged. But the third rope was still moving; being so light, the child was still alive. . . .

For more than half an hour he stayed there, struggling between life and death, dying in slow agony under our eyes. And we had to look him full in the face. He was still alive when I passed in front of him. His tongue was still red, his eyes were not yet glazed.

Behind me, I heard the same man asking:

'Where is God now?'

And I heard a voice within me answer him:

'Where is He? Here He is—He is hanging here on this gallows. . . '

(Elie Wiesel, *Night*, New York, Bantam Books, 1982, 61–62)

Rebellion in the Camps

On the eve of *Rosh Hashanah*, the last day of that accursed year, the whole camp was electric with the tension which was in all our hearts. In spite of everything, this last day was different from any other. The last day of the year. The word 'last' rang very strangely. What if it were indeed the last day?

They gave us our evening meal, a very thick soup, but no one touched it. We wanted to wait until after prayers. At the place of assembly, surrounded by the electrified barbed wire, thousands of silent Jews gathered, their faces stricken.

Night was falling. Other prisoners continued to crowd in from every block, able suddenly to conquer time and space and submit both to their will.

'What are you, my God,' I thought angrily, 'compared to this afflicted crowd, proclaiming to you their faith, their anger, their revolt? What does your greatness mean, Lord of the universe, in the face of all this weakness, this decomposition, and this decay? Why do you still trouble their sick minds, their crippled bodies?'

Ten thousand men had come to attend the solemn service, heads of the blocks, *Kapos*, functionaries of death.

'Bless the Eternal. . . '

The voice of the officiant had just made itself heard. I thought at first it was the wind.

'Blessed be the Name of the Eternal!'

Thousands of voices repeated the benediction; thousands of men prostrated themselves like trees before a tempest.

'Blessed be the Name of the Eternal!'

Why, but why should I bless him? In every fiber I rebelled. Because he had thousands of children burned in his pits? Because he kept the six crematories working night and day, on Sundays and feast days? Because in his great might he had created Auschwitz, Birkenau, Buna, and so many factories of death? How could I say to him: 'Blessed art thou, eternal, master of the universe, who chose us from among the races to be tortured day and night, to see our fathers, our mothers, our brothers, end in the crematory? Praised be thy holy name, thou who has chosen us to be butchered on thine altar?'

I heard the voice of the officiant rising up, powerful yet at the same time broken, amid the tears, sobs, the sighs of the whole congregation:

'All the earth and the universe are God's!'

He kept stopping every moment, as though he did not have the strength to find the meaning beneath the words. The melody choked in his throat. . .

Once, New Year's Day had dominated my life. I knew that my sins grieved the eternal; I implored his forgiveness. Once, I had believed profoundly that upon one solitary deed of mine, one solitary prayer, depended the salvation of the world.

This day I had ceased to plead. I was no longer capable of lamentation. On the contrary, I felt very strong. I was the accuser, God the accused. My eyes were open and I was alone—terribly alone in a world without God and without man. Without love or mercy. I had ceased to be anything but ashes, yet I felt myself to be stronger than the Almighty, to whom my life had been tied for so long. I stood amid that praying congregation, observing it like a stranger.

The service ended with the *Kaddish*. Everyone recited the *Kaddish* over his parents, over his children, over his brothers, and over himself.

We stayed for a long time at the assembly place. No one dared to drag himself away from this mirage. Then it was time to go to bed and slowly the prisoners made their way to their blocks. I heard people wishing one another a Happy New Year!

I ran off to look for my father. And at the same time I was afraid of having to wish him a Happy New Year when I no longer believed in it.

He was standing near the wall, bowed down, his shoulders sagging as though beneath a heavy burden. I went up to him, took his hand and kissed it. A tear fell upon it. Whose was that tear? Mine? His? I said nothing. Nor did he. We had never understood one another so clearly.

The sound of the bell jolted us back to reality. We must go to bed. We came back from far away. I raised my eyes to look at my father's face leaning over mine, to try to discover a smile or something resembling one upon the aged, dried-up countenance. Nothing, not the shadow of an expression. Beaten.

Yom Kippur. The Day of Atonement.

Should we fast? The question was hotly debated. To fast would mean a surer, swifter death. We fasted here the whole year round. The whole year was *Yom Kippur.* But others said that we should fast simply because it was dangerous to do so. We should show God that even here, in this enclosed hell, we were capable of singing his praises.

I did not fast, mainly to please my father, who had forbidden me to do so. But further, there was no longer any reason why I should fast. I no longer accepted God's silence. As I swallowed my bowl of soup, I saw in the gesture an act of rebellion and protest against him.

And I nibbled my crust of bread.

In the depths of my heart, I felt a great void.

(Elie Wiesel, *Night*, New York, Bantam Books, 1982, 63–66)

Discussion

1. Where was God in the boy hanging on the gallows?
2. Is Wiesel's despair similar to Job's response to God in Scripture?

David H. Hirsch: The Holocaust and Camp Songs

David H. Hirsch has served as Professor Emeritus of English and Judaic Studies at Brown University. In 'Camp Music and Camp Songs', he discusses music that was written in the camps. Here he discusses the collection of songs recorded by Aleksander Kulisiewicz. One of these songs, composed anonymously, is a lament of despair at God's absence at Birkenau.

Birkenau Song

Kulisiewicz was, in his own right, an extraordinary being. Born in Krakow in 1918, he aspired to become a musical performer. In October 1939, however, soon after Germany had invaded Poland, he was picked up in a Gestapo dragnet and incarcerated in the Sachsenhausen concentration camp, near Berlin, where he remained until liberated on May 2, 1945. As a prisoner,

> Alex helped organize and himself performed in numerous illegal poetry readings and sings. When an informer denounced him to the authorities as a 'nightingale' SS doctors employed 'scientific' means to try and shut him up. Three times they injected him with diphtheria bacilli to destroy his hearing and three times comrades managed to smuggle in the antidote. Finally the doctors gave up. 'Let the dog sing,' they laughed.[1]

For a brief period in 1944 Kulisiewicz worked in the SS canine training centre (SS *Hundenzwinger Kommando*), where he contracted an infection of animal origin and nearly lost his sight. In addition to collecting songs, he composed 54 camp songs, 15 of which included both the words and music. In June of 1945, following his liberation, he spent more than three weeks dictating camp songs he had memorized, a total of 716 typed pages. At the time, he was a patient in the tubercular clinic in Krakow, and dictated the songs from a hospital bed. The doctors thought Alex was mad. After his recovery, Kulisiewicz performed the camp songs around the world. . .

This is music from another world. More precisely, Kulisiewicz refers to his repertory as songs from Hell. . . The lyrics of some of these songs are so revolting as to make listening to them not only painful, but almost unbearable. But they are, after all, songs, and the bare lyrics do not do

47

them justice. Not only are the words inseparable from music, but the songs are inseparable from the singer, whose raspy voice is a legacy of his captors' efforts to silence him by injecting him with diphtheria bacilli. Kulisiewicz's rendition of the songs projects a sense of total authenticity that no one seems likely to match. . .

Birkenau

Accursed scrap of earth,
Where people are nothing but numbers
Where base brother oppresses brother,
Where bony death stretches out his palm,
Where everything is drenched in blood and tears,
Where you wake up screaming in the watches of the night.

If one should ask,
'Where,
'Oh where is Hell?'
You can surely answer,
'Birkenau, accursed Birkenau.'

Bathed in blood and tears,
Birkenau, forgotten by God,
Godforsaken hellhole, Birkenau,
Thorny path,
Where millions of victims lie
In a common grave.
Birkenau, evil kingdom,
Where there is no God.
This is Birkenau.

Crematoria consuming human carcasses,
Pestilential stench of human flesh,
Chimneys belching reddish smoke,
This is the journey's end,
The end of all suffering.

And you, my friend,
Will be a handful of ashes,
Swept away by the prairie wind.

But it doesn't matter.
You're one of many
Forgotten by this beastly world.

Birkenau, accursed Birkenau,
Drenched in blood and tears,
Forgotten by God
Birkenau, thorny path,
Where millions of victims lie
In a common grave,
Kingdom
Without God.
This is Birkenau. . . [2]

The author of this song was perhaps not a theologian, but in the next lines he raises questions that theologians studying the Holocaust have pondered for the last fifty years. Birkenau is a Godforsaken hellhole, an 'evil kingdom. . . where millions of victims lie in a mass grave. . . .A kingdom where there is no God, This is Birkenau.' A kingdom without a king. Is this not, perhaps, the author's definition of Hell, 'a world without God'? The anonymous author seems to be saying that where God does not exist, there Hell does.

(David H. Hirsch, 'Camp Music and Camp Songs' in G. Jan Colijn and Marcia Sachs Littell (eds), *Confronting the Holocaust*, Lanham, Maryland, University Press of America, 1997, 161–165)

References

1. Peter Wortsman, 'Aleksander Kulisiewicz: A singer from Hell', in *Sing Out! The Folk Magazine* (25:3, 1977), 15
2. *Piesni Obozowe*, Polskie Nagrania: Muza, SX1715

Discussion

1. In what respects did Birkenau and other concentration camps constitute an earthly hell?
2. How did God's seeming absence manifest itself at Birkenau?

Alexander Donat: The Holocaust and Human Perplexity

Alexander Donat was a survivor of Auschwitz and Majdanek. In 'The Holocaust Kingdom', he recounts the tragedy of the onslaught against the Warsaw ghetto. Once the Nazis began deportations of Jews living in the ghetto, the population became deeply alarmed. As Jews faced the terror of resettlement, they began to question their own actions, the intention of world leaders, and God's concern for his people. Yet, in succumbing to Nazi violence, the Jewish people suffered from self-delusion.

Deportation and Confusion

After the first sorrow came the soul searching. How had it all come to pass? How could 300,000 people have let themselves be led to slaughter without putting up a fight? How could young healthy parents hand over their children without bashing in the criminal skulls of guards and executioners alike? Was it not a father's first, most elemental duty to save his children's life even at the cost of his own? Or for a son to die defending his mother? Why had we not lain in wait, axes in our hands, for the assassins? There is a time to live and a time to die, and when the time to die comes, we must stand up and accept death with dignity. Over and over, the ghetto Jeremiahs asked each other aloud, 'Why didn't we go out into the streets with whatever we could lay our hands on—axes, sticks, kitchen knives, stones? Why hadn't we poured boiling water on the murderers or thrown sulphuric acid? Why hadn't we broken out of the ghetto walls and scattered all over Warsaw, all over Poland? Perhaps 20,000, even 50,000 of us would have been slain, but not 300,000! What a disgrace, what an unspeakable shame!'

(Alexander Donat, 'The Holocaust Kingdom' in Albert Friedlander (ed.), *Out of the Whirlwind*, New York, Schocken, 1976, 176)

Nazi Terror and the Lack of Resistance

It was an agonizing self-appraisal. We were bitter to the point of self-flagellation, profoundly ashamed of ourselves, and of the misfortunes we had endured. And those feelings intensified our sense of being abandoned alike by God and man. Above all we kept asking ourselves the age-old question: why? why? What was all that suffering for? What had we done to deserve this hurricane of evil, this avalanche of cruelty?

Why had all the gates of Hell opened and spewed forth on us the furies of human vileness? What crimes had we committed for which this might have been calamitous punishment? Where, in what code of morals, human or divine, is there a crime so appalling that innocent women and children must expiate it with their lives in martyrdoms no Torquemada ever dreamed of?

In vain we looked at that cloudless September sky for some sign of God's wrath. The heavens were silent. In vain we waited to hear from the lips of the great ones of the world—the champions of light and justice, the Roosevelts, the Churchills, the Stalins—the words of thunder, the threat of massive retaliation that might have halted the executioner's axe. In vain we implored help from our Polish brothers with whom we had shared good and bad fortune alike for seven centuries, but they were utterly unmoved in our hour of anguish. They did not show even moral human compassion at our ordeal, let alone demonstrate Christian charity. They did not even let political good sense guide them; for after all we were objectively allies in a struggle against a common enemy. While we bled and died, their attitude was at best indifference, and all too often 'friendly neutrality' to the Germans. 'Let the Germans do this dirty work for us.' And there were far too many cases of willing, active, enthusiastic Polish assistance to the Nazi murderers.

(Alexander Donat, 'The Holocaust Kingdom' in Albert Friedlander (ed.), *Out of the Whirlwind*, New York, Schocken, 1976, 176–177)

The Holocaust and Self-Delusion

The basic factor in the ghetto's lack of preparation for armed resistance was psychological; we did not at first believe the Resettlement Operation to be what in fact it was, systematic slaughter of the entire Jewish population. For generations East European Jews had looked to Berlin as the symbol of law, order and culture. We could not now believe that the Third Reich was a government of gangsters embarked on a programme of genocide 'to solve the Jewish problem in Europe.' We fell victim to our faith in mankind, our belief that humanity had set limits to the degradation and persecution of one's fellow man. This mentality underlay the behaviour of the Jewish leadership at the very beginning of Resettlement, when the overwhelming majority voted against armed resistance. Some felt we ought to wait for a joint rising with the Poles. Others were resigned to sacrificing 70,000 Jews rather than jeopardizing the entire community of 400,000—the Nazi policy of collective responsibility was very much alive in our memories. Still others were religious Jews, committed to the tradition of *Kiddush Hashem*: that is, a martyr's death in the name of God. They believed that, when the enemy came for us, we should be dressed in our prayer shawls and phylacteries, poring over the holy books, all our thoughts concentrated on God. In that state of religious exaltation, we should simply ignore all Nazi orders with contempt and defiance; resistance, violence, only desecrated the majesty of martyrdom in sanctification of the Lord's name.

(Alexander Donat, 'The Holocaust Kingdom' in Albert Friedlander (ed.), *Out of the Whirlwind*, New York, Schocken, 1976, 179–180)

Discussion

1. Were Jews guilty of passivity in the face of the Nazi onslaught?
2. Did pious Jews who faced death with confidence suffer from self-delusion?

Sherwin Wine: The Rejection of God

An American-born Humanistic rabbi, Sherwin Wine has served as the rabbi of the Birmingham Temple in Detroit, Michigan, and is the founder of the Society For Humanistic Judaism. In Judaism Beyond God, *he argues that in a post-Holocaust world belief in God must be abandoned. In his view, Jews today should dispense with any form of supernaturalistic belief. In the past Jews employed religion to explain the course of historical events. In the modern world, however, such theistic interpretations should be replaced by a naturalistic perspective.*

The Age of Reason

The age of reason is the age without God. While nostalgia preserves him in the vocabulary of the powerful, he has lost his substance. The terrifying heavenly superfather has been replaced by a dispensable philosophical abstraction. He has lost his ability to intimidate and to attract. The world he supposedly created is now more interesting than he is. Science has replaced theology as the intellectual commitment of modern times. If science and modern theology appear compatible, it is hardly a tribute to religion. Liberal religion has produced a God too vacuous to be taken seriously. Fundamentalist religion, as the surviving popular resistance to the age of reason, may be rude and assaultive. But, at least, its God is worth noticing. The God of the fundamentalists can enforce what he commands.

The problem in the contemporary world is not the power of God. It is the power of people. The technology that is born of science has given humanity the intimidating force that was formerly reserved for divinity. In a time of biological engineering and computer slaves, now 'deities' of knowledge and power have emerged. The natural world, all by itself, provides us with access to overwhelming might.

In the age of science, the leaders of humanity are faced with the question only gods used to ask: 'How do we use the terrifying power we possess?' The tricks of old Yahveh on mountaintops are now easily duplicated by run of the mill military establishments. And the non-traditional electric switch has turned 'Let there be light' into a routine human experience.

No redefining the word God will change the reality we now perceive. The world that reason has revealed to us may give us more anxiety than we want. Or it may fill us with the pleasant anticipation of new adventure and opportunity. But its new face cannot be easily denied.

(Sherwin Wine, *Judaism Beyond God*, Farmington Hills, Michigan, Society for Humanistic Judaism, 1985, 35–36)

Naturalism and Jewish History

A humanistic approach to Jewish history needs a naturalistic perspective. The supernaturalist approach of the priestly and rabbinic theologians who edited the Bible and the Talmud is unacceptable. And the semi-supernaturalist approach of contemporary historians who describe Jewish survival as a unique 'mystery' is equally unacceptable. The causes of Jewish behaviour and Jewish endurance are open to public investigation. If they are presently unknown, they are not permanently unknowable. 'Mystery' and 'enigma' are contemporary coverups for supernatural direction. They suggest that the causes are beyond rational inquiry.

The laws of the Bible and the Talmud, the stories of sacred scriptures, the petitions of the prayerbook are of human creation. They are the products of human insight, human desire, and human vested interests. They are reflections of particular times and particular places. They are a passionate propaganda in religious and political arguments. The stories of King Saul were written by the priestly employees of his enemy King David. The tale of Jezebel was composed by her prophetic opponents. The sacrificial ritual of Leviticus was designed by the priests who would benefit from it.

Human need—no divine aloofness—is responsible for what Jews did and said. It is also responsible for distorting what Jews did and said. The motivation for recording events and happenings was no dispassionate desire to keep a diary. It was the obvious need to use history to push political programs and religious ideologies. Is the story of the covenant between Abraham and Yahveh a journalistic observation or an actual event? Or is it their justification for the Jewish claim to all of ancient Canaan?

Holidays are not the children of supernatural decrees. They have their beginnings in the human response to natural events. Passover is not the spontaneous invention of a heavenly king. It is an evolving festival that served the nationalistic fervour of patriotic rulers. Nor is *Yom Kippur* the creation of a judgemental god. It is a priestly device to increase the dread of Yahveh. The supernatural did not use the natural to promote its agenda. The human used the supernatural to advance its vested interests.

Seeing God behind all events is not necessary to explain what happens; human desire and natural laws do quite well. It is also potentially embarrassing. If Yahveh arranged for the Exodus, he also arranged for the Holocaust. The theological mileage that one can get from Jewish history is definitely limited. Theology is always more interesting when it is relegated to its appropriate niche in the department of anthropology, a study of human fear and human imagination.

(Sherwin Wine, *Judaism Beyond God*, Farmington Hills, Michigan, Society For Humanistic Judaism, 1985, 118–119)

Discussion

1. Is it no longer credible to believe in a God who acts?
2. Can a religious ceremony devoid of reference to God still be spiritually meaningful?

Michael Oppenheim: The Holocaust and Religious Language

Michael Oppenheim has served as Associate Professor of Religion at Concordia University, Montreal. In Speaking/Writing of God, *he discusses the contributions of Holocaust theologians to the dilemmas posed by the Nazi onslaught against the Jews. In his view, it is possible to use religious language in relation to God's presence in the world.*

Jewish Philosophy and the Holocaust

A number of Jewish philosophers have insisted that the community's struggle with the Holocaust could be meaningfully expressed only in the context of the covenantal relationship with God. Still, except for a few small writings—including those by Martin Buber and Abraham Heschel—the philosophical silence concerning the Holocaust only ended, as it did for Jewish communities throughout the world, with the 1967 Six-Day War. From that time, major works by such innovative Jewish thinkers as Richard Rubenstein (with some earlier pieces), Arthur Cohen, Emil Fackenheim, and, particularly, Elie Wiesel, have appeared and been widely discussed. Fackenheim's clarion call of 'If all present access to the God of history is wholly lost, the God of history is himself lost',[1] vividly reflects the place of religious language in confronting the Holocaust. Many of the most powerful insights of Jewish philosophers can be aligned in terms of that statement, with Fackenheim and Wiesel telling stories about a paradoxical and fragmented presence, while Rubenstein and Cohn discuss the ramifications of God's absence. The establishment of the state of Israel and its ongoing struggle for existence has offered occasions for a more limited and less well-known development of philosophical *midrash* or story about God's presence and action. Fackenheim has described the impact of the 1967 Six-Day War as the experience of 'a wonder at a singled out, millennial existence which, after Auschwitz, is still possible and actual'.[2] However, it is Heschel's wrestling with the right words to use in exploring the meaning of the creation of Israel that best exemplifies the wider way in which Jewish philosophers are sometimes forced, as it were, to reach for religious language. He wrote:

We have not even begun to fathom the meaning of the great event.

We do not fully grasp its message for us as a community and as individuals. It has not penetrated our capacity for representing its meaning in our daily lives. . . For all who read the Hebrew Bible with biblical eyes the State of Israel is a solemn promise of God's trace in history. It is not fulfilment of the promise, it is not the answer to all the bitter issues. Its spiritual significance, however, is radiant.[3]

It is important to note that, in relation to both the Holocaust and the state of Israel, the need to return to religious language is felt by the wider Jewish community as well as by Jewish philosophers. Jews throughout the world recognize a transcendent dimension—in Heschel's terms, a radiance of meaning—in their attempt to come to terms with these subjects. This is being expressed in the most dramatic forms available within the Jewish communal repertoire. Days are set aside—*Yom Ha-Shoah* (Holocaust Day), *Yom Ha-Atzmaut* (Israel Independence Day), *Yom Yerushalayim* (Jerusalem Day)—as religious remembrances and celebrations. Many Jews include special references to the Holocaust and Israel in their Passover *Haggada*. There are other liturgic expressions—most strikingly, the Sabbath prayer for the State of Israel that sees the emergence of that nation as marking 'the dawn of deliverance'.

(Michael Oppenheim, *Speaking/Writing of God*, Albany, State University of New York Press, 1997, 3–4)

Religious Language and the Holocaust

These expressions of religious language do not ignore the intense challenges to religious meaning that have punctuated the lives of all moderns. Perhaps the greatest challenge to the significance and vitality of contemporary religious language, at least for Jews, reverberates from the Holocaust. The discussion of the ramifications of the Holocaust by such philosophers as Emil Fackenheim, Richard Rubenstein, Arthur Cohen, Irving Greenberg, and others has detailed the extent of this threat. Notions of God's providential direction of history, as well as Israel's covenant with God, seem to have been shattered in the wake of the murder camps. However, this is not the only test of Jewish religious language that has appeared in the modern period. Secularism—that is, the view that everyday experience together with the findings of science define the contours of reality—threatens to dissipate every encounter with the divine into a mere feeling. If, following secularism, such encounters are reduced to hallucinations, or some type of isolated subjective sensations, then the concept of revelation has been unequivocally undermined. . .

Jewish religious language that features the life with others both reflects and responds to this contemporary situation. Levinas's discussion of the God who is found within by the person who takes up *Torah* in the struggle for justice is a poignant response to the Holocaust. This is also evident in the concluding statement of his essay, that 'loving *Torah* even more than God means precisely having access to a personal God against whom one may rebel—that is to say, for whom one may die'.[4] Rosenzweig's refrain about trust in God, oneself, the tradition, and the community arises from a deep encounter with the secular world. He insists that God's presence is not cut off today. However, his is not just a language of assurance or certainty. Rosenzweig knows that there are moments of silence, and, equally significant, he discerns God's presence not in extraordinary interventions, but in the love of the neighbour. . .

A Midrash

Isaiah: 43:10, 'You are my witnesses, says the Lord'. The rabbis interpreted this as meaning: 'If you are my witnesses, I am God, but if you are not my witnesses, I am not God'. . .

Contemporary Jewish philosophers have reaffirmed and extended the lesson of the ancient *midrash*. To accomplish this, they have been compelled to describe our lives with and obligations to others. In the face of the radical challenges of modernity, they have found that this speaking/writing of God still uncovers—it even elicits—the presence of the divine. Carried by this language, they offer glimmers of hope and trust, reminding us that, only through ethical testimony to God's presence, can we prevail.

(Michael Oppenheim, *Speaking/Writing of God*, Albany, State University of New York Press, 1997, 155–163)

References

1. Emil Fackenheim, *God's Presence in History*, New York, Harper and Row, 1972, 79
2. Ibid., 95
3. Abraham Joshua Heschel, *Israel: An Echo of Eternity*, New York, The Noonday Press, 1969, 219–220

4. Emmanuel Levinas, *Difficult Freedom: Essays on Judaism*, Baltimore, Johns Hopkins University Press, 1990, 145

Discussion

1. In what ways is religious langauge still of relevance in a post-Holocaust era?
2. How does ethical testimony reveal God's presence in history?

Steven T. Katz: The Uniqueness of the Holocaust

An American-born Orthodox Jew, Steven T. Katz has served as Professor at Cornell University and as Director of Boston University's Centre for Judaic Studies. In Post-Holocaust Dialogues, *he argues that the Nazis displayed a unique intentionality. Killing Jews, he argues, is not a new phenomenon; nonetheless, the Nazi onslaught against the Jews was a new form of genocidal assault. Even though Jewish theologians have not been able to provide an adequate explanation for God's seeming inaction during this tragic period of Jewish history, further explorations are urgently needed.*

Nazi Genocide

Killing Jews is not a new phenomenon in history. For more than two thousand years Jews have died because of and for their faith, either out of choice or someone else's necessity. Thus, the Nazi onslaught stands at the end of a long series of such tragedies and, indeed, would have been unthinkable without this prehistory. Yet, in order to begin to try and understand what happened specifically to the Jews of twentieth-century Europe, both in the context of modern and world history as well as in the context of Jewish history, we have to push beyond the recognition of an old pattern of Jew-hatred resulting in murder and ask whether there is anything different about the Nazi experience. In answering this question one category... becomes of primary significance: intention. Even more pointedly, what emerges as central is the specifically genocidal intent of the Nazis. That is to say, Nazism was an organized human and societal event that had as an integral part of its purposive behaviour the total eradication of world Jewry. In so doing was Nazism 'unique'? Indeed, does the very 'uniqueness' of Nazism lie in its genocidal intent against the Jewish people...

In light of this preliminary discussion it begins to appear that the strong form of the 'argument from genocidal intention' is substantive evidence in favour of viewing the Nazi experience as at least 'unique' in the context of Jewish history. However, the particularity of this conclusion must be underscored, for up until this point all we have attempted to investigate is the Jewish historical context without enquiring into possible parallels in world history. We must now pursue our enquiries into this wider domain, for there exists at least *prima facie* evidence that the Nazi experience is not without precedent there. . .

In the midst of this analytic review one last tragedy, that provides a crucial 'test' of our entire thesis, must be explored. I refer to the treatment of the Gypsies under the Nazis, which is often cited in the literature as a direct, if not exact, duplicate of the Jewish reality under the same regime. . . The Nazis did not ontologize the Gypsy into their metahistorical antithesis, nor did they make the elimination of all Gypsies from history a primal part of either their historic 'mission' or their metaphysical 'mythos'. . .

(Steven T. Katz, *Post-Holocaust Dialogues*, New York, New York University Press, 1983, 287–308)

The Need for Theological Inquiry

Each of the four responses to the Holocaust which we have considered (Richard Rubenstein, Emil Fackenheim, Ignaz Maybaum, Eliezer Berkovits) has seen the relevant events from a different perspective, with alternate presuppositions and faith commitments. Among the many lessons our four thinkers teach us, though not necessarily by intention, two especially call for a concluding comment. The first is that there is no simple set of 'facts' that can be easily seized upon and manipulated in order to get a result which is both meaningful and possesses integrity. The 'facts' are in large part determined by the premises and methodology one uses; heterogeneous preconditions and asymmetrical beginnings produce very different conclusions. Thus, our first thinker philosophizes from a psychoanalytic and anthropological centre through which everything must be judged; he therefore discovers transcendental as compared to anthropological and psychological value wanting. The second begins with an existentialist supernaturalism and so finds existential and supernatural elements even at Auschwitz. The third holds a deep faith in progress and the values of modern liberalism and thus detects God's acting in history, even in the Holocaust, to realize these personally prized ends. The fourth begins with traditional halachic and metaphysical commitments and thus finds the data more susceptible and amenable to a conservative approach in which God is, at least partially, vindicated.

Secondly, as a necessary corollary, it must be noted that each of the reactions considered, and others which have been suggested, all represent, at best, fragmentary accounts, partial descriptions, and limited and imperfect solutions to the major and most pressing questions raised by Auschwitz. Given the nature of the Holocaust, this is not surprising. Each response, even optimally, can be seen to be only incomplete in the face of the reality, quality and magnitude of evil—evil absolute and unimaginable—in our time.

In conclusion, therefore, while we cannot point to any definitive, or even agreed, results, either with regard to a starting point or to shared results, it should not be thought that the investigation of responses to the Holocaust is devoid of significance. To begin with, our review has brought the major elements crucial to any and all thinking about the Holocaust into sharp focus. Secondly, we have been given sound instruction as to how one can begin to go about giving shape to these elements—though it must be recognized that any new, more definitive account will have to go beyond the positions studied above. Third, and of no small importance, the now familiar variety found in what is to be counted as 'data' and 'evidence' and the pluralism of the responses already offered has the virtue of both guiding and warning future thinkers that the Holocaust—whatever its precise parameters and whatever its meaning—will not yield to any conceptual oversimplification. Auschwitz raises the most fundamental, and at the same time, the most difficult intellectual, phenomenological, and existential issues with which reflective men have to deal.

(Steven T. Katz, *Post-Holocaust Dialogues*, New York, New York University Press, 1983, 168–169)

Discussion

1. Was the Holocaust a unique event?
2. In what ways do events of the Nazi era give rise to multiple interpretations?

Jakob Jocz: Judaism after the Holocaust

Jakob Jocz has served as Professor Emeritus of the Chair of Systematic Theology at the University of Toronto. In 'Israel after Auschwitz' he addresses two central issues connected with the Holocaust: Where was God? Where was man? In his view, these two issues have profoundly altered Jewish consciousness.

Religious Belief after Auschwitz

The question regarding God's absence occurs in much of Jewish literature. Many Jewish writers have taken a radical position. God is not. A leader among the radicals is Richard L. Rubenstein, formerly a liberal rabbi and now professor of religion at Florida State University.

Rubenstein's reaction to Auschwitz is definite and uncompromising: to believe in God after Auschwitz is not only unreasonable but indecent: 'we have lost all hope, consolation and illusion'. History means chaos and the universe makes no sense. Man is left an orphan and the values he needs he must create for himself. There is no higher instance of appeal. This does not mean that religion is at an end. Man must reconstruct a religion without God. There are many intellectuals who take a similar view.

An even more difficult problem arises for the still believing Jew. His quest of a theodicy after Auschwitz puts a heavy burden upon his conscience. The Orthodox Jew is hard pressed to square the facts of Auschwitz with what he has been taught to believe about the God of Israel. Rabbi Eliezer Berkovits writes from an Orthodox point of view. His theodicy is supposedly the first effort on the part of an Orthodox Jew to justify God's ways before men.

Rabbi Berkovits is sorely tried to account for the disaster which befell God's chosen people, in view of his goodness and his omnipotence. In order to do so he falls back upon human freedom, but has to admit that this is insufficient to exonerate God from responsibility as Lord and Creator. Yet in spite of this he holds that no Jew dare doubt God's presence. . .

An outstanding figure caught between faith and despair is Elie Wiesel. By reason of his personal experience of four concentration camps and his great literary ability he occupies an almost prophetic position in the spiritual crisis of our age. . . The dominating ingredient in Wiesel's literary output is his experience of Auschwitz. Like Albert

Camus, Wiesel is the rebel *par excellence*. He has a perennial quarrel with God. Wiesel has been described as the Job of the twentieth century. . .

(Jakob Jocz, 'Israel after Auschwitz' in David W. Torrance (ed.), *The Witness of the Jews to God*, Edinburgh, Hansel Press, 1982, 60–61)

Human Responsibility

The case with man is even worse. Traditionally Judaism leans heavily towards humanism. It takes the *imago Dei* concept seriously. Man is the bearer of the image of God. Judaism denies the concept of original sin. Man is born blameless and pure and with the ability to keep the law. He therefore needs no salvation, only repentance. The keyword is *teshuvah* (turning to God) and not conversion in the Christian sense. Every man is his own redeemer. The secular form of self-redemption is aestheticism: emphasis upon education, culture, the fine arts. This was the characteristic mark of assimilated Germany Jewry. They adored German culture, music and literature. They felt at home with Goethe's dictum: '*edel ist der Mensch, hilfreich und gut*—man is noble, helpful and good'. The collapse of faith in man equals the collapse of faith in God.

The museum of the Holocaust in Jerusalem, *Yad Va-Shem* with its vast collection of photographs, documents and exhibits recording the tragedy called 'Auschwitz', stands as a devastating monument to human degradation. The dream which turned into a nightmare discredited once and for all every form of facile humanism. The lie about man, Wiesel expresses in the words of a father beyond the grace addressing his son: 'we were naive, innocent, so innocent that we refused to believe that evil exists. We were incapable of believing that human beings could fall so low.'[1] The rude awakening to the stark facts about man's capacity for evil is at the heart of the spiritual crisis which tears at the soul of contemporary man. Auschwitz is not merely a Jewish tragedy, it is a tragedy of mankind. Humanity is profoundly involved in the Holocaust. Those who perished in the gas ovens of Auschwitz were human beings put to death by human beings. Richard Rubenstein is well aware of the impact of the tragedy: 'Although Jewish history is replete with disaster, none has been so radical in its total import as the Holocaust. Our images of God, man and the moral order have been permanently impaired. No Jewish theology will possess even a remote degree of relevance to contemporary Jewish life if it ignores the question of God and the death camps.'[2] The effect of Auschwitz stretches far beyond the Jewish people and affects the rest of humanity. Wiesel rightly says 'The Holocaust has left its mark on more than one generation, in a way mankind came close to suicide in Auschwitz.'[3] He is aware that a radical change has taken place in the human situation; that the war against Jews is a war against mankind. 'Now we know that all hate means self-hate, that the annihilation of the Jews is bound to end in self-destruction. . . '[4]

The absence of God and the absence of man are logically related. The believing Jew asks: Where was God? The secularised Jew asks: Where was man? Because man has abysmally failed God has become a casualty. The result is an encounter with evil as the overwhelming Jewish experience of our age. Not that Judaism was unfamiliar with evil before the Holocaust. But it believed that rational man can cope with it and control it. Since Auschwitz this is now in doubt. The ugly face of evil stares at modern man from every corner. Its influence is pervasive.

(Jakob Jocz, 'Israel After Auschwitz' in David W. Torrance (ed.), *The Witness of the Jews to God*, Edinburgh, Hansel Press, 1982, 63–66)

References

1. Elie Wiesel, *A Jew Today*, 140
2. Richard Rubenstein, *After Auschwitz*, Indianapolis, Bobbs Merrill, 1966, x
3. Wiesel, op. cit., 183
4. Ibid., 182

Discussion

1. Are the absence of God and the absence of man logically related?
2. In what ways should our view of human psychology change in light of the Holocaust?

Harry James Cargas: The Holocaust and Christian Responsibility

Harry James Cargas served as Professor of Literature and Language at Webster College, Missouri. In Shadows of Auschwitz: A Christian Response to the Holocaust, *he emphasizes that the Holocaust raises fundamental questions about Christian history. Christians, he argues, must face their responsibility in the vilification of the Jews from ancient times to the present. Recognizing the atrocities that have been unleashed upon the Jewish community, they must seek to counter the legacy of anti-Semitism which fuelled Christian antipathy to Jews through the ages. In addition Christians must reassess some of the central doctrines of the faith.*

The Challenge of the Holocaust

To call myself a Roman Catholic is to describe my spiritual development incompletely. It is more honest for me to say at this time in my life that I am a post-Auschwitz Christian, in the wider context of Western Christianity. The Holocaust event requires my response precisely as a Christian. The Holocaust is, in my judgment, the greatest tragedy for Christians since the crucifixion. In the first instance, Jesus died; in the latter, Christianity may be said to have died. In the case of Christ, the Christian believes in a resurrection. Will there be, can there be, a resurrection for Christianity? That is the question that haunts me. Am I a part of a religious body that in fact is a fossil rather than a living entity? Can one be a Christian today, given the death camps that, in major part, were conceived, built, and operated by a people who called themselves Christians?. . .

(Harry James Cargas, *Shadows of Auschwitz: A Christian Response to the Holocaust*, New York, Crossroad, 1990, 1)

Religious Questioning

Questioning, of course, is an absolute necessity today. As a friend told the young Elie Wiesel, just before Wiesel was to be shipped to a death camp: 'I pray to the God within me that he will give me the strength to ask the right questions.' Novelists and philosophers known as the Absurdists ask questions from despair. This seems appropriate for those in the class of persecutors. What is amazing is that the victims—the

Jews—are mainly able to ask their questions in a framework of hope.

However, the hope has its roots in experience and is not naive childish desire. I heard someone ask Wiesel if he believed in God. His reply should be known to all Christians. 'If I told you that I believe in God, I would be lying; if I told you that I did not believe in God, I would be lying. If I told you that I believe in man, I would be lying; if I told you I did not believe in man, I would be lying. But one thing I do know: the Messiah has not come yet.' In *The Crucifixion of the Jews*, Protestant theologian Franklin H. Littell has written, from his Christian perspective:

> The truth about the murder of European Jewry by baptized Christians is this: it raises in the most fundamental way the question of the credibility of Christianity. Was Jesus a false messiah? No one can be a true messiah whose followers feel compelled to torture and destroy other human persons who think differently. Is the Jewish people, after all and in spite of two millennia of Christian calumny, the true Suffering Servant promised in Isaiah?[1]

(Harry James Cargas, *Shadows of Auschwitz: A Christian Response to the Holocaust*, New York, Crossroad, 1990, 160–161)

Reassessing Christian Doctrine

Let me offer a series of points that I feel we, as Christians, might implement in order to bring us closer to our Jewish brothers and sisters, people we have violently alienated for so long. Basically, the suggestions are aimed at institutional actions rather than individual. This is intentional, because it would be presumptuous for one Christian to tell another how to best react to history. That will have to be a personal approach. But because we are all a part of the church, it is not only appropriate but imperative that we require of the church certain acts in our name. . .

Jesus should be recognized as a link between Jews and Christians. . . Too often Jesus has been offered as a stumbling block between Christians and Jews, as a rationale for mutual exclusion. Here is an excerpt from a document written under the sponsorship of the Commission on Faith and Order of the National Council of Churches and the Secretariat for Catholic–Jewish Relations of the National Conference of Catholic Bishops:

The Church of Christ is rooted in the life of the People of Israel. We Christians look upon Abraham as our spiritual ancestor and father of our faith. . . The ministry of Jesus and the life of the early Christian community were thoroughly rooted in the Judaism of their day, particularly in the teachings of the Pharisees. The Christian Church is still sustained by the living faith of the patriarchs and the prophets, kings and priests, scribes and rabbis, and the people whom God chose for his own. Christ is the link. . . enabling Gentiles to be numbered among Abraham's 'offspring' and therefore fellow-heirs with the Jews according to God's promise. . . [2]

Traditional Christian theologies of history need to be reexamined. Generally, history has been regarded as the unfolding plan of God for humanity, or as a *Weltanschauung* based on the providential action of God in human affairs. For many today, it is difficult to see how the Holocaust fits into such concepts. Karl Rahner, one of the most influential Christian thinkers of our era, says that many questions regarding the theology of history require considerable study. Among those he indicates are the purposive unity of human history, the theology of history before Christ, the sanctification of the entire sphere of the 'profane' through the Christian church and much more, including the very basic problem of the theological meaning of a theology of history. Those of us who are nearly overwhelmed by Auschwitz feel a terrible inability to put its relevance into any pattern. Many feel it is outside of any overall plan. If true, that must be reflected in our analysis of the meaning of history. . .

We might look to see if a redefinition of the notion of inspiration in Christian Scripture is appropriate. Gregory Baum wrote this as a priest: 'If the Church wants to clear itself of the anti-Jewish trends built into its teaching, a few marginal correctives will not do. It must examine the very centre of its proclamation and reinterpret the meaning of the gospel for our times.'[3] He presses further and insists that 'what the encounter of Auschwitz demands of Christian theologians, therefore, is that they submit Christian teaching to a radical ideological critique.'[4] Some Christian theologians admit of no anti-Jewish bias in their Bible, but that seems indefensible today. Others see this bias but maintain that this comes not from inspiration, but by interpolation of early Christians to meet certain contemporary exegeses. An eloquent current voice on this subject is Rosemary Radford Ruether, whose book *Faith and Fratricide* has caused many to ask for a more complete exploration of Christian teachings on biblical inspiration.

(Harry James Cargas, *Shadows of Auschwitz: A Christian Response to the Holocaust*, New York, Crossroad, 1990, 162–170)

References

1. Franklin Littell, *The Crucifixion of the Jews*, New York, Harper and Row, 1975, 168
2. Michael McGarry, *Christology after Auschwitz*, New York, Paulist Press, 1977, 57–58.
3. In the Introduction to Rosemary Radford Ruether, *Faith and Fratricide*, New York, 1974, 6–7
4. Ibid., 7

Discussion

1. Are the horrors of the Holocaust the greatest tragedy for Christians since the Crucifixion?
2. Should Christians now re-examine the tenets of the faith in the light of the events of the Nazi period?

John Roth: The Holocaust and Religious Perplexity

John Roth has served as Russell K. Pitzer Professor of Philosophy at Claremont McKenna College, California. In 'It Started with Tears', he explores the ways in which the Holocaust has influenced his development as a Christian religious writer. In his view, the issues raised by the events of the Nazi period constitute important challenges for both Jews and Christians.

Religious Influences

Three writers have influenced my perspectives on the Holocaust more than any others. Although each one is Jewish—indeed perhaps because each one is Jewish—they think very differently, even in ways that may be in conflict. It is fitting that this meditation should conclude by amplifying how each of them continues to influence immensely my Holocaust thinking.

At the beginning of *Night*, the classic memoir that details his experiences as a man-child in Auschwitz, Elie Wiesel introduces one of his teachers. His name was Moshe, and the year was 1941. Although the Holocaust was under way, it had not yet touched Wiesel's hometown directly. One day the twelve-year-old Wiesel asked his teacher, 'And why do you pray, Moshe?' The reply Wiesel heard was, 'I pray to the God within me that he will give me the strength to ask him the right questions'. Wiesel adds, 'We talked like this nearly every evening'. . . [1]

Wiesel's brief description of his conversation with Moshe in 1941 stands out for me, for Holocaust studies have driven home to me how some questions are much more important than others. Specifically, I began to discover, questions do not give us the insight they can provide when they are posed abstractly and without reference to real human experiences and their histories. The writings of Elie Wiesel showed me that. So have Raul Hilberg's. . .

Raul Hilberg has spent his life detailing how such things happened. Thus, in his first appearance in the Lanzmann film, he observes that 'In all of my work I have never begun by asking the big questions, because I was always afraid that I would come up with small answers; and I have preferred to address these things which are minutiae or details in order that I might then be able to put together in a *gestalt* a picture which, if not an explanation, is at least a description, a more full description of what transpired'.[2]

As a philosopher who keeps encountering the Holocaust, I also keep in mind Hilberg's statement—indeed his warning—about 'big questions'. He does not deny that the Holocaust raises them—first and foremost the question Why? Contrary to much human expectation, however, the fact that a question can be asked does not mean that it can be answered well, if at all, particularly when the questions are 'big'— fundamental and sweeping ones of the kind that typically characterize philosophical and religious inquiries. So Hilberg concentrates on details instead. Those minutiae, however, are much more than minutiae. Their particularity speaks volumes and forms a terribly vast description. So full of life distorted and wasted, its accumulated detail makes the 'big' questions less easy and simple to raise but all the more important, too.

Put into perspective by work like Hilberg's, the 'big questions' become what Elie Wiesel's teacher, Moshe, called the 'right questions', and thus they command the respect they deserve. That respect enjoins suspicion about answers that are small—inadequate for the facts they must encompass. The same respect also focuses awareness that the big questions raised by the Holocaust nonetheless need to be kept alive. For the political scientist's detail and the historian's minutiae, far from silencing the questions, ought to intensify wonder about them. Otherwise we repress feeling too much and deny ourselves insight that can only be deepened by asking the 'right questions'.

There is another statement that keeps me thinking about questions that are properly called big and right: The Holocaust demands interrogation and calls everything into question. Traditional ideas and acquired values, philosophical systems and social theories—all must be revised in the shadow of Birkenau. . .

One of the important points those words make is this: Whatever the traditional ideas and acquired social systems and social theories that human minds have devised, whatever religions have been believed or gods have been worshipped, they were either inadequate to prevent Auschwitz or, worse, they helped pave the way to that place.

(John Roth, 'It Started with Tears' in Carol Rittner and John Roth (eds), *From the Unthinkable to the Unavoidable*, London and Westport, Connecticut, Greenwood Press, 1997, 198–199)

Philosophy and Holocaust Studies

What about philosophers and the discipline of philosophy in relation to Holocaust studies? I think philosophers and philosophy have avoided the Holocaust and Holocaust studies because so much history is involved. To encounter the Holocaust philosophically, one must study what has happened, to whom, where, when, and how. Reckoning with detail and particularity of that kind is not what philosophers are trained or naturally inclined to do. So it is likely that relatively few of us philosophers—maybe those who have grown impatient with the abstraction and distance from history that most contemporary philosophy reflects—will immerse ourselves in this field of study. Once there, however, we are unlikely to want to be anywhere else, for the work is so intense and important.

Think of the big questions that now and forever will need to be explored and that must be handled with great care if they are to be the right questions: How did the Holocaust happen? Who is responsible for it? How can we best remember this history? What can words say? What about God and religion after Auschwitz? What about human rights and morality in a post-Holocaust world? What can I know, what should I do, for what may I hope in the shadow of Birkenau?. . .

As I think about all the Holocaust study that still needs to be done, Richard Rubenstein's work continues to loom large. I am particularly concerned about what I call 'Rubenstein's dilemma'. This dilemma is important for every person and for every community, but is especially provocative for us Americans who have a tradition that speaks of 'self-evident' truths about 'inalienable rights' to life, liberty, and the pursuit of happiness. . .

As Rubenstein assesses the situation, the Holocaust, genocide, and related instances of state-sponsored population elimination suggest that 'there are absolutely no limits to the degradation and assault the managers and technicians of violence can inflict upon men and women who lack the power of effective resistance'.[3] A key implication of this point of view, adds Rubenstein, is that 'until ethical theorists and theologians are prepared to face without sentimentality the kind of action it is possible freely to perpetuate under conditions of utter respectability in an advanced, contemporary society, none of their assertions about the existence of moral norms will have much credibility'[4]. . . the Holocaust, he contends, sadly shows that there is little or no penalty for their violation.

(John Roth, 'It Started with Tears' in Carol Rittner and John Roth (eds), *From the Unthinkable to the Unavoidable*, London and Westport, Connecticut, Greenwood, 1997, 200–201)

References

1. Elie Wiesel, *Night*, New York, Bantam Books, 1986, 3
2. Claude Lanzmann, *Shoah: An Oral History of the Holocaust*, New York; Pantheon Books, 1985, 70
3. Richard L. Rubenstein, *The Cunning of History: The Holocaust and the American Future*, New York, Harper Torchbooks, 1987, 90
4. Ibid., 67

Discussion

1. What are the major issues raised by the Holocaust?
2. Does the Holocaust call everything into question?

PART II
Faith in the Death Camps

Chapter 2: Religious Faith   **73**

Yaffa Eliach: Faith among the Hasidim   73

Pesach Schindler: Hasidim and the Holocaust   75

Zvi Kolitz: Faith in the Ghetto   78

Leo Baeck: The Holocaust and Faithfulness   80

Nissim Nadav: The Holocaust and Jewish Heroism   83

Dror Schwartz: The Holocaust and Sanctification of Life   86

Irving Greenberg: The Dialectic of Faith   89

Chapter 3: The Holocaust and Divine Providence   **93**

Bernard Maza: The Holocaust and the Torah   93

Ignaz Maybaum: The Holocaust and Modernity   96

Sha'ar Yashuv Cohen: The Holocaust and the Messiah   98

Hayyim Kanfo: The Holocaust and Redemption   101

Yosef Roth: The Holocaust and Providence   103

Chapter 4: The Holocaust and Mystery   **106**

David Ariel: Divine Mystery   106

Neil Gilman: The Holocaust and Transcendence   109

Chapter 5: Faithfulness and Suffering   **112**

Irving Rosenbaum: The Holocaust and Law   112

Norman Solomon: The Holocaust and the Jewish Tradition   115

David Patterson: The Holocaust and Recovery   117

Ulrich Simon: The Holocaust and Sacrifice   120

CHAPTER TWO

Religious Faith

Yaffa Eliach: Faith among the Hasidim

Yaffa Eliach has served as Professor of Judaic Studies at Brooklyn College, New York. In her anthology, Hasidic tales of the Holocaust, *she recounts tales that are related to her depicting religious faith in the death camps. During the Holocaust, as Jews were systematically murdered throughout Europe, the Hasidim created magnificent tales of courage in ghettos, hiding places and camps. Despite the scope of the onslaught against the Jewish people, Hasidim did not lose their belief in humanity and faith in God. Such dedication is a testimony of the enduring confidence in God's inscrutable plan despite the horrors of the Nazi period.*

Hasidim and the Holocaust

The anonymous, ordinary Hasid, whose only distinction is his unlimited faith in his *zaddik*, also finds it easier because of that faith to come to terms with the Holocaust. He believes that a blessing uttered in the distant past promises survival, that because of the *zaddik's* blessing, even the Auschwitz number tattooed on his forearm may assume a mystical message of life. . . .

These tales are not merely the personal stories of a particular Hasidic rabbi or of individual *Hasidim*; because of the conditions that gave birth to them, they assume the dimensions of moral and social reflections and commentary. At a time when human beings were stripped naked of everything, even of their names, the only resource remaining to them was their inner spiritual strength. This was the very essence of their existence, and it is this the tales record. For the *zaddik*, this resource was his faith; for the *Hasid*, it was often his faith in his *zaddik*. It alone could provide a continuum of history and humanity amidst a distorted chaotic new order. . . .

The Hasidic tale is by its very nature capable of coming to terms with the reality of the concentration-camp universe and its aftermath. When, as Rabbi Nachman said—long before the Holocaust—lines of communication between man and his fellow man are broken, when men of faith are lonely, lost, solitary figures and the familiar social order is shattered, the Hasidic tale can offer solace to those whose faith has failed them, whose prayers seem not to be heard. The tales can restore the vital communication link between man and man, between heaven and earth.

(Yaffa Eliach, *Hasidic Tales of the Holocaust*, New York, Oxford University Press, 1982, xix–xx)

Faith Before Death

Among the thousands of Jews on that field in Janowska was the Rabbi of Bluzhov, Rabbi Israel Spira. He was standing with a friend, a freethinker from a large Polish town whom the rabbi had met in the camp. A deep friendship had developed between the two.

'Spira, all of our efforts to jump over the pits are in vain. We only entertain the Germans and their collaborators, the Askaris. Let's sit down in the pits and wait for the bullets to end our wretched existence,' said the friend to the rabbi.

'My friend,' said the rabbi, as they were walking in the direction of the pits, 'man must obey the will of God. If it was decreed from heaven that it be dug and we be commanded to jump, pits will be dug and jump we must. And if, God forbid, we fail and fall into the pits, we will reach the World of Truth a second later, after our attempt. So, my friend, we must jump.'

The rabbi and his friend were nearing the edge of the pits; the pits were rapidly filling up with bodies.

The rabbi glanced down at his feet, the swollen feet of a fifty-three year-old Jew ridden with starvation and disease. He looked at his young friend, a skeleton with burning eyes.

As they reached the pit, the rabbi closed his eyes and commanded in a powerful whisper, 'We are jumping!' When they opened their eyes, they found themselves standing on the other side of the pit.

'Spira, we are here, we are here, we are alive!' the friend repeated over and over again, while warm tears streamed from his eyes. 'Spira, for your sake, I am alive; indeed there must be a God in heaven. Tell me, Rebbe, how did you do it?'

'I was holding on to my ancestral merit. I was holding on to the coattails of my father, and my grandfather and my great-grandfather of blessed memory,' said the rabbi and his eyes searched the black skies above. 'Tell me, my friend, how did you reach the other side of the pit?'

'I was holding on to you,' replied the rabbi's friend.

(Yaffa Eliach, *Hasidic Tales of the Holocaust*, New York, Oxford University Press, 1982, 1–2)

Discussion

1. Does faith make it easier to come to terms with the Holocaust?
2. Can one believe in miracles after the Holocaust?

Pesach Schindler: Hasidim and the Holocaust

Ordained an Orthodox rabbi, Pesach Schindler served as Assistant Professor of Talmud and Rabbinics at the Rothberg International School at the Hebrew University, Israel. In Hasidic Responses to the Holocaust in the Light of Hasidic Thought, *he describes the faith of Hasidic Jews faced with suffering and death in the camps. As he explains, these devout individuals went to their deaths assured of God's abiding presence.*

The Jewish People

One response pattern comprised efforts to justify God's role during the Holocaust. Man's limited perspective does not permit a full grasp of the interrelationship of divine *Din* (justice) and *Rahamim* (compassion), unless it is viewed in the context of God as the source of the ultimate good. Hence, a Jew must accept everything with love (*kabalah be'ahavah*), inspired by *bitahon* (trust) and *emunah* (faith) in God's benevolent relationship to man. Within this framework, man responds to God by cleaving to him in mystical union (*devekut*) and joy (*simhah*). This process leads to the dissolution of the forces of ego (*bittul hayesh*) and a stance of indifference to material and physical adversity (*hishtavut*). Despite (or because of) this special relationship, some responses questioned God's role in the Holocaust, maintaining that it was incompatible with God's purpose in the universe... 'Positive' and 'negative' consequences of suffering were noted. Some significant responses held that the bond between God and his people is forged by mutual suffering. Man's love for God is simultaneously tested and articulated by means of sacrificial devotion (*mesirat nefesh*) in suffering. Noteworthy was the relative absence of responses that saw the Holocaust as retribution for the sins of the Jewish people.

The teachings of Rabbi Israel Ba'al Shem Tov and his disciples focus upon man's duty to accept personal adversity and suffering within a framework of *bitahon* (trust) in God's ways and in his will. Man is to discover the inherent goodness in misfortune and to accept it with love (*kabalah be'ahavah*). Other Hasidic interpretations of suffering are offered, including the mutual suffering of God and man as part of the general interaction and interdependence of God and man. Man is to convert (*hithapkhut*) his concern for himself (*ani*) to a concern for the *tikkun* (restoration) of the *Shekhinah* (God's presence).

(Pesach Schindler, *Hasidic Responses to the Holocaust in the Light of Hasidic Thought*, Hoboken, New Jersey, KTAV, 1990, 115–116)

The Messianic Era

Some Hasidic thinkers related the Holocaust to the *Hevle Mashiah* (the suffering prior to the coming of the Messiah). Generally the 'birth pangs of the Messiah' are to be welcomed. A variant response prefers to delay the coming of the Messiah so that Israel may be spared the suffering. Both activist and quietist notions emphasized the role of the individual in hastening redemption. The activist notion relies on man's initiative to stimulate redemption. The quietist notion views redemption as a supernatural phenomenon outside man's sphere of action. In either case, the responses acknowledged the 'unexpected' sources from which redemption may spring—unexpected as to the time as well as the source of the redemption. Attention was focused on the nature of *Galut* (exile), its negative impact on the personality of the Jew, and its role as breeding ground for tragedies like the Holocaust. Dominant is the bias of Rabbi Teichthal in *Em Habanim Semehah*, supported in *kabbalah* and Hasidism, that man must assume the initiative in countering *Galut* 'realities'. *Eretz Yisrael* (land of Israel) alone can provide the Jew with a national-religious framework of normalcy. Rabbi Teichthal accuses religious and Hasidic leaders of making exile seem normal by establishing the idea of its permanency and by undermining the Zionist initiative in Palestine. The responses invoke classic Hasidic sources to support the centrality of *Eretz Yisrael* in the essential *tikkun* (restoration) process of the *Shekhinah* (God's presence) and *kelal Yisrael* (the totality of Israel), and as a precursor of the *geulah shelemah* (final redemption).

These responses were positively correlated with aspects of Hasidic thought. The classic Hasidic teachers also welcomed the *Hevle Mashiah* as the necessary forerunner of redemption, the 'darkness before the dawn.' Consistent with *kabbalah*, Hasidism urged man to initiate action 'below' in order to arouse a response 'above'. As applied to redemption, this suggested that man's initiative in utilizing material and natural resources would trigger a similar response from the cosmic elements. The 'double directional relationship' . . . thus operates not only in the sphere of man's misfortunes but in the quest for ultimate *tikkun* (restoration). All elements in *kelal Yisrael* must play a role in the redemption process. While *Eretz Yisrael* is central to ultimate redemption, exile inhibits and obstructs the Jewish soul struggling to return to its holy origin.

(Pesach Schindler, *Hasidic Responses to the Holocaust in the Light of Hasidic Thought*, Hoboken, New Jersey, KTAV, 1990, 116–117)

Kiddush Hashem and Kiddush Hahayim

Responses related to *Kiddush Hashem* (the sanctification of God's name) assumed the classic form of Jewish martyrdom as well as forms related to *Kiddush Hahayim* (the sanctification of God in life) in defiance of the enemy's objective to degrade and terminate life. The study noted the concern for the proper stance and attitude a Jew should assume in preparation for *Kiddush Hashem*. The privilege of *Kiddush Hashem* enabled the *Hasid* to anticipate his tragic fate with some comfort and dignity. *Kiddush Hashem* also strengthened the bond between God and his people and between the people and its land. It was the opportunity to counter the satanic and the impure with the elements that were the most difficult to destroy—the spiritual and divine in human existence. *Kiddush Hashem* allowed the Jew to transcend the uneven battle of material forces.

Mesirat nefesh (sacrificial devotion to religious imperatives) is central to Hasidism and related to *Kiddush Hashem*. The Jew should indeed seek the privilege of experiencing *Kiddush Hashem*, which in essence is the ultimate form of *Ahavat Hashem* (love of God). *Kiddush Hashem* is facilitated by achieving the desired state of *devekut* (cleaving to God in search of a mystical union with the divine). Though *Kiddush Hashem* in martyrdom is unquestionably a religious imperative, the Hasidic teachers, especially Rabbi Nahman of Brazlav, seem to prefer *Kiddush Hashem* as articulated in *Kiddush Hahayim*. This tendency is consistent

77

with the Hasidic concept of *avodah begashmiut* (worshipping God through the mundane and material).

(Pesach Schindler, *Hasidic Responses to the Holocaust in the Light of Hasidic Thought*, Hoboken, KTAV, New Jersey, 1990, 117–118)

Discussion

1. Should Jews accept with love everything that occurred in the death camps?
2. Should the Holocaust be related to the birth pangs of the Messiah?

Zvi Kolitz: Faith in the Ghetto

Yossel Rakover was a pious Jew who died in the Warsaw ghetto. Although he did not leave any written record, the theatre producer Zvi Kolitz composed a reconstruction of the last moments of his life. As the Nazis razed the city, Yossel Rakover is depicted as writing his final reflections on the meaning of his death. Despite his despair over the fate of his people, he remains convinced of the promise of the world to come, and loyal to God who, he believes, will reunite him with his loved ones in a better world.

Perplexity and Faith

I believe in you, God of Israel, even though you have done everything to stop me from believing in you. I believe in your laws even if I cannot excuse your actions. My relationship to you is not the relationship of a slave to his master but rather that of a pupil to his teacher. I bow my head before your greatness, but I will not kiss the lash with which you strike me. . .

You assert that you will yet repay our enemies? I am convinced of it! Repay them without mercy? I have no doubt of that either! I should like you to tell me, however—is there any punishment in the world capable of compensating for the crimes that have been committed against us?

You say, I know, that it is no longer a question of sin and punishment, but rather a situation in which your countenance is veiled, in which humanity is abandoned to its evil instincts. But I should like to ask you, O Lord—and this question burns in me like a consuming fire—what more, O, what more must transpire before you unveil your countenance again to the world?

I want to say to you that now, more than in any previous period of our eternal path of agony, we, we the tortured, the humiliated, the buried alive and burned alive, we the insulted, the mocked, the lonely, the forsaken by God and man—we have the right to know what are the limits of your forbearance.

I should like to say something more: Do not put the rope under too much strain, lest, alas, it snaps! The test to which you have put us is so severe, so unbearably severe, that you should—you must—forgive those members of your people who, in their misery, have turned from you.

(Zvi Kolitz, 'Yossel Rakover's Appeal to God' in Albert Friedlander (ed.), *Out of the Whirlwind*, New York, Schocken, 1976, 396–397)

Beyond Despair

Death can wait no longer. From the floors above me, the firing becomes weaker by the minute. The last defenders of this stronghold are now falling, and with them falls and perishes the great, beautiful, and God-fearing Jewish part of Warsaw. The sun is about to set, and I thank God that I will never see it again. Fire lights my small window, and the bit of sky that I can see is flooded with red like a waterfall of blood. In about an hour at the most I will be with the rest of my family and with the millions of other stricken members of my people in that better world where there are no more questions.

I die peacefully, but not complacently; persecuted, but not enslaved; embittered, but not cynical; a believer, but not a supplicant; a lover of God, but no blind amen-sayer of his.

I have followed him even when he rejected me. I have followed his commandments even when he castigated me for it; I have loved him and I love him even when he hurls me to the earth, tortures me to death, makes me an object of shame and ridicule. . .

God of Israel, I have fled to this place in order to worship you without molestation, to obey your commandments and sanctify your name. You, however, have done everything to make me stop believing in you. Now lest it seem to you that you will succeed by these tribulations to drive me from the right path, I notify you, my God and the God of my father, that it will not avail you in the least! You may insult me, you may castigate me, you may take from me all that I cherish and hold dear in the world. You may torture me to death—I shall believe

79

in you, I shall love you no matter what you do to test me.

And these are my last words to you, my wrathful God: nothing will avail you in the least. You have done everything to make me renounce you, to make me lose my faith in you, but I die exactly as I have lived, a believer!

Eternally praised be the God of the death, the God of vengeance, of truth and of law, who will soon show his face to the world again and shake its foundations with his almighty voice.

Hear, O Israel, the Lord our God the lord is one.

Into your hands, O Lord, I consign my soul.

(Zvi Kolitz, 'Yossel Rakover's Appeal to God' in Albert Friedlander, *Out of the Whirlwind*, New York, Schocken, 1976, 398–399)

Discussion

1. Does it make sense to think that God will repay the enemies of the Jews?
2. What conditions could lead one to renounce belief in God?

Leo Baeck: The Holocaust and Faithfulness

Leo Baeck was President of the Reichsvertretung, the representative body of German Jews during the Holocaust. In 'In Memory of Two of Our Dead' he wrote about a prayer that he had composed during the Nazi era. Determined to stand firm against the Nazi attack on German Jewry, Baeck turned to God in faithfulness to the tradition. In This People Israel, *he reiterates this theme of loyalty to God.*

Jewish Prayer in the Third Reich

The present writer must mention one personal experience with deep gratitude. He had been arrested in the autumn of 1935 and taken to the SS prison, because he had composed a prayer for the Jewish communities which tried to express Jewish pride before men and Jewish humility before God. . .

Kol Nidre Prayer

In this hour all Israel stands before God, the judge and the forgiver. In his presence let us examine our ways, our deeds, and what we have failed to do.

Where we have transgressed, let us openly confess: 'We have sinned!' and, determined to return to God, let us pray: 'Forgive us.'

We stand before our God.

With the same fervour with which we confess our sins, the sins of the individual and the sins of the community, do we, in indignation and abhorrence, express our contempt for the lies concerning us and the defamation of our religion and its testimonies.

We have trust in our faith and in our future.

Who made known to the world the mystery of the Eternal, the One God?

Who imparted to the world the comprehension of purity of conduct and purity of family life?

Who taught the world respect for man, created in the image of God?

Who spoke of the commandment of righteousness, of social justice? In all this we see manifest the spirit of the prophets, the divine revelation to the Jewish people. It grew out of our Judaism and is still growing. By these facts we repel the insults flung at us.

We stand before our God. On him we rely. From him issued the truth and the glory of our history, our fortitude amidst all change of fortune, our endurance in distress.

Our history is a history of nobility of soul, of human dignity. It is history we have recourse to when attack and grievous wrong are directed against us, when affliction and calamity befall us.

God has led our fathers from generation to generation. He will guide us and our children through these days.

We stand before our God, strengthened by his commandment that we fulfil. We bow to him and stand erect before men. We worship him and remain firm in all vicissitudes. Humbly we trust in him and our path lies clear before us; we see our future.

All Israel stands before her God in this hour. In our prayers, in our hope, in our confession, we are one with all Jews on earth. We look upon each other and know who we are; we look up to God and know what shall abide.

'Behold, He that keepeth Israel doth neither slumber nor sleep.' (Psalm 121:4).

'May He who maketh peace in His heights bring peace upon us and upon all Israel.' (Prayer book).

(Leo Baeck, 'In Memory of Two of Our Dead' in Albert Friedlander, *Out of the Whirlwind*, New York, Schocken, 1976, 131–132)

Divine Mystery

The great task of dark days, and the greater one of bright hours, was to keep faith with the expectation. Man waits for God, and God waits for man. The promise and the demand speak here, both in one: the grace of the commandment and the commandment of grace. Both are one in the One God. Around the One God there is the concealment. He does not reveal himself, but he reveals the commandment and the grace. And he, the Eternal One, has given mortal man freedom of will and has shown him a goal for his will. But the ultimate remains concealed from man. Thus the prophet announced the word of God: For my thoughts are not your thoughts, neither are your ways my ways, saith he-who-is (Is. 55:8). The great reverence was exalted in this, and it always clung to this, even when men dared the supposition that their ways were God's ways. The mystery surrounds God. He is not the revealed God, but he is the revealing God. Wherever the great reverence lives in a man and the great readiness for God rises out of it, there and then, man is near to God. . .

Man lives within the universe and within history. This people understood that history and universe testify to a oneness, and reveal a totality and order. One word has dared to be the one expression for that which keeps everything together: 'covenant'—'the enduring,' the covenant of the one God. It is the covenant of God with the universe, and therefore with the earth; the covenant of God with humanity and therefore with this people contained in it; the covenant with history and therefore with every one within it; the covenant with the fathers and therefore with the children; the covenant with days which were and therefore with days which are to come. 'As true as my covenant is'— this was the word of the Eternal One heard by the prophet when he thought about his people in a time of oppression and dark destiny, and certainty entered him. The question of all questions, that of the entrance of the eternal, the unending, the one, in to the domain of the many, the terrestrial, the passing, this question in which the searching, the thinking, the hope of this people has always lived, in which it once grew and in which it was ever reborn—this question itself possesses the answer: 'As true as my covenant is.'

(Leo Baeck, 'This People Israel' in Albert Friedlander (ed.), *Out of the Whirlwind*, New York, Schocken, 1976, 527–533)

Discussion

1. Was Baeck naive to trust in God during the German onslaught against the Jews?
2. Does the belief in divine mystery resolve the dilemmas of the Holocaust?

Nissim Nadav: The Holocaust and Jewish Heroism

In 'The Lights of Faith and Heroism in the Darkness of the Holocaust', the Jewish writer Nissim Nadav, a yeshivah student at Yeshivat Kiryat Shemonah in Israel, emphasizes that the Holocaust constitutes a major challenge to Jewish belief. Yet, in his view the faith of pious Jews in the camps illustrates the power of faith to withstand the greatest tragedies.

The Religious Dilemma

The believing Jew is in great spiritual distress as he attempts to understand the ways of divine providence, which permitted the wicked ones to exterminate the majority of the Jewish people in Europe, including the major centres of Torah learning for generations past. One of the more extreme views regards the Holocaust as punishment for the heavy sin of the Jewish people, especially that of falling prey to the enticements of the *Haskalah* (Enlightenment) and assimilating in European culture. The proponents of this view state that the source of the tragedy was in Germany, where the walls of faithful Judaism were first breached by secular education and non-Jewish culture.

The believing Jew obviously cannot abandon the principle of divine providence and the direction of the world on the basis of reward and punishment. After the cessation of prophecy, however, are we capable of interpreting every occurrence in our time? Does anyone in our generation have the audacity to claim that the intent of the creator and the plans of divine providence are known to him? Inherent in such a claim is the danger that any interpretation of the divine will would be influenced by the personal worldview of the interpreter. Consequently, many philosophers and educators argue that we must renounce any attempt to provide a rational explanation of the Holocaust, and instead accept the fact that it remains an unsolvable enigma within the context of the Lord's direction of his people.

(Nissim Nadav, 'The Lights of Faith and Heroism in the Darkness of the Holocaust' in Yehezkel Fogel (ed.), *I Will Be Sanctified*, Northvale, New Jersey, Jason Aronson, 1998, 26)

Jewish Heroes

Unquestioning acceptance of the underlying cause of the Holocaust does not exempt us from learning the facts of the Holocaust. A study of the memoirs and testimonies by Jews in the Holocaust is likely to upset accepted conceptions in our understanding of this terrible period. . . Observant Jews provided an outstanding example of the aspiration to realize Jewish life even under the greatest duress. The attempt to maintain *Torah* observance was extremely difficult and was fraught with danger, since observant Jews were the first to be killed by the Germans, who regarded them as the backbone of the Jewish people. . .

The experience of *Kiddush ha-Shem*, in the broad sense of the realization of expressly Jewish life, left its mark on the behaviour of many Jews. They desired to live and die as their religious way of life demanded of them, by sanctifying the divine name through the fulfilment of the commandment of *Kiddush ha-Hayyim*. They consciously went to their deaths, with head held high, as Jews and as humans, in complete contrast to the manner in which the Nazis sought to portray them to themselves and to others. . .

There are innumerable examples of religious heroism in the Holocaust, even at the entrances of the gas chambers. . . It was a Saturday afternoon. A large number of Jews had been assembled at the train station, to be transported to Auschwitz, where most would be put to death immediately. When they realized that it was time for *seudah shalishit* (the third Sabbath meal), the Jews searched for a bit of water and bread, washed their hands, recited the blessing over the bread, and began to sing songs for *seudah shalishit*.

A second instance: a group of fifty young men were brought into the hall where they undressed before the 'showers'. While in this hall, they said to one another: 'Today is *Simhat Torah* (literally, the Rejoicing of the Torah). Let us celebrate the holiday before we die. We have no *Torah* scroll, but the Holy One, blessed be he, is with us—let us rejoice with him.' They began the traditional dancing and singing, with great fervour. The Nazis standing outside could not comprehend what was taking place before their eyes. . .

Faith has never been challenged so seriously as in our generation. We are the generation of the Holocaust, the generation of the Binding, but we also were privileged to witness the establishment of the State of Israel. There can be no greater proof of the truth of our faith than the rebirth of the Jewish state. In the past, it was commonly stated that the physical and spiritual presence of the Jewish people could not be understood without a belief in divine providence. The presence of the people of Israel in the State of Israel only reinforces this wisdom.

(Nissim Nadav, 'The Lights of Faith and Heroism in the Darkness of the Holocaust' in Yehezkel Fogel (ed.), *I Will Be Sanctified*, Northvale, New Jersey, Jason Aronson, 1998, 26–30)

Heroism in the Camps

The first anti-Jewish decrees of the murderers were directed against the spiritual leadership: rabbis, *yeshivah* heads, and their students. *Torah* centres flourished among the millions of Jews in Eastern Europe and spread their light upon the entire community. Jews faithfully fulfilled the instructions issued by their rabbis, who headed their flocks and directed their lives. Torah scholars and Hasidic *rebbes* stated their opinions openly, and those wearing the 'crown of *Torah*' served as the community's leaders. The murderers were well aware of this reality, and therefore they sought to first eliminate the community's spiritual leaders. The Jewish masses would then be easy prey for the Nazi plans. Wherever the Nazi jackboots trod, the rabbis, *yeshivah* students, ritual slaughterers, cantors, and other religious functionaries were the first to be killed, in order to prevent the formation of a religious leadership that would unite the community and stiffen its resolve. Anyone whose external appearance identified him as a possible member of the religious elite was a candidate for elimination. Many Jews were compelled to cut off their beards because of this danger. The rabbis faced a difficult predicament in these times. Many of their followers sought to save their leaders' lives and smuggle them beyond the sphere of Nazi control. The religious leadership withstood this test and refused to abandon their communities, whom they continued to guide, despite the ever-present danger this entailed.

Their leadership was even more essential when the mass murders began. In these difficult moments of despair, when the members of their flock were sent on their last way, the rabbis marched at the head of their congregations, encouraging them to walk with head high and die with honour, as is proper for Jews who die because of their Jewishness and thereby sanctify the divine name.

(Nissim Nadav, 'The Lights of Faith and Heroism in the Darkness of the Holocaust' in Yehezkel Fogel (ed.), *I Will Be Sanctified*, Northvale, New Jersey, Jason Aronson, 1998, 34)

Discussion

1. Is the quest to comprehend God's will during the Nazi era a heretical quest?
2. Was it folly to sanctify God in the middle of suffering?

Dror Schwartz: The Holocaust and Sanctification of Life

In 'The Heroism of Masada and the Martyrs of the Holocaust', Dror Schwartz, a yeshival student at Yeshivat Kiryat Shemonah in Israel, describes the principle of 'sanctification of life'. As he explains, in the ghettos and death camps Jews were determined to live so as to defeat the Nazis' plan of destroying the Jewish people.

Sanctification of Life

The concept of *Kiddush ha-Hayyim*, the 'sanctification of life', first appeared in the Holocaust, and originated in the concept of *Kiddush Hashem*. Until the Holocaust, the concept of *Kiddush Hashem* was understood to mean self-sacrifice. In other words, the way to sanctify the name of the Holy One, blessed be he, in the world consisted of dying for one's belief in him; however, this explanation greatly limited the concept. . .

There are two categories of *Kiddush Hashem*. One consists of publicizing the name of the Holy One, blessed be he, by sacrificing ourselves when faced with an attack on our religion. The other consists of preventing *Hillul Hashem* when there is a danger of this. The return of the Jewish people to its land is an example of the second category, for exile constitutes a desecration of the divine name, because the non-Jews regard this as the weakness of the Lord of Israel and their victory over him. In such a situation, action by the people of Israel to frustrate the machinations of its enemies is to be regarded as *Kiddush Hashem*. This is connected to the Jewish people's being the people of God, a conception that is shared by the non-Jewish peoples. The defeat of the Jewish people, its inability to oppose its enemies, also is regarded by the latter as the defeat of its God. . .

It is patently clear that when the goal of our adversary is to take our lives, his success would constitute *Hillul Hashem*. Accordingly, it is incumbent upon us to remain alive as long as possible, so that we frustrate the designs of our enemy; this constitutes *Kiddush Hashem*.

There is no question that the intent of the Nazis was the total systematic annihilation of the Jewish people. The Nazis also viewed this as the idealized victory of the chosen Aryan race over the inferior Jewish race and all that the latter represents. Consequentially, the sanctification of the Name of God during the Holocaust consisted of *Kiddush ha-Hayyim*; in other words, remaining alive. The first to adopt this approach was Rabbi Nissenbaum:

> And then the piercing saying of Rabbi Yitzhak Nissenbaum was cast into the air of the ghetto: 'This is the hour of *Kiddush ha-Hayyim*, and not of *Kiddush Hashem* by dying. Formerly, our enemies demanded the soul and the Jew offered his life for *Kiddush Hashem*; now, the adversary demands the Jewish body, and it is the duty of the Jew to defend it, to protect his life.' A survivor of the Holocaust testifies that a fierce desire to life surfaced among the inhabitants of the ghetto, replete with hidden powers which could not be imagined in normal life. This desire for life expressed itself in the cultural realm. . . Against Hitler's evil design to destroy and annihilate stood the will of the Jews, specifically to live. . . In an organized fashion, and to an even greater extent not in an organized manner, spontaneously, the Jewish population revealed vitality and a will to live so fierce that it is difficult to describe. . . [1]

This intense desire to live, and thereby frustrate the plans of the Nazi adversary, was responsible for the survival of many, and gave Jews the strength to endure the suffering the likes of which were experienced only by those who lived in this period. This then explains why the Jews of the Holocaust chose life, in contrast to the Jews of Masada. The imperative of their time was to live, and thereby rob the Germans of their victory, which would have led to *Hillul Hashem* in the world. Unlike the Germans, the Romans sought to destroy the honour of the Jews, and therefore the considerations of the Jews at Masada were different.

The resolve to live is also expressed in the poems written in the ghettos and the extermination camps. The fact that such determination appears in poems written by children demonstrates the degree to which the imperative was ingrained in their parents, who transmitted this message to their children. An example of this is the poem written by a girl named Eva Pitzkova in the Theresienstadt camp:

The Struggle

Typhus, like a serpent, chokes the girl.
Father is bent over, his heart beats once.
Mother covers her face with her hands
And we stand, confused
But we cling to this world,
Struggling with our last powers against our suffering.
Not to die, but live we are commanded,
To live, to live, in the name of God!

It should come as no surprise, then, why the Jews complied with the degrading and excruciatingly difficult orders of the Nazi officers. The Jews worked hard, suffered dreadful humiliations—all in order to remain alive, and thereby be victorious over the enemy. The Jews encouraged each other: We shall outlive them!. . .

The desire to live was not limited to the realm of physical survival, but encompassed the entire Jewish experience: to live as Jews, as they had before the war. The Jews in the ghettos and death camps did not forgo continued cultural life. Religious Jews continued to observe the commandments, despite the many difficulties they faced. One had to endanger his very life for *Torah* study and observance, but this did not deter religious Jews from deceiving the Germans and establishing yet another *heder* or *yeshivah*, in order to clandestinely maintain religious life. . .

In conclusion: the Jews in the Holocaust sanctified the divine name by their choice of life. Indeed, if they had taken their own lives in order to maintain their personal honour, they would have presented the Nazis with a victory on a silver platter. The Jewish masses did not adopt this course; they aspired to upset the enemy's plans—and to live.

(Dror Schwartz, 'The Heroism of Masada and the Martyrs of the Holocaust' in Yehezkel Fogel (ed.), *I Will Be Sanctified*, Northvale, New Jersey, Jason Aronson, 1998, 151–154)

References

1. N. Eck, *Those Wandering on the Paths of Death*, 37 and 244

Discussion

1. Was the response of the Jews of Masada inferior to the response of those who struggled to endure the Nazi onslaught?
2. Did suicide in the camps constitute a victory for the Nazis?

Irving Greenberg: The Dialectic of Faith

Irving Greenberg is an Orthodox rabbi, and has served as Professor of Jewish Studies at City College of New York, President of the National Jewish Center for Learning and Leadership, and President of the Jewish Life Network. In 'Cloud of Smoke, Pillar of Fire: Judaism, Christianity and Modernity after the Holocaust', he argues that the Holocaust poses a fundamental challenge to both Judaism and Christianity since it calls into question the central affirmations of these faiths. In his view, adherents of these traditions must re-examine their beliefs in the light of the events of the Nazi era. What is required is an acceptance of the dialectic of the Holocaust in which both light and darkness are present. To live with this dialectic, the image of Job is of central importance: out of the whirlwind he experienced God's presence.

The Challenge of the Holocaust

Both religions (Judaism and Christianity) have always sought to isolate their central events—Exodus and Easter—from further revelations or from the challenge of the demonic counter-experience of evil in history. By and large, both religions have continued since 1945 as if nothing had happened to change their central understanding. It is increasingly obvious that this is impossible, that the Holocaust cannot be ignored.

By its nature, the Holocaust is obviously central for Jews. The destruction cut so deeply that it is a question whether the community can recover from it. When Adolf Eichmann went into hiding in 1945, he told his accomplice, Dieter Wisliceny, that if caught, he would leap into his grave laughing. He believed that although he had not completed the total destruction of Jewry, he had accomplished his basic goal—because the Jews could never recover from this devastation of their life centre. . . .Since there can be no covenant without the covenant people, the fundamental existence of Jews and Judaism is thrown into question. For this reason alone, the trauma of the Holocaust cannot be overcome without some basic reorientation in light of it by the surviving Jewish community. . .

For Christians, it is easier to continue living as if the event did not make any difference, as if the crime belongs to the history of another people and faith. But such a conclusion would be and is sheer self-deception. The magnitude of suffering and the manifest worthlessness of human life radically contradict the fundamental statements of human value and divine concern in both religions. Failure to confront and account for this evil, then, would turn both religions into empty, Pollyanna assertions, credible only because believers ignore the realities of human history.

(Irving Greenberg, 'Cloud of Smoke, Pillar of Fire: Judaism, Christianity and Modernity after the Holocaust' in Eva Fleischner (ed.), *Auschwitz: Beginning of a New Era?*, New York, KTAV, 1977, 8–9)

The Holocaust and Israel

I have saved for last the most important reason why the moment of despair and disbelief in redemption cannot be final, at least in this generation's community of Israel. Another event has taken place in our lifetime which also has extraordinary scope and normative impact— the rebirth of the State of Israel. As difficult to absorb in its own way and, like the Holocaust, a scandal for many traditional Jewish and Christian categories, it is an inescapable part of the Jewish historical experience in our time. And while it is a continuation and outgrowth of certain responses to the Holocaust, it is at the same time a dialectical contradiction to many of its implications. If the experience of Auschwitz symbolizes that we are cut off from God and hope, and that the covenant may be destroyed, then the experience of Jerusalem symbolizes that God's promises are faithful and his people live on. Burning children speaks of the absence of all value—human and divine; the rehabilitation of one-half million Holocaust survivors in Israel speaks of the reclamation of tremendous human dignity and value. If Treblinka makes human hope an illusion, then the Western Wall asserts that human dreams are more real than force and facts. Israel's faith in the God of history demands that an unprecedented event of destruction

90

be matched by an unprecedented act of redemption.

(Irving Greenberg, 'Cloud of Smoke, Pillar of Fire: Judaism, Christianity and Modernity after the Holocaust' in Eva Fleischner (ed.), *Auschwitz: Beginning of a New Era?*, New York, KTAV, 1977, 31–32)

Job and the Holocaust

What, then, are the theological models that could come to the fore in a post-Holocaust interpretation of the relationship between God and man? One is the model of Job, the righteous man from whom everything is taken: possessions, loved ones, health. It is interesting that his wife proposes that Job 'curse God and die'; his friends propose that he is being punished for his sins. Job rejects both propositions. . . The ending of the book, in which Job is restored and has a new wife and children, is of course, unacceptable by our principle. Six million murdered Jews have not been and cannot be restored. But Job also offers us a different understanding. His suffering is not justified by God, nor is he consoled by the words about God's majesty and the grandeur of the universe surpassing man's understanding. Rather, what is meaningful in Job's experience is that in the whirlwind the contact with God is restored. That sense of Presence gives the strength to go on living in the contradiction.

The theological implications of Job, then, are the rejection of easy pieties or denials and the dialectical response of looking for, expecting further revelations of the Presence. This is the primary religious dimension of the reborn State of Israel for all religious people. When suffering had all but overwhelmed the Jews and all but blocked out God's Presence, a sign out of the whirlwind gave us the strength to go on, and the right to speak authentically of God's Presence still.

(Irving Greenberg, 'Cloud of Smoke, Pillar of Fire: Judaism, Christianity and Modernity after the Holocaust' in Eva Fleischner (ed.), *Auschwitz: Beginning of a New Era?*, New York, KTAV, 1977, 34–35)

Human Responsibility in a Post-Holocaust Age

We also face the urgent call to eliminate every stereotype discrimination that reduces—and denies—this image in the other. It was the ability to distinguish some people as human and others as not that enabled the Nazis to segregate and destroy the 'subhumans' (Jews, Gypsies, Slavs). The ability to differentiate the foreign Jews from

French-born Jews paved the way for the deportation first of foreign-born, then of native, French Jews. This differentiation distilled conscience, stilled the church, stilled even some French Jews. The indivisibility of human dignity and equality becomes an essential bulwark against the repetition of another Holocaust. It is the command rising out of Auschwitz.

This means a vigorous self-criticism, and review of every cultural or religious framework that may sustain some devaluation or denial of the absolute and equal dignity of the other. This is the overriding command and the essential criterion for religious existence, to whoever walks by the light of the flames. Without this testimony and the creation of facts that give it persuasiveness, the act of the religious enterprise simply lacks credibility. To the extent that the religion may extend or justify the evils of dignity denied, it becomes the devil's testimony. Whoever joins in the creation and rehabilitation of the image of God is therefore participating in 'restoring to God his scepter and crown.' Whoever does not support—or opposes—this process is seeking to complete the attack on God's presence in the world.

(Irving Greenberg, 'Cloud of Smoke, Pillar of Fire: Judaism, Christianity and Modernity after the Holocaust' in Eva Fleischner (ed), *Auschwitz: Beginning of a New Era?*, New York, KTAV, 1977, 44)

Discussion

1. Is the creation of the State of Israel a solution to the religious problems presented by the Holocaust?
2. Does God's response to Job provide a basis for hope after the events of the Nazi era?

CHAPTER THREE

The Holocaust and Divine Providence

Bernard Maza: The Holocaust and the Torah

Bernard Maza is an Orthodox rabbi and theologian. In With Fury Poured Out, *he argues that the Holocaust was the result of divine providence. In his view, God brought about the Holocaust in order to insure that Jews returned to Torah Judaism.*

The Religious Dilemma of the Holocaust

When the cantor began to chant the blessing *Shehecheyonu*, 'Thou hast given us life,' the silence was broken by wild screams from a dark corner at the edge of the tent.

'Lies, lies, it's all lies!'

The congregants began to knock on the wooden benches with their fists and they said, 'Oy, oy, desecration and blasphemy! Sh! Quiet! On the eve of *Kol Nidre*?! Quiet!'

However, the man paid no attention to their protests. He raised his voice above their banging and quieted them.

The man was Reb Chaim, a righteous and holy man, who had led a pious and holy life for all of his sixty years, and who had never turned away from the ways of the *Torah*. In the last slaughter, all of his family had been taken away. By a miracle he had remained alive, and he could not explain why only he, the old man, had remained, while his young sons and daughters had been led to the death pits behind the city.

Only one Jew dared interrupt the words of Reb Chaim. A young man stepped forward. The worshippers made way for Leibele Brodsky who came to face his opponent.

Who in the city did not know Leibele Brodsky, the *yeshivah* student who had strayed from the Torah's ways. He had become a public desecrator of the Sabbath, a man who mocked the customs of Israel and all who observed them. But from the day the Nazis began their murders he had repented. All day he sat in his house and recited Psalms.

'Jews,' said Leibele. 'You know that I was a blasphemer, a mocker of Israel, a lost soul. And I tell you, yes, there is a G-d in heaven. Here we have seen fulfilled the words of the Prophets and their curses. All the curses have fallen upon us—not one is missing'. . .

Leibele raised his voice and said, 'Behold our eyes have plainly seen the hand of G-d raised to punish his people who betrayed their mission and rejected him and his *Torah!*'

Leibele looked to every side with an air of victory. The listeners had listened to the fiery words of the 'new *tzaddik*' and now waited for the response of Reb Chaim who had stood silently with his eyes closed when Leibele was speaking.

Reb Chaim clapped his hands and began to speak in a soft voice as though from the depths.

'My teachers, you heard, G-d destroys his people from off the face of the earth because of their sins. Isn't it foolish to believe that? If this were a punishment from heaven because of our sins, why did all the rabbis, the pure and holy *tzadkim* who were full of Torah and good deeds, why did they die?'

(Bernard Maza, *With Fury Poured Out*, New York, KTAV, 1986, 3–4)

The Holocaust and Divine Providence

For generations their faith remained firm, their loyalty to the Torah unswerving. And in 1939 this generation, as earlier generations, was steady and undoubting.

But human beings have their limits and the Jewish people had reached theirs. The Jews of succeeding generations could no longer bear to be the shame and ridicule of nations, as a sheep led to slaughter. They would forget the name of *Hashem*. . .

In the twentieth century there was descending upon the Jewish people the desire to be like all other nations. The younger generation of the scattered remnants of the Jewish people were seeking other values. The young *chalutzim* of Eastern Europe were seeking European socialism and secular Zionism. The children of the immigrants in America were seeking the materialism of the 'Golden Land.'

But it was the will of *Hashem* that the Jewish people, the bearers of the Torah, would not forsake the Torah. The present generation of righteous would not be the last. The ambition of the coming generation to be like all the nations of the world would not be.

Hashem knew that the oppression of the Jewish people had to end or the sun of *Torah* would set. The Jewish people had to be redeemed and returned to the land of Israel. Only in the land of Israel would they find freedom from the suffering that was inevitably their lot in the lands of their exile.

When they would be returned to their land and the burden of oppression lifted from their backs, the heaviness would be removed from their hearts. When their hearts and minds would be free, they would seek and find themselves. The *'pintele yid'*, the spark of Judaism that is in the heart of every Jew, would be awakened. The sunshine of Torah would rise.

This was therefore the moment in the divine history of the Jewish people that *Hashem* judged to be the time for redemption from oppression. . .

The prophet Ezekiel had said:

'As I live,' says the Lord, 'that only with a strong hand and an outstretched arm, and with fury poured out will I be King over thee.'

The road to the Kingdom of *Hashem*, beginning with redemption from oppression, would be preceded by 'fury.' Not just fury, but a fury of unprecedented magnitude—a 'fury poured out.'

The beginning of redemption was to be ushered in with all of its prophetic accompaniments. It meant the coming of the fury. It meant a holocaust.

Hashem knew that this was the last generation of the exile that lived in the spirit of Rav Nachman, that had the sanctity to sing '*Ani Maamin*' with their last breath. *Hashem* chose this generation for martyrdom. Their martyrdom would bring the blessing of *Hashem* upon the work of those they left behind. And with their deeds the Jewish people would be redeemed from the oppression of their exile and the sunshine of Torah would rise again.

Hashem hid his face and he did not protect his people from the evil that was in the hearts of his enemies.

(Bernard Maza, *With Fury Poured Out*, New York, KTAV, 1986, 124–127)

Discussion

1. If the Holocaust is a divine punishment, why did righteous victims die along with those who were wicked?

2. Is the revitalization of *Torah* Judaism a sufficient reason for the Holocaust to have occurred?

Ignaz Maybaum: The Holocaust and Modernity

An Austrian-born Reform rabbi, Ignaz Maybaum was actively involved in providing support for the Berlin Jewish community prior to the Second World War and later served as rabbi of Edgware Reform Synagogue in London. In The Face of God After Auschwitz, *he argues that the Holocaust was part of God's providential plan. In his view, Hitler served as a divine instrument for the reconstruction of modern Jewish life.*

Jewish Progress

The first *churban*, the destruction of Jerusalem at the hand of Nebuchadnezzar, the second *churban*, the destruction of Jerusalem in the year 70 by Rome, and the third *churban*, the destruction suffered by Jewry in the years 1933–1945, these catastrophes are 'a small moment', 'a little wrath', measured against the eternal love which God showers on his people.

After every *churban*, the Jewish people made a decisive progress and mankind progressed with us. After the first *churban* we became the people of the diaspora proving to the gentiles that a people can exist without the heathen attachment to its land. After the second *churban*, after the loss of the Temple, we made worship dependent on the spoken word alone. After the third *churban*, that of our own time, the Jewish diaspora is no longer limited to Ashkenazi and Sephardi regions, but has become a world-diaspora. The medieval organisation outside which God was not supposed to be found has been destroyed. You can be a Jew outside the *din*, outside the religious organisation as defined in the codes. The Middle Ages have come to an end. It is the same for us as it is for the Christian. He can be a Christian outside the Roman Church: at least we can all be citizens living in freedom. That is the blessed end of the Middle Ages, the end of the Empires, through the rise of democracy. . .

Thus Hitler came. He, the Nihilist, did what the progressive should have done but failed to do, he destroyed the Middle Ages, but did so by destroying the old Europe. The sins of a stagnant Europe, the sins of an isolationist America, the sins of the democracies, failing to progress towards the solution of the new problems gave birth to Hitler. Of Nebuchadnezzar, the destroyer of Jerusalem, the word of God in the book of Jeremiah says: 'Nebuchadnezzar, my servant' (Jeremiah 27:6). Of Ashur who destroyed Samaria, Isaiah says that God himself called him to come. Would it shock you if I were to imitate the prophetic style and formulate the phrase: Hitler, my Servant!? In the Book of Job, Satan is there, among the servants and messengers of God. Hitler was an instrument, in itself unworthy and contemptible. But God used this instrument to cleanse, to purify, to punish a sinful world; the six million Jews, they died an innocent death; they died because of the sins of others. Western man must, in repentance, say of the Jew what Isaiah says of the Servant of God: 'Surely, our diseases he did bear, and our pain he carried. . . he was wounded because of our transgressions, he was crushed because of our iniquities.' (Isaiah 53:4–5).

(Ignaz Maybaum, *The Face of God after Auschwitz*, Amsterdam, Polak and Van Gennep, 1965, 66–67)

The Holocaust and Sacrifice

When the catastrophe came and the Davidic chapter of history came to an end with the destruction of Jerusalem and Samaria, the prophets said: it is our God who did it, the God of Israel. It was his judgement over the past. It was 'The Day of the Lord.' By saying so, the prophets found the formula for survival. When Samaria, the capital of Israel was destroyed in 722 BCE, the Jewish people, who suffered greviously, had, with the help of their prophets—as we read in our Hebrew Bible—the religious strength to celebrate God's victory over an evil, decadent chapter of history and to confess as suffering victims with no cooperation with the real leaders, their share in the sins of the condemned age. Therefore they survived and progressed hopefully to the next chapter of history.

We live now in the post Auschwitz era and look back to the *ante* Auschwitz era. It was, what Amos calls, 'the Day of the Lord', which created the division into a condemned past and into a new era. Before Auschwitz, there were various ideologies of political messianism, in which many thought they could shape the pattern of the future; they thought they could make history as they arranged their front gardens. They thought that they themselves and they alone could do it. They looked forward into the future which they regarded as a happy playground for their creative enterprise, forgetting the Creator, the

Maker of man and the Maker of history. The day of the Lord came: it was darkness and not light, it was a day of judgement which destroyed the pride of man and taught him his utter dependence on God. The six million who died innocently, died because no man is an island, because everyone is responsible for everyone else. The righteous are responsible for the sinners. The innocent who died in Auschwitz, not for the sake of their own sins, but because of the sins of others, atone for evil and are the sacrifice which is brought to the altar and which God acknowledges favourably. The six million, the dead of Auschwitz and of other places of horror, are Jews whom our modern civilisation has to canonise as holy martyrs; they died as sacrificial lambs because of the sins inherent in Western civilisation. Their death purified Western civilization so that it can again become a place where man can live, do justly, love mercy, and walk humbly with God.

Auschwitz closes a past for everyone, for us Jews, of course, too. There are people amongst us who preach the same doctrines and talk in the same ideologies and party slogans which are familiar to us from pre-Auschwitz days. These people of yesterday offend our martyrs, they ignore their sacrifice. The day of the Lord, as a day of judgement, condemns the past. But in doing so, it opens the door to a new future. The martyr dies to give us, the Remnant, an atoned future, a new day, wonderful like every morning in which God renews his creation.

(Ignaz Maybaum, *The Face of God after Auschwitz*, Amsterdam, Polak and Van Gennep, 1965, 83–4)

Discussion

1. Is it blasphemous to conceive of Hitler as God's instrument?
2. Should those who died in the camps be viewed as sacrifical victims?

Sha'ar Yashuv Cohen: The Holocaust and the Messiah

Sha'ar Yashuv Cohen served as Chief Rabbi of Haifa. In 'Hester Panim in the Holocaust versus the Manifest Miracles in our Generation', he rejects the contention that the Holocaust is a punishment for sin. Rather, he argues that the Holocaust should be understood as part of the birth pangs of the Messiah initiating the redemption of the Jewish people.

The Holocaust and the Righteous

In 1943, when the first reports about the Holocaust arrived—these were not complete reports of the full extent of the Holocaust, but they already contained the terrible news of thousands and tens of thousands who went to the gas chambers and the crematoria—I was a student in the Merkaz ha-Rav Yeshivah, which had been founded by Rabbi Kook. I went up to the head of the *yeshivah*, Rabbi Charlap, the outstanding pupil of Rabbi Kook. . . I gathered my courage, went in, and raised the following question: one of the foundations of our faith is that we are the people chosen by God. . . Then how was it possible that this chosen people must suffer more than any other people, to the extent that hundreds of thousands and millions of its sons were sacrificed on the altar, with no explanation of reward and punishment?. . .

Rabbi Charlap said, it would seem that all of our educational and public activity aspires to inculcate the awareness that we suffer because we have forsaken the ways of the Lord; in consequence, we are punished, and all these evils come upon us; and the proper response to this is to repent. . . If so, it is proper for the people of Israel to say, 'in that day: "Have not these evils come upon us because our God is not among us?" and why we should receive an even greater punishment for this, namely, "And I will surely hide my face in that day."'

Rabbi Charlap explained this question and the statement that 'our God is not among us' as follows: tribulations and sufferings are beyond the bounds of nature. They are a decisive proof for the believing Jew that we are not a people like all the others, but rather, 'Thus is the way of this nation: when they go up, they ascend to the heavens; and when they go down, they descend to the dust'. We are not like the other peoples regarding the profundity of the sufferings, tragedies and sacrifices we endure, nor are we similar to the non-Jewish peoples regarding the destiny of Israel. Great things await us; great things have happened to us in the past, and even more wondrous things will be our lot in the future. We have no explanations for any of these events, but we must understand that this is apparently the last phase in the birth pangs of the Messiah, before the redemption that will come for us. Casting doubt upon this fundamental of faith is the most extreme form of *Hester Panim*, the act of concealing—but it is intended to cause the people of Israel to repent. This repentance is not only to the Torah of Israel, and not only to the commandments, but it is also to the land of Israel. There is no graver sin than Jews living in the diaspora, despite their being able to come to Israel.

(Sha'ar Yashuv Cohen, '*Hester Panim* in the Holocaust versus the Manifest Miracles in our Generation' in Yehezkel Fogel (ed.), *I Will Be Sanctified*, Northvale, New Jersey, Jason Aronson, 1998, 1–3)

Messianic Deliverance

The instinctive and spontaneous response of the myriads who walked to the gas chambers singing 'I believe with perfect faith in the coming of the Messiah' assaults our sensibilities, but it issued from the profound awareness that they were living in the generation of the birth pangs of the Messiah, who will bring the redemption after these tribulations. These sufferings will be unbearable, and as one of the *Amoraim* declared, 'Let it (the redemption) come, but I do not want to witness it', because of these upheavals. We perhaps, after the fact, are only now beginning to understand that the threat of annihilation, which recurs in every generation, and the losses we suffer are, as the rabbis said, proof that we are living in a great period. Our time is one of unparalleled suffering, but also of unprecedented joy, for the redemption that shall speedily come. . .

I completely reject the explanations of the Holocaust given both by the opponents of Zionism and by its proponents. The former state that the Holocaust was punishment for the sin of hastening the End of Days. . . The Rabbi of Satmar, the outstanding talmudic scholar Rabbi Isaac Hutner, and others have attempted to explain the Holocaust as punishment for our attempting to speed the redemption by Zionism and the establishment of the State of Israel and by not wanting to wait for the Messiah, thereby violating the oaths that the Holy One, blessed be He, imposed upon us.

Religious Zionist thinkers, in contrast, have cast the blame for the Holocaust on the opponents of Zionism: because they did not heed the call to leave the diaspora for *Eretz Israel*, but rather told their pupils that it was forbidden to immigrate to *Eretz Israel*, they were responsible for the deaths of these Jews. This is the gravest sin that a Jew is capable of committing: not permitting other Jews to immigrate to *Eretz Israel*. The resulting punishment was the Holocaust. Each of these two opposing groups thus attempts to explain the Holocaust as punishment for the actions of the rival camps. . .

I conclude from this that we are all living in a generation too sublime for human comprehension. We cannot understand the suffering we have endured, and we have similar difficulty in fathoming the salvation and redemption we have received. If we know how to believe, how to trust in the Lord, and how to appreciate those who regarded all this suffering as a prelude to the 'beginning of the flowering of our redemption'—then the *Hester Panim* of the Holocaust will be transformed into the magnificent revelation of miracles in our time, before our eyes.

May it be the will of the one who assured us 'Even when they are in the land of their enemies, I will neither reject nor abhor them, to destroy them and to break my covenant with them' (Lev. 26:44) to fulfil his promise. May it be his will that the Holocaust and the wars for *Eretz Israel* will constitute the entire measure of the birth pangs of the Messiah, and that from now on we will receive the salvation and the consolation of the Holy One, blessed be He, for the people of Israel, and witness the complete redemption, speedily in our days.

(Sha'ar Yashuv Cohen, '*Hester Panim* in the Holocaust versus the Manifest Miracles in our Generation' in Yehezkel Fogel (ed.), *I Will Be Sanctified*, Northvale, New Jersey, Jason Aronson, 1998, 6–14)

Discussion

1. Should the suffering of the Holocaust be regarded as a punishment for sin?
2. Is it a sin for Jews to live in the diaspora?

Hayyim Kanfo: The Holocaust and Redemption

In 'Manifestation of Divine Providence in the Gloom of the Holocaust', a yeshivah student at Yeshivat Neveh Dekalim, Hayyim Kanfo, argues that God's presence was manifest in the Holocaust. The terrors of the Nazi onslaught against the Jews were part of the redemptive process.

The Function of the Holocaust

With divine inspiration, the rabbis foresaw the terrible tribulations that would befall the Israelite nation on the eve of the redemption. They even related the death throes to be experienced by the Jews, as is depicted in a *midrash*:

'The Lord shall answer you in the day of trouble' (Psalm 20:2): this is comparable to a father and his son who were walking along, and the son became tired. He asked his father, 'Where is the city?' He replied: 'My son, let this be a sign for you: if you see a cemetery, know that you are close to the city.' Thus says the Holy One, blessed be he, to Israel: If you see that troubles envelop you, at that moment you are redeemed. (*Midrash Shoher Tov* 20)

Death and sufferings constitute preparation for the redemption of the nation. In his vision of the End of Days, Isaiah declares: 'For as the earth brings forth her growth, and as the garden causes the things that are sown in it to spring forth, so the Lord God will cause victory and glory to spring forth before all the nations' (Isaiah 61:11). The prophet compares the redemption to a seed that has been planted. Just when it is close to rotting, it renews itself, sprouts and blossoms. The exile in its entirety is an ongoing state of decay in the life of the nation, culminating in the terrible Holocaust. Precisely at the apex of this chain of events, a new, fresh shoot springs forth, with a great future before it.

In a similar vein, Isaiah compares the redemption to birth:

Before she travailed, she brought forth; before her pain came, she gave birth to a male child. Who has heard of such a thing? Is a land born in one day? Is a nation brought forth at once? For as soon as Zion travailed, she brought forth her children. Shall I bring to the birth, and not cause to bring forth? says the Lord. (Isaiah 66:7–9)

Zion is compared to an expectant mother whose labour pains reach a peak close to the birth that she awaits; it is not coincidental that the sufferings of redemption are called the 'birth pangs of the Messiah'.
(Hayyim Kanfo, 'Manifestation of Divine Providence in the Gloom of the Holocaust' in Yehezkel Fogel (ed.), *I Will be Sanctified*, Northvale, New Jersey, Jason Aronson, 1998, 21–22)

The Dawn

These basic principles teach that divine providence encompasses the historical course of events from the beginning of time to the end, and divine direction leads the world toward its state perfection, namely, the universal acknowledgment of God and his kingship.

Within this context, the Holocaust constitutes the darkness and terrible absence that will cause the events of salvation to spring forth.

The previous condition of the Jewish people—the debasement of the diaspora and the severance from *Eretz Israel*—was excised, so that a new, fresh shoot for which we hope may come forth: the shoot that will constitute the foundation for the restoration of the Davidic line and the return of the Divine Presence to Zion.

This process in the life of the nation is of a general and public nature, and therefore requires many unblemished public sacrifices (a reference to a type of sacrifice offered in the Temple). All the great Torah scholars and children were patently without flaw; they served as public sacrifices for the entire world.

It was decreed that our generation pass through the seven chambers of purgatory. It was not chosen for this purpose because it was inferior. To the contrary, it is exalted, a generation that has endured the tortures of the Holocaust and the darkness. It is this generation that goes forth from darkness to light, from destruction to national revival, from exile to redemption.

We are privileged to be part of this generation, not as Ulla and Rabbah, who said: 'Let him (the son of David) come, but let me not see him,' but as Rav Joseph, who hoped to be in the generation of redemption, despite the many sufferings this entailed (Sanhedrin 98b). Rabbi Kook explained that Rav Joseph understood the profundities of this exalted concept. . . Indeed, with our own eyes we witness the light of salvation as it expands and spreads, in the rebuilding of the Land and in the restoration of its ruins.

(Hayyim Kanfo, 'Manifestation of Divine Providence in the Gloom of the Holocaust' in Yehezkel Fogel (ed.), *I Will Be Sanctified*, Northvale, New Jersey, Jason Aronson, 1998, 22–23)

Discussion

1. Should the Holocaust be viewed as the gloom before the light of deliverance?
2. Is it sensible to view the great Torah scholars as unblemished sacrifices?

Yosef Roth: The Holocaust and Providence

In 'The Jewish Fate and the Holocaust', Yosef Roth, a yeshivah student at Yeshivat Maale Edumim in Israel, surveys various traditional approaches to the

Holocaust. In his view, the tragedy of the Nazi era should be understood as part of the unfolding of God's plan for the Jewish people.

Traditional Theodicy

Rabbi Eliezer Berkovitz does not regard the Holocaust as a unique occurrence, but rather as a link in a chain of tragic events in Jewish history. The reason for these ordeals is the divine attribute known as *Hester Panim*. According to Berkovitz, *Hester Panim* is a condition for man's free choice; in other words, the ability to choose between good and evil, free of divine intervention. Since God does not interfere, but man has the freedom to choose, he uses this freedom in a negative manner. . .

Other important thinkers connect the Holocaust with redemption—the establishment of the State of Israel. According to this approach, the lack of proportion between the sin and its punishment is explained by the end of the exile and the establishment of the State of Israel. The holders of this view regard the Holocaust as a divine 'treatment' meant to release the Jewish people from its adherence to the exile. This hypothesis is based on the chronological fact that the establishment of the State of Israel immediately followed the conclusion of the Holocaust. . .

Another view regards the Holocaust and national revival as events connected to the period of the end of the exile. This approach is based on the rabbinical teaching that at the end of the exile the advent of the Messiah will be preceded by the 'birth pangs of the Messiah' (Sanhedrin 98b). Consequently, the Holocaust is to be regarded as these 'birth pangs', and the establishment of the State of Israel, as the redemption. . .

Dr. Yonah Ben Sasson describes an additional approach in his essay 'The Religious Significance of the Holocaust' as containing 'an explanation of the suffering and destruction, not in the context of sin and punishment, but as a necessary disruption of Jewish existence, and as an imperative of the Jewish misson.'. . . In conclusion: this approach views the Holocaust as essential for the continued existence of the Jewish religion and nation, and as intertwined with the advancement of Jewish life. . .

Some authorities regard the Holocaust as punishment for our nonobservance of the commandments of the Torah. . . A view prevalent among the anti-Zionist circles of Torah scholars maintains that the establishment of the Jewish state was one of the primary causes of the Holocaust. . . A slightly different view maintains that the Holocaust was mainly caused by the pretentions of our people to return to its land on its own and thereby bring an end to the period of exile, without awaiting the advent of the Messiah. . .

(Yosef Roth, 'The Jewish Fate and the Holocaust' in Yehezkel Fogel (ed.), *I Will Be Sanctified*, Northvale, New Jersey, Jason Aronson, 1998, 49–59)

Divine Providence

The Holocaust led a portion of the faithful to question the presence of God, or the possibility of his direction of human history. This question, like others connected with the ways of divine providence, does not have an unequivocal answer that can be attained by humans, 'for my thoughts are not your thoughts' (Isaiah 55:8), and we cannot know the intent of the Master of the Universe. Our comprehension is limited, and cannot plumb the profundities of the will of the king of all worlds. Our reckoning is a human one, within the limitations of time, while the divine reckoning spans all time.

Despite these limitations, this question is so central and important that the attempt to seek an answer must be undertaken. Prominent in any consideration of the Holocaust as a unique event are three interrelated focal points: faith, divine providence, and the national revival in *Eretz Israel*. Notwithstanding all this, it must be emphasized that the thought of the Master of the Universe is unfathomable. This enigma regarding the direction of the world by the creator must remain unresolved. The faithful Jew, however, believes that within the hidden there are clear manifestations of the divine plan. If the believing Jew has not yet reached this level, this does not detract from his faith, which is not conditional upon an understanding of the ways of the Lord.

This, then, is the source of self-sacrifice of many in the Holocaust due to their perfect faith, they were ready for any sacrifice, and their faith was only strengthened by the sufferings they underwent.

(Yosef Roth, 'The Jewish Fate and the Holocaust' in Yehezkel Fogel (ed.), *I Will Be Sanctified*, Northvale, New Jersey, Jason Aronson, 1998, 59–60)

Discussion

1. Is *Hester Panim* a precondition for human freedom?
2. Are there clear manifestations that the Holocaust was part of the divine scheme?

CHAPTER FOUR

The Holocaust and Mystery

David Ariel: Divine Mystery

David Ariel has served as President of the Cleveland College of Jewish Studies, Ohio. In What Do Jews Believe?, *he argues that there can be no rational explanation for the terrible events of the Nazi regime. In his view, God's purposes are unfathomable.*

Job's Answer

God's answer to Job is the classical answer of Judaism to the question of human suffering. God is transcendent and his nature is unknowable. We can relate to Job's anguish and loneliness. God's silence about the fairness or injustice of his fate leaves him in a state of religious despair. Trust in God can never again be taken for granted. Yet the voice within the tempest strangely brings Job the desolate peace of a man who accepts his fate and the abyss between human and divine understanding. The very existence of God as creator of the universe gives our lives meaning. The only way to make life bearable when we cannot find answers is to recognize that some answers are beyond us. This is also the conclusion of the rabbinic tradition: Rabbi Yannai said, '(The reason) why the guilty prosper or the innocent suffer is not within your grasp.'

Job meets a face of God that is awesome, remote and terrifying; it is beyond the categories of human experience. Job, however, emerges from his trials a wiser man. Never again will he expect life to provide him with predictable answers. Job learns from his experience because he is open to what God can teach him. Although this story does not offer easy answers about human suffering, it points to the human capacity that ever astounds us—the ability to continue life after tragedy and even to grow in compassion and wisdom. The story of Job inevitably brings us back to the world of human activity, the only arena in which we can live.

(David Ariel, *What Do Jews Believe?*, London, Rider, 1996, 105)

Suffering and Sin

Can we accept the idea that there is no sufficient answer to the question of human suffering in the Holocaust? Some religious traditionalists have argued that our sins are so overwhelming that we have eclipsed God and caused God to withdraw from us. Modern Hasidism continues to see mass suffering as a form of divine retribution for sins and as a form of punitive divine withdrawal (*hester panim*, 'hiding the face') from the Jewish people. Hasidic survivors of the Holocaust frequently see the destruction of their own families as divine retribution for their own sins and the collective sins of the Jewish people. They often single out the violation of the *mitzvot* which they equate with the growth of non-Orthodox Judaism—including Zionism—and assimilation as the reason for divine retribution in the Holocaust. Some Christian theologians take a similar tack in positing a collective punishment for Jews.

These extreme theological positions horrify us with their willingness to view innocent victims as object lessons for a fundamentalist agenda. The rabbis took the myth of sin and punishment to its limits and beyond in an effort to find answers to unanswerable questions. We cannot accept the traditional rabbinic explanation that the victim's supposed guilt is the cause of his suffering. This explanation becomes obscene when confronted with the murder of six million men, women and children.

(David Ariel, *What Do Jews Believe?*, London, Rider, 1996, 105–106)

Jewish Despair

For many contemporary Jewish theologians, the traditional notion that an active personal God is responsible for reward and punishment is obsolete. The view of one modern Jewish theologian, Richard Rubenstein, is that God is dead. If God is not dead, at least belief in God is dead. To the writer and Holocaust survivor Elie Wiesel, God's silence at Auschwitz and every other killing site is an ongoing challenge to God's goodness. In his play *The Trial of God*, Wiesel invokes the Jewish tradition of convening a *bet din*, or rabbinical court, and charging

God as the defendant. He wants to force God to answer out of the silence that intensifies despair. In the void between the extreme positions of Rubenstein and Wiesel, we realize that humanity as a whole has to assume full responsibility for those tragedies that result from human actions or the failure to act.

(David Ariel, *What Do Jews Believe?*, London, Rider, 1996, 106)

The Holocaust and Tragedy

The mystery of how God could have permitted the Holocaust remains inexplicable. The only viable explanation is that the Holocaust, and all evil, pose a challenge to us all. When confronted by evil, we must oppose it without compromise, without temporizing, without hesitation. All evil challenges us for a response that sees each victim or potential victim as created in the image of God. Only the absolute conviction that he who saves one life saves the entire world can offer meaning in the face of absolute evil. The certainty that evil challenges us to total and uncompromising moral action is rooted in the imperative to mend the world through resistance to evil.

Jewish thinkers today reject the view of blaming the victim or looking for the source of evil in human sin. In a much broader sense, however, the rabbinic emphasis on human responsibility for the evils of the world pertains. Human beings are ultimately responsible for the actions of their own governments. In the Holocaust, there were perpetrators, collaborators, and bystanders, as well as governments that failed to act to end the atrocities. There were also heroic individuals who resisted the Nazis at great personal risk. Although we cannot ultimately explain why evil persists, we can agree on the human imperative to actively resist it. We are responsible for the world and for each other. Still, the vexing spiritual question remains, 'Why did God not intervene to prevent the suffering?' This is a question we cannot presume to answer, but within a purposeful universe we cannot avoid the asking.

(David Ariel, *What Do Jews Believe?*, London, Rider, 1996, 106–107)

Discussion

1. Is the belief that the Holocaust was divine retribution for Israel's sin an obscene idea?
2. Should humanity assume full responsibility for the tragedies of the Holocaust?

THE HOLOCAUST AND MYSTERY

Neil Gillman: The Holocaust and Transcendence

Neil Gillman is Aaron Rabinowitz and Samuel H. Rifkind Professor of Jewish Philosophy at the Jewish Theological Seminary, New York. In Sacred Fragments, *he surveys the various religious responses to the tragedy of the Nazi era. In his view all these theodicies are ultimately inadequate. For this reason, the Jewish tradition affirms that God's ways are beyond human understanding.*

Religious Responses

With the Holocaust, the problem of evil acquires a new and terrifying urgency. Jewish theological responses to the Holocaust can be grouped into two broad classes.

The first sees the Holocaust as one more instance of human cruelty, perhaps more massive than ever but not intrinsically different and hence not posing significantly new theological or religious challenges. The death of six million Jews and countless other human beings is not necessarily more problematic than the death of one innocent child. The Jewish theological tradition, in this view, has developed resources to deal with the problem and these resources are applied to the Holocaust.

The other view sees the Holocaust as totally unprecedented. The sheer scope of the massacre, the malevolence with which it was perpetrated, the machinelike efficiency of the Nazi death camps, the active involvement and passive acquiescence of countless, ordinary human beings, the fact that the world of Auschwitz was conceived and carried out by the most cultured of European nations—any or all of these factors make the Holocaust totally unique. In this view, the resources that the tradition has evolved for dealing with suffering are simply inadequate. We can not write this trauma off as one more instance of human cruelty. The vexing theological question 'Where was God?' will not go away by simply postulating human freedom. In fact, it is made all the more poignant by Judaism's cardinal claim that God and Israel share a unique intimacy. Indeed, then, where was he? Why did he let it happen?

One response that is almost universally rejected by all thinking segments of the community is that the Holocaust is God's punishment for Israel's sin. If the Holocaust accomplished anything, it effectively killed the doctrine of retribution as the key to Jewish theodicies. It may have worked for centuries, but today it is viewed as an obscenity. It has not been invoked by any but the most traditionalist wings of the Jewish community, by those who maintain the sanctity of the past, come what may. To everyone else, the sheer disparity between the 'explanation' and the event is so wide that it just does not merit serious consideration. This is our paradigmatic instance of the death of a portion of the Jewish myth. It must be replaced—but by what?

(Neil Gillman, *Sacred Fragments*, Philadelphia, Jewish Publication Society, 1990, 201–202)

Beyond Theodicy

This survey of positions has shown that the enterprise that has come to be called Holocaust theology, but a few decades old, has already produced a rich and diversified literature. But the second dimension of the challenge, the attempt to develop a more generalized religious response to the event through liturgy and ritual, has not proven nearly as fruitful. A glance at the various ways in which we celebrate *Yom Ha-Shoah* will confirm that our community has not as yet reached a consensus on a memorial that is Holocaust specific. Thus far, we have been drawing on other familiar patterns. . .

This should not be surprising. Liturgy and ritual are infinitely more complex to work out, particularly on a communal basis, and particularly when we haven't as yet reached a consensus on the theological issues. What should the liturgy say? What should be the implicit message of the ritual? Until those questions are answered, we are all groping in the dark. But we are also desperately in need of a set of religious responses, so we draw from the familiar patterns of our past.

The Holocaust is simply too close to us. But it is not too much to expect that the same vitality that enabled our ancestors to develop elaborate ceremonial pageants for *Passover, Hanukkah, Purim*, and *Tishah b'Av* will, in time, enable us to develop equally gripping memorials for this event as well.

If the ultimate impulse behind a religious perspective on the world is to introduce a sense of cosmos, order, or harmony into our experience of the world, then suffering and evil are properly perceived as profoundly threatening. In fact, the problem of evil is the greatest theological problem because it threatens the central function of any religious system as a whole. It represents the eruption of the chaos that destroys our cosmos.

When that happens, we can respond in two ways. Intellectually, we try to account for the evil, explain why it had to be so, and thereby integrate it into our cosmic pattern. In effect, we reknit the pattern with the evil included. This is properly the task of theodicy. The evil becomes God's punishment, or the result of God's self-limitation to make room for human freedom, or it will be rectified in some eschatological future. These are all intellectual accountings, designed to maintain the integrity of our fabric of understanding.

But sometimes these explanations just don't work. To return to one of our initial distinctions, they may provide objective explanation and yet leave us with a sense of emotional irresolution. Heschel, for example, can insist that the Holocaust is our failure, not God's, and objectively that may be perfectly true. But on some other level, it explains nothing at all. We are still haunted by questions: Why did this have to happen? Why does this have to be the price we pay for our freedom? Why is the world this way?

At this point, our response to chaos has to move in a different, less intellectual, and more affective direction—or, to use our earlier distinction, a 'religious' direction. At that point, we stop trying to explain, and instead, somehow existentially affirm our conviction that our cosmos will be restored intact. Jews say the *Kaddish*, which in its last line becomes a prayer for an eschatological *shalom*, for harmony, for cosmos in human affairs. . .

In the final analysis, most theodicies are inadequate. That's probably why the Book of Job is in the Bible. It's almost as if our ancestors said, 'We really don't have any conclusive answer for why human beings are doomed to suffer. So here's another approach.' The genius of most ancient and rich religious traditions is that they give us multiple ways of accomplishing the same purpose.

(Neil Gillman, *Sacred Fragments*, Philadelphia, Jewish Publication Society, 1990, 209–211)

Discussion

1. Is the Holocaust our failure?
2. Are all theodicies inadequate to account for the events of the Nazi era?

CHAPTER FIVE

Faithfulness and Suffering

Irving Rosenbaum: The Holocaust and Law

In The Holocaust and Halakhah *the Jewish scholar Irving Rosenbaum surveys the range of halakhic decisions reached during the Holocaust. In his view the continuation of the halakhic tradition within the camps enabled Jews to face suffering and death.*

Halakhah in the Camps

It has become almost an article of faith that the Holocaust was without precedent in Jewish experience. It was not! But the mistaken assumption that it was has not only spawned an entire literature of 'Holocaust theology', but also has been responsible for an almost total unawareness of the role played by the *Halakhah* in the lives and deaths of the Holocaust's victims. It has been estimated that more than half of the millions of Jews caught up in the Holocaust observed the *mitzvot*, the commandments of the Torah, in their daily lives prior to the advent of the Nazis. Did this commitment to the *Halakhah*, the 'way' of Jewish religious law, crumble and disintegrate under the pressures of the final solution? Or did the *Halakhah* continue to bring not only some semblance of order, but of meaning, sanity, and even sanctity into their lives?

Precisely because the Holocaust was not without precedent, and because the *Halakhah* had confronted, dealt with, and transcended similar situations in the past, it was able to guide and sustain those who lived and died by it during the bitter and calamitous times of the German domination of Europe. While much of its technology was novel, the Holocaust simply duplicated on an extensive and enormous scale events which had occurred with melancholy regularity throughout Jewish history. The concept of the 'final solution', it may

112

be argued, differed in kind from earlier attempts at the destruction of Jews; but this could make little difference in the reaction of its victims, who were unaware of the comprehensive nature of the plan. Pillage, psychological degradation, exclusion from society, mass murder, mass graves, burning, torture, beatings, cremation, forced labour, imprisonment, death marches, infanticide, enforced prostitution, rape, and expulsion had all been experienced by Jewish communities in the past. Long, long before the Holocaust, the *Halakhah* had developed its theoretical 'theology' and its practical course of action when confronted with such tragic events.

The *Halakhah* was, therefore, uniquely equipped to adjust to death and suffering as well as to life and joy. It would be blasphemous effrontery for anyone who did not himself experience the terrors and the madness of the Holocaust to speak rapturously of the supportive and sustaining power of the *Halakhah* during the insane and diabolical period. But the vivid and compelling testimony of survivors, the literary testaments of victims, even the eyewitness accounts of the SS and those in league with them, clearly indicate the significant and ennobling role of Jewish religious observance in the Holocaust kingdom. In the face of events which would make Job's trials seem trivial, Jews retained their confident belief in a just Creator, whose secret purposes they might not be able to fathom, but whose revealed and clear dictates in the *Halakhah* they were bound to observe

(Irving Rosenbaum, *The Holocaust and Halakhah*, New York, KTAV, 1976, 1–2)

The *Halakhah* and Jewish Belief

In almost all the halakhic literature of the Holocaust there is hardly any attempt at questioning, let alone vindicating, the justice of the Almighty. To some extent this avoidance of theodicy may be explained by the apothegm attributed to the great spiritual leader of East European Jewry, Rabbi Israel Meir HaCohen, the Hafetz Hayyim: 'For the believer there are no questions; and for the unbeliever there are no answers.' But the more essential reason was that personal and national tragedies had long since prompted the raising of all the possible questions. They are strewn throughout the Bible, the *Talmud*, the *Midrash*, and the post-Talmudic literature. The answers, however unconvincing or unsatisfying or even contradictory they might be, were well known to anyone at all familiar with Jewish tradition. The *Halakhah* maintained that the only tenable response of the believing

Jew to the chastisements of God—deserved or not—was that of Moses himself, who, after describing God's outpouring of wrath upon his people, declared, 'The secret things belong unto the Lord our God, but the things that are revealed belong unto us and to our children forever, that we may do all the words of this law' (Deut. 29:28). The one course of action which remained mandatory under even the most calamitous circumstances was the fulfilment of the *mitzvot*.

This basic principle was applicable no less to the Holocaust than it was to every personal and national tragedy that preceded it. It was clearly enunciated in the second century in the response of the Sages to the apostasy of Elisha ben Abuyah. Observing that the consequences of the fulfilment of the commandment of *shiluah ha-kan* (not taking fledglings in the presence of the mother bird) (Deut. 22:6) and *kibbud av* (parental honour) (Ex. 20:12) were not, as the *Torah* promised, 'well-being and length of days,' but, at least on one occasion, violent and untimely death, Elisha concluded. . . 'there is no justice and no Judge', and abandoned the *Halakhah*. Rabbi Jacob, however, declared that the 'well-being' and 'long life' promised by the Torah to those who observed its commandments were not necessarily to be enjoyed in this world, but in the next. As Rabbi Yannai summed it up, 'It is not in our power to explain either the prosperity of the wicked or the afflictions of the righteous' (*Avot* 4:19). Whether one met with sorrow or suffering or happiness and rejoicing, he was still obligated to praise and bless God (*Berakhot* 48b).

But a Jew did not need to be a talmudic or rabbinic scholar to know that the *Halakhah* provided for and was operative in death and pain as it was in life and joy. The beloved and well-known texts of the *siddur* (prayerbook), the *tehilim* (Psalms), the *humash* (Pentateuch), the *selihot* (penitential prayers) and the *kinot* (elegiac prayers for *Tisha b'Av*) had familiarized him with the lot which had befallen pious Jews in the past with no consequent impairment of their piety. It may be said that in a very real sense this daily, albeit vicarious, experience of suffering prepared the observant Jew for the agonies of the Holocaust. Conversely, the 'culture shock' of the alienated and emancipated Jew of the Western world was infinitely greater when he was confronted with the actual experience of the Holocaust, or even with a mere historical account of its events. The Jew who lived by the *Halakhah*, reciting the 137th Psalm each weekday before saying grace, was aware that the ancient Babylonians had dashed Jewish infants to death upon the rocks. In the daily *tahanun* (petitionary prayers) he proclaimed, 'Our

114

soul is shrunken by reason of the sword and captivity and pestilence and plague and every trouble and sorrow. . . O God, sunken is our glory among the nations, and they hold us in abomination, as of utter defilement'. . .

Halakhic Judaism had not obliterated the memory of these tragedies. On the contrary it had reinforced them, so that at least on a subliminal level, and generally on a conscious level as well, Jews who observed the Torah and its commandments were aware that the *Halakhah* had enabled their predecessors to survive, and even to surmount, the enemies and afflictions of earlier times. Thus, in the ghettos of Kovno, Warsaw, and Lodz, in the concentration camps of Auschwitz, Bergen-Belsen, and Malthausen, they were able to face life with dignity, death with serenity—and sometimes even ecstasy.

(Irving Rosenbaum, *The Holocaust and Halakhah*, New York, KTAV, 1976, 5–8)

Discussion

1. Was the *Halakhah* uniquely equipped to adjust to suffering and death?
2. Is it true to say that for believers there are no questions, and for unbelievers there are no answers?

Norman Solomon: The Holocaust and the Jewish Tradition

An English Orthodox rabbi, Norman Solomon served as Director of the Centre for the Study of Judaism and Jewish–Christian Relations at Selly Oak College in Birmingham, and Lecturer in Modern Judaism at Oxford University. In Judaism and World Religion, *he argues that there is no need for a new theology to emerge in a post-Holocaust world. Rather, he points out that suffering has been a constant feature of Jewish history. Jews have been able to survive such tragedies because of their faith in God. It is still possible to have confidence in an all-good and all-powerful Deity despite the religious challenges posed by the Nazi onslaught against the Jews. What is required is loyalty to God's commands.*

The Quest for a New Jewish Theology

If the *Shoah* does not itself demand a new theology, and the demands for new theologies made by post-*Shoah* theologians do not result in anything really new, why have so many of them felt impelled to distance themselves from traditional Jewish theologies of suffering? There are two main reasons.

First the traditional theologies of suffering never were satisfactory. In the words of the second-century rabbi Yannai, 'It is not in our power to explain either the prosperity of the wicked or the affliction of the righteous.' Yannai's words did not stop rabbis in his own or later generations speculating on the problem of evil. Indeed, though none of the answers is satisfactory, they may all contribute, if only a little, to the upholding of faith in the face of evil.

Second, the reason why non-Orthodox Holocaust theologians reject traditional answers may be something quite other than the intrinsic inadequacy of those answers. . . the traditional interpretations of suffering depend heavily for such cogency as they may have on the belief in life after death and/or the transmigration of souls. Equally, they depend upon a belief in the inerrancy of scripture and in the authenticity of its rabbinic interpretation. These beliefs have been under attack in modern times for reasons which have nothing to do with the *Shoah*. Jews, like Christians, have been challenged by, for instance, modern biblical studies, which tend to undermine the traditional type of scriptural belief and demand a new kind of attitude to the authority of the Bible. Likewise, modern intellectual developments, such as the radical questioning of Cartesian dualism, have placed new strains on the concept of life after death. These changes have so weakened the traditional arguments justifying the ways of God with humankind that the *Shoah* has provided the *coup de grâce* to lead the modernist wing of Judaism to abandon traditional theodicy altogether.

Thus it is not that the *Shoah* poses a new challenge to theology, but rather that the *Shoah* came at a time when theology was already in a greater ferment than ever before in its history, a ferment occasioned by the intellectual movements of the modern world. This explains why earlier tragedies, such as the expulsion from Spain, occasioned not the abandonment but the development of traditional modes of response to suffering.

It is dangerously misleading for Holocaust theologians to base their challenge to traditional beliefs on the fact of the *Shoah*. The serious intellectual issues of faith in the modern world thereby become submerged in a deep emotional trauma which prevents them from being directly faced. The agenda for Jewish theologians ought to comprise not only the broad social issues which confront theologians of all faiths in contemporary society, but also the intellectual problems which lie at the root of theistic, revelation-based faith. It would be superficial to ignore the *Shoah* in these contexts, but to centralise it distorts the very framework of the Jewish faith.

It is a remarkable fact that, notwithstanding a long and continuous tradition, from the Bible onwards, of theology and suffering, and notwithstanding a history of martyrdom second to none, suffering has not in the past been the focus of Jewish theology. In rabbinic Judaism, certainly, the focus has consistently been God and his commandments. I submit that there is no reason for this to change even after the *Shoah*.

(Norman Solomon, *Judaism and World Religion*, London, Macmillan, 1991, 198–200)

Discussion

1. Does the Holocaust pose a new challenge to Jewish theology?
2. Should the Holocaust be understood as simply another manifestation of malevolence against the Jewish nation?

David Patterson: The Holocaust and Recovery

David Patterson has served as Professor of Russian and European Literature at Oklahoma State University. In Sun Turned to Darkness, *he maintains that what is at stake in Holocaust memoirs is the recovery of the divine being that sanctifies all human life.*

Memoir and Recovery

In a sense, then, recovery—both of tradition and from illness—is consummated with the realization that it cannot be completed? Why? Because, in the words of Levinas, 'the more I answer the more I am responsible'.[1] Each act of response increases my capacity for response, so that I always have something more to offer that I fail to offer; I fall behind what my voice brings to bear from within myself. And so, Levinas concludes, 'In approaching the other I am always late for the meeting. But this singular obedience. . . prior to all responsibility, this allegiance before any oath, this responsibility prior to commitment, is precisely the other in the same inspiration and prophecy, the passing itself of the Infinite.' Here, perhaps more clearly than ever, one sees that the recovery from the illness of indifference is linked to the recovery of the God of tradition, of the *En Sof* or the Infinite One, for whom one expresses one's love through one's love for one's neighbour. 'Man changes', writes Wiesel, 'whenever he confronts his fellow-man, who, in turn, undergoes an essential change. Thus every encounter suggests infinity. Which means: the self is linked to infinity only through the intermediary of another self, another consciousness.'[2]

It is the infinity of God that makes the two forms of recovery forever incomplete. And it is the promise of God, the covenant with God, that makes the two forms of recovery forever needful. Here it proves helpful to recall André Neher's insight that 'for the man of the Promise, God suddenly vanishes to the rear, but there is no purpose in seeking him in that rear. . . for God is already waiting out there in front, on the horizon-edge of a promise which only restores what it has taken, without ever being fulfilled.'[3] The horizon-edge that Neher invokes is the edge of time where, in the words of Levinas, 'time means that the other is forever beyond me, irreducible to the synchrony of the same. The temporality of the interhuman opens up the meaning of otherness and the otherness of meaning.'[4] And once meaning is opened the God who had vanished to the rear, left hanging on the gallows of Buna, rushes to the horizon of time, invisibly 'out there.' Hence, Levinas insists, 'time is the most profound relationship that man can have with God, precisely as a going towards God. . . "Going towards God" is meaningless unless seen in terms of my primary going towards the other person.'[5] The open-ended nature of the Holocaust memoir does not lie simply in the necessary miscarriage of any liberation for the survivor. Much more than that, it is rooted in the essence of this memory as a movement toward a humanity and a divinity that has 'receded' to the horizon of the yet-to-be. The memory that has lost a sense of chronology, therefore, can regain it not through the proper reconstruction of a sequence in the past but through the time regained in the dialogical, human pursuit of the divine along the horizon of the future. . .

The realm of the yet-to-be, the horizon of time and eternity from which the summons arises, looms in the light of a history—or a breach in history—that would eclipse such a horizon. 'God', Levinas suggests, 'is perhaps nothing but this permanent refusal of a history which would come to terms with our private tears.'[6] But the tears that stain the pages are not just private tears shed in a world whose sun has lost its shining. They contain a world, like the tears of truth in the legend about the

Angel of Truth that Simon Wiesenthal relates in *The Sunflower*. The Angel opposed the creation of man, and so God cast him to the earth, banishing him from heaven. When he was finally allowed to return to the heavenly host, he brought along a clod of earth soaked with his tears. From that clod God created man, adding to the clod, perhaps, a tear of his own. Perhaps, then, the tears of these victims are the tears of God himself, shed in his infinite longing for himself. Because God longs for himself in human longing for him, 'our desire for God', says Levinas, 'is without end or term: it is interminable and infinite because God reveals himself as absence rather than presence'.[7] Yet the not–here of God's absence is the not-yet of God's presence, and the Holocaust memoir operates within this dialectic of time, which, Levinas points out, 'is the very dialectic of the relationship with the other, that is, a dialogue'[8]. . . That is what the Holocaust memoir is about: this memory of the death of the self is undertaken for the sake of a new birth—for the self, for the other, and for God. It vibrates on the edge of time and eternity where the already said breaks on the cusp of the saying it summons. And there is no engaging this dialogue within the memoir without being engaged in a dialogue with the memoir.

(David Patterson, *Sun Turned to Darkness*, Syracuse, Syracuse University Press, 1998, 29–32)

References

1. Emmanuel Levinas, *Otherwise Than Being or Beyond Essence*, The Hague, Martinus Nijhoff, 1981, 93
2. Elie Wiesel, *The Oath*, New York, Avon, 1973, 88
3. André Neher, *The Exile of the Word*, Philadelphia, Jewish Publication Society, 1981, 123
4. Emmanuel Levinas, 'Dialogue with Emmanuel Levinas', in Richard A. Cohen, (ed.), *Face to Face with Levinas*, Albany, SUNY Press, 1986, 21
5. Ibid., 23
6. Emmanuel Levinas, *Nine Talmudic Readings*, Bloomington, Indiana University Press, 1990, 20
7. Emmanual Levinas, 'Dialogue with Emmanuel Levinas', in Richard A. Cohen, (ed.), *Face to Face with Levinas*, Albany, SUNY Press, 1986, 32
8. Emmanuel Levinas, *Existence and Existents*, The Hague, Martinus Nijhoff, 1978, 93

Discussion

1. Were the tears of victims in the camps the tears of God?
2. Does God reveal himself as absence rather than presence?

Ulrich Simon: The Holocaust and Sacrifice

Ulrich Simon was Professor of Christian Literature at King's College, London. In A Theology of Auschwitz, *he views the Holocaust as a sacrificial offering. In the light of Christ's death, the death of millions of Jews should be perceived as an act of sacrifice.*

Golgotha

Like the victim of Golgotha these dead leave for the most part no children, no report, no property. Few of them leave even a name. Obscurity is the only memorial. Yet the transformation starts here also with the fulfilment of Scriptures. In as much as they died innocently, they became one with the suffering servant, the Israel of God. The spirit seals their transitory lot with the stamp of eternal purpose.

Seen in this light Auschwitz becomes a spiritual challenge in which the visible phenomenon must be reinterpreted according to the great tradition of prophetic expectation and priestly ritual. Thus we escape from the purely tragic evaluation and negative despair. This holocaust is no less a sacrifice than that prefigured in the Scriptures. Here again the circle closes, and the lives of the many are given for the sins of the world.

This acceptance of death as sacrifice was particularly experienced by those trained in the spiritual tradition of Judaism and Christianity. They never doubted the providential nature of their course. This heroic vision was brought to a fine point by a few martyrs who substituted themselves for others in going to death. In the terms of the Bible they regarded their lives as a ransom, their bodies as sin offerings, their death as redemptive.

By seeing their death within the cultic pattern they were transforming death itself. The mechanics of murder were turned into a godward oblation. This spiritual achievement enabled them to 'die unto God', not as animals, caught up in the mechanics of slaughter, but with a freedom of self-giving. This power of transformation is itself a token of the divine Presence in death. The act of transformation shows the intimate connection between the work of the spirit and the human will.

The basis of this transformation is God's love for man, given by the eternal promise in creation and redemption. It is not merely an ecstatic self-assertion of the higher self, or a feverish fantasy to meet a desperate situation, but the objectively grounded union with God which death cannot interrupt. It is not man at Auschwitz, but God who incorporates the terror into the pattern of meaningful sacrifice.

This meaning, however, is perceptible only to faith. It is grounded in the belief that God has himself entered human history in the sacrifice of Jesus. Thus the Church could interpret the death of Christ in terms of ancient ritual. Christ, the victim on the Cross, was seen as the high-priest from whom all sacrifice derives. Moreover, though killed once and for all, he was known to continue his priestly sacrifice eternally with God. Thus the tremendous themes of atonement were translated from temple ritual and annual observance to a celestial sanctuary where outside the limitations of man-made and temporary ceremonies he fulfils the whole cultic tradition. He who stood in need of no purification enters this sanctuary with his own blood to make restitution for the whole of mankind. The death of Jesus is therefore the very denial of an avoidable, though tragic, death, and his resurrection is more than the vindication of virtue. Rather the cosmic perfection depends upon his abiding work of sacrifice.

We can appropriate this pattern partly for the victims of Auschwitz, not in the sense that they are now gods or that their work aspired to perfection. No such claim can be made for any man, Christian, Jew, or devoutly virtuous members of other cults. The claim is that all these, at the point of life-giving, enter into the supreme sacrifice by the way of a sharing analogy. . .

This argument may appear less difficult when we take the scapegoat motif from the day of atonement. The complicated ritual of Leviticus xvi summarizes not only the Jewish but the whole human need to get rid of sin. Here survived an act by which the community solemnly and penitentially transferred its burden of guilt to the animal which was then taken to a cliff from which it was hurled to death, or to wander in the wilderness to take its load of sins to the home of the mystery of all evils, where it also died. Although not a few thinkers and pious leaders declared much of the institution of sacrifice to be of doubtful value, if not downright unnecessary and perverse, the core of the great need remained and demanded a sacrifice for sin. . .

The ritual of the bitter herbs and sweet food accentuates the ambiguity of Passover. It is terrible and delightful, the Cross and Auschwitz reveal the depth of the darkness to be crossed, but the meal of the unleavened bread also brings out the deathlessness and joy of the communion of the Passover. It is not only a feast of remembrance, but also a firm resolution to have done with darkness and despair. Though sacrificial, it is really a feast, and the Christian is bidden to celebrate the feast because 'Christ our Passover is sacrificed'. The casting out of the leaven symbolizes the decisive ethical step not to submit to natural fermentation and corruption. Thus also the Cross and Auschwitz are not meant to hand on to the future patterns of unending cruelty, but rather the ending of the torment. Just because they have endured to the end like sheep for the slaughter they plead for the abolition of malice and wickedness, the old leaven of the old man.

(Ulrich Simon, *A Theology of Auschwitz*, London, SPCK, 1978, 83–89)

Discussion

1. At Auschwitz did God incorporate terror into the pattern of meaningful sacrifice?
2. Can the Jewish community draw inspiration from the image of the cross as God's self-giving sacrifice?

PART III

Wrestling with the Holocaust

Chapter 6: The Suffering of God   **127**

Paul Fiddes: The Holocaust and Divine Suffering   127

Dorothee Sölle: Divine Pain   129

Marcus Braybrooke: Suffering Love   132

Colin Eimer: Jewish and Christian Suffering   135

Hans Jonas: God after Auschwitz   138

Franklin Sherman: Theology and Suffering   140

Marcel Jacques Dubois: The Holocaust and the Cross   144

David Tracy: Theodicy of Suspicion   147

Kalonymus Kalman Shapira: The Holocaust and Divine Suffering   150

Chapter 7: Human Free Will   **153**

Eliezer Berkovits: The Holocaust and Human Free Will   153

Jonathan Sacks: Evil, Free Will and Jewish History   157

André Neher: The Holocaust and Human Free Will   160

David Birnbaum: The Holocaust and Freedom   162

Didier Pollefyt: The Holocaust and Evil   166

Chapter 8: The Holocaust and Christian Faith   **170**

Graham Keith: The Holocaust and Jewish Christianity   170

Hugh Montefiore: The Holocaust and the Cross   173

David Stern: The Holocaust and Evangelism 176

Chapter 9: The Holocaust and the Kingdom **178**

Richard Harries: The Holocaust and the Kingdom of God 178

Seymour Siegel: The Holocaust and Messianism 180

Dan Cohn-Sherbok: The Holocaust and the Hereafter 183

Chapter 10: The Holocaust and Covenant **186**

Eugene Borowitz: Covenant and Holocaust 186

David Weiss: Holocaust and Covenant 189

Chapter 11: The Holocaust and Human Evil **192**

Alan T. Davies: Overcoming Nihilism 192

Paul van Buren: Auschwitz and Moral Responsibility 195

Immanuel Jakobovits: The Holocaust and Human
Responsibility 198

Jack Bemporad: The Holocaust and Human Nature 199

Abraham Joshua Heschel: The Holocaust and Sin 202

Allan R. Brockway: Religion and Faith 204

Nicholas de Lange: The Holocaust and Human Sin 206

Julio de Santa Ana: The Holocaust and Liberation 209

Marc Ellis: The Holocaust and Atrocity 212

Chapter 12: The Holocaust and Jewish Survival **216**

Robert Weltsch: Zionism and Jewish Survival 216

Emil Fackenheim: The Holocaust and the Commanding Voice 218

Lionel Rubinoff: The Holocaust and God's Presence 221

Byron Sherwin: Jewish Survival and the Holocaust   223

Michael Goldberg: The Holocaust and Survival   225

Roberta Strauss Feuerlicht: The Holocaust and Israel   229

Primo Levi: The Holocaust, the Doomed and the Saved   232

Jacob Neusner: The Holocaust and Redemption   234

Chapter 13: Reconstructing Judaism   **237**

Oliver Leaman: The Holocaust and Evil   237

David Blumenthal: Theology and Protest   240

Arthur A. Cohen: A Detached God   242

Melissa Raphael: The Holocaust and Jewish Feminism   245

Susan Shapiro: The Holocaust and Negation   248

Harold Schulweis: The Holocaust and Evil   251

Zachary Braiterman: Jewish Thought after Auschwitz   254

Steven Jacobs: The Holocaust and Jewish Faith   256

Edward Feld: The Holocaust and Spirituality   260

Eliezer Schweid: The Holocaust and Jewish Thought   263

Robert Reeve Brenner: Holocaust Survivors and Religious
    Belief   265

CHAPTER SIX

The Suffering of God

Paul Fiddes: The Holocaust and Divine Suffering

Paul Fiddes has served as Principal of Regent's Park College, Oxford. In The Creative Suffering of God, *he argues that the key to understanding the Holocaust is to accept that God suffers with humanity. Yet, he contends that a careful examination is needed of what it means to talk about the suffering of God which avoids the danger of a merely sentimental belief. It is his aim therefore to describe the nature of God who suffers supremely yet is still the kind of God to whom the Christian tradition has witnessed. In discussing the existence of evil, he affirms that God freely chooses to limit himself, to suffer change, and to journey through time and even experience death while remaining the living God.*

Human Suffering and God's Presence

One obvious response to the challenge of reconciling a universal and a particular suffering of God would be to weaken the meaning of the suffering of God altogether. But the task I hope to confront in this book is to speak consistently of a God who suffers eminently and yet is still God, and a God who suffers universally and yet is still present uniquely and decisively in the sufferings of Christ.

This double task might be summed up by critical reflection upon a story which has been often quoted and diversely used. A survivor from the Nazi concentration camp at Auschwitz, Elie Wiesel, relates in his book *Night* how one day the SS guards hanged two Jewish men and a young boy in front of the whole camp. The men died quickly, but the child did not:

> 'Where is God? Where is He?' someone behind me asked. . . But the third rope was still moving; being so light, the child was still alive.

For more than half an hour he stayed there, struggling between life and death, dying in slow agony under our eyes. And we had to look him full in the face. . .

Behind me, I heard the same man asking: 'Where is God now? And I heard a voice within me answer him: 'Where is He? Here He is—Hanging here on this gallows. . . '

This last phrase makes a fitting counterpoint to the epigram with which we began. There indeed 'goes God' in his grace, there goes God, as Barth says, 'into the far country'. But in what sense is God there, hanging on the gallows?. . .

(Paul Fiddes, *The Creative Suffering of God*, Oxford, Clarendon Press, 1988, 3–4)

The Transcendent Suffering of Christ

To say that God overcomes non-being by using it to define his own being does not mean that this definition happens solely in the cross of Jesus. Throughout human history, indeed from the beginning of creation, God has been encountering death and making it serve him. But the depth of alienation God experiences in the death of Jesus, due to the depth of relationship between the Father and this Son, means a corresponding clarity of definition. The most dreadful assault of non-being has become the most articulate word about God. We can speak therefore of a transcendent suffering of God in Christ, which is witnessed to by the way our own language about death has been transformed in the light of the death of Jesus. . .

This verbal phenomenon brings us to a second aspect of God's negation of non-being. It means that the permanent impression of death upon God contributes to the life-giving quality of the being of God for his world. . . We encounter God as the one who participates in our estrangement, and this has a persuasive power, moving us to trust him. In our trust of God, non-being loses its aggressive power over us; death becomes the place where we trust God to preserve our relationships with him and others, rather than being the place of the curse where all relationships are broken. Death is changed in the sense that our perception of it has changed and because we ourselves are changed. The sign of the resurrection of Jesus affirms that God does something new for his creation in the face of the finality of death. He creates new possibilities and relationships where, from a human point of view, life has come to an end.

There is, then, no mechanically causal link between God's experience of death and the offering of resurrection life, as if God had literally met and killed an enemy being called 'death'. That would be to remythologize death and non-being. Yet, from another angle, it is true that resurrection happens, overcoming death, because death has entered into the being of God. It is true in a compressed sense. If we unpack this affirmation it will be something like this: by responding to the self-giving love displayed in God's encounter with death, we are enabled to co-operate with God in new possibilities for life which he eternally offers to human personalities, in this life and the life to come. So God wins our response to him, the response that nullifies non-being where our lack of response had given it power over us.

Again, we cannot and must not suppose that death only enters into the being of God in the cross of Jesus or that God only overcomes death there. Wherever trust in God is created, death ceases to be the instrument of hostile non-being. But in the cross the encounter of God with death reaches its uttermost pitch, and so his suffering becomes most creative and persuasive. Here God goes furthest in speaking his word of acceptance to us, so that his offer can truly be named a 'new covenant', and through the cross he calls out a new word from us to him. In his humility, this is the conversation of the Spirit that God desires and suffers to create.

(Paul Fiddes, *The Creative Suffering of God*, Oxford, Clarendon Press, 1988, 266–267)

Discussion

1. Can God suffer and still remain divine?
2. Does the cross offer both Jews and Christians a means of coming to terms with the death of six million Jews?

Dorothee Sölle: Divine Pain

Dorothee Sölle is a radical German theologian and has served as Professor at Union Theological Seminary, New York. In 'God's Pain and Our Pain', she argues that the traditional doctrine of an all-loving, omnipotent Deity must be modified in the light of the terrible events of the Holocaust. No longer is it possible to believe that God possesses these attributes. Instead, we must conceive of God as all-loving, but not all-powerful. In her view, God should be perceived as on the side of the victims, sharing their suffering.

129

The Problem of Theodicy

In a relatively short period of the history of Western philosophy, the proponents of theodicy have attempted to reconcile three qualities of God: omnipotence, love and intelligibility. The result of the debate can be summarized in that only two of these three theologoumena are conceivable at any one time, while the remaining one must always be excluded.

The first position is that God is omnipotent and intelligible. God stands, metaphorically speaking, at the head of the universe as the great disposer, the organizer, the one who is really responsible; as the one who can step in and end the torment of humankind, assuming, of course, that God wishes to. In this context we often speak of the suffering of the innocent, of children, for example, who are tortured. But in a deeper sense all people are innocent. No one deserves to starve and of the six million gassed, not one of them ever, even a liar or thief, 'deserved' the suffering that was inflicted upon them.

An omnipotent God, who imposes suffering, who benignly looks down on Auschwitz from above, must be a sadist. That kind of God stands on the side of the victors, and is, in the words of a black American theologian, 'a white racist.' This is the position of Satan in Wiesel's play: he always appears where murder is committed. He is the advocate of submission. His God is pure power. And a theology that conceives of such a supreme ruler, organizer, responsible provoker and creator, reflects the sadism of those who invented it.

The second position conceives of God indeed as omnipotent and all-loving, but at the same time as unintelligible God eludes us. Belief in God becomes absurd or, at best, a paradox. 'I lost my belief in God at Verdun' is a well-known expression of mass atheism. If God has become completely unintelligible, God can no longer be held fast to in the long term, even in paradoxical belief.

What does this tenet from the First World War mean for the things that happened after? I suspect that after Auschwitz, from the point of view of the Germans (for whom I alone can speak here), nothing like this was said, not only because God had long been forgotten, but also because the element of guilt, even if not confessed to, makes the innocence of the first tenet impossible. In view of the Holocaust I cannot talk simply of 'losing' God: chance participation compels one to other forms of speaking of God and must lead beyond the omnipotent and all-loving God.

The third position conceives of a God of love, but not as omnipotent. Between the victors and the victims, God is credible only if God is on the side of the victims, if God is capable of suffering. This position is represented today by such different Jewish philosophers as Elie Wiesel, Abraham Heschel, and Hans Jonas, but also by a popular theologian such as Rabbi Kushner. On the Christian side I can name, above all, Dietrich Bonhoeffer, who became increasingly close to the suffering God while in prison. I can also mention litigation theology which articulates God's indigence and growth, and I can mention the theology of liberation both in its Latin American and in its feminist forms.

(Dorothee Sölle, 'God's Pain and Our Pain' in Otto Maduro (ed.), *Judaism, Christianity and Liberation*, New York, Orbis, 1991, 112–113)

God's Suffering

In the following I wish to think of the suffering godhead, which is the only possible response to the question of the suffering of the innocent. I do not wish to respond to the question of theodicy, but to show it to be a false question. The religious question of suffering is no longer the one so often heard: How can God permit that? but a more difficult one, which first has to be studied: How does our pain become God's pain and how does God's pain appear in our pain? In speaking of 'God's' pain', I am liberating myself from the compulsory concepts of the patriarchs: God as dictator, God at the head of hierarchical thought, God as omnipotent—I find these theological notions of the patriarchs distasteful and despicable. And an unchanging eternal God, who is utterly self-sufficient and beyond need and vulnerability cannot, or, at least, can only cynically, answer the question of human suffering. Such a God must be prosecuted and our desire to defend God disappears. Under the spiritual terms of the patriarchs, under the theology of the omnipotent God, the argument about theodicy is still the best that can emerge. In attempting to introduce God's pain, I am setting this false concept right. I am not speaking of anything that God could avoid or abolish. When we speak of the pain of God, then we no longer see God in a purely masculine presentation. God is then our mother who cries about what we do to each other and about what we brothers and sisters do to animals and plants. God consoles us as a mother does, she cannot wave away pain magically (although that occasionally happens!), but she holds us on her lap, sometimes until we stand up again, our strength renewed, sometimes in a darkness without light. To call this darkness the 'darkness of God', to be able to call it this, is the real difficulty of a theological discussion after the Holocaust: not to yield this darkness to an anti-God, to a different, dualistically opposed, principle, that is the challenge of theology after Auschwitz.

God cannot comfort us if she were not bound to us in pain, if she did not have this wonderful and exceptional ability to feel the pain of another in her own body, suffering with us, existing with us.

(Dorothee Sölle, 'God's Pain and Our Pain' in Otto Maduro (ed.), *Judaism, Christianity and Liberation*, New York, Orbis, 1991, 113–114)

Discussion

1. Is an omnipotent God who imposes suffering and looks down on Auschwitz a sadist?
2. Does it make sense to conceive of God entering into the pain of those who died in the camps?

Marcus Braybrooke: Suffering Love

Marcus Braybrooke has served as Vicar of Marsh Baldon, Oxfordshire, and Chairman of the World Congress of Faiths. In 'The Power of Suffering Love', he acknowledges that the Holocaust poses a fundamental challenge to Christian belief. Yet in Braybrooke's view, the religious perplexities of the Holocaust can be resolved by appealing to the concept of suffering love. The picture of Jesus suffering on the cross, he argues, can serve as the framework for comprehending the tragedy of the Nazi era.

The Church and the Holocaust

Can the church be redeemed?. . . The question which the American Harry James Cargas asks himself in his *Shadows of Auschwitz* is likely to haunt any Christian who acknowledges the depth of Christian complicity in the *Shoah*. Eleven million people were murdered by the Nazis. Six million of them were Jews. One million of the Jews were children. They were murdered in the heartland of Christian Europe. Those who harried the Jews and most of the guards and those who administered the policy of death were baptized Christians. Even Hitler, a baptized Catholic, was never excommunicated.

Nazism was anti-Christian, but it is clear that it was only able to take root in Germany because of centuries of Christian anti-Jewish teaching. In other parts of Europe, many people colluded with the Nazis and only a few actively resisted their persecution of the Jews.

The *Shoah*, although the most horrific attack on the Jews, was not an isolated event. The history of Christian Europe is marred by persecution, massacre and pogrom.

Increasingly, Christians are acknowledging that much of their teaching over the centuries has been false. It was wrong to blame the Jews for the death of Jesus ('deicide'). The New Testament picture of the Pharisees is a caricature. The church has not replaced the Jews as 'the people of God'. All this is being recognized in official statements of the churches, even if it is still not widely known by members of those churches.

Yet even if the churches rid themselves of overt anti-Judaism—and Jewish friends may think there is still a long way to go—will this cure the sickness? I fear there is a triumphalism close to the centre of much Christian preaching which sees the other as a threat, an opponent of God, to be converted, suppressed or even destroyed. I have been moved by feminist theologians who have seen the oppression of the Jews and the oppression of women as both being an expression of this triumphalism. People of other faiths and people not of European origin have suffered too at the hands of Christian Europeans. Indeed they continue to suffer economic exploitation.

The church in many centuries and in many places—not quite 'everywhere and always'—has been an oppressive and persecuting body. Is it just that the church has failed to check human sinfulness and that Christianity has never been tried? Is it that the church has colluded with the abuse of power? I suspect the latter is true, and that too often Christians have ascribed despotic power to God and then behaved in the image of this god.

(Marcus Braybrooke, 'The Power of Suffering Love' in Tony Bayfield and Marcus Braybrooke (eds), *Dialogue with a Difference*, London, SCM, 1992, 81–82)

The Power of Suffering Love

The picture of God as suffering love has become increasingly important to me. As it has done so, my understanding of others of faith has been changed. I begin to see that to emphasize God's suffering love implies rejecting traditional descriptions of God as omnipotent, impassable, and omniscient. It follows that prayer does not change God, but us. Further this picture of God suggests that the future is in our hands and, if we are to shape a more just and peaceful world, we should imitate God's way of suffering love.

I am conscious that the concept has become more central for me as I have pondered the implications of the *Shoah*. The *Shoah* hangs over all Christian–Jewish dialogue 'as a dark, powerful and accusing cloud'. A prerequisite for honest conversation is acknowledgment by Christian participants of their churches' share of responsibility for Jewish suffering. Even then, there is a proper hesitancy about speaking of suffering that nobody who was not there can comprehend. There is a hesitancy, too, about theologizing as a Christian about what was primarily a Jewish tragedy of appalling dimension and of appearing to apply to it ways of thinking drawn from the Christian tradition. Yet, the horror of the Holocaust challenges all faith in God's goodness. I cannot forget the horror when I speak of God or speak to God. Inevitably, too, my thinking is moulded by the Christian tradition that has shaped me.

In one sense this is nothing new. Several passages in the Bible affirm that God is with us in our sufferings (Ps. 23.4; Ps. 139). The crucifixion has suggested to Christians God's deep involvement in human pain. There is a saying in the *Talmud* that 'when God remembers his children who dwell in misery among the nations of the world, he causes two tears to fall into the ocean and the sound is heard from one end of the world to the other'. . .

In the shadow of the *Shoah*, only a suffering God is credible to me. A God who could have acted and did not is not worthy of worship. I recognize that my picture of God as suffering love is shaped by an understanding of the death of Jesus which has come to me through some of the Christian tradition. Jesus accepted cruelty and mockery without answering bitterness. Words of Isaiah were soon used to describe his death: 'He was afflicted, he submitted to be struck down and did not open his mouth' (Isa. 53–7). The object of hatred, there was not hatred in him. He prayed for those who caused his death. The hope is that such vulnerability and acceptance of enmity eventually drains it of its power. Hatred which is absorbed without response loses its venom.

Love, which through suffering absorbs evil and is completely vulnerable, is of its very nature indestructible. Such love cannot be defeated by evil and death, whereas enmity eventually exhausts itself.

The resurrection of Jesus, beyond questions about what happened, is the recognition of the invincible character of self-giving love. In such love, I believe that the deepest meaning of life is revealed. The cross, therefore, for me discloses the nature of God and the way to life.

(Marcus Braybrooke, 'The Power of Suffering Love' in Tony Bayfield and Marcus Braybrooke (eds), *Dialogue with a Difference*, London, SCM, 1992, 85–86)

Discussion

1. Does the Holocaust hang over Jewish and Christian dialogue as a threatening cloud?
2. Is a God who could have acted but refrained from doing so not worthy of worship?

Colin Eimer: Jewish and Christian Suffering

Colin Eimer has served as Rabbi of the Southgate and District Reform Synagogue, England. In 'Suffering: A Point of Meeting', he argues that the Jewish tradition speaks of a God who suffers with his chosen people. Drawing on midrashic and kabbalistic traditions, Eimer contends that God restrains himself so that human freedom can be exercised. Yet there are important differences between Jewish and Christian views of suffering.

A Suffering God

Is there a sense, then, in which a Jew can talk of the power of suffering love? If we speak of a God who cares, who loves his people, of God as a loving parent, then we have also to speak of God who suffers. In the same breath that the biblical prophets establish a connection between abandonment of the covenant and consequent suffering, they also speak of God's continuing love. The *Shekhinah*, the divine presence, has gone into exile with the people. God will be with them, will not abandon them and will ultimately return them to their land and former glory. To match the tears we weep by the waters of Babylon, God also weeps.

It is in the 2000-year-old tradition of *midrash*, the world of homily and parable, of the 'God as it were' analogy, that we find this idea most fully developed. Rabbi Jose, relates one *midrash*, entered the ruins of the Temple in Jerusalem. He wept there for the glory that was lost. In the midst of his anguish, he heard a *bat kol*, a voice from heaven, lamenting: 'Woe is me, for I have destroyed my house, burned my Temple, and exiled my children!'

Out of such statements developed the idea of *hester panim*, the idea that God, as it were, hides his face. This can be understood in a number of ways. God hides his face, turns away from the people because of the wrong they do. God can no longer tolerate what his people have done and turns away, angry and disappointed. That was the sense of abandonment the people felt at the time of exile.

Such a view posits a God like the parents of a very young child. When they see the child moving towards the danger they rush over and rescue it. But children must grow up and bear the consequences of their actions. They move beyond direct parental intervention. The parents can only watch in pain and anguish as their loved child damages itself in some way. But they can do no more. That, too, is part of *hester panim*. God is not angry or disappointed, but constrained by human freedom—the very power he has granted to his creation. It is not free-will at all if we expect God to bail us out when things go wrong. If there is *hester panim*, turning away, it is to hide the grief and pain at what humans do. Even the enormity of the *Shoah* is beyond his reach. Like the earthly parent, all he can do is suffer in silence and be there—accessible to his beloved children should they wish to come to him.

(Colin Eimer, 'Suffering: A Point of Meeting' in Tony Bayfield and Marcus Braybrooke (eds), *Dialogue with a Difference*, London, SCM, 1992, 99)

Different Theologies

There are many ways, therefore, whereby a Jewish and Christian response to the *Shoah* can join hands. But where we would part company is when, for example, Marcus Braybrooke writes of 'the glory of the cross.' In Jewish thinking the words 'pain' and 'suffering' sit very uncomfortably with the word 'glory'—divine or human. The cross and the resurrection have been, and still are, used to preach Christian triumphalism, 'proofs' of the rightness of the Christian message. One of the dangers of such triumphalism, of course, is the coercive imperative many feel it bestows. The connection between universalism and despotism is well established—if you feel you have the truth for all humanity, you will not be overconcerned if, along the way, you have to coerce a few people to accept your truth. . .

The *Shoah* gave the lie to non-violence. It works on the assumption that the adversaries have moral limits, the lines that even they will not cross, and confronts them with those limits. The Nazis, however, knew no such boundaries and were unfettered by any moral considerations. When that situation exists, non-violent resistance becomes almost suicidal, and loses touch with reality. . .

In the face of suffering, we can both speak of hope—for Marcus Braybrooke of a Second Coming, for me of The Coming. The devout Jew repeats Maimonides' formulation daily: 'I believe with perfect faith in the coming of the messiah—and though he tarry, I still believe.' It is reported that Jews sang those words in the gas-chambers of Auschwitz—not blind faith, surely, for there can be none of that at such a moment, but a certainty of sorts. The Jew lives daily on the edge of that hope, and (or but) does not despair at midnight when it has not happened. . .

Suffering is part of the 'birthright' of all people. Judaism can speak of a God who suffers with his creation but not for, or on behalf of it. God is the great Unity and the great Unifier. In our dialogue we can come together to hear the authentic voice of the Other. Together we can grope, in humility, towards a deeper shared understanding. Together we can evolve a vocabulary which is rigorous enough to stand up to the questions raised by the *Shoah* and the experience of suffering. The most minimalist lesson to be drawn from the *Shoah* must be that 'tired', trite pre-*Shoah* theology and theological categories are simply inadequate to face up to what the *Shoah* represents.

(Colin Eimer, 'Suffering: A Point of Meeting' in Tony Bayfield and Marcus Braybrooke (eds), *Dialogue with a Difference*, London, SCM, 1992, 101–103)

Discussion

1. Does it make sense to believe that God was present in Auschwitz suffering with his people?
2. Does the Holocaust illustrate the futility of non-violent resistance?

Hans Jonas: God after Auschwitz

Born in Germany, Hans Jonas served as Professor in the Philosophy Department of the New School for Social Research in New York. In 'The Concept of God after Auschwitz', he argues that the concept of divine impassibility must be set aside in a post-Holocaust age. Instead, it should be recognized that God is not an omnipotent Deity. Rather, he is limited and suffers when evil overwhelms human goodness.

The Nature of the Divine

First, and most obviously, I have been speaking of a suffering God—which immediately seems to clash with the biblical conception of divine majesty. This is, of course, a Christian connotation of the term 'suffering God', with which my myth must not be confounded; it does not speak, as does the former, of a special act by which the deity at one time, and for the special purpose of saving man, sends part of itself into a particular situation of suffering (the incarnation and crucifixion). If anything in what I said makes sense, then the sense is that the relation of God to the world from the moment of creation, and certainly from the creation of man on, involves suffering on the part of God. It involves, to be sure, suffering on the part of the creature too, but this truism has always been recognized in every theology. Not so the idea of God's suffering with creation, and of this I said that *prima facie* it clashes with the biblical conception of divine majesty. . .

Then, the myth suggests the picture of a becoming God. It is a God emerging in time instead of possessing a completed being that remains identical with itself throughout eternity. Such an idea of divine becoming is surely at variance with the Greek, Platonic, Aristotelian tradition of philosophical theology which, since its incorporation into the Jewish and Christian theological tradition, has somehow usurped to itself an authority to which it is not at all entitled by authentic Jewish (and Christian) standards. Trans-temporality, impassibility, immutability have been taken to be necessary attributes of God, and the ontological opposition maintained by classical thought between being and becoming, with the latter characteristic of the lower, sensible world, excluded every shadow of becoming from the pure, absolute being of the Godhead. But this Hellenic concept has never accorded well with the spirit and language of the Bible. . .

Bound up with the concepts of a suffering and becoming God is that of a caring God—a God not remote and detached and self-contained but involved with what He cares for. Whatever the 'primordial' conditions of the Godhead, He ceased to be self-contained once He let himself in for the existence of a world or letting it come to be. God's caring about His creatures is, of course, among the most familiar tenets of Jewish faith. But my myth stresses the less familiar aspect that this caring God is not a sorcerer who in the act of caring also provides the fulfilment of His concern; He has left something for other agents to do and thereby made His care dependent on them. He is therefore also an endangered God, a God who risks something. Clearly that must be so, or else the world would be in a condition of permanent perfection. The fact that it is not bespeaks of one of two things: that either there is no God at all, or there is a God who has given a chance and authority to something other than Himself about which that which is a concern of his.

(Hans Jonas, 'The Concept of God after Auschwitz' in Albert Friedlander (ed.), *Out of the Whirlwind*, New York, Schocken, 1976, 468–470)

A Suffering Deity

The elimination of divine omnipotence which follows from our discussion of power leaves us with the alternatives of either some preexistent—theological or ontological—dualism, or of God's own self-limitation through the creation from nothing. The first alternative might take the Manichaean form of an active force of evil opposing the divine purpose in the universal scheme of things (a two-god theology), or the Platonic form of a passive medium imposing imperfection, no less universally, on the embodiment of the ideal in the world (a form–matter dualism). The first is plainly unacceptable to Judaism. The second answers at best the problem of imperfection and natural causality—the use of the latter in the hands of responsible agents (Auschwitz rather than the earthquake of Lisbon)—with which Jewish theology has to contend at this hour. Only with creation from nothing do we have the oneness of the divine principle combined with that self-limitation which then permits (gives 'room' to) the existence and autonomy of a world. Creation was that act of absolute sovereignty with which it consented, for the sake of self-determined finitude, to be absolute no more.

Certain ethical conclusions follow from the myth and its

adumbrations. The first is the transcendent importance of our deeds, of how we live our lives. If man, as our tale has it, was created 'for' the image of God, rather than 'in' his image; if our lives become lives in the divine countenance—then our responsibility is not defined in mundane terms alone, by which often it is inconsequential enough, but registers in a dimension where efficacy follows transcausal norms of inner essence. Further, as transcendence grows with the terribly ambiguous harvest of deeds, our impact on eternity is for good and for evil—we can build and we can destroy, we can heal and we can hurt, we can nourish and we can starve divinity, we can perfect and we can disfigure its image. . .

What about those who never could inscribe themselves in the Book of Life with deeds either good or evil, great or small, because their lives were cut off before they had their chance, or their humanity was destroyed in degradations most cruel and most thorough such as no humanity can survive? I am thinking of the gassed and burnt children of Auschwitz, of the defaced, de-humanized phantoms of the camps, and of all the other, numberless victims of the other man-made holocausts of our time. . . this I take to believe: that there was weeping in the heights at the waste and despoilment of humanity; that a groan answered the rising shout or ignoble suffering and wrath—the terrible wrong done to the reality and possibility of each life thus wantonly victimized.

(Hans Jonas, 'The Concept of God after Auschwitz' in Albert Friedlander (ed.), *Out of the Whirlwind*, New York, Schocken, 1976, 472–475)

Discussion

1. Does it make sense to believe that God is not omnipotent?
2. Is it plausible to believe that there was weeping in the heights concerning the Holocaust?

Franklin Sherman: Theodicy and Suffering

Franklin Sherman served as Professor of Christian Ethics at the Lutheran School of Theology in Chicago. In 'Speaking of God after Auschwitz', he offers a critique of various attempts to account for the Holocaust. In his view, the only solution to the religious dilemmas posed by the Nazi regime is to believe in a suffering God.

Divine Punishment

Is it possible to think of the Holocaust as God's judgment upon the Jews, or as his vengeance upon them? One's heart and mind and soul instinctively reject such a thought. Even to mention it is bitter to the tongue. Yet Christians must recognize that for centuries the church promoted just such a theory to explain the fall of Jerusalem and the destruction of the Jewish state. The besieging Romans, it was taught, were God's instrument of judgment upon the Jews for not accepting the Messiah.

It is true that some Jewish thinkers themselves accepted the theory that Israel's suffering and its dispersal by the Romans was to be interpreted as punishment for its sins. That does not make the theory any more correct. Its inadequacies must be clearly exposed. Toward this end, the statement of the Second Vatican Council which lifts from the Jews and Judaism as such the charge of responsibility for the crucifixion makes a great contribution, as do the similar Lutheran statements. But much remains to be done through education among the broad masses of church membership to break the last threads of this guilt-and-punishment theory. This must be done as preventive therapy, lest at any time in the future there is a temptation to apply it once again.

(Franklin Sherman, 'Speaking of God after Auschwitz' in Paul D. Opsahl and Marc H. Tanenbaum (eds), *Speaking of God Today*, Philadelphia, Fortress Press, 1974, 147–148)

Providence

If we return to John Hick's analysis for a moment, we find that although he adopts, on the whole, the Irenaenan viewpoint that the sufferings of this present time are justified by their eventual result, it is precisely the Holocaust which he acknowledges cannot fit within this context of explanation. He has to allow it to remain as absurd, as something unexplainable. . .

When we ask such a question today we almost inevitably think of the Nazi programme for the extermination of the Jewish people, with all the brutality and bestial cruelty that it involved and evoked. What does that ultimate purpose and activity mean for Auschwitz and Belsen and the other camps in which, between 1942 and 1945, between four and six million Jewish men, women, and children were deliberately and

141

scientifically murdered? Was this in any sense willed by God?

The answer is obviously no. These events were utterly evil, wicked, devilish and, so far as the human mind can reach, unforgiveable; they are wrongs that can never be righted, horrors which will disfigure the universe to the end of time, and in relation to which no condemnation can be strong enough, no revulsion adequate. . . Most certainly God did not want those who committed these fearful crimes against humanity to act as they did. His purpose for the world was retarded by them and the power of evil within it increased.[1]

(Franklin Sherman, 'Speaking of God after Auschwitz' in Paul D. Opsahl and Marc H. Tanenbaum (eds), *Speaking of God Today*, Philadelphia, Fortress Press, 1974, 150–151)

Mystery

If the first theory speaks of God as the God of judgement, the second speaks of God as the God of creative purpose. But neither is adequate to explain, much less to justify, Auschwitz. Neither, in fact, was found adequate by Job to explain his own suffering. The only answer Job receives is the theophany: an experience of the overwhelming majesty and awfulness of God. In this sense, the answer to Job's question is that there is no answer: I am God and you are man; and the fact that you are man is reflected precisely in the fact that you cannot comprehend my ways. Job bows to the dust, in humility and faith.

What does this mean for our speaking about God? It means that we speak of God as the God of mystery; that we acknowledge the inscrutability of God. . . There is a category in Lutheran theology which is intended as an acknowledgment of this mystery, this inscrutability. This is the notion of the *Deus absconditus*, the hidden God. . . For Luther, the will of God is most evident in the ordinary course of world events. His will is known only where he chooses to make it known; only in revelatory moments, not in life as a whole. We live by those moments, but in so doing, we walk by faith, not by sight. And faith is usually contrary to experience. . .

Let us recapitulate the discussion thus far. The problem of Auschwitz, like the problem of evil as such, is the problem of how such things can happen if God is both good and powerful. If he is not good, then he looks upon these matters with indifference or even, if this is conceivable, with delight. But such a God would in no way be the God we worship. . . If the goodness of God is not to be given up, if he is truly all-loving and at the same time all-powerful, then Auschwitz cannot be explained. It remains in the domain of mystery.

(Franklin Sherman, 'Speaking of God after Auschwitz' in Paul D. Opsahl and Marc H. Tanenbaum (eds), *Speaking of God Today*, Philadelphia, Fortress Press, 1974, 150–152)

Divine Suffering

We have reviewed three 'solutions' to our problem which left the divine sovereignty unimpaired, but thereby failed to answer the question of how the reality of God and the fact of Auschwitz can be held together. These were the sin-and-punishment theory, the character education theory, and the theory that declines to answer the question, leaving the matter in the realm of mystery. . .

With all this, however, we still have not spoken of God in the way that corresponds most closely to the nature of the problem, and that corresponds too to the deepest insights of the Christian—and also, I believe, of the Jewish—faith. This is to speak of the suffering God. . .

This is for me, religiously, the solution to the problem. God participates in the sufferings of men, and man is called to participate in the sufferings of God. . . For Christianity, the symbol of the agonizing God is the cross of Christ. I think that it is tragic that this symbol should have become a symbol of division between Jews and Christians, for the reality to which it points is a Jewish reality as well. I mean the reality of suffering and martyrdom.

(Franklin Sherman, 'Speaking of God after Auschwitz' in Paul D. Opsahl and Marc H. Tanenbaum (eds), *Speaking of God Today*, Philadelphia, Fortress Press, 1974, 156–157)

References

1. John Hick, *Evil and the God of Love*, New York, Harper and Row, 1966, 397

Discussion

1. Is it conceivable that the Holocaust could be divine judgement upon the Jews?
2. Can the symbol of the cross bind Jews and Christians together in a post-Holocaust world?

Marcel Jacques Dubois: The Holocaust and the Cross

Marcel Jacques Dubois was Professor of Medieval Philosophy at the Hebrew University in Jerusalem. In 'Christian Reflection on the Holocaust', he discusses the piety of faithful Jews during the terrors of the Nazi regime. As he explains, these religious individuals were assured of God's abiding presence despite their suffering. In his view, Jews and Christians can be united in the recognition that the tragedy of the Holocaust can be understood in the light of the cross.

The Sanctification of the Name

The Jewish people thus confronted, in the very name of its faith and of its memory, with what Martin Buber rightly called 'the eclipse of God', experienced a terrible dilemma, a dilemma resumed by Richard Rubenstein in a form so pessimistic that it bears the accent of despair: 'either a cruel God or none.' Yet here, once again, this trial which involves God gives to the Jewish experience a value that is exemplary for all human experience.

The Holocaust was for the Jewish conscience a paradigm of the ever-recurring problem of evil and of injustice whose perpetual presence in the world seems to deny the existence of a God who is good. Against this stumbling block many Jews fell. Some became disorientated. Hence Richard Rubenstein's cold reply to the dilemma mentioned above: 'Jewish paganism is the most visible religious option available to contemporary Jews.' For him the immeasurable monstrosity of the Nazi crimes definitely destroys all possibility of belief in the presence and action of God in history. It follows paradoxically that if the tragic experience in which six million Jews were massacred has an exemplary meaning, the meaning is that the universe and human existence are radically absurd. If there is a certitude to which Israel can witness, it is the certitude that there is no God. Jewish destiny confirms the philosophy of Sartre and of Camus because the Holocaust is the definitive manifestation of the absurd.

And yet there was a very different response from those Jews who, in the very abyss of anguish and of night, seemingly abandoned, turned their desperate hope to God. Far from evading the bewilderment of the contradiction, they found in their faith the strength to cry forth to God 'out of the depths'. . . The Jewish people had throughout the ages lucidly confronted and denounced the apparent absurdity of existence,

144

the insolent victory of injustice and of evil. From the story of Abraham in Genesis to the interpolations of the prophets and the Psalms, the Bible is full of this daring contestation. Israel calls God to account in the name of God's past promises, of God's mercy, or of God's justice. The book of Job will forever be the compendium of this protestation of humankind against the incomprehensible injustice and the wickedness of people, and the most striking thing about it is that God, far from being offended, praises Job for his ruthless honesty (Job 42:7). There the very anguish becomes, in the name of faith, a warrant to challenge the Almighty.

(Marcel Jacques Dubois, 'Christian Reflection on the Holocaust' in Katharine T. Hargrove (ed.), *Seeds of Reconciliation*, North Richland Hills, Texas, Bibal Press, 1996, 168–169)

The Cross

How can one compare the Holocaust with the Cross! The Cross brandished in the pogroms by murderers, and, for so many Jews, the symbol of intolerance, oppression and hatred! How can one find in the Jewish hope of the victory of life a certitude that evokes that of the victory of Christ over death! Such things cannot be expressed in human language. How can they be formulated without sullying or blurring their ineffable secret, the mystery contained by the comparison. May my Jewish friends pardon me if here I seem to annex to the Passion of Christ an ocean of suffering whose abyss they alone know. Yet, as a Christian addressing Christians, I must tell them of my conviction and ask them to consider it, and try with them to understand a little better what our human hearts are capable of understanding. The transcendent intelligibility of the Holocaust can be granted only by light from above, and for us Christians that light passes through the mystery of Golgotha.

This is an inexpressible truth which language can only suggest to our hearts because language is incapable of revealing all its mystery! It is infinitely difficult to speak of anguish and death, our personal suffering, because all efforts to be objective seem but to open ways of escape for the living reality that the words are trying to capture. How can one speak of death to those who are threatened with it or who are already experiencing its sting? Even if one believes that it is possible to provide a metaphysical explanation of the problem of evil, what value can justifications and reasons have for all those whose lives are shipwrecked and who are lost in an unbounded ocean of suffering?. . . Even if we share their dismay, even if our heart bleeds with theirs, is it possible to express compassion to those whom the senselessness of the sufferings has imprisoned in an impenetrable and incommunicable solitude?

And yet if we believe in Christ's victory over death, if the mystery of the Cross means for our faith that by his death the Lord has vanquished all death, there is no human suffering, no presence of death that is not at this very moment part of the metamorphosis of Transfiguration. Because Christ has experienced them for us, agony, torment and death are but the mysterious crucible of a resurrection already operative. Every home visited by death, death of body, of heart, of family, of people, of everything that is our flesh and blood is called to become the hidden victory tent of the one who is life. This certainty should help the Christian to transfigure the universe, and first of all his or her own life, by giving to every suffering, to every form of death, its ultimate and authentic meaning.

Everywhere in the world there is an infinite mass of suffering, of wretchedness—an immense capital of distress and agony which risks becoming emptiness, nothingness, despair unless Christ's victory comes to save it and by saving it to give it meaning. The Cross of Christ thus appears as an immense sacrament reaching through time and permeating all the secret places of human existence. Its application certainly depends on the penetration of our faith and the intercession of our prayer, but we are assured by this certainty that many people will be saved by the Cross which they bore without knowing it and which in their death-ravaged lives was the pledge and the sacrament of resurrection.

What then can be said of the death camps and of the long agony of the Jewish people?

It is a striking fact that Judaism itself in the spontaneity of its deepest resilience has answered this question. The answer contains such an unexpected presentiment of the mystery of the Cross that Christians cannot fail to notice and to be struck by it. . . Jewish tradition. . . recognizes in the suffering destiny of Israel, in its uniqueness and in its mystery, a value for the salvation of the world. It is true to say that this conviction belongs to the tradition of Jewish wisdom. For this reason, it would not astonish those who understand the very strong sense of responsibility, both human and cosmic, implicit in the fidelity of Israel to its vocation. . . Thus do the destinies of Jesus and of Israel meet in the same figure. How is it possible not to be struck by the resemblance of these two countenances? What the Christian can truly say is that to the eye of faith, Jesus fulfils Israel in its destiny of Suffering Servant and that Israel, in its experience of solitude and anguish, announces and represents, even without knowing it, the mystery of the Passion and of the Cross.

(Marcel Jacques Dubois, 'Christian Reflection on the Holocaust' in Katharine T. Hargrove (ed.), *Seeds of Reconciliation*, North Richland Hills, Texas, Bibal Press, 1996, 172–176)

Discussion

1. Was the Holocaust a manifestation of the absurd?
2. Is it plausible that without knowing it, the Jewish experience of suffering reveals the mystery of the passion?

David Tracy: Theology of Suspicion

David Tracy served as Andrew Thomas Greeley and Grace McNichols Greeley Distinguished Service Professor of Catholic Studies at the University of Chicago Divinity School. In 'Religious Values After the Holocaust: A Catholic View', he argues that in a post-Holocaust age Catholic theologians must engage in a theology of suspicion in which traditional religious assumptions are called into question. As far as the Holocaust is concerned, Tracy argues that Christians must reject previous distortions of Jews and Judaism. In addition, they must subject classical theism to criticism; in Tracy's view, God must be understood as a suffering God who is pained by the tragedy of the Nazi era.

Hermeneutics of Suspicion

To retrieve those prophetic and eschatological Jewish strains in Christianity is to demand that a major part of contemporary Christian theological interpretation should be a hermeneutics of suspicion upon the actual realities of the religious tradition, a tradition recognized theologically as fundamentally trustworthy yet also recognized theologically as ambiguous and demanding constant prophetic self-reform. The route from the anti-Judaic statements of the New Testament through the revolting anti-Jewish polemics of John Chrysostom and others in the patristic period through the explicit (and yet more deadly, the implicit) 'teaching of contempt' tradition in the Christian tradition to the virulent, revolting anti-Semitism that can pervade and clearly has pervaded many a Christian unconscious are merely the most obvious examples of the radical ambiguities within the Christian religious tradition.

(David Tracy, 'Religious Values after the Holocaust: A Catholic View' in Abraham J. Peck (ed.), *Jews and Christians after the Holocaust*, Philadelphia, Fortress Press, 1982, 89)

The Holocaust and Christian Suspicion

I submit that the Holocaust is the classic negative event of our age, an event that bears the religious dimension of the *tremendum*; an event that does not displace the founding religious events of either Judaism or Christianity; yet an event that demands the release, for Christians, of a profound Christian hermeneutics of suspicion upon many traditional interpretations of the Christian tradition. . .

The fact remains, however, that the hermeneutics of suspicion released by the Holocaust can and should become for Christians a demand for a Christian theological hermeneutics of suspicion upon both tradition and world. In the light of that suspicion, we may yet find the possibilities for new hermeneutics of retrieval of half-forgotten or even repressed aspects of the Christian tradition.

Allow me to give some examples of both the suspicions raised by the Holocaust and the possibilities of retrieval of sometimes forgotten aspects of the tradition which the reality of the Holocaust discloses. I will concentrate my major attention on the fundamental doctrines of salvation, Christ, and God. Before those more controversial aspects of my proposal, however, allow me to note some prior issues that demand further and continuous reflection.

The first factor is the most obvious and perhaps the most deadly: Christianity has explicitly allowed in the writings of some of its most cherished fathers of the faith. . . a long teaching of contempt for the Jews and for the Jewish religion. Christianity has implicitly allowed more popular expressions of this contempt to endure even in its catechisms and its popular piety. The liturgical reforms of the Good Friday service initiated by Pope John XXIII and the catechical reforms initiated since Vatican II are merely the first expressions of the suspicions that must be cast on this revolting tradition of both implicit and explicit teachings of contempt. . .

Moreover, the painful, repressed memories of Christian anti-Semitism have also been aided by the anti-Judaic statements of the New Testament, especially but not solely in the Gospel of John. If those scriptural statements cannot be excised, then minimally they should

148

always be commented upon whenever used in liturgical settings and noted critically in every Christian commentary on the Scriptures. . .

To release a Christian hermeneutics of suspicion. . . can also release a Christian hermeneutics of retrieval. These first examples of suspicion, in fact, also suggest the necessity of retrieval. In a real sense, this has begun to occur powerfully among Christian theologians. . . who have begun to recognize the profoundly Jewish character of Christianity itself. The Christian God is none other than the God of Israel, the God of Abraham, Isaac and Jacob. Our Christ is none other than Jesus the Jew of Nazareth. Our sacred texts are none other than the Hebrew Scriptures, which also serve as our Old Testament, and the apostolic writings—the apostolic writings of the early Jewish Christians, which we call the New Testament.

Yet to retrieve the Jewishness of Christianity is also to retrieve the possibility of recalling, on Christian grounds, that for the Christian the Jews are and will remain God's chosen people. The Christian as Christian can and, I believe, must affirm that chosenness of the Jews as a theological reality.

(David Tracy, 'Religious Values after the Holocaust: A Catholic View' in Abraham J. Peck (ed.), *Jews and Christians after the Holocaust*, Philadelphia, Fortress Press, 1982, 93–95)

Divine Suffering and Love

Even those theologians like myself who continue to believe that process categories are, in fact, more philosophically coherent than classically theistic categories; that they are more appropriate categories for understanding the scriptural affirmation of God as a God of love; and that they are more existentially resonant to our postclassical understanding of change and process as anthropological constants and marks of perfectibility, not imperfection, cannot after the Holocaust rest in an affirmation of a process understanding of God, much less a process theodicy. What those theologians who accept these process categories. . . can do, I suggest, is to radicalize the process and understanding of God as love. . .

For myself that means that we must rethink anew the reality of suffering in the reality of God's own self as the self who is love. I believe, with Dietrich Bonhoeffer, that 'only a suffering God can help us now'. I believe, with the often-repressed strains of the Scriptures of both traditions, Jewish and Christian, that our God is none other than pure, unbounded love—the God who radically affects and is affected by (that is, suffers) the evil we, not God, persist in inflicting upon God's creation. I believe, therefore, that the unspeakable suffering of the six million is also the voice of the suffering of God.

(David Tracy, 'Religious Values after the Holocaust: A Catholic View' in Abraham J. Peck (ed.), *Jews and Christians after the Holocaust*, Philadelphia, Fortress Press, 1982, 105–106)

Discussion

1. Can only a suffering God help humanity come to terms with the horrors of the Nazi regime?
2. After Auschwitz, can one believe that God is none other than unbounded love?

Kalonymus Kalman Shapira: The Holocaust and Divine Suffering

Kalonymus Kalman Shapira was the rebbe of the Warsaw ghetto. In The Holy Fire, *he rejects the explanation that the Holocaust was due to Israel's sins; instead, he argues that God suffers on behalf of his chosen people.*

The Birth Pangs of the Messiah

Let us understand, in our diminished circumstance, the meaning of the birth pangs of the Messiah. The simple explanation of the function of these sufferings is that they serve to cleanse us of our sins before the revelation of the Messiah's advent. But why should the generation of the Messiah have to suffer for the sins of past generations?

Rather: After the sin of Adam, God said, 'In pain shall you bring forth chidren' (Genesis 3:16). This is not simply a kind of vengeance. . . Rather, after the sin the world became corporeal, so that each individual has a separate existence. In consequence, it is impossible for anything to give birth—i.e., to be the vehicle for the elicitation and revelation of new light—without the annihilation of a portion of the light of the individual self. In other words, it is impossible for anything to reveal the divine light without self-annihilation. Before a seed manifests a new creation—a tree with branches, leaves, and fruit, which is many orders of magnitude greater than the seed—the being of the seed must first be annihilated. That is why every seed must decompose in the ground, as a kind of death. This is precisely the meaning of 'in pain shall you bring forth children.' It refers to death, or pain approaching death, for the forces which need to achieve annihilation before the birth of a new creation. . . .

This, then, is the way we may understand the birth pangs of the Messiah. For what, after all, is redemption? It is a divine revelation wherein God will manifest his light and holiness. Now this revelation takes place by means of Israel. That is why redemption and the time of redemption, depend upon Israel. So in order that Israel merit that such light be manifested through them, it is necessary that certain of their capacities be annihilated; that is what is called the birth pangs of the Messiah.

(Kalonymus Kalman Shapira, *The Holy Fire: The Teachings of Rabbi Kalonymus Kalman Shapira, the Rebbe of the Warsaw Ghetto*, ed. Nehemiah Polen, Northvale, New Jersey, Jason Aronson, 1994, 111–112)

Divine Suffering

Now the Jew who is tormented by his afflictions thinks that he alone suffers, as if all his personal afflictions and those of all Israel do not affect above, God forbid. Scripture states, however, 'In all their troubles he was troubled' (Isaiah 63:9), and the Talmud states: When a person suffers, what does the *Shekhinah* say? 'My head is too heavy for me, my arm is too heavy for me.' Our sacred literature tells us that when a Jew is afflicted, God, blessed be he, suffers as it were much more than the person does. It may be that since he, blessed be he, is not subject to any limitation—for which reason no conception of him is possible in the world—therefore his suffering from Israel's troubles is also boundless. It is not merely that it would be impossible for a person to endure the experience of such great suffering, but that even to conceive of his suffering, blessed be he—to know that he, blessed be he, does suffer, to hear his voice, blessed be he: 'Woe for I have destroyed my house and have exiled my children'—is impossible, because he is beyond the confines of the human.

(Kalonymus Kalman Shapira, *The Holy Fire: The Teachings of Rabbi Kalonymus Kalman Shapira, the Rebbe of the Warsaw Ghetto*, ed. Nehemiah Polen, Northvale, New Jersey, Jason Aronson, 1994, 116)

Human Suffering

God, blessed be he, is to be found in his inner chambers weeping, so that one who pushes in and comes close to him by means of studying *Torah*, weeps together with God, and studies *Torah* with him. Just this makes the difference: the weeping, the pain which a person undergoes by himself, alone, may have the effect of breaking him, of bringing him down, so that he is incapable of doing anything. But the weeping which the person does together with God—that strengthens him. He weeps—and is strengthened; he is broken—but finds courage to study and teach. It is hard to raise one's self up, time and again, from the tribulations, but when one is determined, stretching his mind to connect to the *Torah* and divine service, then he enters the Inner Chambers where the blessed Holy One is to be found; he weeps and wails together with him, as it were, and even finds the strength to study Torah and serve him.

(Kalonymus Kalman Shapira, *The Holy Fire: The Teachings of Rabbi Kalonymus Kalman Shapira, the Rebbe of the Warsaw Ghetto*, ed. Nehemiah Polen, Northvale, New Jersey, Jason Aronson, 1994, 119)

Discussion

1. Should innocent victims have to suffer for the sins of past generations?
2. Is it plausible to believe that God is affected when a Jew is afflicted?

CHAPTER SEVEN

Human Free Will

Eliezer Berkovits: The Holocaust and Human Free Will

A Romanian-born Orthodox rabbi, Eliezer Berkovits was Chairman of the Department of Jewish Philosophy at the Hebrew Theological College in Chicago. In Faith after the Holocaust, *he argues that religious belief is possible after the nightmare of the crematoria. In his view, the problem of faith can be solved by appealing to the free will argument. If God did not respect human freedom, not only would morality be abolished, but men and women would cease to be human. Freedom and responsibility are the very essence of humanity—if human beings are to exist, they must be allowed to sin. In this light, the Holocaust must be seen as an expression of human evil, a tragedy inflicted by the Nazis on the Jewish people. God did not intervene to save the Jewish nation because he had bestowed free will on humanity at creation. In the face of the Holocaust, the Jew must adopt a Job-like stance, believing in God's goodness despite the flames of the crematoria. In a later work,* With God in Hell, *he depicts those who remained faithful in the death camps.*

Free Will and the Hidden God

We have to concern ourselves with the question of the absence of God, the problem of *El Mistater*, the hiding of God. For the radical theologian the absence of God means the death of God. Altizer discusses this aspect of our subject in the following terms:

> God is not simply hidden from view, nor is he lurking in the depth of our unconscious or on the boundaries of our infinite space, nor will he appear on the next turn of an historical wheel. Totally committed as he is to the full epiphany of faith in the concrete moment before him, the contemporary Christian accepts the death of God as a final and irrevocable event.[1]

153

Here too, as so often, Altizer's meaning is somewhat obscure. As other passages in his writing show, Altizer believes that the Christian dogma of God's descent into the flesh represents the death of God as an event in history. At that moment, the transcendental God actually collapsed into imminent humanity. Thus he perished. He is unique among the radical theologians with his interpretation. But they have all in common the inability to acknowledge the concept of a 'hiding God' so important, for instance, in the theology of an Isaiah. We believe that this too is the result of their original Christian background. The 'hiding God' can hardly be an authentic Christian idea. The entire purpose of the incarnation in Christianity is salvation, to lift man out of his profane existence and give him reality as a new being in the realm of eternity. This is the function of the saviour, to be accomplished in the epiphany of the Christian faith. By its very nature it can be achieved by a God who reveals himself; by the visible breaking of the transcendental into the realm of the profane. This very nature of this God incarnate is divinity made manifest. This God cannot hide for he saves by his self-revelation. A Saviour-God cannot not save. If he is in hiding, he does not save. If he does not save, he is not; his death is final and irrevocable.

The hiding God is present; though man is unaware of him, He is present in his hiddenness. Therefore, God can only hide in this world. But if this world were altogether and radically profane, there would be no place in it for Him to hide. He can only hide in history. Since history is man's responsibility, one would, in fact, expect him to hide, to be silent, while man is about his God-given task. Responsibility requires freedom, but God's convincing presence would undermine the freedom of human decision. God hides in human responsibility and human freedom. However, where there is no room for history, where redemption lies, not in a process of sanctification, but in the transfiguration of a profane existence into a new birth in eternity, there God cannot hide. He must be visible in the miracle of salvation; he saves by his epiphany. There is no room in Christianity for the hiding God. If he does not walk with me, if he does not talk to me, if he is absent, he is not, he is dead. This is the conclusion drawn correctly by the radical theologian from the absence of God.

(Eliezer Berkovits, *Faith after the Holocaust*, New York, KTAV, 1973, 63–64)

Job and the Modern Jew

The questioning of God's providence in the death camps was taking place within the classical tradition of Judaism. Unfortunately, unlike the case of Job, God remained silent to the very end of of the tragedy and the millions in the concentration camps were left alone to shift for themselves in the midst of infinite despair. To this day, theologians are arguing about the meaning of God's answer to Job. Be that as it may, one thing is certain: in the denouement God appears to Job; He makes himself known to him. Thus Job is able to find peace with God in the words: 'I had heard of Thee by the hearing of the ear; But now mine eye seeth Thee; Wherefore I abhor my words, and repent, Seeing I am dust and ashes.' No such denouement to the drama of faith took place in the camps. To the very end God remained silent and in hiding. Millions were looking for him—in vain. They had heard of Him by the hearing of the ear, but what was granted to their eyes to behold was 'dust and ashes,' into which they—and everything dear to them—were turned.

There were really two Jobs at Auschwitz: the one who belatedly accepted the advice of Job's wife and turned his back on God, and the other who kept his faith to the end, who affirmed it at the very doors of the gas chambers, who was able to walk to his death defiantly singing his '*Ani Maamin*—I believe.' If there were those whose faith was broken in the death camp, there were others who never wavered. If God was not present for many, He was not lost to many more. Those who rejected did so in authentic rebellion; those who affirmed and testified to the very end did so in authentic faith. Neither the authenticity of rebellion nor the authenticity of faith is available to those who are only Job's brother. The outsider, the brother of the martyrs, enters on a confusing heritage. He inherits both the rebellion and the witness of the martyrs: a rebellion not silenced by the witness; a witness not made void by the rebellion. In our generation, Job's brother, if he wishes to be true to his God-given heritage, 'reasons' with God in believing rebellion and rebellious belief. What is it then he may hope for? He is not searching for an understanding, in terms of his faith, of what had befallen his people. He is not attempting to steal a glance at 'the hand' of the Almighty in order to be able to appreciate what meaning the senseless destruction of European Israel might have in the divine scheme. To understand is to justify, to accept. That he will not do. . . He desires to affirm, but not by behaving as if the holocaust had never happened. He knows that this generation must live and believe in the shadow of the holocaust. He must learn how this is to be done. If his faith is to remain meaningful, he must make room for the impenetrable darkness of the death camps within his faith. The darkness will remain, but in its 'light' will he make his affirmations of faith, and it will accent his affirmations. The inexplicable will not be explained, yet it will become a positive influence in the formulation of that which is to be acknowledged. The sorrow will stay, but it will become blessed with the promise of another day for Israel to continue on its eternal course with a new dignity and a new self-assurance. Thus, perhaps in the awful misery of man will be revealed to us the awesome mystery of God. But when this happens, who can say that it will not be we who, seeking his consolation, in consoling Him shall find our comfort.

(Eliezer Berkovits, *Faith after the Holocaust*, New York, KTAV, 1973, 69–70)

Loyalty to God in the Face of Death

In a volume of Holocaust eyewitness testimonies published by the labour movement in Israel, the point is made that although the Jews in Europe knew well what had happened to many of their brethren, and what was awaiting them should they, too, be caught, many of them did not depart from their customary ways. In numerous places in the ghettos one could see through the windows Jews studying, or wearing *tallit* (prayer shawl) and *tefillin* (phylacteries), praying the daily services in the midst of the required quorum of at least a *minyan* (ten men). On the High Holy Days they would put on the traditional *kittel* (white robe) and would pray with loud voices. Some of them even permitted themselves to walk in the streets clad in prayer shawls as if they were living in Jerusalem. It was as if Jews had ceased being afraid.

(Eliezer Berkovits, *With God in Hell*, New York, Sanhedrin Press, 1979, 1)

References

1. Thomas J.J. Altizer, *Radical Theology and the Death of God*, New York, Bobbs-Merrill, 1966, 126

Discussion

1. Can one believe that God did not intervene on behalf of the Jewish people because he had granted humans free will?
2. Was God present at Auschwitz even though he was hidden?

Jonathan Sacks: Evil, Free Will and Jewish History

Jonathan Sacks has served as Chief Rabbi of the United Hebrew Congregations of the Commonwealth. In Tradition in an Untraditional Age, *he explains his earlier reluctance to explore the religious issues raised by the Holocaust. Yet, he insists that the questions raised by this tragedy must now be faced by contemporary Jewish writers. After discussing a range of interpretations, he draws on the theology of Eliezer Berkovits, arguing that the Holocaust was the result of human free will. In Sacks's view, the only lesson one can derive from the murder of six million Jews is that human beings are capable of horrendous acts. When human beings perpetrate evil, he writes, it is these individuals who are to blame, not God. Confronting the question how God can thus be known, Sacks asserts that there is no other witness that God is present in history but the history of the Jewish people.*

Confronting the Holocaust

The holocaust is a mystery wrapped in silence. For almost twenty years afterwards, little was said, still less written about it. Like many others of the post-holocaust generation, I was reluctant to presume on so unfathomable a subject. The questions insist on being asked: How could one dare to speak? And how could one dare not to speak? The conflict is part of the continuing presence of the holocaust, so it is here that I begin.

First, I and others of my generation are too far away from that time. Which of us who were born after the holocaust, which of us who did not lose family in the holocaust can speak about the holocaust?. . . We are too far away to speak. But secondly, in an important sense we are also too close. Just as we now ask questions about the holocaust, so tradition tells us that we would ask questions about the exodus from Egypt and the events that preceded it. . . We will not go far wrong if we say that the Biblical time-scale applies to the holocaust too: we should expect it to take forty years even to find the right question, let alone expect an answer. Third: just as we resist looking too long at the sun for fear of being blinded, we resist from looking too long at the blinding darkness of Auschwitz for fear of being driven to despair. . .

These then are the three reasons why I and many others confronted by the holocaust, respond as did the Israelites at Sinai. . . They saw and trembled and stayed at a distance. This feeling will govern what I have

157

to say, but cannot altogether inhibit it. Because theology must perform the dual task of respecting such sentiment on the one hand and wrestling with it on the other. To respect it is to admit that we are not yet in sight of the time when the holocaust is intelligible within the classic terms of Jewish history. We are not yet ready to say where it belongs in the drama between God and His people. . .

(Jonathan Sacks, *Tradition in an Untraditional Age*, London, Vallentine Mitchell, 1990, 139–141)

Human Freedom and Evil

Which brings us to the final thinker I want to consider and the one who, to my mind, most accurately embodies an authentic Jewish response; namely, Eliezer Berkovits. Berkovits disputes the central argument of Fackenheim, that the holocaust is unique. It may indeed be unique from some perspectives, but not in a way that is relevant to faith.

The problem of the *tzaddik ve-ra lo*, the 'righteous who suffers', is one as old as Abraham. *Hashofet kol ha'aretz lo ya'asheh mishpat*: 'Shall the judge of all the earth not do justice?' The answer given by tradition applies to the holocaust, too. God, in giving man the freedom to choose to be good, at the same time necessarily gives him the freedom to be evil. God teaches us what goodness is. But He does not intervene to force us to be good or to prevent us from being wicked. This is the extraordinary Jewish conception of the power of God. God is powerful not through His interventions in history but through His self-restraint. . .

So when human beings perpetrate evil it is human beings who are to blame, not God. But then the crucial question arises. Where do we witness God in history? Berkovits answers: God reveals His presence in the survival of Israel. Not in His deeds, but in His children. There is no other witness that God is present in history but the history of the Jewish people.

Hence the demonic character of the Nazi project. the final solution, says Berkovits, was an attempt to destroy the only witness to the God of history. The ingathering of exiles after the holocaust and the creation of the state of Israel revealed God's presence at the very moment when we might have despaired of it altogether. The rebirth of the state came at a moment in history when nothing else could have saved Jews from extinction through hopelessness. The miracle that testifies that God exists is that the people of Israel exist. Though they walked through the valley of the shadow of death, *am yisrael chai*, the people of Israel lives.

The only meaning to be extracted from the holocaust is that man is capable of limitless evil. The religious meaning of six million deaths is no more and no less than that they, as other Jews had done before them, died *al kiddush ha-Shem*, for the sanctification of God's name, suffering, as Isaiah saw the servants of God would always suffer, until the world finds in its heart not to afflict the children of God. We find meaning not in the holocaust but in the fact that the Jewish people survived the holocaust. The existence of the state of Israel does not explain the *Shoah*, but it gives us faith despite the *Shoah*.

That is perhaps as near as we will come to a theology of the holocaust. It helps to explain why Orthodox Judaism has been reluctant to create a new fast for *Yom Ha-Shoah*, and why thinking about the holocaust has played a less prominent part in Orthodox circles than elsewhere. Not because Orthodoxy has felt it less acutely than others: on the contrary, no other group lost so much as the worlds of the *yeshivah* and the *Hasidim*. Rather it was because the traditional Jewish response has been not to sanctify suffering but instead to rebuild what was broken. Indeed it was the ultra-Orthodox groups in particular who have tacitly insisted that the one command to come from Auschwitz was: Let there be more Jewish children. Who is to say that this was not the deepest response of all?

One writer about the holocaust records that he met a rabbi who had been through the camps, and who, miraculously, seemed unscarred. He could still laugh. 'How', he asked him, 'could you see what you saw and still have faith? Did you have no questions?' The rabbi replied: 'Of course I had questions. But I said to myself: If you ever ask those questions, they are such good questions that the Almighty will send you a personal invitation to heaven to give you the answers. And I preferred to be here on earth with the questions than up in heaven with the answers.' This too is a kind of theology.

(Jonathan Sacks, *Tradition in an Untraditional Age*, London, Vallentine Mitchell, 1990)

Discussion

1. Are human beings—not God—responsible for the Holocaust?
2. Is the only lesson to be extracted from the Holocaust that human beings are capable of limitless evil?

André Neher: The Holocaust and Human Free Will

André Neher served as Professor of Biblical and Jewish studies at the University of Strasbourg. In 'The Exile of the Word: From the Silence of the Bible to the Silence of Auschwitz', he argues that after Auschwitz there can only be silence. This catastrophic event cannot be comprehended. Yet, theologically Auschwitz illustrates the limits of human freedom. In this light, human beings rather than God were responsible for the suffering caused during the Nazi regime.

Auschwitz and Silence

Now Auschwitz is, above all, silence. This has been doubtless better understood by the poets than by the philosophers. . . First, there is the silence of the 'concentrational' city closed in upon itself, its victims, and its executioners, separated from the outside world by concentric circles of Night and Fog ('night and fog' was the term used by the Nazis to describe the policy of secrecy and concealment surrounding the concentration camps). This first form of silence, this gulf between Auschwitz and the world, as impenetrable as the deep, should never be forgotten when we mention Hiroshima, Dresden, or Coventry in the same phrase or in the same breath as Auschwitz. There is simply no comparison to be made; one cannot possibly compare Auschwitz to anything else. . .

Then there is the silence of those few who finally understood, but who took refuge in an attitude of prudence, perplexity and incredulity. This was the silence of the beholder, transgressing the iron law of Leviticus 5:1.

Lastly there is the silence of God, which continues when the other rings of silence have been broken, and by that very fact is all the more serious and alarming. The approaches to this triple silence lead, if not to an impasse, then at least to a full-scale inversion of values, none of which can any longer claim to express reality as such, except through a total change of significance, forcing men to search where nothing can be found. . .

Auschwitz is like some perilous passage between the rocks where the millennial adventure of human thought met with absolute disaster. It went down in darkness, without even the ray of a lighthouse to indicate where it had been. It is a return to chaos, which we must first have the courage to enter if we wish to find our way out of it; otherwise

160

there can be only false exits, spurious thought without any grasp of reality. Perhaps, moreover, entering into Auschwitz may encourage thought to make its dwelling there, and will spur it on to renew itself from within and to take, at last, the first step, which alone is absolutely free and which consists of self-creation out of nothingness. Did the world not spring up *ex nihilo*, out of such a creative act? The first step after Auschwitz then seems to be the one which would place us at the exact moment when nothing any longer exists but when all may be again. It is the moment of Silence, of that Silence which once, at the beginning of the world, held back the Word while also being its womb; of that Silence which at Auschwitz but a short while ago was identified with the history of the world.

(André Neher, 'The Exile of the Word: From the Silence of the Bible to the Silence of Auschwitz', in John K. Roth and Michael Berenbaum (eds), *Holocaust: Religious and Philosophical Implications*, New York, Paragon House, 1989, 9–10)

Auschwitz and Human Freedom

In creating man free, God introduced into the universe an element of extreme incertitude which no divine or divinatory wisdom, no mathematic calculation, no prayer even, could foresee or anticipate or incorporate into a predetermined design. Free man is improvisation made flesh and history; he is the absolutely unforeseeable; he is the limit which the directive forces of the creative plan encounter, and no one is able to foretell whether this limit may be crossed or whether, because of the mighty barrier it raises against them, it will compel these creative forces to retreat, by this shock of repercussion endangering the whole plan of the creation. Free man is God's dividing of the waters: those below, separated from those above, are henceforward to live from themselves.

According to the Jewish tradition, the inception of this risk of God's is to be found in the curious statement *na'ase adam*, 'let us make man,' in Gen. 1:26. Whom is God addressing in this weighty moment of decision, when the plan of creating man hardly seems possible without the cooperation of some force other than the divine creative force? The angels? The world? Himself? Without dismissing prematurely any of these possibilities, the Sages finally suggest that God's call is addressed to man, to the potential Adam who is envisaged in God's plan but who can be brought into being only through a cooperation between man and God. 'Let us make man,' the two of us—you, man and Me, God—

and this Covenant establishes forever the liberty of man, whom it makes forever the partner of God.

Thus the initial phases in the unfolding drama of history are stages in the apprenticeship in liberty. It is as though God were testing man, were forcing him to prove his liberty like a resistant steel, as though God had decided to try this creature He had endowed with freedom, and, having put him through the test, sought means of strengthening him further; of identifying him even more closely with his liberty. There was a risk, however, that the point might be reached where man was completely unified with his liberty and that henceforth, with all the consequences it would inevitably entail, the angelic as well as the bestial condition would be definitely barred to man. There was a risk, as Maimonides acutely observed, that liberty would become man's physical law not only potentially but in act, that this liberty which God had envisaged for man would invest him in a real and actual garment, that it would remain with him day by day, that it would accompany him in his thoughts, his history, and his sufferings, and that he would now be bound only by a single constraint, that, precisely, of being free. . .

But it can also at any moment overflow, burst the barriers, explode, and, up to the very end of days and the limits of space, threaten to invade, destroy, or sublimate the creation, to wrench it away from God with a brutal gesture or to restore it to Him in a completely new springtime, to offer it up to damnation or redemption.

(André Neher, 'The Exile of the Word: From the Silence of the Bible to the Silence of Auschwitz' in John K. Roth and Michael Berenbaum (eds), *Holocaust: Religious and Philosophical Implications*, New York, Paragon, 1989, 12–13)

Discussion

1. Is it a mistake to compare Auschwitz with other events?
2. Does human freedom limit God's knowledge of the future?

David Birnbaum: The Holocaust and Freedom

David Birnbaum is a yeshiva-educated scholar, and has served as a member of the faculty of the New School of Social Research in New York. In God and Evil, *he maintains that Jews must transcend their dependence on God—instead, they must accept that the Divine is 'Holy Potential', allowing through the process of contraction space for the exercise of personal freedom. In his view, human beings are able to attain spiritual maturity in the exercise of such liberty and thereby attain their fullest possible potential. This view serves as the basis for reconciling the horrors of the Holocaust with a traditional understanding of God's nature.*

Evil and Freedom

Redemption must be achieved from a base of freedom, which also implies an environment of ascendant evil. As man's intellectual base advances, both of these criteria become more manifest. The Hasidic *rebbe* who consoled his flock, en route to their impending doom in a Nazi camp, by interpreting their travail as a harbinger of the coming of the Messianic age, was not necessarily out of line philosophically. For 'redemption' cannot be seized from an environment of either slavery—or bliss. And out of the depths of evil, the potentialities of good can conceivably be snared.

Free man is obliged to protect his freedom and dignity. When man—created in the image of God—yields, however slightly, on his dignity, he also yields on the dignity of the God who created him. When man allows himself to be dragged into slavery—and does not obsessively resist to the utter limits of the plausible—he yields on Divine dignity.

Man, who has been granted the infinitely precious gift of freedom, must guard it with obsessive vigilance. Granted that we are geniuses in retrospect, nevertheless the lessons must be ingrained into the cumulative consciousness. For the Jew, in particular, has learned that, incredible as it might be to conceptualize, the forces of evil will, in one way or another, ultimately coalesce yet again to strike at man's freedom and dignity.

(David Birnbaum, *God and Evil*, Hoboken, New Jersey, KTAV, 1989, 161–162)

A Unified Theory

The United Formulation fits well with the general trend of Jewish history, with the concept of the ascent of man, and with the intellectually vigorous thrust of Jewish history. It fits well with our concepts of freedom and privacy, while not limiting the potential total omniscience of the Primal Force. It reconciles manifest intervention in Pharaoh's Egypt and apparent nonintervention in Hitler's Europe.

It validates the authentic views of those who went to their deaths at the hands of the Nazis fully believing in the God of Israel, and those who went to their deaths finally and completely rejecting the classic watching God of Israel. For in a sense both were correct.

God, indeed, is not sitting outside the crematorium watching while infants are being burned alive. Because it is an abomination to the essence of *El Moleh Rachamim* (God full of compassion). It must be presumed that God is in a state of contracted real-time consciousness for the higher purpose, elected by man, of allowing the totality of infants and men to grow up in a state of *bona fide* personal freedom, so that they may grasp for the totality of their potentialities. The price, however, is often high, too high.

Man of reason, man of *Halachah*, and *homo religiosus* can all relate to our formulation, albeit on different levels. Our formulation introduces an element of structure into a mysterious world and almost incomprehsensible existence. It offers hope for the further ascent of man and his ultimate realization of potential. Thus the theme of potential can be carried through all stages of historical/religious development both on a cosmic, theistic, and human level. . .

Can Judaism survive with a God of contracted real-time consciousness? Is our religious fervour not undercut? Can Judaism survive without the authoritarian God standing in the room with us, holding God's sledgehammer, watching our deeds and thoughts in all times in all states? Can Judaism survive if prayer is less efficacious than the literal meaning of the words might indicate?

On the other hand, can Judaism truly be comfortable with the formulation of an infinitely manifested, omnipotent, omnimerciful, omnipresent God who observed, albeit in his mysterious ways, the debasement, enslavement, and murder of a third of his people? What ultimate purpose did a God watching in real-time calculate as the gas pellets were dropping, hundreds of God's children nakedly, painfully, humiliatingly, and desperately being asphyxiated, hour after hour, day after day, year after year? Does Judaism just shrug its shoulders and go on to other, less intractable matters? Would the Patriarch Abraham who argued so tenaciously for invidious Sodom, have been satisfied with consigning the Holocaust to the netherworld of the 'unfathomable'?

We have attempted to make the case that potential/knowledge/ evil/good/freedom/privacy/human dignity/Providence/Divine consciousness/ are all interlocked with each other in a cosmic dynamic geometric relationship, with man as the protagonist; that as man ascends in knowledge and implicitly in his demand for greater freedom, the Divine Face of *Rachamim* (Mercy) is pre-empted by the Divine core of Potential.

(David Birnbaum, *God and Evil*, Hoboken, New Jersey, KTAV, 1989, 164–165)

The Post-Holocaust Jew

In a sense, the post-Holocaust Jew is also the freest Jew in history. He has survived in spite of the fact that he is Jewish. His coreligionists have undergone some of mankind's most nefarious depravity. Indeed, depravity within depravity. Post-Holocaust Jews can be tempted to charge God with a breach of the covenant. Our commonly accepted image of the God of Israel does not truly survive the Holocaust intact. Certainly, traditional concepts of reward and punishment were once again brutalized along with the innocent victims.

Yet if we postulate a God of Israel wholly directed towards opening the gates to man's infinite potential by granting him ascending levels of freedom as he ascends intellectually, and if we grant a God of Israel contracting his real-time consciousness to grant man this crucial freedom, then our outlook is clearer. A Deity exercising contraction of real-time consciousness for the greater good, man's freedom and potential, clearly—not inscrutably—commits no crimes of breach of covenant or complicity of silence. He is guilty only of the crime of increasing man's freedom—an option exercised by man at Eden.

The Nazi force, which subverted science for its nefarious ends, was a perversion of the dynamics of the Tree of Knowledge and of creation itself. It was anti-individualistic, anti-freedom, anti-privacy, anti-dignity. It claimed the right to enslave and terminate innocent life at will. It was a challenge to God itself.

Ultimately 'this thousand year Reich of Aryan supermen' would be ended by a secular nation-state whose coin of the realm bears the mottos 'Liberty' and 'In God We Trust'. And a thousand years after the dismemberment of the Third Reich, a later generation of Jewish five year olds will undoubtedly be taking out their notebooks and learning the *aleph-bet*. . .

Man simultaneously wants total freedom and the total security of the womb. Yet mankind gave priority to freedom/potential at Eden, and it must be presumed that this is the only route for the cosmos to attain its full realization.

(David Birnbaum, *God and Evil*, Hoboken, New Jersey, KTAV, 1989, 165–167)

Discussion

1. Should contemporary Jews charge God with a breach of the covenant?
2. Does creation need human freedom for the cosmos to attain its realization?

Didier Pollefyt: The Holocaust and Evil

Didier Pollefyt has been a Doctoral Researcher at the National Fund for Scientific Research at the Catholic University, Louvain. In 'Auschwitz or How Good People Can Do Evil', he confronts the horrors of the Holocaust. In attempting to explain how the Nazis could have committed acts of horror, he argues that in extreme circumstances normal individuals can be driven to disregard ordinary modes of ethical behaviour.

Fragmentation

The behaviour of most of the Nazi perpetrators looks very incoherent; both humane feelings and cruelty can easily be found in one and the same person. The commandant Kramer of Bergen–Belsen, for example, wept with emotion listening to his favourite music, but could mercilessly kill a Jew who did not obey his orders. Kramer declared in his trial that 'he did not feel emotions during these crimes.' This disunity or 'doubling' in the lives of most of the perpetrators points to a radical discontinuity in their inner lives between the public and the private. During the day in the camps they did the cruelest of things, but in the evening in their rooms they wrote very romantic letters to their spouses. Their minds seem to have been compartmentalized like the waterproof bulkheads of a submarine. On Christmas night 1943 the *Einsatz-kommando* IIb received an order to kill 3000 Jews and Gypsies in Russia. The order was executed doubly quick in order to enable the soldiers to go to Midnight Mass. During the Nuremberg trials, the Nazi criminal Speer declared that 'on the affective level he only had sentimental reactions, but on the level of decisions only rational principles count for much.' Such fragmentation is the creation of a difference in the inner life between various spheres of life, so that human compassion can no longer interfere with public work (genocide), while the private life remains intact. On the basis of fragmentation it becomes clear how

166

normal human beings can become mass-murderers and how a member of a totalitarian system can (try to) reconcile his submission to immoral orders with the preservation of his private moral self-respect.

(Didier Pollefyt, 'Auschwitz or How Good People Can Do Evil' in G. Jan Colijn and Marcia Sachs Littell (eds), *Confronting the Holocaust*, Lanham, Maryland, University Press of America, 1997, 98)

Depersonalization

For totalitarian ideologies human beings are never considered as goals in themselves (philosophically) nor as images of God (theologically). Individuals are always thought in terms of a bigger cosmic project (such as Hitler's thousand-year Reich) in which they themselves are of no importance. For Todorov, one of the goals of totalitarianism is depersonalization: the reduction of individuals to merely ingredients of an enormous project that completely transcends them. The camps were the first and foremost place to experiment with this process of depersonalization.

Yet the transformation of human beings to non-humans is not immediately evident, requiring the overcoming of a great deal of inner moral resistances. Therefore the Nazis used (modern) techniques to neutralize the 'appeal of the face of the other'. . . thereby wiping out the humanity of the other. These techniques might be illustrated with some examples that make clear how the evil of Auschwitz was more the result of depersonalization than of sadistic monstrosity. . .

A first technique was the deprivation of victims of their clothing just prior to killing them. Normally we do not see naked people in groups. Since clothing is an expression of humanity, by stripping victims of their clothes, it became much easier to consider them non-human. This technique made it more difficult for the perpetrators to identify with the victims and easier for them to kill with a clear conscience. Another technique was to make people live in their own waste without food or sanitation, so that they became completely unrecognizable and, like animals, preoccupied only with food. . .

A third technique consisted in the reduction of persons to numbers tattooed on their arms. In this way, a person loses his or her name, the first indication of his or her being human. . . A fourth technique was the continuous use of large quantities. It is more difficult to kill two persons than to kill two thousand. A last technique was the avoidance of direct confrontation with the victims. . .

(Didier Pollefyt, 'Auschwitz or How Good People Can do Evil' in G. Jan Colijn and Marcia Sachs Littell (eds), *Confronting the Holocaust*, Lanham, Maryland, University Press of America, 1997, 99–100)

Power

A third characteristic of the anthropology of the perpetrator is the enjoyment of the exercise of power. This is a kind of depersonalization in which the other is reduced to only a means, while the power-holder remains an end. . . Of course, one can also enjoy making someone else happy. There is, however, an asymmetry between the effects of making someone else happy and unhappy. By making someone else unhappy, one receives a much stronger proof of one's power over that person. But when one makes someone else happy, one can never be sure that this person's happiness is not also thanks to his or her own will. When one makes someone else unhappy, one can be more certain about the effectiveness of one's power, because normally no one wants to be unhappy. Killing the other is the absolute proof of my power over that person (but at the same time the absolute limit of my power!). Yet it is not the suffering of the other itself that causes my enjoyment, as in sadism, but the consciousness of having had power over the other. Instead of sadism, then, it was the enjoyment of power that was the central passion behind the evil of Auschwitz. There are not many proofs for this claim in the biographies of perpetrators because most of these were written with apologetic purposes. We can nonetheless see that perpetrators in camps became angry when, for example, an order was not executed quickly or the victim risked to look into the eyes of the executioner. What was new for the camps was that this enjoyment of power was no longer limited by any legal or moral boundary. The only boundary left was the death of the other person. The desire to exercise such power over the victim was for the most part the consequence of the perpetrators' own restriction of freedom with the system. Many perpetrators within the totalitarian system were tyrants to those below because they were slaves to those above.

(Didier Pollefyt, 'Auschwitz or How Good People Can Do Evil' in G. Jan Colijn and Marcia Sachs Littell, *Confronting the Holocaust*, Lanham, Maryland, University Press of America, 1997, 101–102)

Discussion

1. Were the perpetrators of evil suffering from fragmented personalities?
2. Was the evil of Auschwitz the result of depersonalization rather than sadism?

CHAPTER EIGHT

The Holocaust and Christian Faith

Graham Keith: The Holocaust and Jewish Christianity

Graham Keith is a Christian writer and has taught at the James Hamilton Academy in Ayr, Scotland. In Hated Without a Cause, *he traces the history of anti-Semitism from ancient times to the present. In his view, anti-Semitism should not be understood simply as a human event, but as instigated by Satanic forces. What is required today, he contends, is a more nuanced account of the history of anti-Semitism which recognizes the importance of leading the Jewish people away from unbelief to an acceptance of Jesus as Lord and Saviour of humankind.*

Satan and Anti-Semitism

If Christians are to pursue a 'meta-historical' line on anti-Semitism they might do better to explore the notion of anti-Semitism as satanic—perhaps a ploy to hinder the Jewish people from re-assessing their relationship to Jesus of Nazareth and his disciples as well as from bringing blessing to the other nations of the world. The advantage of such an approach would be this: Christian anti-Semitism could be included under this heading. No less a person than Simon Peter, Jesus' leading disciple, became a mouthpiece of Satan in his own ignorant devotion to Jesus and tried to deter Jesus from the cross. I would suggest that Christian leaders may have performed a similar role in sanctioning an unduly severe and uncharitable line toward the Jewish people if they appeared to persist in stubborn unbelief and to question or ridicule cardinal Christian doctrines. . .

To resort to the devil as an explanation, however partial or tentative, might seem a step into the unknown or at least into an arena where assertions become unproveable. But in this case it is not inappropriate seeing that the Christian Scriptures, which were often used against the

170

Jews, do present something of the character and activities of the devil. In fact, the passage from John's gospel where Jesus accuses a group of Jews of being children of the devil has acquired notoriety as the text with the most anti-Semitic potential in the whole of the New Testament, because its highly charged language has often been applied to the whole Jewish nation without qualification.

(Graham Keith, *Hated Without a Cause: A Survey of Anti-Semitism*, Carlisle, Paternoster Press, 1997, 270)

The Holocaust and Jewish Witness

Since the Holocaust the churches, particularly in western Europe and North America, have attached renewed importance to their relations with the Jewish people. Some theologians have been bold enough to assign the Holocaust a revelatory significance from God. But this rather extreme position, in my view, distracts from the more urgent task of detecting the roots of anti-Semitism which formed the backcloth to the Holocaust.

It is a good sign that most churches have acknowledged that Christians bear some responsibility for anti-Semitism, though it is unfortunate that they have not yet reached accord on the precise nature of that responsibility. Again, there is welcome agreement that the Jewish people still stand in a special relationship to God. Due account is thus taken of the Apostle Paul's affirmation—'As far as election is concerned, they are loved on account of the patriarchs, for God's gifts and his call are irrevocable.' A general consensus, however, is harder to find on the ecclesiastical and missiological implications of this.

At the same time the other strand of Paul's declaration—that the Jews are 'enemies' on account of the gentile believers—is underplayed. Effectively this brings contemporary churches to almost the polar opposite position from that of the medieval church, where it was held that the Jews were indeed enemies of God, but this was so interpreted as to put the Jews into a special class of unbelievers who were virtually beyond redemption. Today some churches veer to a position where the attitude of Jews to Jesus has almost become an irrelevance.

With liberal Christians the underplaying of Jewish unbelief is evident in a tendency altogether to replace mission, which makes its goal the recognition of Jesus as the Messiah, with dialogue, which emphasizes learning from one another and the identification of common moral concerns. It also means that Messianic Jews have been ignored, even though this is an increasing movement both in Israel and especially among Jews of the Dispersion. These groups, which endeavour to wed Christian beliefs to an affirmation of Jewish identity, raise awkward questions. They remind the churches that there are Jews in this generation, as in previous generations, who believe Jesus of Nazareth is the fulfilment of authentic Judaism, and so the rest of their countrymen are in serious error. . .

An incorrect diagnosis of anti-Semitism will lead to wrong strategies. For instance, unreserved support for the Jewish leadership in Israel will neither promote justice among the peoples of the Middle East nor further the claims of Jesus of Nazareth among the Jewish people. It will also gloss over the harassment accorded groups of Messianic Jews by Jewish leaders who dislike their stance and their proselytism. This is ironic because the emergence of a sovereign Jewish state has seemingly provided a context in which a distinctively Jewish church can re-emerge. . .

It has been widely suggested that an independent national life is a vital precondition if a Jewish church is to develop roots. With no assimilationist pressures the church will be free to develop its own witness and ministry to the wider Jewish community. This will pose a challenge not only to the mainstream of Jewish society but to Christian churches. What attitude are they to have to those Messianic Jews? Are they to align with them as examples of the believing Jewish remnant of which the Apostle Paul speaks? Or are they to overlook them in preference for the main pillars of Jewish society in the fear that any other policy would be dismissed as anti-Semitic? If the latter policy is pursued, the gentile churches will be treating Jewish unbelief as somehow different from that of other men. They will be guilty of the reverse of the medieval position when Jewish unbelief was regarded as far more pernicious than that of others. The present danger is that it may be treated as innocuous.

Clearly it is as difficult today as at any time for the gentile churches to hold in balance the two elements of Paul's perspective in Rom. 11:28. Yet, they must strive to do so. If they forget that the Jewish people are beloved of God and their election is irrevocable, inevitably they will slip into anti-Semitic attitudes and practices. On the other side of the coin, to ignore the reality of Jewish unbelief and the fact that it makes them enemies of God means that the Jewish people will be deprived of the greatest service the gentile Christians can give them—the testimony to Jesus of Nazareth as the Saviour of Israel.

(Graham Keith, *Hated Without a Cause: A Survey of Anti-Semitism*, Cumbria, Paternoster Press, 1997, 278–283)

Discussion

1. Does it make sense to conceive of Satan as the source of anti-Semitism?
2. Does Jewish unbelief regarding the Messiahship of Jesus make Jews the enemies of God?

Hugh Montefiore: The Holocaust and the Cross

Hugh Montefiore served as Anglican Bishop of Birmingham. In On Being a Jewish Christian, *he explores a variety of responses to the Holocaust. In his view, the death of Jesus provides a means of coming to terms with the murder of six million Jews at the hands of the Nazis.*

The Holocaust and the Jewish People

The attempted genocide of Jewry by the Nazis has shaken the civilised world, but it has also left an indelible mark on Jewry as a whole, which Christians can hardly appreciate. There have of course been genocides in the history of mankind, and even today we have been shown on our television screens the appalling sight of mass killings, measured in hundreds of thousands, in Africa. But it was the cold-blooded planning of the Nazis and the scale and efficient administration of their mass slaughter, using modern technology, that has been so hateful and repulsive that no words can describe it. Jews have been used to violence and repression throughout their long history. Usually this has had a religious cause. But although the anti-Semitism that the Nazis showed had its origins in earlier Christian anti-Judaism, it was a secular version of racial hatred rather than a religious kind of oppression. Although the Church may be accused of being silent and slow to help in this Jewish catastrophe, the *Shoah* cannot itself be blamed upon Christians.

The *Shoah* does, however, pose terrible questions for Jews about divine providence. In the past it has been customary for them to account for their persecution by the visitation of divine wrath on their disobedience of divine Law. But this cannot apply to an attempted genocide, which applied indiscriminately to all with Jewish blood.

How then could God have allowed it to happen. Are not the Jews his chosen people—how can he allow his elect to be treated in such a terrible way? Some have been forced to give up their belief in God... Others have fallen back on the explanation that God grants humans freedom to sin, although this does not of course exonerate God from all responsibility... Perhaps God is not omnipotent: God did not will Auschwitz, he wept over it... Even to pose the question has been agonizing. 'The *Shoah* is a challenge to all belief in God'... To suggest that God is not loving is to deny the whole of the earlier history of his self-disclosure in the Old Testament. To put forward the concept of a suffering God does not really give an answer... Elie Wiesel in his despair accuses God of indifference. It has even been suggested that there was a 'divine interruption', God interrupting his providence for a time, almost as though his attention was elsewhere.

(Hugh Montefiore, *On Being a Jewish Christian*, London, Hodder and Stoughton, 1998, 94–95)

Jesus and Auschwitz

Here I would like to make a personal suggestion. Could it be that the pattern of life through death, which the Messiah reluctantly accepted at his father's hands, makes sense of the *Shoah*, which is otherwise inexplicable? If it is true that life through death gives us the deepest insight into spiritual reality, and if this is what Jesus himself had to undergo, is it altogether inconceivable that this same pattern of life through death is ordained not merely for the Messiah, but also for God's chosen people?...

For Christians to suggest that Jews are fulfilling the role of Suffering Servant in no way means that 'they array themselves at the head of the ranks of those who would like to repeat the Holocaust'... If this fate has come upon the Jews, it is because they are the chosen people of God: it has not been willed in any way by them, nor have they been conscious of the reasons why they have suffered so terribly down the ages and in particular at the hands of the Nazis. Such a concept in no way reduces the appalling evil of the Nazi regime. The *Shoah* becomes the latest and most terrible instance of their suffering. If Jesus was indeed the Jewish Messiah, it is not (as been alleged) 'a profound offence against the sanctity of the unique suffering of Holy Israel' to set one man's death alongside the deaths of six million Jews, especially if chapter 53 of Isaiah can be interpreted as referring both to the Messiah and to the Jewish people. . . . It has been said that 'when it (Christianity) presses Judaism into its own construct, denying Jewish integrity and identity, and when it utilizes and misuses Auschwitz in a celebration of Christian triumphalism and supersessionalism, we take issue with Christianity'[1]. . . . I hope that I am not doing this. I am merely trying to say what, as a Jewish Christian, is the only way in which I can make any sense out of an event so utterly frightful as the *Shoah*.

I am not saying that the end justifies the means: God forbid! But it is a matter of fact that for the Jewish people new life has come from these terrible experiences of the past. They have emerged from these persecutions, sufferings and murders, with what seems renewed vitality. Is it mere coincidence that post-Enlightenment Jews, out of all proportion to their numbers, have today become leaders in so many fields of life: industry, commerce, medicine, philosophy, sociology, art, music, politics and so on? Persecution, far from blotting them out, seems to have given them new energy and inner resources. Prejudice, far from keeping them down, has been the springboard from which in so many fields they have risen to the top, often by so doing incurring envy on the part of their Gentile neighbours.

(Hugh Montefiore, *On Being a Jewish Christian*, London, Hodder and Stoughton, 1998, 95–97)

References

1. Albert Friedlander, 'Against the Fall of Night', Council of Christians and Jews, 1984

Discussion

1. What is the relationship between Christian anti-Semitism and Nazi antipathy to the Jewish people?
2. Do Jesus's life and death provide an acceptable framework for understanding the Holocaust?

David Stern: The Holocaust and Evangelism

David Stern is a Messianic Jew and served as a Professor at the University of California, Los Angeles. In Messianic Jewish Manifesto, *he argues that the Holocaust has not ruled out the need for Christians to evangelize Jews. In his view, this obligation remains a central feature of the Messianic movement.*

The Jewish Messiah

There are also people who call themselves Christians who not only neglect Jews and refuse to evangelize them, but do so on purpose and believe that they are right.

Some are simply afraid of being rejected, since it is well known that many Jewish people are not open to considering the claims of Yeshua and the New Testament. If that is their only reason, they can be encouraged to drop their fear, pray that God will bless their efforts, and then obey the Great Commission by reaching out to the Jews with the offer of God's love and forgiveness through the Messiah.

Others feel they should respect the sensibilities of Jewish people who say they do not want to hear about Yeshua. For them the remedy is to give Scripture heavier weight than their feelings and to renew their efforts—tactfully, sensitively, as the Lord leads—at communicating the truth of the Gospel to Jews. I owe my salvation in part to a young man who was quite unaware of my sensibilities but told me the truth about Yeshua anyway.

However, there are those who do not rely on emotions but attempt to rationalize steering clear of Jewish evangelism by marshalling facts. A common justification for not evangelizing Jews is the Holocaust. Six million Jews died at the hands of the Nazis. During Hitler's twelve-year rule the state churches were notoriously silent and weak in the face of the visible evil; moreover, mainstream Christian theology, if not actually antisemitic, was sufficiently cold toward Jews and Judaism to allow virulent antisemitism to express itself unchecked. Many well-meaning Christians ask how, in the face of such sin by the Church, do we dare tell Jews they should believe in Jesus?

The answer is twofold. On the one hand, the answer to the question, 'How?' is: 'Humbly'. A Christian should be willing to shoulder the burden of the Church in respect to Jews. He should not say, 'The bad Christian theology was done by liberals, and they weren't real Christians. The state churches were not run by real Christians.' Instead, he should admit, 'It is possible that people who are my brothers in Christ committed horrors against Jews. I don't know for certain that they really are my brothers, but I will not massage my own conscience by denying the possibility categorically.'

Moreover, his stance toward Jews in regard to the Holocaust should be one of seeking forgiveness without expecting it. He should acknowledge that the Church sinned. And he should ask forgiveness. But why should a Jew grant it? What has the Church done to earn the Jewish people's forgiveness? An element in forgiveness is restitution. How can the Church, or anyone, make restitution for the death of six million people? Ultimately, the answer is that only God can make restitution. The Holocaust is too horrible to allow that any human act or combination of human acts could pay for it. Only God, in his miraculous way, through the healing that Yeshua the Messiah brings, can restore the hearts of the living to the point where they can forgive. No Christian has a right to expect Jewish forgiveness for the Holocaust, and in fact he will probably not get such forgiveness from Jews whose hearts have not been healed by Yeshua the Messiah.

Nevertheless, a Christian should bring the Gospel to the Jews. Why? Because it is true, and because it is necessary—without Yeshua Jewish people, like Gentile people, are destined for eternal destruction; moreover, without Yeshua the true Messiah of the Jewish people, the Jewish people will not achieve its own glorious goals promised by Scripture. Not to preach the Gospel to Jews is the worst antisemitic act of all. Therefore, in spite of the Holocaust—and the Inquisition, and the pogroms, and all the other horrors—Christians must take up the Gospel and bring it to the Jews. For without Yeshua, the Jewish people (and other peoples), individually and collectively, have no hope.

(David Stern, *Messianic Jewish Manifesto*, Clarkesville, Maryland, Jewish New Testament Publications, 1997, 254–256)

Discussion

1. Should the Holocaust serve as a reason for not evangelizing the Jewish community?
2. Can the Church make restitution for its sins during the Holocaust?

CHAPTER NINE

The Holocaust and the Kingdom

Richard Harries: The Holocaust and the Kingdom of God

Richard Harries has seved as the Anglican Bishop of Oxford. In 'Theodicy Will Not Go Away' he argues that the theological questions evoked by the terrible events of the Nazi regime must be confronted. Today many Christians and Jews find it difficult to assert that there is hope beyond the grave, yet such a vision is central to a true understanding of God's ways. Only by accepting that God's Kingdom is upon us can we hope to make sense of the persistence of evil in the modern world.

The Problem of Theodicy

The problem of theodicy is posed by the fact that life is such an inextricable mixture of happiness and misery. If life were entirely a burden, the problem of theodicy would not arise. We would know it was the product of an evil or indifferent power. It is because (at least for some of the time) we experience life as a blessing and want to give thanks to a good creator that the evil we see around us appears as such a contradiction of what we otherwise know. The questions that lie behind traditional theodicy, far from being misconceived, take on, in the light of the *Shoah*, a new intensity for Christians. The evil we have to face is not just an evil permitted by God but one that came into the world in the wake of Christ's Incarnation. The faith we have to go on is not just our own but that of the Jewish people, who despite everything continue to bless God for their creation.

It is clear that in their respective responses to the problem of evil Jews and Christians will want to say many of the same things, even though sometimes in different language. Christians talk about God's will to create beings with genuine free choice and the limitations this imposes on what God can do without contradicting his fundamental

178

purpose. The Jewish mystical tradition suggests that God could only make space for human beings by a voluntary withdrawal. With the all-embracing cape of his presence he makes a small space where he is not, in order that human beings might be with a life of our own. . . Yet God does do more than this. He is ceaselessly active, seeking to draw good out of evil and inviting us to co-operate with him in the task. He does not do this in a remote and distanced manner but, through his spirit, from within the flux of human events. For he is with us and for us, striving in our striving, suffering in our suffering.

(Richard Harries, 'Theodicy Will Not Go Away' in Tony Bayfield and Marcus Braybrooke (eds), *Dialogue with a Difference*, London, SCM, 1992, 106–107)

Beyond the Grave

When Christ is first depicted on the cross, as in a series of four ivory panels dating from about 420 CE in the British Museum, he is strong and triumphant. Christ as a suffering, battered figure did not emerge for a further 400 years. What spoke to the condition of Christians in the first 900 years was the strong Christ who saves us from fate, evil, all forms of malevolent power and death.

It is quite clear that millions of people do not find their proper fulfilment in this life. They die young, are born mentally ill, are crushed by circumstances and so on. If there is a loving and wise power behind this strange life of ours then his purposes cannot be limited to this earth. There must be the possibility of further growth, especially in the knowledge and love of God himself, beyond the spatio-temporal order. . .

For hope is one of the vital elements which Jews and Christians share in their response to suffering and the *Shoah*. As the Chief Rabbi Dr. Jonathan Sacks said in conversation, this is neither the best of all possible worlds nor the worst of all possible worlds but 'the worst of all possible worlds—in which there is hope'. As the 1988 Lambeth Conference of Anglican Bishops put it:

Christians and Jews share one hope, which is for the realization of God's Kingdom on earth. Together they wait for it, pray for it and prepare for it. This Kingdom is nothing less than human life and society transformed, transfigured and transparent to the glory of God. Christians believe that this glory has already shone in the face of Jesus Christ. In his life, death and resurrection the Kingdom of God, God's just rule, has already broken into the affairs of this world. Judaism is not able to accept this. However, Christian belief in Jesus is related to a frame of reference which Christians and Jews share. For it is as a result of incorporation into Jesus Christ that Christians come to share in the Jewish hope for the coming of God's Kingdom... [1]

We are not concerned so much with the meaning of life as for the realization of God's purposes in relation to the whole of his creation. We look for the coming of his kingdom, his just and gentle rule. So we seek to stand together in practical endeavour of all kinds, the well-being of the Jewish community, upholding human rights wherever they are violated and working for the elimination of poverty both in this country and amongst the one billion people in the world now living at or below starvation level. There is practical work to be done together. There is also for the Christian community a particular responsibility at this time for correcting in its teachings all distortions of Judaism.

(Richard Harries, 'Theodicy Will Not Go Away' in Tony Bayfield and Marcus Braybrooke (eds), *Dialogue with a Difference*, London, SCM, 1992, 108–110)

References

1. 'Jews, Christians and Muslims: The Way of Dialogue', in *The Truth Shall Make You Free*, The Anglican Consultative Council 1989, para 14, 302

Discussion

1. In light of the Holocaust, can one believe that God ceaselessly seeks to draw good out of evil?
2. Does belief in the Kingdom resolve the problems raised by the Nazi onslaught against the Jews?

Seymour Siegel: The Holocaust and Messianism

Seymour Siegel has served as Professor of Theology and Ethics at the Jewish Theological Seminary, New York. In 'Response to Emil Fackenheim' he argues that Messianism, Zionism and the Holocaust are interrelated. Modern Zionism, he believes, has brought about a fundamental change in the traditional concept of Messianism by abandoning the belief in divine intervention in history. Such a view was confirmed by the Holocaust. Nonetheless, Siegel maintains, the creation of the Jewish state should be perceived as a prelude to the coming of the Messianic kingdom.

Redemption and Human Action

To the two elements of Messianism and chosenness, a third element was to be added: the concept of the land. The land is the Land of Promises. It is also the Land of Beginnings. It is where Judaism began and where the great culmination will occur. The land is the thread which runs throughout all of Jewish history. The God of Israel is a universal God. But Jewish history reflects a dialogue with the land, even when the people reside outside of it. 'The love of this land was due to an imperative, not to an instinct, not to a sentiment. There is a covenant, an engagement of the people to the land. We live by Covenants. We could not betray our pledge or discard the promise.'

Thus three interrelated themes—prominent in Jewish theology—intertwined to form Zionist ideology: Messianism, chosenness, and the land. They were transmuted, transformed, and translated into secular terms. But their power was reflected in the movement of return and renascence.

The events of the Holocaust did not create Zionism. They confirmed the insights of Zionism.

The nations of the world showed their ferocious enmity. The withdrawal of the Jewish people from history had resulted in destruction, degradation, and the Holocaust. We are only now beginning to understand the awesome dimensions of the enmity of the nations toward Jacob. The Hitlerian butchers were the prime criminals. But there were others who stood by while six million died. There were those who were silent in the Vatican even when the dimensions of the slaughter became know. There were the rulers of the 'workers' paradise', who made a pact with Hitler, and who can now refuse to acknowledge the fact of Jewish suffering. Nor can we forget the complicity of the Arabs, some of whom openly sided with Hitler, among them the grand mufti of Jerusalem, who was given a place of honour in the courts of the butchers of the Jews. The need for active participation, for the transformation of the passive Jew into one who would fight for his physical existence with force and with blood; one who would seek political power in order to defend himself against the demons which seem to possess the nations of the world when they deal with the House of Jacob—this need became vividly clear.

The events of the Holocaust have confirmed that while ultimately our trust is with the God of Jacob, He will, apparently, not protect us unless we protect ourselves.

(Seymour Siegel, 'Response to Emil Fackenheim' in Eva Fleischner (ed.), *Auschwitz: Beginning of a New Era?*, New York, KTAV, 1977, 220–221)

Israel and the Messianic Kingdom

It should be noted that a secular Messianism is not the sum total of Jewish Messianism. The fulfilment of Zionism is not the Messianic kingdom. The dream of Jewish Messianism cannot be severed from the dream of universal peace from the generation of human nature and the incursion of the Transcendent to heal the lesions of nature and the cosmos. We must stand on guard against premature Messianism. The Messianic idea is subject to two distortions: pessimism and quietism in which we wait for God to redeem us, and utopianism where we think we can achieve the complete redemption. The one expects too little of us, the other too much. The Jews, even those in Israel, live in an unredeemed world. They share the human predicament of estrangement and sin. They know too well the lack of universal brotherhood. The State of Israel is salvation, but not redemption. Because Israel is not the Messianic kingdom, it must use secular means to deal with the concrete problems of security and boundaries. Israel as a secular political structure cannot endanger its national life even for universal aims. Borders have to be set by diplomacy in light of considerations of security and of realistic hopes for peace. Israel came into being as a result of the Messianic vision. However, because the Messiah has not come, Israel must use secular means to protect itself and, if possible, find a *modus vivendi* with its neighbours, using the ordinary procedures of sovereign states.

What does all this mean for Christians? If we are indeed younger and elder brothers, then you share with us the divine patrimony. We are members of one family. Christians, therefore, have a responsibility to protect the Jewish people from its enemies—to help insure that the Jewish body and the Jewish soul will have a secure resting place. The establishment of the state is one step in the long road toward the redemption of the world. The Messianic dream, the challenges of the covenant have resulted in the return of the Jewish people as active participants in the historical process.

These achievements, precarious as they now seem to be, are not a call to be at ease. How could one be at ease, especially in Zion?—for God is beckoning us to be restless until his fulfilment comes.

(Seymour Siegel, 'Response to Emil Fackenheim' in Eva Flesichner (ed.), *Auschwitz: Beginning of a New Era?*, New York, KTAV, 1977, 222–223)

Discussion

1. Did the events of the Holocaust confirm the insights of Zionism?
2. Should the State of Israel be perceived as a prelude to the coming of the Messianic Kingdom?

Dan Cohn-Sherbok: The Holocaust and the Hereafter

Dan Cohn-Sherbok is Professor of Judaism at the University of Wales. In Holocaust Theology, *he argues that belief in the afterlife offers the only solution to the problem of the Holocaust. In his view, this central tenet of the Jewish faith sustained generations of Jews who endured suffering and persecution. In the camps as well, such a conviction provided a source of consolation for those who went to their deaths.*

The Sanctification of God and the Holocaust

In the concentration camps many religious Jews remained loyal to the tradition of *Kiddush ha-Shem*. Joining the ranks of generations of martyrs, they sanctified God with unshakable faith. As they awaited the final sentence, they drew strength from one another to witness to the God of Israel. A survivor of the Holocaust recounted an experience of such dedication at Auschwitz:

> Fourteen hundred boys who were locked in a block and condemned to the gas chambers found out that I had a *shofar*. They begged and implored that I go to them and blow a hundred blasts of the *shofar*. After the blowing of the *shofar* one young man arose and said: 'Dear friends, the rabbi has given us his words of strength. He has told us the words of the *Talmud* that even if a sharp sword is placed at the neck of a man he must not despair of God's mercy. I say to you we can hope for the best. But we must be ready for the worst. For the sake of God let us not forget at our last moment to say "*Shema Yisrael*".' And they all recited with intense feeling the sentence '*Shema Yisrael*'.

183

Another survivor wrote that during *Succos* he saw an old Jew sitting in a *succah* in one of the camps singing *zmirot* in a loud voice. He entered the *succah* and asked the old man if he were aware of the great danger of what he was doing. The old man continued to sing and after some time said: 'What can they do to me? They can take my body but not my soul. Over the soul they have no authority. Here they are powerful but in the Other World they are powerless.'

In the camps many Jews faced death silently. When their last moments arrived they died without fear. They neither grovelled nor pleaded for mercy since they believed it was God's judgment to take their lives. With love and trust they awaited the death sentence. As they prepared to surrender themselves to God, they thought only of the purity of their souls. . . Implicit in the determination of these Holocaust victims to sanctify God's name was an absolute faith in the life beyond death. Instead of viewing earthly life as the brief interlude between two eternal states of darkness, they saw their suffering and death as a prelude to a more glorious future. In the life beyond the gas chambers and mass graves, God would reward the righteous of Israel— this was the eternal destiny of His chosen people.

(Dan Cohn-Sherbok, *Holocaust Theology*, London, Lamp, 1991, 124–126)

Death and the Afterlife

On the basis of the belief in eternal salvation which sustained the Jewish people through centuries of persecution, it might be expected that Holocaust theologians would attempt to explain the events of the Nazi period in the context of a future life. . . This has not occurred. Instead these writers have set aside doctrines concerning messianic redemption, resurrection and final judgment. This shift in orientation is in part due to the fact that the views expressed in rabbinic literature are not binding. All Jews are obliged to accept the divine origin of the Law, but this is not so with regard to theological concepts and theories expounded by the rabbis. Thus it is possible for a Jew to be religiously pious without accepting the central beliefs of mainstream Judaism.

Given that there is no authoritative bedrock of Jewish theology, Holocaust theologians will no doubt have felt fully justified in ignoring various elements of traditional rabbinic eschatology which have ceased to retain their hold on Jewish consciousness. . . Because of this shift of emphasis in Jewish thought, it is not surprising that Jewish Holocaust theologians have refrained from appealing to the traditional belief in other-worldly reward and punishment in formulating their responses to the horrors of the death camps. Yet without this belief, it is simply impossible to make sense of the world as the creation of an all-good and all-powerful God. Without eventual vindication of the righteous in Paradise, there is no way to sustain the belief in a providential God who watches over His chosen people. The essence of the Jewish understanding of God is that He loves His chosen people. If death means extinction, there is no way to make sense of the claim that He loves and cherishes all those who died in the concentration camps, for suffering and death would ultimately triumph over each of those who perished. But if there is eternal life in a World to Come, then there is hope that the righteous will share in a divine life. Moreover, the divine attribute of justice demands that the righteous of Israel who met their death as innocent victims of the Nazis will reap an everlasting reward.

Here then is an answer to the religious perplexities of the Holocaust. The promise of immortality offers a way of reconciling the belief in a loving and just God with the nightmare of the death camps. As we have seen, this hope sustained the Jewish people through centuries of suffering and martyrdom. Now that Jewry stands on the threshold of the twenty-first century, it must again serve as the fulcrum of religious belief. Only in this way will the Jewish people who have experienced the Valley of the Shadow of Death be able to say, in the ancient words of the Psalmist: 'I shall fear no evil, for thou art with me.'

(Dan Cohn-Sherbok, *Holocaust Theology*, London, Lamp, 1991, 127–128)

Discussion

1. Is belief in an afterlife a solution to the problem of the Holocaust?
2. Can the belief in life after death serve as a basis for modern Jewish life?

CHAPTER TEN

The Holocaust and Covenant

Eugene Borowitz: Covenant and Holocaust

Eugene Borowitz has served as the Sigmund L. Falk Distinguished Professor of Jewish Religious Thought at the Hebrew Union College/Jewish Institute of Religion, New York. In Choices in Modern Jewish Thought, *he expresses his commitment to the doctrine of Covenant. In his view, the Jewish people stands in relation to God though God's covenantal bond with Israel. Adopting a liberal interpretation of this tenet of the faith, he asserts that the problem of evil can be resolved within this context. Although Jews have found it increasingly difficult to believe in life after death, they can be sustained by the belief in Covenant despite the horrors of the Nazi era.*

Liberal Judaism and Divine Presence

The fundamental relationship in which the Jew stands is Covenant. However, it was made and is maintained primarily with the people of Israel and not the individual Jew. To be sure, the people of Israel is not an entity outside of its individual members and no claim is made that it possesses some folk-soul or national-will of its own. Nonetheless the individual Jew's direct personal relationship with God is not begun by that Jew but by the historic experience of the Jewish people into which the contemporary Jew is born. . . Individual Jews, then, are immediately involved in a dialectic not only of self and God. . . but of the self and the Jewish people in relation to God. . .

This sets the agenda for contemporary liberal Jewish apologetic theology. As against all secular interpretations of being a Jew, commitment to the Covenant insists that a relationship to God is primary to the life of the Jewish people and the individual Jew. The first concern of our apologetics, then, needs to be the recapture of the living reality of God in individual Jewish lives and thus in the Jewish

186

community. The major target in this regard is the crypto-agnosticism with which most Jews have evaded this issue for a generation or more. In the face of contemporary nihilism, I am convinced, the old hope of serious values without commitment to God is increasingly untenable. The second concern of our apologetics is to help the individual Jew identify personally with the people of Israel. That is somewhat easier in our present time of high regard for ethnic difference and the search for one's own folk roots. Yet the primary model most people use in their thinking remains the Cartesian one of the detached self seeking truth without preconceptions or commitments. This has particular appeal to Jews since it immediately releases them from Jewish attachment in accord with the social pressures on any minority to assimilate to the majority.

(Eugene Borowitz, *Choices in Modern Jewish Thought*, New York, Behrman House, 1983, 281–282)

Covenant Theology and Evil

The notion of relationship provides an approach to living with the problem of evil and specifically, the Holocaust. Relationships exist not only when there is immediate confirmation of them but also in its absence. To trust means that the relationship is considered still real though no evidence for it is immediately available. One also believes such confirmation will yet be forthcoming. The practice of Judaism, the life of *Torah*, is an effort to build a strong relationship with God. Within the context of such closeness, Jews have largely been able to live with the evils of the world.

There are special reasons why it has been difficult to continue this approach in modern times, most notably the loss of our belief in personal survival after death. The Holocaust raised our problems in this regard to an unprecedented level of tension, for some to the point of breaking the relationship with God. It remains stupefyingly inexplicable. Yet, perhaps to our surprise, it has not destroyed the Covenant. For most Jews the ties with the people of Israel are far stronger than anything we had anticipated. The absence of God during the Holocaust cannot be absolutized. It should not be used to deny that God has since been present in our lives as individuals and in that of the people of Israel. . .

The perception of a transcendent demand upon us to preserve the people of Israel, the affirmation of a transcendent ground of value in the face of contemporary nihilism, have led some minority of Jews to a restoration of our relationship with the other partner in the Covenant, God. The absence of God and the hurt we have felt are not intellectually explained. Yet it is possible, despite them, to continue the relationship. For the intellectually determined the most satisfactory way of dealing with this issue is to say that God's power is limited. For those to whom this raises more problems than it solves, there is acceptance without understanding. Both positions are compatible with relating to God in Covenant. I find myself constantly tempted to the former though mostly affirming the latter, a dialectic I find appropriate to affirming the Covenant.

(Eugene Borowitz, *Choices in Modern Jewish Thought*, New York, Behrman House, 1983, 284–285)

Covenant and Torah

As to *Torah*, our sense of Jewish duty emerges from standing in relationship to God as part of the people of Israel. Various theories of revelation might be appropriate to accepting relationship as basic to our existence. For me, the personalist teaching of God's presence as commanding permits me to retain my autonomy while setting me in an individual bond with the people of Israel. I find it especially harmonious with Judaism seen as existence in relationship and my experience trying to live it. However, it should be understood, as against strictly antinomian interpretations of such revelation, that I take the Jewish self not to be atomistic, unattached and individual when standing in relationship with God, but as one of the Jewish people. Hence, responding to the Divine presence cannot only be a matter of what is commanded to me personally at this moment. . . but what is commanded to me as one whose individuality is not to be separated from my being one of the historic Jewish people.

(Eugene Borowitz, *Choices in Modern Jewish Thought*, New York, Behrman House, 1983, 286)

Discussion

1. Can one believe in the Covenant in the light of the Holocaust?
2. Given the events of the Holocaust, can one believe that the Jewish people stand in a special relationship to God?

David Weiss: Holocaust and Covenant

Born in Vienna, David Weiss has served as the Chairman of the Lautenberg Centre for General and Tumor Immunology at the Hebrew University Hadassah Hospital in Jerusalem. In 'The Holocaust and the New Covenant', he argues that the Holocaust was not a unique event; rather it is a modern manifestation of anti-Jewish sentiment which has existed throughout Jewish history. In his view, the covenant remains unchanged in a post-Holocaust world.

Rejecting New Covenants

The incumbency of a radically new Judaic theology has been argued with growing insistence during the past thirty years. Pivotal to the claim is the imputed uniqueness of the European holocaust of 1939–1945. The horror visited on the Jewish people during these years has been, it is claimed, a wholly singular experience, and one that signals the beginning of a new era. The classic Judaic delineation of the relationship between God and the House of Israel is no longer tenable, perhaps, indeed, has not been since the destruction of the Second Temple and Jewish commonwealth. The covenant that was, or the illusion of this covenant, has been abrogated in the German death camps. What is demanded of the survivors is a new covenant, a unilateral, voluntary assertion by the House of Israel of the will to continue Jewish existence in the face of an indifferent, changeable, or non-existent deity. . .

Certainly, this last havoc demands a searching, penetrating reaffirmation of faith and commitment, as there have been urgent gropings for renewed meaning in the wake of earlier holocausts. The striving for new perspectives and new apperceptions is indeed a constant demand of the spirit on every Jew, at all times. But a 'new covenant', a 'new epoch'—that is a closing of the book of Judaism. Whatever their sincerity, their love of Israel, their loyalties to Jewish practice, the prophets of the new covenant call not to a revitalization but to denial of the God of Israel and annulment of the Jew's *raison d'être* in the world. That, too, is not unique. Not all the gropings after preceding desolation remain anchored in the covenant that is. Those that were not, led into apostate movements and disappearance. . .

The advocates of new covenants will not halt the salvation history of the Jewish people, but they can add to the century's attritions. They

189

must not go unchallenged, therefore. It must be told unequivocally: they are advocates not of a reaffirmed Judaism, but of something other than the religion eternal of a God eternal.

(David Weiss, 'The Holocaust and the New Covenant' in John K. Roth and Michael Berenbaum (eds), *Holocaust: Religious and Philosophical Implications*, New York, Paragon House, 1989, 71–74)

A Covenant People

The Jew must struggle to come to grips with ravage and loss on two distinct levels, that of the people collectively and that of the individual.

For the people, the covenant is indissoluble, and its conditions have been spelled out: 'See, I have set before thee this day life and good, and death and evil. . . I command thee this day to love the Lord thy God, to walk in his ways, and to keep his commandments. . . Then thou shalt live and the Lord thy God shall bless thee in the land into which thou goest. . . But if thy heart turn away. . . and shalt worship other gods. . . I announce to you this day, that thou shalt surely perish, and thou shalt not prolong your days upon the land. . . I call heaven and earth to witness this day against you, that I have set before thee life and death, blessing and cursing. Therefore choose life. . . And the Lord said to Moses, Behold, thou shalt sleep with thy fathers; and this people will. . . go astray after the gods of the. . . land into which they go. . . and break my covenant which I have made with them. Then. . . I will forsake them, and I will hide my face from them, and they shall be devoured. . . so that they will say on that day, are these evils not come upon us, because our God is not among us? And I will surely hide my face on that day for all the evils which they shall have perpetrated.' (Deut. 30.15–20; 31.16–18)

This is a clear blueprint of Jewish history, in promise and realization. The terms of the covenant are repeated, again and again, throughout Scripture and rabbinic literature, and their fulfilment is historical record. The people that chose and was chosen to bear witness to the God that is revealed in the affairs of mankind cannot survive at ease the betrayal of that God and the forcing him to turn his face. We are given the choice to make God's presence large in the world of man or to banish the *Shechinah*, but we cannot avoid the consequences of then being alone in a godless world. God's banishment paves the way to holocausts. . .

The privilege of being a covenantal people is transcendent. The consequences of violation are agonizing. Many Jews have individually reasserted their allegiance to the collective covenant, even in bitter experience of its terms. I ask myself whether I should have the strength for such personal reassertion, had I endured them fully in my being. But I do know this: The covenant has unfolded for the people, and continues to unfold, in panlucid verity. It has not been broken by God, nor has he permitted the people to shake it off.

(David Weiss, 'The Holocaust and the New Covenant' in John K. Roth and Michael Berenbaum (eds), *Holocaust: Religious and Philosophical Implications*, New York, Paragon House, 1989, 74–75)

Discussion

1. Was the Holocaust a unique event?
2. Is a new Jewish theology now required?

CHAPTER ELEVEN

The Holocaust and Human Evil

Alan T. Davies: Overcoming Nihilism

Alan T. Davies has served as Professor in the Department for the Study of Religion at the University of Toronto. In 'Response to Irving Greenberg', he disputes the view that it is no longer possible to believe in the God of Scripture in a post-Holocaust world. According to Davies, history does not play the same role in Judaism and Christianity: for the Jew the Exodus is primary whereas for the Christian the cross/resurrection is the central orienting event. This means that Christians find ultimate meaning beyond rather than within history. The Holocaust therefore should not overwhelm Christian belief. Nonetheless, Davies contends that Auschwitz poses serious theological problems for the Christian community.

A Challenge to the Christian Faith

If to speak of the Holocaust is painful for Jews, to speak of the Holocaust is also painful for Christians. Because the disaster erupted in Christian Europe, on soil fertilized for centuries by Christian ideas, because the Nazis, when not Christians themselves, were the baptized children of Christians, and because the German churches permitted themselves to be seduced too willingly by Nazi dreams and visions, the terrible question of Christian complicity is instantly ventilated. The subject is threatening, for the intrinsic worth of the Christian faith itself is brought under judgment. Generations of Christian theologians and preachers have proclaimed with assurance that Judaism 'died on the cross'. Now ironically, the dictum can be reversed, for, with much greater justification, Jewish theologians are raising the possibility that Christianity died at Auschwitz! An awesome suggestion. One reads it, for example, in Eliezer Berkovits' polemical but powerful indictment of Christianity, *Faith after the Holocaust,* in which the Christian religion is charged with a total moral and spiritual bankruptcy, as the true source of the Nazi genocide. The fact that Berkovits almost certainly overstates his case by claiming that a direct rather than an indirect line extends from the Council of Nicaea to the death camps does not mitigate the agonizing crisis of conscience which the entire issue poses for the Christian churches. It is not without reason that Franklin Littell has described the Holocaust as a basic event in Christian history, 'of the same order as the Exodus, Sinai and the fall of Rome', and therefore a serious challenge to Christian theology.

(Alan T. Davies, 'Response to Irving Greenberg' in Eva Fleischner (ed.), *Auschwitz: Beginning of a New Era?*, New York, KTAV, 1977, 57)

Christianity and History

For Christians, generally speaking, God's mode of relating to history is perceived somewhat differently. There is no midrashic framework of Christian belief. This is not because Christians have not as a matter of habit interpreted the Christian ages in terms of God's overarching design. On the contrary, ever since Lactantius regarded the triumph of the Christian church in the Roman *imperium* as a vindication of the true religion over its rivals, Christian thought has been coloured by an ideological understanding of providence. Of late, with the disintegration of Christendom, most Christians are inclined to show much greater caution toward any attempt to decipher the presence of God in the events of history, a scepticism which, because of past distortions, is probably healthy. Even when the preoccupation with providence ran strong, however, these great theologians who dealt with the subject, such as Augustine, always operated from a different orientating experience than rabbinic Judaism: not the Exodus, but the birth, death, and resurrection of Christ supplied the paradigmatic symbol. The cross, however (which includes the resurrection), unlike the Exodus, is both a historical and transhistorical event. . .

One must, of course, be careful in stating this contrast between Judaism and Christianity. It would be abhorrent for a Christian to minimize historical tragedy, especially when Jews are involved, by an otherworldly appeal to transcendental symbols. . . Nor must the cross ever be employed by Christians in order to avoid the scandal of the Holocaust: a genuine temptation, reflected in any triumphalist theology of our age. Nor, I think, should Christians approach the subject as untroubled theists because, on this analysis, they are relieved of the necessity of scanning history for the signs of God's continuing presence. All profound theistic (and biblical) faith embraces doubt as one of its elements.

(Alan T. Davies, 'Response to Irving Greenberg' in Eva Fleischner (ed.), *Auschwitz: Beginning of a New Era?*, New York, KTAV, 1977, 61–62)

The Holocaust and Crucifixion

Must faith require a sign out of the whirlwind before its response is possible? Or can the Gordian knot which the Holocaust poses remain unsevered, leaving us with fragmentary rather than final meanings, because history supplies no final meanings? Out of the Holocaust, which defies final explanation, there nevertheless emerge many fragments of meaning. Elie Wiesel, for example, has described with great poignancy the beauty and heroism of Jewish martyrs in the midst of death, and Berkovits has affirmed his faith in the future of man because of the extraordinary nobility of some of Hitler's victims. These fragments of meaning in a meaningless situation overcome, in part, the larger meaninglessness of the Holocaust. Given this fragmentary sense of meaning, it is, I think, possible to live without nihilism. . .

Perhaps it is legitimate for Christians to see in the Holocaust a more terrible revelation of the human condition, which, in turn, adds a new dimension to the cross as a revelatory symbol linked to evil and suffering. I would like some gifted Christian artist to paint a crucifixion scene portraying Jesus as an Auschwitz Jew, including the yellow badge Jude on his body, against the barbed wire of a death camp. In this sense, the religious meaning of the central symbol of Christianity has been forever transformed and deepened for me, and no theological response would be complete which does not recognize this fact. At the same time, and for the same reason, I agree with Irving Greenberg that it is more imperative than ever for Christians to struggle with the Christian sources of the Holocaust, the ideological roots of anti-Semitism in the structures of classical Christian theology, and the attitudes of historic Christendom. These painful events have made the Holocaust a basic event in Christian history and an unprecedented crisis for the Christian conscience.

(Alan T. Davies, 'Response to Irving Greenberg' in Eva Fleischner (ed.), *Auschwitz: Beginning of a New Era?*, New York, KTAV, 1977, 63–64)

Discussion

1. Did Christianity die at Auschwitz?
2. Is it possible to overcome the meaninglessness of the Holocaust?

Paul van Buren: Auschwitz and Moral Responsibility

Paul van Buren served as Professor at Temple University, Pennsylvania. In Discerning the Way: A Theology of the Jewish–Christian Reality, *he argues that in a post-Holocaust world fundamental questions have been posed about the nature of God and divine providence. In his view, the Holocaust calls for a reconstruction of Christian theology. Using the image of the way, he argues that the Gentile Church has been called by the God of Israel through the Jew Jesus to join the Jewish people on a path through history. Together they are to cooperate in building God's kingdom on earth.*

The Negative Message of Auschwitz

The Holocaust negatively raises the issue of human responsibility for history by throwing a floodlight on a failure of human responsibility. What happened could have been prevented, humanly prevented, and it was not. That may be evidence that God will not intervene to do what He expects us to do for ourselves—and for Him. Earlier in this century Protestant theologians exposed us to a theology of 'the mighty acts of God,' without sufficient attention to the fact that the acts in question were all in the distant past. Such a theology helped to make it increasingly difficult to speak of the living God in the present tense. Had we been listening more to the Jews, we might have paid more attention to *Torah* and so noticed how it ends. Mighty acts and signs had been done in Egypt all right, but they are not quite so simply denoted God's acts as this strand of Protestant theology led us to think. On the contrary, the last book of *Torah* concludes with Israel's verdict concerning Moses which bears repeating:

> There has never yet risen in Israel a prophet like Moses, whom the Lord knew face to face: remember all the signs and portents which the Lord sent him to show in Egypt to Pharaoh and all his servants and the whole land; remember the strong hand of Moses and the terrible deeds which he did in the sight of all Israel (Deut. 34:10–12)

195

It has been pointed out that the major literature of Judaism produced during the Holocaust was not focused on the problem of theodicy, the question of what God was doing to justify Himself in that event. The major literature was Halachic: questions concerning how Jews ought to act when faced with some of the agonizing choices with which they were confronted by the prospect of mass murder.

(Paul van Buren, *Discerning the Way: A Theology of the Jewish–Christian Reality*, New York, Seabury Press, 1980, 180–181)

The Holocaust and the Church

The Holocaust does indeed have something new to say to us in the church. It asks about our responsibility for what took place and so about our responsibility for the future. It tells us what Dietrich Bonhoeffer discovered in the midst of the horror, that it is God Himself who is forcing us to live in His world as if it were our own world, which indeed by the gift of Creation it is. It is God Himself who is forcing us to live in this world as if the God of our theological tradition, the one classically defined in Latin, e.g., as *actus purus*, were not there (*etsi deus non daretur*) to do for us what He expects us to do for ourselves and for His creation. Had more Christians come to this realization earlier, perhaps millions murdered by Hitler might have been saved. The new in the revelation from Auschwitz, then, is that God requires that we take unqualified responsibility before Him for His history with us.

If the Holocaust is a negative revelation of God's requirement of human responsibility, the founding of the state of Israel says the same thing in a positive form. Israel was founded not by divine intervention from heaven or the sending of the messiah, but by Jewish guns and Jewish effort against seemingly insuperable numerical and material odds. Had the early pioneers, the fugitives from the Holocaust or the supporters of the project from the Diaspora waited upon a so-called act of God instead of daring to be the act of God, they would in all likelihood be waiting still, those who were still alive. This event which has begun to reorient the church, this event of the founding of Israel and Jewish return to the Land, was one of humanly assumed responsibility for history, yes, for God's history with His people and their history with Him.

(Paul van Buren, *Discerning the Way: A Theology of the Jewish–Christian Reality*, New York, Seabury Press, 1980, 181)

Jews and Christians

For Christians there is revealed a relationship between God and His creatures more nearly in line with Jewish Halachic faithfulness than with our idea that all that happens does so solely by God's action. If we are to continue to speak of 'by grace alone', then we shall need to allow for the fact that, by the grace of Creation, the grace of Sinai and the grace of Jesus Christ—all and each unfinished events—God has really turned over into our hands the Way into the future which He has promised. We can move ahead in hope, but it will be a hope that calls us to cast our efforts into God's plan for this world. Redemption has been promised. The creation shall be completed. But this is something which will not happen apart from the efforts of God's people and God's Gentile church. What is new in the revelation of our days is that God will not deal with us as a 'problem-solver.' He is God, and not man; His ways are higher than our 'problem-solving' ways and His thoughts are to deal with us as a loving Father who genuinely expects us to stand on our feet and struggle to do our part, which may be the largest part for all we now know, in bringing closer the age of redemption for which we long.

(Paul van Buren, *Discerning the Way: A Theology of the Jewish–Christian Reality*, New York, Seabury Press, 1980, 183)

Discussion

1. Is it possible to believe that God acts in history, given the horrors of the Holocaust?
2. Is the Holocaust a negative revelation of God's requirement of human responsibility?

Immanuel Jakobovits: The Holocaust and Human Responsibility

Of German origin, Immanuel Jakobovits has served as Chief Rabbi of the United Hebrew Congregations of the Commonwealth. In 'Where Was Man at Auschwitz?', he argues that the most important question to ask after the terrible events of the Nazi era is: Where was man? Why did the majority of Germans support the Nazi quest to create a new society based on racial principles?

The Holocaust and the Absence of Moral Values

When I am asked, Where was God at Auschwitz? I too have no answer. Perhaps there is none. Indeed, infinity of suffering cannot be multiplied, whether it affects six million, or one million, or a single innocent life. Every time an infant's life perishes in a cot-death, turning young parents into mourners, the same question arises: 'Where was God?'

Maybe the question is inscrutable—in the words of one of our great medieval philosophers: If I knew him, I would be him; or, if I could comprehend divine justice, I would myself be divine.

The real question is: 'Where was man at Auschwitz?' Where was the humanity of a cultured nation mesmerised by a rabble-rouser, to turn into millions of mass-murderers and their accomplices? Where was man when numerous civilised nations remained silent and closed their borders to those fleeing from fiendish persecution? Where were the leaders of great faiths when the cries of the tormented evoked no response? Where was man when millions were shipped here in cattle trucks for the crime of being born as Jews?

Auschwitz has been liberated from the Nazi barbarians. But the world has not yet been completely liberated from Auschwitz. When neo-fascists can still form powerful parties in countries like Russia and Italy, when Nazi propaganda can still be freely disseminated in many parts of the world, and when the cloak of respectability can be claimed by fake historians who deny that the Holocaust ever took place, we have the ultimate evidence that, fifty years on, the legacy of Auschwitz—city of death—is not yet dead. If Auschwitz never existed, where—I ask—are my aunts and uncles, my cousins and numerous other relatives, together with most of my teachers and classmates who were deported there?

(Immanuel Jakobovits, 'Where Was Man at Auschwitz?' in Helen Fry (ed.), *Christian–Jewish Dialogue*, Exeter, University of Exeter Press, 1996, 65–66)

Discussion

1. Is the central question posed by the Holocaust: Where was man?
2. Has the world been liberated from Auschwitz?

Jack Bemporad: The Holocaust and Human Nature

Of Italian origin, Jack Bemporad served as a Reform rabbi and Director of the Centre for Interreligious Understanding in Englewood, New Jersey. In 'The Concept of Man after Auschwitz', he explores the nature of human beings in the light of the Nazi era. In his view, men and women are not inherently good or evil. Rather, they have the capacity to act ethically.

The Holocaust and Human Despair

The holocaust has given rise to a temper of absolute despair—despair, because man has used his most precious knowledge his reason, science, and technology, the achievements of the scientific spirit, for genocide, for mass murder. And yet this surrender to despair is much too facile; it does not adequately account for the value of what has been lost. The holocaust has shaken us not because it shows that nothing has meaning—in such a situation, the loss of the meaningless and useless is no cause for dismay. The tragedy is that so very much that had so much meaning could be lost—and was lost. It demonstrates for us the possibility of the perversion of all that is dear. It indicates to us the potential demonism in man, and it has awakened us from the optimistic slumber of the nineteenth century. . .

On the psychological level, the holocaust has shown us the effects of a totalitarian system on its subjects—both persecuted and persecutor. The concentration camp provides an agonizingly clear example of how a totalitarian state can deform and depersonalize all people under its rule.

The Nazis depersonalized and dehumanized their victims in a variety of ways, beginning with mass arrests, often awakening and terrorizing victims at night, herding them by the hundreds and thousands into stifling cattle cars, taking away all their belongings, shaving their heads, and assigning them numbers in place of names. The list goes on and on. Suffice it to say that any attempt at individuality and spontaneity was immediately and ruthlessly punished. The camp was geared to reducing man to a purely sub-human animal existence, an animal existence with but one aim—to survive at any cost, and the final result of the process of dehumanization and depersonalization was that in time, those who did survive often adopted Nazi attitudes, identifying themselves with their persecutors, judging themselves by Nazi standards. . .

The depersonalization and dehumanization characteristic of the Nazis. . . was the culmination of a process whose roots went back to the sixteenth century. Implicit in the triumph of modern science and the dualism that ensued between matter and mind concomitant with its rejection of teleology, the universe became completely divorced from any reference to human ends. . .

Left alone with his own will without any reference to a physical or spiritual cosmos, man simply becomes a creature of desires, of needs and passions. This philosophical result fits in well with the triumph of Darwinism which viewed man as a high grade animal whose reason in no way elevated him or separated him from the rest of the animal kingdom. Reason in evolutionary thought was viewed as an instrument for survival and became a tool of the life process. It thus became a means and once reason becomes merely a means, all ends are irrational.

(Jack Bemporad, 'The Concept of Man after Auschwitz' in Albert Friedlander (ed.), *Out of the Whirlwind*, New York, Schocken, 1976, 478–482)

Human Nature

For some it appears that this human condition, this general malaise whose ultimate expression culminated in the holocaust reinforces the Augustinian Christian belief in original sin: man is by nature corrupt and through his own devices can only destroy himself. The only hope is an otherworldly salvation. Only a depraved being, this view maintains, born with original sin could have committed such heinous crimes.

It seems that we have gone full circle from the rational optimistic doctrine of man rooted in Greek and Enlightenment thought to an irrationalist pessimism rooted in classic Augustinian, Lutheran Christianity conjoined with some aspects of contemporary biology.

The holocaust has indeed demonstrated that man can destroy himself. It has shown that man in a dehumanized state is capable of doing untold and unbelievable harm. It has also shown that man is not by nature good. It has not, however, demonstrated that man is by nature evil. It has shown us that his awesome potentialities are for both good and for evil. It forces us to look at what contemporaneously is leading to dehumanization and depersonalization, and to do our best to prevent its coming to be. We must emphasize all those aspects which stress man's spirituality as a being with dignity and value related to an objective structure of values at the basis of his existence. We must strive to preserve man's integrity and foster those personal and social elements that make for human integration. We must strenuously reject those doctrines that see man as merely a creature of needs and desires—a complicated or high grade animal and nothing more. I believe that no one would deny that man has passions and needs, that he is inclined to self-centredness and egotism, to idolatry and that he can often be manipulated and used inhumanly especially in a conformist and totalitarian social structure so that he is alienated from that element within him that can respond to the true, the good and the beautiful, to the sacred and the holy. A view that sees man as a high grade animal sees only part of the truth. The other aspect is that man is also responsive and related to a world of values and rationality that leaves far behind his animal status. It is in fact only because of the impact of bifurcationist theories that such a dualistic view of man has become prevalent. Man is indeed not an animal and only by abstracting certain aspects of his nature can one see him in this aspect. Man is a human living being whose humanity which is represented by his capacity to symbolize, to think, to be self-concious, to project the future, to transcend himself, qualifies his animal status. All those elements that one identifies with animal are completely transmuted in human beings since they are conjoined with man's symbolic self-transcending nature. Once we recognize that man is by nature neither good nor evil and that both his good and his evil are human qualities and that man has the freedom to actualize either good or evil, then we are able to recognize the traditional Jewish teaching with respect to the nature of man.

(Jack Bemporad, 'The Concept of Man after Auschwitz' in Albert Friedlander (ed.), *Out of the Whirlwind*, New York, Schocken, 1976, 482–483)

Discussion

1. Does the Holocaust demonstrate the potential despotism of men and women?
2. Are human beings inherently good?

Abraham Joshua Heschel: The Holocaust and Sin

Of Polish descent, Abraham Joshua Heschel taught at the Hochschule für die Wissenschaft des Judentums in Berlin and later served as Professor of Jewish Ethics and Mysticism at the Jewish Theological Seminary, New York. In 'The Meaning of This Hour', he argues that the world was plunged into darkness during the Second World War as a result of human wickedness. What is now required is for human beings to assume responsibility for their actions in accordance with God's decrees.

Human Wickedness

Emblazoned over the gates of the world in which we live is the escutcheon of the demons. The mark of Cain in the face of man has come to overshadow the likeness of God. There has never been so much guilt and distress, agony and terror. At no time has the earth been so soaked with blood. Fellow men turned out to be evil ghosts, monstrous and weird. Ashamed and dismayed, we ask: Who is responsible?

History is a pyramid of efforts and errors; yet at times it is the Holy Mountain on which God holds judgment over the nations. Few are privileged to discern God's judgment in history. But all may be guided by the words of the Baal Shem: If a man has beheld evil, he may know that it was shown to him in order that he learn his own guilt and repent; for what is shown to him is also within him.

We have trifled with the name of God. We have taken the ideals in vain. We have called for the Lord. He came. And was ignored. We have preached but eluded him. We have praised but defied Him. Now we reap the fruits of our failure. Through centuries His voice cried in the wilderness. How skilfully it was trapped and imprisoned in the temples! How often it was drowned or distorted! Now we behold how it gradually withdraws, abandoning one people after another, departing from their souls, despising their wisdom. The taste for the good has all but gone from the earth. Men heap spite upon cruelty, malice upon atrocity.

The horrors of our time fill our souls with reproach and everlasting shame. We have profaned the word of God, and we have given the wealth of our land, the ingenuity of our minds and the dear lives of our youth to tragedy and perdition. There has never been more reason for man to be ashamed than now. Silence hovers mercilessly over many

202

dreadful lands. The day of the Lord is a day without the Lord. Where is God? Why didst Thou not halt the trains loaded with Jews being led to slaughter? It is hard to rear a child, to nourish and to educate. Why dost Thou make it so easy to kill? Like Moses, we hide our face; for we are afraid to look upon Elohim, upon his power of judgment. Indeed, where were we when men learned to hate in the days of starvation? When raving madmen were sowing wrath in the hearts of the unemployed?

(Abraham Joshua Heschel, 'The Meaning of This Hour' in Albert Friedlander (ed.), *Out of the Whirlwind*, New York, Schocken, 1976, 488–489)

Wickedness and Responsibility

Our world seems not unlike a pit of snakes. We did not sink into the pit in 1939, or even in 1933. We had descended into it generations ago, and the snakes have sent their venom into the bloodstream of humanity, gradually paralysing us, numbing nerve after nerve, dulling our minds, darkening our vision. Good and evil, that were once as real as day and night, have become a blurred mist. In our everyday life we worshipped force, despised compassion, and obeyed no law but our unappeasable appetite. The vision of the sacred has all but died in the soul of man. And when greed, envy and the reckless will to power came to maturity, the serpents cherished in the bosom of our civilization broke out of their dens to fall upon the helpless nations. . .

The conscience of the world was destroyed by those who were wont to blame others rather than themselves. Let us remember. We revered the instincts but distrusted the prophets. We laboured to perfect engines and let our inner life go to wreck. We ridiculed superstition until we lost our ability to believe. We have helped to extinguish the light our fathers had kindled. We have bartered holiness for convenience, loyalty for success, love for power, wisdom for information, tradition for fashion.

We cannot dwell at ease under the sun of our civilization as our ancestors thought we could. What was in the minds of our martyred brothers in their last hours? They died with disdain and scorn for a civilization in which the killing of civilians could become a carnival of fun, for a civilization which gave us mastery over the forces of nature but lost control over the forces of our self. . .

God will return to us when we shall be willing to let Him in—into our banks and factories, into our Congress and clubs, into our courts and investigating committees, into our homes and theatres. For God is everywhere or nowhere, the Father of all men or no man, concerned about everything or nothing. Only in His presence shall we learn that the glory of man is not in his will to power, but in his power of compassion. Man reflects either the image of His presence or that of a beast. . .

There is a divine dream which the prophets and rabbis have cherished and which fills our prayers and permeates the acts of true piety. It is the dream of a world rid of evil by the grace of God as well as by the efforts of man, by his dedication to the task of establishing the kingship of God in the world. God is waiting for us to redeem the world. We should not spend our life hunting for trivial satisfactions while God is waiting constantly and keenly for our effort and devotion.

(Abraham Joshua Heschel, 'The Meaning of This Hour' in Albert Friedlander (ed.), *Out of the Whirlwind*, New York, Schocken, 1976, 490–492)

Discussion

1. After the Holocaust, has the vision of the sacred died in our midst?
2. Is the prophetic dream of a world rid of human evil a fruitless hope in the light of the Nazi period?

Allan R. Brockway: Religion and Faith

Allan R. Brockway has served as Courtesy Professor at the University of South Florida. In 'Religious Values after the Holocaust: A Protestant View', he argues that a distinction must be drawn between religion and faith. In his view the Holocaust was the result of religious values which had been misused by the Nazis during the Third Reich. Faith, however, extols and protects individual rights. In the modern world, human beings must learn from the tragedy of the Holocaust and insure that faith guides human beings in their dealings with one another.

Beyond Religion

The distinction that Karl Barth made between religion and faith, which I learned about most explicitly through Dietrich Bonhoeffer, who wrote about 'religionless Christianity', has yet to make its way fully into our thinking about values. But the Holocaust says nothing to us if it does not insert that distinction indelibly into our collective consciousness. For it was the preeminence of religious values that produced the Holocaust, religious values that forced humanistic and humanitarian values into a secondary and finally nonexistent role. These latter, the humanitarian values, I wish to argue, are at the heart of the Christian value system based on faith, but they are foreign to religion, Christian religion in particular. The former, the religious values, were at the heart of Hitler's final solution.

It is true, of course, that Hitler's religion was not Christianity, despite his formal allegiance to Catholicism. Instead, his was a religion founded on race and blood, that fed upon the historic pragmatic religion of Christianity. But it was religion, nevertheless, because it placed idealistic, even transcendent, values above those of human beings and of peoples. Hitler demonstrated in the most horrible fashion imaginable that religious values made absolute are demonic.

Christianity has been prone, more than most religions, to just such demonism. Torquemada's Inquisition is a beautiful example, during which Jews and others were made to 'confess' Jesus Christ or suffer painful deaths. The people, the individuals, were unimportant; what happened to them as persons made no difference. The only things that mattered were the transcendent values of the religion. But Hitler took the religious value system one crucial step further. For him, religion was not a matter of belief, it was a matter of being. 'Being precedes essence', the existentialists have told us, but for Hitler being and essence were identical. If a man or woman was 'Aryan', this was sufficient for salvation (literally). Otherwise, particularly if one were a Jew, one's essence denied existence—and it was the Nazi religious duty to actualize that denial of existence, which is, of course, just what the death camps did.

(Allan R. Brockway, 'Religious Values after the Holocaust: A Protestant View' in Abraham J. Peck (ed.), *Jews and Christians after the Holocaust*, Philadelphia, Fortress Press, 1982, 55–56)

Values of Christian Faith

It is instructive to note that Hitler did not generally imprison, murder, or otherwise persecute those who were merely adherents of the Christian religion (*Deutsche Christen*). But he fully recognized the danger from those of Christian faith. These latter refused not only to participate in the expression of the Nazi folk religion but, more importantly, actively held to the values of their own faith, values that could never be harmonized with those of the Nazi regime and religion.

What were, and are, those values? They are what might be called horizontal values, those that make real, live people more important that abstractions, more important than religious belief. The value system of Christian faith does not differ from that of any enlightened humanity, it should be observed, save in one important particular: Christian faith is grounded in the conviction that active dedication to the infinite worth of the created universe in general and specific human individuals in particular is the first, last, and only test of one's faith in God. No one loves God who does not love those loved by God—which includes every single human being, of whatever colour, belief, nationality, sex, or age. Nothing could have been farther from the Nazi creed. And nothing could be farther from the Christian religion when religion takes precedence over faith.

I need not chronicle again the dismal record of the Christian churches and the majority of individual Christians when confronted with the fact of Hitler's mass murder of their friends and neighbours— the Jewish business people, secretaries, accountants, homemakers, factory workers, schoolteachers, labourers, and children of Europe. What is important for us to note today is that there was little in the history of the Christian religion to prompt a response other than that of the *Deutsche Christen*. For centuries the church had taught that the Jewish people had been written out of God's plan of salvation. It was not merely a peripheral religious tenet; it was central to the Christian religion itself, for from the earliest days of the church religion had displaced faith.

(Allan R. Brockway, 'Religious Values after the Holocaust: A Protestant View' in Abraham J. Peck (ed.), *Jews and Christians after the Holocaust*, Philadelphia, Fortress Press, 1982, 57)

Discussion

1. Were religious values at the heart of Hitler's final solution?
2. What are the values of religious faith?

Nicholas de Lange: The Holocaust and Human Sin

Nicholas de Lange is a Reform rabbi and has served as Reader in Hebrew and Jewish Studies at Cambridge University. In 'Jesus Christ and Auschwitz', he surveys both Jewish and Christian theological responses to the Holocaust. In his view, the central task facing both the Jewish and Christian communities is to acknowledge the different ways in which their sinfulness was responsible for the events of the Nazi era.

Religious Responses to the Holocaust

For Jews as well as Christians, the Holocaust, or *Shoah*, is of overwhelming significance. According to a number of Jewish thinkers the destruction of six million Jews by the Nazis was a unique event— the Final Solution was the first systematic genocidal assault in human history. Likewise, a number of Christian writers have stressed the centrality of this tragedy. How can one make sense of this modern calamity? From both the Christian and Jewish sides there has been a variety of theological responses. According to some Jewish thinkers, the Jews died in the concentration camps for the sins of humankind as God's suffering servant and sacrificial lamb. A second Jewish approach to the Holocaust is to see in the death camps a manifestation of God's will that his chosen people survive. Another Jewish response to the Holocaust is to reject any kind of explanation; instead, the events of the Holocaust are seen as part of God's inscrutable plan.

Paralleling such Jewish speculation a number of Christian thinkers have formulated theories grounded in Christian theology. Among Christian writers one of the most important developments has been the desire to reinterpret the doctrine of divine impassibility. For these writers, to recognize God in the crucified Christ means to grasp the trinitarian history of God and to understand oneself and this whole world with Auschwitz as existing in the history of God. God is not dead. Death is in God. He suffers by us and with us. While most Jews would have difficulties with such a Christological approach to the Holocaust, these theories illustrate the current Christian sensitivity to the religious perplexities of the Holocaust. No longer is the Church prepared to stand by silently as the Jewish people endure persecution and death; instead, many Christian theologians are acutely aware of the horrors of the death camps and the Church's share of responsibility for these atrocities.

(Nicholas de Lange, 'Jesus Christ and Auschwitz' in Dan Cohn-Sherbok (ed.), *The Future of Jewish–Christian Dialogue*, Lewiston, New York, Edwin Mellen, 1999, 9)

The Holocaust and Human Failure

The narrative of the death of Jesus in the Gospels is, in a strange way, an allegory of the story of the destruction of the Temple. It is a drama in which every step is guided by divine destiny, yet in which human choice and human responsibility play a full part. And it is clear that groundless hatred and wickedness play a large part in bringing the drama to its disastrous conclusion. It happened *mipnei hataeinu*, because of our sins. It is this aspect that lends such poignancy to Jesus' prayer, 'forgive our sins' (Luke 11:4): if only their sins could have been forgiven, they might have been delivered from the evil.

Is it really possible to say that destruction came 'because of our sins'? According to Maybaum, it is not.

> After Auschwitz Jews need not say this. Can any martyr be a more innocent sin-offering than those murdered in Auschwitz? The millions who died in Auschwitz died because of the sins of others.[1]

I agree with Maybaum: it seems grotesque to say that Auschwitz happened 'because of our sins.' And yet if the Jesus of the Gospels can pray to God 'Forgive us our sins' he throws down a challenge that we must take up. There are two ways that the Jew of today can read these words. On one level, they sound like a plea to Jews in our post-Auschwitz generation to forgive Jesus himself and all those who have persecuted us in his name. This is a thought I leave to others to comment on: it does not accord with my own understanding either of the Gospels, as documents of history, or of the Jewish view of 'forgiveness.' The second interpretation is more fruitful, potentially, for me. *Het* is not only wrongdoing, it is also shortcoming or failure. It is in this sense that I can understand the phrase *mipnei hataeinu*, in relation to the Babylonian *churban*, the Roman *churban*, and also the Third *churban*. The Jews who died in the *Shoah* were collectively innocent of wrongdoing. They were vicarious victims of the wrongdoings of others. Yet were they not also guilty of failure, as we all are? If the Jewish people had succeeded in making its message of humanity and compassion heard in the world, the *Shoah* could not have taken place. This is what I understand Maybaum to be saying. *Hatanu*: 'We have failed.' The 'we' embraces not only the Jews but also the Christians who were true to the message of the Old Testament and the Gospel.

Jesus was not an upholder of power and the established order. On the contrary, he strove to overturn the established order. He proclaimed freedom and compassion. In this he was a typical and prophetic Jew. It is the real tragedy of Jesus that the established order seized him and turned him into an implement of its own power. The name of Jesus became the false currency of Nazi antisemitism, as it had previously been attached to the Crusades, the Inquisition, the conquest of the Indies and all the other European empires. The Christian Church became the accomplice of the Nazi state.

In facing up together to the question 'Where was Jesus Christ at Auschwitz?', we must recognize the complexity of the question, and we must listen attentively to Jesus who says 'Forgive us our sins.' It was our failure that made the *churban* possible—the Christians who allowed the name of Jesus to be used as an instrument of oppression, the Jews who failed to make their message of mercy and humanity heard in a cruel and uncaring world. *Mipnei hataeinu*: the Holocaust happened, in part at least, because of our failure.

(Nicholas de Lange, 'Jesus Christ and Auschwitz' in Dan Cohn-Sherbok (ed.), *The Future of Jewish–Christian Dialogue*, Lewiston, New York, Edwin Mellen, 1999, 17–19)

References

1. Ignaz Maybaum, *The Face of God after Auschwitz*, Amsterdam, Polak and Van Gennep, 1965, 35

Discussion

1. Were both Jews and Christians responsible for the Holocaust?
2. In what ways was the Christian Church an accomplice of the Nazi state?

Julio de Santa Ana: The Holocaust and Liberation

Julio de Santa Ana has served as Director of the Ecumenical Centre of Services for Evangelization and Popular Education in Sao Paulo, Brazil. In 'The Holocaust and Liberation', he challenges contemporary Holocaust theologians. In his view, it is now necessary for Jews critically to examine the policies of the state of Israel. For de Santa Ana, the events of the Holocaust call for the liberation of all oppressed people.

Contemporary Holocaust Theology

This liberation calls for overcoming every type of bitterness. And the

209

need to overcome bitterness leads to a consideration of the emphasis given by a good deal of contemporary Jewish theology to the Holocaust. Some theology of the Holocaust is still marked by bitterness, in reaction to that horrible moment when the Jewish people suffered such cruelty. The problem of bitter people is that they do not liberate themselves from the force that struck out against their person, their being. The bitter have injected this force into their own life. They have not liberated themselves from this force. For this reason, they use it against others. Some strains of the theology of the Holocaust try to theologically legitimate bitterness, by trying to justify an aggressive power for the state of Israel, which in one form or another shows itself to be oppressive and unjust to the Palestinian people. The worst evil that oppressors can commit is to pour out their own guilt feelings— which they inevitably have in virtue of their practice of oppression —onto the oppressed person. The oppressed, then, takes over the same orientation in life as the oppressor. If the oppressor sought to dominate the other, using any means possible, the oppressed almost mechanically and unconsciously repeats the attitude of the dominator. In other words, the oppressed do not transcend their situation.

For this reason, Marc Ellis is correct when he says the theology of the Holocaust should be replaced by a theology of solidarity, through which the Jewish people would give a full expression to their universal vocation. The emphasis should be on the extension of the faith, and not on its exclusivity. This practice of solidarity begins with those who are closest. The other, the Palestinian, calls for recognition, dialogue, life with open relationships. This is what is written in the *Torah*. More than a Jewish liberation theology, it is a challenge to the Jewish people to develop a profound practice of liberation. Solidarity, beginning with the Palestinians, will be indelible proof that bitterness has been overcome. And, let us not forget, the Holocaust was a horrifying expression of bitterness— something that should never be repeated, not even by the Jews.

(Julio de Santa Ana, 'The Holocaust and Liberation' in Otto Maduro (ed.), *Judaism, Christianity, and Liberation*, New York, Orbis, 1991, 44–45)

Holocaust Theology and Theology of Liberation

A very important point in common between the theology of the Holocaust and the theology of liberation is the recognition that an oppressor exists. The oppressor talks of freedom, but imposes laws in an authoritarian manner. The only freedom that the oppressor recognizes in practice is the freedom of the market. The market, with its providential and 'invisible hand', eliminates all suffering. Unfortunately, this is not true. The proof is there: Auschwitz and Treblinka are part of bourgeois bad conscience, they cannot be erased. In the same manner, the deterioration of the quality of life, the gradual death of African, Latin American, Pacific, and other Third World peoples—remember also, along these lines, what is happening in the Amazon jungle, so pillaged by the demands of the market—all are things that reveal bourgeois bad conscience. And when we speak of bad conscience, we are speaking of guilt.

The trick of oppressors has been to give that bad conscience to the oppressed. For example, indebted peoples are judged for not being able to pay even the interest on their external debt. There is no mercy for them. They must pay, even if this means less life for them. The guilt of the irresponsible creditor is passed on to the powerless debtor. In these cases, the temptation to bitterness is very strong.

That temptation must be overcome. To do so, both Jewish theology and liberation theology have sufficient resources. Yahweh, the God of Jesus, is the God of life, the God who listens to the cry of the oppressed. God is certainly a warrior God. But God's combat is for justice for the poor. God's struggle is a liberating struggle. And in this sense, both Jewish and Latin American liberation theology affirm that the agents of liberation rise from the people.

(Julio de Santa Ana 'The Holocaust and Liberation' in Otto Maduro (ed.), *Judaism, Christianity, and Liberation*, New York, Orbis, 1991, 46–47)

Liberation Theology and Israel

The State of Israel came into being after the tragic experience of Nazi persecution and Jewish genocide in concentration camps. This took place in the threatening context of the beginning of the 'cold war' and the hostility of most of the Arab world. The state of Israel was clearly vulnerable and weak. Israel feared that the Holocaust could be repeated in a different way. This fear and the bitterness from the sufferings at the hands of fascist Nazism were extremely important factors that led Israel to adopt the behaviour of its former oppressors. It based this policy on a 'realistic' view of the world. *Si vis pacem, para bellum*—if you want peace, prepare for war. As we know, it is difficult to only prepare for war. Very often the will for national security leads to aggression.

The state of Israel has proven that many times: oppression of the Palestinian masses; three open wars with Egypt, in two of which Israel was the party directly responsible for beginning hostilities; permanent arms race in the region, certainly one of the most militarized on the planet; development of armed nuclear capacity; active arms producer; open support for regimes that define themselves as reactionary and conservative... A will that denies dialogue, negotiation. In sum, a practice that takes a definite stance against the liberation of many oppressed peoples...

To sum up, that is the great challenge that Latin American liberation theology presents to Jewish theology today. It undoubtedly implies the demand to transcend the theology of the Holocaust, or a theology that is fundamentally priestly. It is a request that theology also free itself, that it cease to be exclusive, and that it live in a practical way the extension of the gift—a life that not only nourishes from memory, but also, and especially, nourishes itself from promise. The promise of God that opens the future to all human beings.

(Julio de Santa Ana, 'The Holocaust and Liberation' in Otto Maduro (ed.), *Judaism, Christianity, and Liberation*, New York, Orbis, 1991, 49–51)

Discussion

1. Have Jews in modern society become oppressors as they were once oppressed?
2. Does the Holocaust call for a theology of liberation?

Marc Ellis: The Holocaust and Atrocity

Marc Ellis has served as Professor of American and Jewish Studies at Baylor University, Texas. In Unholy Alliance, *he argues that Holocaust theology has been largely concerned with the perpetuation of the Jewish tradition and the State of Israel. Yet in his view, the lessons of the Holocaust have not been absorbed by the Jewish people—the treatment of Palestinians is a continuation of inhumanity in the modern world.*

Holocaust Theology and Israel

After 1967, the Holocaust and Israel became central to Jewish life as a package, and the discussion about one is seen to be at the same time a discussion about the other. In the twinning of Holocaust and Israel, insights are gained and lost. A continuity is established between experiences of suffering and empowerment. Weak and helpless in the Holocaust, Jews are now strong. In this way, Jewish identity and self-respect are strengthened; a pride emerges where once there was ambivalence and shame. One can see other effects as well, however. With the increasing power of Israel, the Holocaust too becomes empowered, almost militarized. In speech and action the Holocaust becomes an exclusive Jewish property, a property in need of a theology to articulate its uniqueness and justify its owners. The result is the development of Holocaust theology, a theology that seeks to guide the Jewish community through despair, celebration, and over the years through an increasingly ambivalent empowerment. In the end, this theology looks forward to empowerment rather than critically engaging it, and celebrates Jewish survival while neglecting the disaster that befalls the Palestinian people. In Holocaust theology, Jewish empowerment remains essentially innocent.

Here we reflect on the generation of theologians who came to prominence after the 1967 war. Though they are pictured together as a harmonious group, with contributions from each coming together into an overall interpretation, their consensus is retrospective. Harvesting the insights of Holocaust theologians as they are absorbed in Jewish memory testifies to the power of their thought while glossing over the struggle for the heart and soul of the Jewish people. The seeming inevitability and acceptance of their theological insights is similarly a myth. For like the Eichmann trial, Holocaust theology was initially a battleground with dramatic stakes: Jewish survival, continuity, tradition, and even God. After the death camps, could Jews believe in a God of history? After Auschwitz, could one affirm a covenantal relationship as the essence of Jewish life? What did it mean to be Jewish after the Holocaust? Was empowerment of the Jewish people, especially in Israel, a Jewish commandment, after powerlessness led to mass death?

(Marc Ellis, *Unholy Alliance*, London, SCM Press, 1997, 11–12)

The Jewish People after Auschwitz

It may be that the Jewish people have already lost their opportunity to heal the break with the human and God because of their life and policies after Auschwitz. Is it possible that the survivors of the barbarism in

Europe appear, at least to the Palestinians, as purveyors of barbarism in Palestine? If it is true that barbarism prevailed in the very heart of Christian humanism, Renaissance culture, and classic rationalism—a barbarism that continues to haunt these traditions more than fifty years after the Holocaust—then it must be said that barbarism prevails at the very ground of Jewish humanism and religion. Steiner is right when he posits the seemingly implausible, that some who devised and administered Auschwitz read Shakespeare and Goethe. . . Yet it also is true that the later among those who occupied, displaced, and tortured—as well as those who covered over and denied these realities—are Jews learned in Jewish history and Jewish texts, that is, Jews within the concentric tradition of reading that defines the essence of Judaism. It could be, at another level, that this tradition not only fails to prevent the misuse of Jewish power after the Holocaust, but in its misuse shields Jews from this very realization, thereby impeding the ability to stop before it is too late.

(Marc Ellis, *Unholy Alliance*, London, SCM Press, 1997, 33)

Holocaust and Atrocity

After Auschwitz to be sure, but now after Bosnia and Rwanda, the question of humanity is as difficult to answer as the question of God. For while God remains a mystery, an assertion in need of debate and questioning, humanity is here, within and before us. No matter its political and religious legitimation, atrocity is carried out by human beings on the bodies of other humans. God may be other, or elucidation, or right relations; humans are us, named and awaiting naming, strong and vulnerable, young and old, male and female. At Auschwitz we reached the end of humanity by ourselves, and with only ourselves, and perhaps this is why the call for God is so insistent, to save us from the vision of what we have become. It could be that the lament over the end of God is really a lament over the end of humanity. If we say that we came face to face with the end of humanity at Auschwitz and therefore realized what it was to come to the end, then how did we allow the cycle to continue in the killing fields of Cambodia, Bosnia, and Rwanda? One wonders if the desire to kill human beings is also somehow the desire to kill humanity, or at least that part of us which aspires to life beyond injustice and atrocity. Does the continuation of atrocity, this pursuit of the eschatological end of humanity, represent a desire to murder the eschatological possibility of

God? This much is certain: the Christian legitimation of atrocity murders the narrative of Christian salvation, just as the Israeli policies of expropriation and torture murder the Jewish covenant. Will both Judaism and Christianity become available to us again once the cycle of atrocity comes to an end? The answer will come when atrocity ends. In our exploration at least, the possibility of Judaism and Christianity being participants in the coming age where atrocity ceases to exist is highly doubtful. Though for some they remain a comfort in this journey at the eschatological end of humanity, for others they are a source of the tragedy itself. Judaism and Christianity are part of the end for millions upon millions of people historically and in the present; despite renewal movements, or even because of them, the future is unlikely to be radically different. . . And what can Judaism proclaim today? When Jews pronounce the end of humanity in Auschwitz, do they also proclaim it in the prison cells where Hebrew-speaking soldiers torture Palestinian men and women? If God was absent in the death camps, is God present in those nights when the screams echo in the walls of prisons constructed by Jewish hands, speech, and even theology?

(Marc Ellis, *Unholy Alliance*, London, SCM Press, 1997, 192–193)

Discussion

1. Have the lessons of the Holocaust been learned by the Jewish people?
2. Is the Holocaust an exclusive property of the Jewish community?

CHAPTER TWELVE

The Holocaust and Jewish Survival

Robert Weltsch: Zionism and Jewish Survival

Robert Weltsch was a leading Zionist and journalist in Germany during the Second World War. In 'Wear the Yellow Badge with Pride' published in 1933, he argued that the onslaught of Nazism constitutes a challenge for German Jewry to reassess its future. In his view, the only solution to the problem of anti-Semitism is for Jews to settle in Palestine. In making this claim, he implies that God will not intervene to rescue his people from calamity; instead, they must save themselves by establishing a Jewish state.

The Rise of Nazism and the Jewish People

The first of April, 1933, can be a day of Jewish awakening and Jewish rebirth—if the Jews want it to be; if the Jews are ripe for it and possess inner greatness; if the Jews are not as they are depicted by their adversaries.

Having been attacked, Jewry must avow its faith in itself.

Even on this day of extreme excitement, when the most tempestuous emotions fill our hearts in the face of the unprecedented phenomenon of the entire Jewish population of a great civilized country being universally outlawed, the one thing we must preserve is our composure. Even though we are staggered by the events of recent days, we must not be dismayed, but must take stock without self-deception. What should be recommended at this time is that the work which witnessed the infancy of Zionism, Theodor Herzl's *The Jewish State*, be disseminated among Jews and non-Jews in hundreds of thousands of copies. If there is still left any feeling for greatness and nobility, gallantry and justice, then every National Socialist who looks into this book is bound to shudder at his own blind actions. Every Jew who reads it would also begin to understand and would be consoled and uplifted by it. Page after page of this booklet, which first appeared in 1896, would have to be copied to show that Theodor Herzl was the first Jew dispassionate enough to examine anti-Semitism in connection with the Jewish question. And he recognized that an improvement cannot be effected by ostrich-like behaviour, but only by dealing with facts frankly and in full view of the world. . .

We Jews who have been raised in Theodor Herzl's spirit want to ask ourselves what our own guilt is, what sins we have committed. At times of crisis throughout its history, the Jewish people has faced the question of its own guilt. Our most important prayer says, 'We were expelled from our country because of our sins.' Only if we are critical toward ourselves shall we be just toward others.

(Robert Weltsch, 'Wear the Yellow Badge with Pride' in Albert Friedlander (ed.), *Out of the Whirlwind*, New York, Schocken, 1976, 120–121)

The Nazi Onslaught against the Jews

Many Jews had a shattering experience last Saturday. Suddenly they were Jews—not out of inner conviction, nor out of pride in a magnificent heritage and contribution to mankind, but through a affixing of a red slip and a yellow badge. The squads went from house to house, pasting them on store fronts and business signs and painting them on windows; for twenty-four hours German Jews were put in a pillory, as it were. In addition to other marks and inscriptions one frequently saw on the shopwindows a large *Magen David*, the Shield of David. This was supposed to be a disgrace. Jews, pick up the Shield of David and wear it honourably!. . .

As recently as thirty years ago it was considered objectionable in educated circles to discuss the Jewish question. In those days the Zionists were regarded as trouble-makers with an *idée fixe*. Now the Jewish question is so timely that every small child, every schoolboy as well as the man in the street have no other topic of conversation. All Jews throughout Germany were branded with the word 'Jew' on April lst. If there is a renewed boycott, the new directives of the boycott committee provide for a uniform designation of all shops: 'German business' in the case of non-Jews, the simple word 'Jew' for Jewish places. They know who is a Jew. There no longer is any evading or hiding it. The Jewish answer is clear. It is the brief sentence spoken by the prophet Jonah: *Ivri anochi*, I am a Hebrew. Yes, a Jew. The affirmation of our Jewishness—this is the moral significance of what is

217

happening today. The times are too turbulent to use arguments in the discussion. Let us hope that a more tranquil time will come and that a movement which considers it a matter of pride to be recognized as the peacemaker of the national uprising will no longer derive pleasure from degrading others, even though it might feel that it must fight them. As for us Jews, we can defend our honour.

(Robert Weltsch, 'Wear the Yellow Badge with Pride' in Albert Friedlander (ed.), *Out of the Whirlwind*, New York, Schocken, 1976, 121–123)

Discussion

1. Are Jews inevitably victims of anti-Semitism?
2. Should German Jews have heeded the Zionists' call to emigrate to Palestine?

Emil Fackenheim: The Holocaust and the Commanding Voice

Born in Germany, Emil Fackenheim was ordained a Reform rabbi and served as Professor at the University of Toronto. In various works, he has argued that God was present in the death camps. Out of the ashes of Auschwitz, he issued the 614th commandment.

The 614th Commandment

What does the Voice of Auschwitz command:

> Jews are forbidden to hand Hitler posthumous victories. They are commanded to survive as Jews lest the Jewish people perish. They are commanded to remember the victims of Auschwitz lest their memory perish. They are forbidden to despair of man and his world, and to escape into either cynicism or otherworldliness, lest they cooperate in delivering the world over to the forces of Auschwitz. Finally, they are forbidden to despair of the God of Israel, lest Judaism perish.

(Emil Fackenheim, 'Jewish Faith and the Holocaust' in Michael Morgan (ed.), *The Jewish Thought of Emil Fackenheim*, Detroit, Wayne State University Press, 1987, 176)

Modern Jewry

I think the authentic Jew of today is beginning to hear the 614th commandment. And he hears it whether, as agnostic, he hears no more, or whether, as believer, he hears the voice of the *metzaveh* (the commander) in the *mitzvah* (the commandment). Moreover, it may well be the case that the authentic Jewish agnostic and the authentic Jewish believer are closer today than at any previous time.

To be sure, the agnostic hears no more than the *mitzvah*. Yet if he is Jewishly authentic, he cannot but face the fragmentariness of his hearing. He cannot, like agnostics and atheists all around him, regard this *mitzvah* as the product of self-sufficient human reason, realizing itself in an ever-advancing history of autonomous human enlightenment. The 614th commandment must be, to him, an abrupt and absolute given revealed in the midst of total catastrophe.

On the other hand, the believer, who bears the voice of the *metzaveh*, in the *mitzvah*, can hardly hear anything more than the *mitzvah*. The reasons that made Martin Buber speak of an eclipse of God are still compelling. And if, nevertheless, a bond between Israel and the God of Israel can be experienced in the abyss, this can hardly be more than the *mitzvah* itself.

The implications of even so slender a bond are momentous. If the 614th commandment is binding upon the authentic Jew, then we are, first, commanded to survive as Jews, lest the Jewish people perish. We are commanded, second, to remember in our very guts and bones the martyrs of the holocaust, lest their memory perish. We are forbidden, thirdly, to deny or despair of God, however much we may have to contend with him or believe in him, lest Judaism perish. We are forbidden, finally, to despair of the world as a place which is to become the kingdom of God, lest we help make it a meaningless place in which God is dead or irrelevant and everything is permitted. To abandon any of these imperatives, in response to Hitler's victory at Auschwitz, would be to hand him yet other, posthumous victories.

How can we possibly obey these imperatives? To do so requires the endurance of intolerable contradictions. Such endurance cannot but bespeak an as yet untenable faith. If we are capable of this endurance, then the faith implicit in it may well be of historic consequence. At least twice before—at the time of the destruction of the First and Second Temples—Jewish endurance in the midst of catastrophe helped transform the world. We cannot know the future, if only because the present is without precedent. But this ignorance on our part can have no effect on our present action.

(Emil Fackenheim, 'The Jewish Return into History' in Michael Morgan (ed.), *The Jewish Thought of Emil Fackenheim*, Detroit, Wayne State University Press, 1987, 159–160)

Religious Duty

The ultimate question is: where was God at Auschwitz? For years I sought refuge in Buber's image of an eclipse of God. This image, still meaningful in other respects, no longer seems to me applicable to Auschwitz. Most assuredly no redeeming voice is heard from Auschwitz, nor ever will be heard. However, a commanding Voice is being heard, and has, however faintly, been heard from the start. Religious Jews hear it, and they identify its source. Secularist Jews also hear it, even though perforce they leave it unidentified. At Auschwitz, Jews came face to face with absolute evil. They were and still are singled out by it, but in the midst of it they hear an absolute commandment: Jews are forbidden to grant posthumous victories to Hitler. They are commanded to survive as Jews, lest the Jewish people perish. They are commanded to remember the victims of Auschwitz, lest their memory perish. They are forbidden to despair of man and his world, and to escape into either cynicism or otherworldliness, lest they cooperate in delivering the world over to the forces of Auschwitz. Finally, they are forbidden to despair of the God of Israel, lest Judaism perish. A secularist Jew cannot make himself believe by a mere act of will, nor can he be commanded to do so; yet he can perform the commandment of Auschwitz. And a religious Jew who has stayed with his God may be forced into new, possibly revolutionary, relationships with him. One possibility, however, is wholly unthinkable. A Jew may not respond to Hitler's attempt to destroy Judaism by himself cooperating in its destruction. In ancient times, the unthinkable Jewish sin was idolatry. Today, it is to respond to Hitler by doing his work.

(Emil Fackenheim, 'Jewish Faith and the Holocaust' in Michael Morgan (ed.), *The Jewish Thought of Emil Fackenheim*, Detroit, Wayne State University Press, 1987, 165)

Discussion

1. Is it plausible that a 614th commandment was issued out of the death camps?
2. Did Jews face absolute evil during the Nazi era?

Lionel Rubinoff: The Holocaust and God's Presence

Lionel Rubinoff served as Professor in the Philosophy Department of Trent University in Canada. In 'Auschwitz and the Theology of the Holocaust', he proposes an authentic Jewish response to the Holocaust based on the theology of Emil Fackenheim. According to Rubinoff, Jews must remain loyal to the tradition so as to ensure the survival of the Jewish nation.

Responding to Auschwitz

How can a Jew respond Jewishly to an event like Auschwitz? This response, according to Fackenheim, takes the form not only of memory but of witness. Not to remember would be blasphemy. Not to be a witness would be a betrayal. For a Jew, to respond through memory and witness is to commit himself to survival as a Jew. To dedicate oneself as a Jew to survival in the age of Auschwitz is in itself a monumental act of faith. To be a Jew after Auschwitz is to confront the demons of Auschwitz and to bear witness against them in all their guises. It is to assert as the basis of one's beliefs the conviction that evil will not prevail and to stake one's life and those of one's children on this conviction. Indeed, as Fackenheim represents it, Auschwitz reexperienced is nothing short of revelation. Through that revelation of reliving Auschwitz the Jew is commanded to survive as a Jew through memory and witness in order that Hitler may not be permitted a posthumous victory. Jews are forbidden to despair of God and of the world as the domain of God lest the world be handed over to the forces of Auschwitz. For a Jew to break this commandment would be to do the unthinkable—to respond to Hitler by doing his work.

(Lionel Rubinoff, 'Auschwitz and the Theology of the Holocaust' in Paul D. Opsahl and Marc H. Tanenbaum (eds), *Speaking of God Today*, Philadelphia, Fortress Press, 1974, 122–123)

Divine Command

The greatest challenge to midrashic thought is the Holocaust whose symbol is Auschwitz. It is difficult enough to comprehend the possibility of a midrashic encounter with the ordinary history of evil. It is utterly incomprehensible how there could be immediacy after reflection on Auschwitz: incomprehensible that is, unless we are to

221

regard Auschwitz not simply as a challenge to the root experience but as itself a root experience. But this is precisely what Fackenheim proposes. Following Elie Wiesel's suggestion that the Holocaust may be compared with Sinai as revelatory significance, Fackenheim, with a boldness and daring unparalleled, I suggest, in the history of recent theology, turns his ear to the Holocaust and listens. And what he hears, through the reenactment of that root experience in accordance with midrashic tradition, is what he refers to as 'the commanding voice of Auschwitz'. Thus is revealed the six-hundred-fourteenth command-ment, according to which the authentic Jew of today is forbidden to hand Hitler yet another posthumous victory.

(Lionel Rubinoff, 'Auschwitz and the Theology of the Holocaust' in Paul D. Opsahl and Marc H. Tanenbaum (eds), *Speaking of God Today*, Philadelphia, Fortress Press, 1974, 130–131)

Beyond Comprehension

Resisting rational explanations, Auschwitz will forever resist religious explanations. . . In particular the attempt to find a purpose in Auschwitz is foredoomed to a total failure. Some have sought refuge in the ancient 'for our sins we are punished.' But it does not require much sophistication to rule this out as totally unacceptable. Secular Jews might even connect the Holocaust with the rise of the state of Israel. But while there is undoubtedly a causal connection here, to translate this into a purpose is intolerable and would constitute a vicious example of the fallacy *post hoc ergo propter hoc* ('after this, therefore because of this'). Equally intolerable would be any attempt to justify Israel on the grounds that it is the answer to the Holocaust. To so link these events together is to diminish them both. If Israel is a free and independent state it is not because of the Holocaust, although it may be out of respect for the Holocaust that Israel assumes its determination to maintain its messianic pledge. Thus we must agree with Fackenheim when he insists that 'a total and uncompromising sweep must be made of these and other explanations, all designed to give purpose to Auschwitz. No purpose or otherwise non-religious, will ever be found in Auschwitz. The very attempt to find one is blasphemous.'[1]

(Lionel Rubinoff, 'Auschwitz and the Theology of the Holocaust' in Paul D. Opsahl and Marc H. Tanenbaum (eds), *Speaking of God Today*, Philadelphia, Fortress Press, 1974, 142)

References

1. Emil Fackenheim, 'Jewish Faith and the Holocaust', *Commentary*, 46, August 1968, 31

Discussion

1. Is dedication to the survival of Judaism an act of faith?
2. Does Auschwitz resist religious explanations?

Byron Sherwin: Jewish Survival and the Holocaust

Byron Sherwin has served as Vice-President and Professor of Jewish Philosophy and Mysticism at Spertus Institute of Jewish Studies, Illinois. In Toward a Jewish Theology, *he argues that American and Israeli Jews have reinterpreted the Holcaust event in new ways. Unable to identify with the notion of martyrdom, they focus instead on acts of resistance which took place under Nazi rule. The danger of such an approach, however, is that it can lead to the abandonment of religious belief.*

Reinterpreting the Holocaust

There can be no *heilsgeschichte*, no 'salvation history' with regard to the Holocaust because this was an event with a history, but with no salvation. Though the Nazis had their 'Final Solution', there is no 'final solution' to explain the Holocaust, especially not a theological one. As the talmudic rabbis said centuries ago, 'It is not in our power to explain either the suffering of the righteous or the prospering of the wicked'. . .

In understanding how Jews today, particularly American Jews, tell the story of the Holocaust, one may see how they understand the story, and how they have understood themselves since the Holocaust occurred. . .

For Americans, America is a new land, a 'promised land.' America is the 'new world.' Europe is the old world, a world left behind. Americans understand themselves to be a new kind of human being in a new world. And, American Jews see themselves as a new kind of Jew, with Europe and its memories of persecutions, poverty, massacres and oppression left behind. Similarly, the Israeli Jew understands himself or herself to be a new kind of Jew, in a way, like the American Jew: free, independent and self-reliant. The American Jew has the American story of the Alamo and the Israeli Jew has Josephus's story of Masada. Rather than identify with the saintly Rabbi Akiva, who was martyred by the Romans, Israelis prefer to identify with the heroes of Masada who went to their deaths fighting against the armies of Rome. For the Israelis, self-reliant self-survival became the essential characteristic and imperative of post-Holocaust Jewish existence. The Holocaust made the State of Israel both possible and necessary. For Zionists, the Holocaust represents the inevitable fate of Jews in the Diaspora, the inevitable history of Jews when they permit themselves to be reliant upon others for their own security and survival. In their view, better to die fighting than to be pushed into a gas chamber and accept a passive death. Better to die a fighting hero than a praying martyr.

(Byron Sherwin, *Toward a Jewish Theology*, Lewiston, New York, Edwin Mellen, 1991, 97–99)

Jewish Survival and Religious Faith

This focus on the Jewish people and its survival, rather than upon the traditional Jewish religious focus on the perpetuation of the spiritual and intellectual traditions of Judaism, inevitably leads to secularization. The 'new' Jew is the secular Jew who is primarily concerned with the perpetuation of his ethnic, national or cultural nature, his religious and spiritual traditions having now been relegated to a lower priority than before. Nevertheless, this stress on Jewish survival, understandable though it is, remains problematic for a number of reasons.

First, the claim that Jewish survival is of paramount importance leads to the view that Judaism is of value because it helps ensure Jewish survival. But this view is theologically problematic. It maintains that the primary values of Judaism are not embodied in the spiritual message that it bears, the ethical lifestyle that it teaches, the theological beliefs it affirms, but that the primary value of Jewish faith is to support Jewish group survival. True, there can be no Judaism without Jews, but as Saadya Gaon, the father of Jewish philosophy, said long ago, 'The Jews are only a people by virtue of the Torah.' According to Jewish religious tradition, Judaism exists for the primary purpose of serving God and his will, and not for the primary purpose of helping to ensure Jewish survival.

Second, to consider Jewish survival as an end in itself is idolatry, theologically speaking. Idolatry may be defined as treating that which is not absolute as if it were absolute. For Jewish faith, only God is

224

absolute. To consider Jewish group survival as an end in itself rather than a means to worshipping God is a form of idolatry, theologically speaking. In other words, Jewish survivalism cannot be, though it tries to become, a substitute for Judaism. For example, the idea that the survival of the Jewish people has replaced Jewish faith in God as the ultimate Jewish value is evident in the song introduced by secular Zionists to celebrate Hanukah. This song is sung today in many synagogues. The lyrics are: 'Who can retell the victories of Israel?' The original lyrics, quoting the Psalms, are: 'Who can retell the victories of God?' (Ps. 106.2). Here the people of Israel not only has replaced God, but has become the instrument of Jewish redemption as well.

Third, the secularization of Jewish existence removes the very *raison d'être* for Jewish existence from a theological point of view. If the Jews are a covenanted people, a holy people, a people by virtue of their having been chosen by God to enter into a special covenant with Him, the notion of Jewish survival for survival's sake means a rejection of the very basis of meaning for Jewish survival. The existence of the relationship of the Jews to God and to His *Torah*—the covenantal relationship—is the why; the basis of the very meaning of Jewish existence. Ultimately, existence presumes meaning.

Fourthly, there is a moral problem. With Jewish survival as an end to itself, as an ultimate value, any deed that is perceived as furthering the cause of Jewish survival becomes permissible and justifiable. Such an approach can potentially have morally and spiritually regrettable implications.

(Byron Sherwin, *Toward a Jewish Theology*, Lewiston, New York, Edwin Mellen, 1991, 101–103)

Discussion

1. Does the focus on Jewish resistance during the *Shoah* lead to an abandonment of faith?
2. Is the quest for Jewish survival a form of idolatry?

Michael Goldberg: The Holocaust and Survival

In Why Should Jews Survive? *the conservative rabbi Michael Goldberg, who has taught at St John's University, Minnesota, discusses the ways in which the Holocaust has influenced the Jewish understanding of history. In his view, the tragic events of the Nazi era have had a profound impact on Jewish self-understanding. Today, Jews fervently proclaim the central importance of Jewish survival. Yet, they have overlooked the reason for such survival: the belief that God will redeem the world.*

Faith in the Holocaust

What has replaced God as civil Judaism's centre of devotion? For those who worship at the Holocaust cult, the object of veneration can be but one thing: survival. Woocher puts it perfectly when he says that for American Jewry, 'Commitment to Jewish survival is an unqualified demand of its civil religion.'[1] So while talk of God has all but disappeared from the various pronouncements of civil Judaism's leaders, 'survival' has become their shibboleth. Once again, civil Judaism has transformed—some might say deformed—traditional Judaism. By making survival Jews' 'consuming passion', it has altered Judaism's most fundamental precept: 'And you shall love survival with all your heart, and all your soul, and all your might'. . .

What a cult worships is best seen through how it worships. Its rites, rituals, ceremonies are all enactments of its fundamental values, beliefs, and stories. The Holocaust cult is no different.

In both Israel and the Diaspora, the Holocaust is remembered ritually through the observance of *Yom Hashoah*. Indeed, in the whole of the Jewish liturgical year, it may be the most communally remembered of all days. Whether Jews share a memory of the Holocaust is debatable; that they share the experience of commemoration is not. In Israel, just as the *shofar* is sounded in ancient times to signal a time of national alarm, on *Yom Hashoah* the blare of an air-raid siren brings the whole country to a standstill. In America, where many Jewish communities are riven the rest of the year by internecine warfare among Orthodox, Conservative, and Reform Jews, *Yom Hashoah* observances mark a one-day truce when all the rabbis in a community can be found sharing a common *bimah* in a common *shul*.

(Michael Goldberg, *Why Should Jews Survive?*, Oxford, Oxford University Press, 1995, 49–50)

The Holocaust and Jewish History

The Holocaust as a master story holds out only two choices for Jewish identity: victim or hero. Seen through the lens of the Holocaust, the

Jewish past is an epic of suffering that culminated in the murder of 6,000,000 men, women, and children. From that perspective, the Jewish people's future will look exactly like its past unless Jews heroically and unrelentingly resist the world's undying anti-Semitism.

Many, perhaps most, contemporary Jews in America and Israel have accepted this Holocaust-framed vision of Jewish history. But the images it provides Jews, particularly the self-images, are malformed. They mutilate Jews' self-understanding and mangle the truer depiction of Jewish existence rendered by the Exodus. . .

After the Holocaust most Jews had little trouble swallowing a story that portrayed all prior Jewish history as a grim saga of powerlessness and passivity. The Jew's unchanging role in that epic of suffering? At worst, a contemptible weakling, at best, a pathetic *nebisch*. Throughout the late forties and fifties, the Nazis' victims evoked more revulsion than sympathy from Jews in Israel and the United States. . .

Nevertheless, the depiction of all Jewish history as one long episode of victimization is profoundly false. Although Jews certainly have suffered many savage episodes of persecution—for a people over three and one half-millennia old, it would be astounding not to find such episodes—a chronicle focusing on such experiences alone fails to yield the whole story. . . In sum, the Holocaust-inspired narration of Jewish history portraying Jews as docile doormats is simply incorrect.

It is also deeply anti-Semitic. Its assessment of Jews essentially agrees with the worst that the enemies of the Jewish people have historically said about us: that we have been spineless, that we have been cowards, that we have been less than human. The Holocaust master story's characterization of our ancestors is at its core character assassination.

(Michael Goldberg, *Why Should Jews Survive?*, Oxford, Oxford University Press, 1995, 121–123)

God and Jewish Survival

Originally, however, the locus of reciting *Kaddish* was not, for example, the house of mourning, but the schoolhouse, the *beit midrash*. After one of the rabbinic masters had delivered his *d'var Torah* (his interpretive discourse on some sacred text), all present would recite *Kaddish*, appropriate after hearing about God's unfolding story with the Jewish people, not because it had anything to do with death or grieving, but because it had everything to do with hope: 'May he establish his kingdom in your life and during your days and in the life of the whole household of Israel, speedily and soon'. Later, *Kaddish* moved beyond the schoolhouse to the synagogue and in a somewhat reformulated fashion became a prayer for those who had suffered the loss of a close relative. The cliché, of course, is that this prayer recited in the face of death never once mentions death. Exactly! For what it asserts in the face of death is God's living presence; even at that most broken of times, of broken hearts, broken lives, and broken worlds, the mourner stands up and declares aloud, publicly, before friends, relatives, and God, the hope that there may yet be 'great peace from Heaven, life for us and for all Israel'.

Kaddish gives voice to why Jews should survive: They are the hope of the world. They embody such hope. If ever any people had a right to feel the world is a hopeless place, it is surely the Jewish people. In that sense, Jews who have taken up a Holocaust master story are right in what they have done. They are wrong, however, in thinking that they can remain Jews while holding such a story. For even as they recite their Holocaust-*Kaddish*, they must scrupulously ignore the one to whom the prayer refers and the hope which it articulates. They must assiduously push into the background the Lord of heaven and earth, being mindful only of a litany of inhuman violence, cruelty, and death. Just as Jews cannot long remain Jews while holding a Holocaust-shaped story—after all, given such a story, why should they?—neither can humankind stay human if such a narrative becomes the paradigm of human existence in this world. If the Jewish people would continue to be the bearer of a master story about redemption— not only theirs, but the world's, not only humanity's, but God's—Jews must come to recite *Kaddish* once more not as a doleful lament, but as a joyous affirmation, proclaiming the hope of its closing line, 'He who makes peace in his heavens, he will make peace for us and for all Israel'.

(Michael Goldberg, *Why Should Jews Survive?*, Oxford, Oxford University Press, 1995, 174–175)

References

1. Jonathan S. Woocher, *Sacred Survival: The Civil Religion of American Jews*, Bloomington, Indiana University Press, 1986, 72–73

Discussion

1. What is the purpose of Jewish survival?
2. Is Judaism in danger of losing the belief in redemption?

Roberta Strauss Feuerlicht: The Holocaust and Israel

Roberta Strauss Feuerlicht is a Jewish author and anti-Zionist. In The Fate of the Jews, *she discusses the emergence of the Jewish state in the light of the Holocaust. As she notes, early Zionists attempted to persuade the Third Reich that it would be in its interest to aid Jews who wished to emigrate to Palestine. Following the war years, Jews throughout the world have come to perceive Israel as a necessary safe-haven for Jewry in persecuted lands.*

Jews and Nazis

Zionists have not only been accused of opposing rescue operations or favouring their own believers, but of offering to collaborate with Nazi Germany. In September 1981, Professor Israel Shahak published an article based on both Hebrew sources and an article by a German historian, Klaus Polkehn, 'The Secret Contacts: Zionism and Nazi Germany, 1933–1941'.[1] According to Shahak, the offer was made by the Zionist terrorists, LEHI, one of whose leaders was Begin's foreign minister, Yitzhak Shamir.

Early in January 1941, LEHI approached the Nazis, using the name of its parent organization, the Irgun (NMO). The naval attaché in the German embassy in Turkey transmitted the LEHI proposal to his superiors in Germany. It read in part:

> It is often stated in the speeches and utterances of the leading statesmen of National Socialist Germany that a New Order in Europe requires as a prerequisite the radical solution of the Jewish question through evacuation.
>
> The evacuation of the Jewish masses from Europe is a precondition for solving the Jewish question, but this can only be made possible and complete through the settlement of these masses in the home of the Jewish people, Palestine, and through the establishment of a Jewish state in its historic boundaries. . .
>
> The NMO, which is well acquainted with the good will of the German Reich government and its authorities towards Zionist activity inside Germany and towards Zionist emigration plans, is of the opinion that:
>
> 1. Common interests could exist between the establishment of a new order in Europe in conformity with the German concept, and the true

national aspirations of the Jewish people as they are embodied by the NMO.

2. Cooperation between the new Germany and a renewed Hebrew nation would be established and—

3. The establishment of the historical Jewish state on an annual and totalitarian basis and bound by a treaty with the German Reich would be in the interest of maintaining and strengthening the future German position of power in the Near East.

(Roberta Strauss Feuerlicht, *The Fate of the Jews*, London, Quartet Books, 1984, 119–120)

The Jewish State

The concept of vicarious suffering and redemption is Christian, not Jewish; in Judaism each individual is responsible for his own conduct. Nonetheless, pained by the Holocaust and the guilt that it entailed, Jews gratefully welcomed what appeared to be the resurrection following a most grievous death: the founding of the state of Israel in 1948.

Zionism has always been a minority position among the Jewish people and remains so. What most Jews support is the concept of Israel as a place of refuge, not as the centre of the Jewish universe.

Before World War II, relatively few American Jews were Zionists; Zionist organizations here had only 12,000 members. But during World War II, when American Jews became concerned with the rescue of European Jews, they began to look more favourably upon the idea of a Jewish state. Leading Zionists like Louis Brandeis and Felix Frankfurter lent credence to the concept, though Brandeis made Zionism more acceptable by misstating its intent.

Central to Zionist theory is that all Jews have a home in Palestine, and any Jew who does not return is in exile, and less a Jew. The First World Zionist Congress in Basel in 1897 stated this unequivocally: 'Zionism seeks to create for the Jewish people a home in Palestine.' Brandeis chose to state this as 'Zionism seeks to establish in Palestine, for such Jews as choose to go there and their descendants, a legally secured home.'

This absolved American Jews of the charge of dual loyalty and the challenge of moving to a new land. It created a class of armchair and chequebook Zionists: Jews who supported Israel as a home for other Jews, but not for themselves. . .

American Jews joined Zionist organizations by the thousands, and contributed millions. By 1945, propagandizing and the Holocaust had made Zionism the only movement that came close to uniting American Jews. . . When World War II ended, there were perhaps half a million Jewish survivors in Europe. Had they been admitted to America and other countries of their choice, there would be no Middle East problem today; if there were, it would be an intra-Arab squabble. The cost would have been trivial compared to lives lost, military aid, oil crises, and the political and economic drain of Third World enmity. There also would have been no need to displace hundreds of thousands of Arabs to make room for hundreds of thousands of displaced Jews.

To serve the Zionist dream, refugees were to be taken from the lands where they barely survived extinction to a land where they faced it again. The Zionists needed them, because you cannot have a land without people. American Jews acquiesced because it seemed a perfect solution for a touchy problem; they did not want the refugees here. . .

With rare exceptions, Jews orphaned by the left joined Jews in the middle or on the right in support of Israel. Not only was it politically safe, but after the destruction of the Jews by both Fascists and Communists, perhaps the only answer to anti-Semitism, the only solution that guaranteed survival, was a Jewish state. . . Without their religion, without their culture, Jews were forgetting how to be Jews. Needing new meaning in their lives, American Jews reached out to the Jewish state. Zionism would become the new religion of American Jews, and Israel would be their new God.

(Roberta Strauss Feuerlicht, *The Fate of the Jews*, London, Quartet Books, 1984, 120–130)

References

1. *The Shahak Papers*, No. 42, 50–51

Discussion

1. Should Jews have negotiated with the Nazis?
2. Is Zionism the new religion of American Jews?

Primo Levi: The Holocaust, the Doomed and the Saved

Of Italian origin, Primo Levi has written a number of novels dealing with the Holocaust. In 'If This is a Man', he depicts the nature of those who were unable to resist the Nazi onslaught. Such individuals are the damned, unable to confront the terror and misery around them. As Mussulmaner, *they were doomed in the camps. Others, however, were able to rise above such despair in the struggle to survive.*

The Doomed

We do not believe in the most obvious and facile deduction: that man is fundamentally brutal, egoistic and stupid in his conduct once every civilized institution is taken away. . . We believe, rather, that the only conclusion to be drawn is that in the face of driving necessity and physical disabilities many social habits and instincts are reduced to silence.

But another fact seems to us worthy of attention: there comes to light the existence of two particularly well differentiated categories among men—the saved and the drowned. Other pairs of opposites (the good and the bad, the wise and the foolish, the cowards and the courageous, the unlucky and the fortunate) are considerably less distinct, they seem less essential, and above all they allow for more numerous and complex intermediary gradations.

This division is much less evident in ordinary life; for there it rarely happens that a man loses himself. A man is normally not alone, and in his rise or fall is tied to the destinies of his neighbours; so that it is exceptional for anyone to acquire unlimited power, or to fall by a succession of defeats into utter ruin. Moreover, everyone is normally in possession of such spiritual, physical and even financial resources that the probabilities of a shipwreck, of total inadequacy in the face of life, are relatively small. And one must take into account a definite cushioning effect exercised both by the law, and by the moral sense which constitutes a self-imposed law; for a country is considered the more civilized the more the wisdom and efficiency of its laws hinder a weak man from becoming too weak or a powerful one too powerful.

But in the Lager things are different: here the struggle to survive is without respite, because everyone is desperately and ferociously alone. If some Null Achtzehn vacillates, he will find no one to extend a helping hand; on the contrary, someone will knock him aside, because it is in no one's interest that there be one more '*mussulman*', dragging himself to work every day; and if someone, by a miracle of savage patience and cunning, finds a new method of avoiding the hardest work, a new art which yields him an ounce of bread, he will try to keep his method secret, and he will be esteemed and respected for this, and will derive from it an exclusive, personal benefit; he will become stronger and so will be feared, and who is feared is, *ipso facto*, a candidate for survival.

In history and in life one sometimes seems to glimpse a ferocious law which states: 'to he that has, will be given; to he that has not, will be taken away.' In the Lager, where man is alone and where the struggle for life is reduced to its primordial mechanism, this unjust law is openly in force, is recognized by all. With the adaptable, the strong and astute individuals, even the leaders willingly keep contact, sometimes even friendly contact, because they hope later to perhaps derive some benefit. But with the *mussulmans*, the men in decay, it is not even worth speaking, because one knows already that they will complain and will speak about what they used to eat at home. Even less worthwhile is it to make friends with them, because they have no distinguished acquaintances in camp, they do not gain any extra rations, they do not work in profitable *Kommandos* and they know no secret method of organizing. And in any case, one knows that they are only here on a visit, that in a few weeks nothing will remain of them but a handful of ashes in some near-by field and a crossed-out number on a register. Although engulfed and swept along without rest by the innumerable crowd of those similar to them, they suffer and drag themselves along in an opaque intimate solitude, and in solitude they die or disappear, without leaving a trace in anyone's memory.

(Primo Levi, *If This is a Man* in Albert Friedlander (ed.), *Out of the Whirlwind*, New York, Schocken, 1976, 209–210)

The Survivors

But beside the officials in the strict sense of the word, there is a vast category of prisoners, not initially favoured by fate, who fight merely with their own strength to survive. One has to fight against the current; to battle every day and every hour against exhaustion, hunger, cold, and the resulting inertia; to resist enemies and have no pity for rivals; to sharpen one's wits, build up one's patience, strengthen one's will power. Or else, to throttle all dignity and kill all conscience, to climb down into the arena as a beast against other beasts, to let oneself be guided by those unsuspected subterranean forces which sustain families and individuals in cruel times. Many were the ways devised and put into effect by us in order not to die: as many as there are different human characters. All implied a weakening of the struggle of one against all, and a by no means small sum of aberrations and compromises. Survival without renunciation of any part of one's own moral world—apart from powerful and direct interventions by fortune—was conceded only to a very few superior individuals, made of the stuff of martyrs and saints.

(Primo Levi, *If This is a Man* in Albert Friedlander (ed.), *Out of the Whirlwind*, New York, Schocken, 1976, 213)

Discussion

1. In the camps did the struggle to survive produce a state of moral suspension?
2. Was neglect of *mussulmans* an ethical defect?

Jacob Neusner: The Holocaust and Redemption

Jacob Neusner has served as Distinguished Research Professor of Religious Studies at the University of South Florida. In Introduction to American Judaism, *he argues that there are two type of Judaisms—the Judaism of the dual* Torah *and the Judaism of Holocaust and Redemption. The first governs the private life of American Jewry while the second serves as the framework for public life.*

Judaism and the Holocaust

In North America, a second Judaic system flourishes alongside the Judaism of the dual *Torah* and is practised by the same Judaists. The Judaism of the dual *Torah* appeals to the myth that at Sinai God revealed the *Torah* to Moses in two media: written (Scripture as we know it) and oral (ultimately written down in the *Mishnah, Talmuds, Midrash,* and related documents). . . The correlative Judaism is the Judaism of Holocaust and Redemption, which has translated the catastrophe of European Jewry from 1933 through 1945 and the founding of the Jewish state in Palestine as the state of Israel of 1948 and the state's successful history from then on into events of transcendent proportions and cosmic meaning: murder, become Holocaust, and the consequent creation of the state of Israel, Redemption.

The ritual of the other Judaism involves political action and enormous communal organization and activity. Its counterpart to the Day of Atonement is the fund-raising dinner of the local Jewish Federation and Welfare Fund and United Jewish Appeal campaign for the state of Israel and other Jewish causes. Its counterpart to the *bar* or *bat mitzvah* is a summer vacation in the state of Israel. Its equivalent to the intense moments of marriage and death is the pilgrimage to Auschwitz followed by a flight to Jerusalem and procession to the Western Wall in Jerusalem. Its places of worship comprise Holocaust museums, and its moments of celebration include commemorations of the Holocaust on a day set aside for that purpose. Its 'study of the *Torah*' involves visits to Holocaust museums and courses on the German war against the Jews and the death factories of Europe. Its memorial of the destruction of the Temple finds expression in recitations of how the Germans massacred the Jews by firing squads, by asphyxiation, and by driving them into a barn and setting it on fire.

(Jacob Neusner, *Introduction to American Judaism*, Minneapolis, Fortress Press, 1994, 109–110)

Public and Private Religion

Why is it that the Judaism of the books, that is, the Judaism of the dual *Torah*, finds a firm position in the shared imagination of Judaists in one part of the social order—the familiar and personal and private—while the Judaism of Holocaust and Redemption occupies the centre of the social order that is public, corporate and communal? I have stressed that those rites of book Judaism that form important components of the North American Judaists' Judaism focus on home and family. . .

If that fact exhaustively characterized the life of Judaists (and other Jews as well), we should plausibly conclude, then, that 'Judaism' has been privatized, and the life of the faith reduced to the dimensions only of home and family. But the facts prove otherwise. Judaic public behaviour extends to what is communal, public, and corporate: 'contribute to Jewish charity', 'give to UJA.' Judaists also are activists in Jewry when shared and public action of a political character is demanded of 'all good Jews.' The consensus of Judaists focuses upon corporate as much as private dimensions of the social order. . .

So the appearance of indifference to the corporate dimensions of the holy life of book should not deceive us. Not only do Jews form a corporate community and share a substantial range of social experience; that shared public life itself takes shape in response to a Judaism and forms a religious system. But. . . it is not the same Judaism, the same religious system, that governs in private life. The reason is that this other Judaism answers the urgent questions that the community at large asks itself, and, it follows, its answers are found self-evidently true, therefore its rites predominate, and other rites for the community fall by the way. . .

What is this other Judaism—the Judaism of Holocaust and Redemption? Let me spell out the worldview and way of life of a Judaism that exercises the power to transform civic and public affairs in Jewry as much as the Judaism of the dual *Torah* enchants and changes the personal and familial ones. In politics, history, and society, Jews in North America respond to the Judaism of the Holocaust and Redemption in such a way as to imagine that they are someone else, living somewhere else, at another time and circumstance. That vision transforms families into an Israel, a community. The somewhere else is Poland in 1944 and the earthly Jerusalem, and the vision turns them from reasonably secure citizens of America or Canada into insecure refugees finding hope and life in the state of Israel. Public events commemorate so that 'we' were there in 'Auschwitz', which stands for all of the centres of the murder of Jews, and 'we' share, too, in the everyday life of that faraway place in which we do not live but should, the state of Israel. That transformation of time and of place, no less than the recasting accomplished by the Passover *seder* or the rite of *berit milah* or the *huppah*, turns people into something other than what they are in the here and now.

The issues of this public Judaism, the civil religion of North American Jewry. . . are perceived to be political. That means, the questions to which this Judaism provides answers are raised by people's public and social experience, not the experience of home and family and the passage through life from birth to death. But the power of that Judaism to turn things into something other than what they seem, to teach lessons that change the everyday into the remarkable—that power works no less wonderfully than does the power of the other Judaism to change me into Adam or one of the Israelites that crossed the Red Sea. . .

(Jacob Neusner, *Introduction to American Judaism*, Minneapolis, Fortress Press, 1994, 110–114)

Discussion

1. Has Judaism been overwhelmed by the ideology of Holocaust remembrance?
2. Has Israel overshadowed Jewish faith in modern society?

CHAPTER THIRTEEN

Reconstructing Judaism

Oliver Leaman: The Holocaust and Evil

Oliver Leaman has served as Zantker Professor of Judaic Studies at the University of Kentucky. In Evil and Suffering in Jewish Philosophy, *he points out that the belief in the uniqueness of the Holocaust leads to a recognition of the distance between God and the world. In the view of some Jewish thinkers, what is now required is a reformulation of Jewish theology in light of God's inactivity during the Holocaust era.*

Uniqueness

Many Jewish thinkers who write about the Holocaust emphasize the essential difference between that event and the other superficially similar disasters affecting other ethnic groups, or even the Jews in previous periods. A good deal of the argument surrounding the Holocaust deals with this issue, and the very concept of the Holocaust or *Shoah* is designed to point to the distinctiveness of the event. Since the event is taken to be unique, the ordinary forms of analysis will not apply to it, since these techniques are designed to cope with the normal events of the world, not the exceptional. To claim that the Holocaust is just one more disaster like previous disasters, and that it falls into the category of extreme persecutions of ethnic minorities is to misunderstand, it is claimed, the very special nature of the event. Now, whatever one might think of this sort of argument, it is worth pointing to its connection with the distant God of Jewish philosophy.

(Oliver Leaman, *Evil and Suffering in Jewish Philosophy*, Cambridge, Cambridge University Press, 1995, 201)

The Absence of God

Perhaps an aspect of the Holocaust's uniqueness is the dramatic way in which it brought into focus the apparent distance of God from us. During the Holocaust God seemed to be distant not just from a portion of the Jewish people, as was the case in the past, but rather from the kernel of Jewish civilization, which was almost entirely destroyed and totally displaced geographically. This is precisely the sort of event which one might expect a deity to prevent or ameliorate through his intervention, and yet there is no indication that he did. This is not to suggest that it is impossible to find religious explanations for the Holocaust—no end of these have been put forward—nor even that nothing good can be seen to have come out of it. Many would argue that the State of Israel is a valuable consequence of the disaster. Yet what the Holocaust did was to bring into stark focus the significance of the distance which separates God and his creation. It seemed to many thinkers that the distance was so great in much Jewish philosophy that it is impossible to ask why God did not prevent the Holocaust, since there is little room for God to prevent anything at all happening in the world.

The apparent inaction of God, together with the idea that he does not intervene in the world anyway, suggests that God is very far away indeed. If even the Holocaust does not elicit a response from the deity one might wonder what role the concept of God can still play in a religious philosophy. Jewish philosophers tend to work with a rather bare notion of God, and they have in the past spent considerable efforts in denuding it even more, to the extent that it seems difficult to explain how God could intervene in the world of generation and corruption at all, where by 'intervention' is meant something close to what we ordinarily mean by intervention. Then along came a disaster of such a magnitude that it seemed incomprehensible that a God could stand by and let it happen, but of course it is not incomprehensible, since previous generations of philosophers had expended much effort in explaining the difficulties in looking for divine intervention. Given the way in which the concept of our relationship with God had been developed, it would have been incomprehensible to have had to deal with an account which described divine intervention.

It is precisely in such circumstances that we should expect to have a rationale for the suffering, together with an analysis of our relationship with God which permits us to understand what has taken place. In stressing the uniqueness of the Holocaust Jewish thinkers are implying that a new theology will need to be constructed to make sense of the event, since the existing conceptual materials are insufficient to do the job. This in part is what is behind the radical approaches which have been taken to elucidating the meaning of the Holocaust, and we must bear this in mind if we are going to be able to put the varying approaches to Holocaust theodicy in context.

(Oliver Leaman, *Evil and Suffering in Jewish Philosophy*, Cambridge, Cambridge University Press, 1995, 201–203)

Radical Theology

So far we have looked at a variety of Jewish responses to the Holocaust, and to a Christian approach. The Jewish responses differ in their assessment of the theological significance of the Holocaust. Some argue that a complete reorientation of thought is required as a result of that traumatic event, while others try to fit it into the pattern of Jewish history. Perhaps the most radical approach is undertaken by Rubenstein, who seems to have abandoned traditional conceptions of the deity in favour of a deity who can be approached through mysticism, but who does not have the ordinary divine characteristics, such as power to influence the world. On this view God is the divine nothingness, and as such is the source of being and existence, since by nothingness he represents a superfluity of being. Death and destruction is just a return to this nothingness from which life later emerges in a different form. . . This god plays no part in history, has no power over the world and cannot be thought of as taking decisions and observing the activities of his creatures.

(Oliver Leaman, *Evil and Suffering in Jewish Philosophy*, Cambridge, Cambridge University Press, 1995, 203)

Discussion

1. Was the Holocaust worse than other tragedies of the Jewish past?
2. If the Holocaust did not elicit a response from the Deity, does God still have a role to play in history?

David Blumenthal: Theology and Protest

David Blumenthal has served as Jay and Leslie Cohen Professor of Judaic Studies at Emory University, Georgia. In 'Despair and Hope in Post-Shoah Jewish Life', he argues that the religious implications of the Shoah *are of fundamental significance. The religious dilemmas posed by the destruction of European Jewry must be faced. In his view, what is now required is a theology of protest.*

Confronting the Holocaust

Who is responsible for the *shoah*? Who bears responsibility for the child's fate in *Au revoir les enfants*? Who is the one we blame for the pregnant woman whose feet were tied together when she went into labour so that both she and the infant died in terrible pain? To whom can we point the finger for the thousands who fell into the pits of excrement and drowned as others, who were forbidden to help on pain of death, had to look on?

Yes, we justly blame the human, or more exactly the subhuman, perpetrators. The nazis are responsible for the cruelty and hatred. There can never be an escape from that, much as deniers, neo–nazis, and even children of perpetrators may wish to deny such responsibility. Humans were worse than bestial, for beasts never act with wanton cruelty.

No, the victims are not responsible, much as some macho observers would like to hold them responsible. The victims were just that— victims of racism, innocent of the 'crimes' of which they were accused. Their 'guilt' lay in their being, in their bloodlines. As all victims of racism are innocent. They do nothing; they be, and that is enough to condemn them to being victims. Perhaps more of the victims should have foreseen what was coming, but hindsight is no blessing.

If one is religious, if 'God' means something to you, who is to blame? If one has lived a life in which God's presence has been felt, if religious ritual has been an important part of your spiritual life, who is to blame? If you are a believer, if one believes that God is not some remote force but is active in our personal and national lives, who is to blame? If one accepts the doctrine of God's providence, if you believe in God's actions in history, who is to blame?

Most religious folk, and most religious thinkers and clergy along with them, do not want to ask this question. They do not want to know that

God is responsible for history, that is, for the bad parts. They do not want to contemplate, not even to think about, how God might be responsible for the *shoah*. They dodge. They avoid. They cite: 'Indeed, our thoughts are not My thoughts and your ways are not My ways' (Is. 55:8). They justify, invoking the sinful ways of the Jewish people. They rationalize, invoking humankind's free will. They make excuses, saying that God's face was hidden. Mostly, they firmly close their eyes, hiding their heads in the sand. They just refuse to confront this question. They piously claim ignorance of God's ways, and change the subject. The theology of Job's comforters, not the theology of Job. They occupy themselves, faithfully and busily, with the needs of the community. Action, not theology. Busyness hiding unwanted questions.

Heretics and atheists think about the question of ultimate responsibility. They know the answer. Some say there is no God of history. There is no God whose will is manifest in human affairs. At least, no good God who is active in history. Not even a bad God who acts in human history, no Jewish God, no God as God is known to Jewish and Christian scriptures. Others say there is no God at all. We are here alone in a neutral, perhaps even hostile world. We do the best we can. We work hard to ensure our survival. We even risk death to do so. We write bitter, bitter poetry. We die, and others take up the task.

(David Blumenthal, 'Despair and Hope in Post-*Shoah* Jewish Life, *Bridges*, Fall/Winter, 1999, 120–121)

God and the *Shoah*

If you are religious, what do you think? Are you among the pious avoiders? Among those who say that God could not have been involved because God gave humankind free will, an act which relieves God of all responsibility? Are you among those who believe that God is too good to be responsible? That God was absent? Or, are you among the heretical avoiders? Among those who deal with this question by denying God? You must take a stand, if God is integral to who you are.

I, too, as a Jew and as a theologian, confronted this terrifying question and I reached the conclusion that God is, indeed, present and responsible even in moments of great evil. God is, indeed, partly responsible for the *shoah*. In a certain sense, God is capable of tolerating, or even causing, great evil. Still, God is also capable of great good, of deep blessing. God's presence is part of our ongoing lives, as persons and as God's people. This leaves us with a God who is not perfect, not even always good, but who is still our God and the God of our ancestors. Jewish tradition advocates this position and reaches the conclusion that protest is the only proper response. Not defensiveness. Not denial. But protest—in thought and in prayer.

But is it working? Am I 'dealing with' the God of history, including the *shoah*? Do I feel more 'secure' with this God against whom I can protest? Are others following this path, traditional though it is? To tell the truth, yes and no. It is working in the sense that, when I have the courage to use the liturgy that I suggested, I know I have done my duty toward God, toward the dead, toward the survivors, and toward Jewish history and religion. When I protest, in liturgy and in teaching, I know that I have done the right thing and that I can face God on the day of judgment. But it is very hard. The others have not followed me. Rather, they have persisted in their. . . heretical denial. See no evil. Hear no evil. Speak no evil—especially of God.

(David Blumenthal, 'Despair and Hope in Post-*Shoah* Jewish Life', *Bridges*, Fall/Winter, 1999, 122–123)

Discussion

1. Is God capable of tolerating or causing evil?
2. Does it make sense to believe one is more secure with a God against whom one can protest?

Arthur A. Cohen: A Detached God

Arthur A. Cohen was a Conservative rabbi and theologian. In Tremendum, *he offers an interpretation of the Nazi regime based on an alternative conception of God. According to Cohen, it is a mistake to long for an interruptive God who can intervene magically in the course of human affairs. If there were such a God, the created order would be an extension of God's will rather than an independent domain brought about by God's creative love. Since humanity is free, God does not interfere in the course of history. Therefore, it is a mistake to hold God responsible for the Holocaust.*

Beyond Understanding

The death camps are a reality which, by their very nature, obliterate thought and the humane programme of thinking. We are dealing, at the very outset, therefore, with something unmanageable and obdurate—a reality which exists, which is historically documented, which has specific beginnings and ends, located in time, the juncture of confluent influences which run from the beginnings of historical memory to a moment of consummating orgy, never to be forgotten, but painful to remember, a continuous scourge to memory and the future of memory and yet something which, whenever addressed, collapses into tears, passion, rage. The death camps are unthinkable, but not unfelt. They constitute a traumatic event and, like all decisive trauma, they are suppressed but omnipresent, unrecognized but tyrannic, silted over by forgetfulness but never obliterated. . .

Whatever we may learn from history, moral philosophy, psychopathology, or political science about the conditions which preceded and promoted the death camps or the behaviour of oppressors and victims which obtained with the deaths damps, is unavailing. All analysis holds us within the normative kingdom of reason, and however the palpable irrationality of the events, the employment of rational analysis is inappropriate. I do not feel the calm of reason to be obscene as some critics of the rational inquiry into the *tremendum* have described it. It is not obscene for human beings to try to retain their sanity before an event which disorders sanity. It is a decent and plausible undertaking. It is simply inappropriate and unavailing. Probative inquiry and dispassionate reason have no place in the consideration of the death camps. precisely because reason possesses a moral vector. To reason, that is to estimate and evaluate, is to imply discernment and discrimination before a moral ambiguity. The *tremendum* is beyond the discourse of morality and rational condemnation.

(Arthur A. Cohen, *Tremendum*, New York, Crossroad, 1981, 1–8)

The Uniqueness of the Death Camps

The uniqueness of the death camps, that which makes them a novelty *in extremis* severed from all normative connections to historical precedent and causality, imparts to them a phenomenological simplicity. The death camps are a reality quite literally *sui generis*. Insofar as their reality is concerned, it is not necessary for us to perform phenomenological surgery, to bracket them, to excise their connections from the welter of historical conditions, to clarify the standpoint of perception in order not to confuse their manifestation with that of any other seemingly comparable phenomenon, like the social institution of the prison or the army. Simply defined (and the simpler the better for our purposes), the death camps were constructed to fulfil one purpose: to kill the greatest number of Jews at the least possible cost in money and material. To the side of Jews were added Gypsies, another 'degenerative and infectious race', and the work was undertaken and, by the war's end, almost completed. It is a task pursued with lethal self-sacrifice since, quite clearly, as many historians have noted, the war effort of the German army was severely impaired by the preference given to the transport of Jews. The simplicity of the phenomenon is no less its enormity. To kill Jews, any and all, defines the reality and clarifies its uniqueness.

(Arthur A. Cohen, *Tremendum*, New York, Crossroad, 1981, 12)

God and Human History

The *cri de coeur* of the memorialists of the *tremendum* is the silence of God. How could it be that God witnessed the holocaust and remained silent, that within the providential plan of God the holocaust should figure among its details, that God is vaunted presentness but was absent, that God is highest manifest reality but recondite and hidden? What, in truth, does the cry contend and require? Nothing less than the interruptive miracle, that the sea open and the army of the enemy be consumed. This is surely what all of us might have dreamt for the miracle of ransom. The ancient model, embedded as the scheme of our redemption from the land of Egypt, is the prefigurement of modern hope. The interruptive God, however, is not ever interruptive even were the sea to part and close or the earth of Auschwitz to open and the murderers to fall in. . .

Can it not be argued no less persuasively that what is taken as God's speech is really always man's hearing, that God is not the strategist of our particularities or of our historical condition, but rather the mystery of our futurity, always our *posse*, never our acts. If we can begin to see God less as the interferer whose insertion is welcome (when it accords with our needs) and more as the immensity whose reality is our prefiguration, whose speech and silence are metaphors for our language and distortion, whose plentitude and unfolding are the hope of our futurity, we shall have won a sense of God whom we may love and honour, but whom we no longer fear and from whom we no longer demand.

God and the life of God exist neither in conjunction with nor disjunction from the historical, but rather in continuous community and *nexus*. God is neither a function nor a cause of the historical nor wholly other and indifferent to the historical. I understand divine life to be rather a filament within the historical, but never the filament that we can identify and ignite according to our requirements, for in this and all other respects God remains God. As filament, the divine element of the historical is a precarious conductor always intimately linked to the historical—its presence securing the implicative and exponential significance of the historical—and always separate from it, since the historical is the domain of human freedom. Given these assumptions, it would follow that the *tremendum* does not alter the relation of God to himself, nor the relation in which God exists to the historical, nor the reality of creation to the process of eternal beginning within God, but it does mean that man—not God—renders the filament of the divine incandescent or burns it out. There is, in the dialectic of man and God amid history, the indispensable recognition that man can obscure, eclipse, burn out the divine filament, grounding its natural movement of transcendence by a sufficient and oppository chthonic subscension. It is this which is meant by the abyss of the historical, the demonic, the *tremendum*.

(Arthur A. Cohen, *Tremendum*, New York, Crossroad, 1981, 95–98)

Discussion

1. Is it a mistake to long for an interruptive God?
2. Is the *tremendum* beyond human discourse?

Melissa Raphael: The Holocaust and Jewish Feminism

Melissa Raphael has served as a lecturer at Cheltenham and Gloucester College of Higher Education. In 'When God Beheld God', she presents a Jewish feminist theology of the Holocaust. In her view, the androcentrism and patriarchal models of God must be transcended in confronting the religious dilemmas posed by the Holocaust. The patriachal model of God, she contends, was the God who failed Israel during the Holocaust. Drawing on the records of women's experiences during the Nazi period, she offers a post-Holocaust theology of relation that affirms the redemptive presence of God in Auschwitz.

Women in the Camps

The feminist historiography of women's experience in the death and concentration camps provides a methodological and substantive groundwork on which a feminist theology might build. Not ultimately dependent, however, on the historical record, I use a traditional Jewish mystical understanding of the presence of exile and restoration within God as a structuring redemptive metaphor by which to interpret the record of (some) women's resistance to the Nazis' profanation of their female personhood by those sacralizing means available to them as (Jewish) women in conditions of absolute physical and spiritual deprivation. I suggest that by means of mutual care, these women summoned *Shekhinah* (the traditional female image of the holy presence of God) into the very abyss of profanity. Because women are made in the image of God, *Shekhinah* suffered in the suffering of women. So that what has been called the 'gender wounding' of Jewish women in the death and concentration camps was also a wounding of God. But conversely, that mutual care by which women restored the divine image to each other also restored God to God. For the erasure of the femaleness of God has divided God from God-self over millennia of patriarchal theological and religious domination. In this sense, the redemption of both women and God from patriarchy was occurring at the same time as their fall into a pit of total darkness: a crisis of such urgency and intensity as to render the former process at least a prefiguration of eschatological judgment on the latter.

No theologian could claim that a redemptive process ascribed to the past is not also at work in the present, if differently mediated. And it seems to me that contemporary religious feminists' struggle to restore the erased female image in God by their comprehensive revalorization of femaleness describes a redemptive process that is continuous with that which took place in the camps and with the entire history of women's resistance to patriarchal violence. In other words, without drawing highly offensive comparisons between Jewish women's religio-political struggles today and the acute suffering of Jewish women during the Holocaust, I offer a feminist post-Holocaust theology that assumes present feminist experience of *Shekhinah* to help us to understand how she might have been present in the past.

(Melissa Raphael, 'When God Beheld God', *Feminist Theology*, 21, 1999, 54–55)

Mystical Theology and Feminism

Jewish mysticism is helpful to a feminist theology of relation (and therefore of its opposite—alienation) because it is premised on two basic notions. First, the medieval kabbalistic notion that the catastrophes that befall the Jews are also catastrophes for God, tearing God apart from God-self. And second that *tikkun* (restoration, reconciliation, healing, completion) in God and the world can be brought about by human activity. This concept of *tikkun* is grounded in the Lurianic doctrine of the 'holy sparks'. In this kabbalistic scheme, when God emerged from concealment in order to create the universe, the vessels of the seven lower *sefirot* (or emanations of God) shattered because they could not contain the divine light or holiness that filled them. This stream of spilled light ran down from world to world until catastrophically, it reached the 'Other Side'. Here, the 'shells' (*kelipot*) or forces of impurity spilled the light and the holy sparks were scattered all about, falling into the impure material world. The redemption of the world is brought about when Jews consecrate the world by their goodness, if necessary by descending into the very abyss of impurity to rescue the hidden or imprisoned sparks, and, by their elevation, return them to God. Human efforts to reunite God with God by the elevation of the sparks have cosmic repercussions. They enable the female *Shekhinah* (also know as *Sefirah Malkhut*—the emanation of God closest to humanity) to be reunited with the male *Sefirah Tiferet* (beauty). This is a sacred marriage bringing peace and harmony to the *sefirot* and enabling the free flow of divine grace to the world.

Much of the kabbalistic scheme is too gnostic, esoteric and dualistically inclined to be of interest to a feminist theology of relation. Also, kabbalists have traditionally taught that redemption or the restoration of divine unity can be achieved by highly focused prayer, study, the observance of the 613 *mitzvot*, and a number of technical ritual practices. Here, though, I argue that *tikkun* cannot be contingent upon orthopraxis because Orthodoxy is profaned by its patriarchal nature. Nonetheless, the basic kabbalistic redemptive myth can serve as a structuring metaphor for the feminist theology of the Holocaust suggested here. That is, each act of 'female' *hesed* can be likened to lighting the Sabbath candles which traditionally invite the *Shekhinah* into the home. Each act of *hesed* elevated the profane spark of the divine image in each woman they supported. That meant the redemptory process was going on in a manner all the more mysterious and powerful to contemplate because it happened there, in a place precisely organized for the profane to overwhelm and extinguish the holiness of human life.

And in different times and places this process continues wherever religious feminist resistance rescues the sparks from the 'shells' of patriarchal oppression by invoking *Shekhinah* and other (subordinated or denied) Jewish female images of the divine. When women identify themselves as manifestations or reflections of *Shekhinah* then the femaleness of God is restored to God because she can behold herself in her creation. The oral tradition of the *Kabbalah* claims that God brought the world into existence because 'God wished to behold God.' Now, if Auschwitz means that God could no longer behold God on earth then her being and her reason for creation was close to destruction. She would become blind to herself. This was the case when God seemed so dispersed by absolute atrocity as to have disappeared altogether. But if God could behold her image even in the smoke-blackened mirror of Auschwitz, then God's original creative purpose was not utterly thwarted. In those moments when God could behold God in the midst of Auschwitz, through the thick scale of our profanization, these were moments of *tikkun*.

(Melissa Raphael, 'When God Beheld God', *Feminist Theology*, 21, 1999, 62–64)

Discussion

1. Did the *Shekhinah* suffer in the suffering of women in the death camps?
2. Is it necessary to discard the patriarchal image of God in confronting the religious dilemmas posed by the camps?

Susan Shapiro: The Holocaust and Negation

Susan Shapiro has been an Assistant Professor at Syracuse University in Syracuse, New York. In 'Hearing the Testimony of Radical Negation', she argues that the Holocaust calls for a recognition of negation. What is now required is the creation of a new hermeneutic which will take into account this major tragedy of the modern world.

The Holocaust and Language

Not only has the subsequent course of history been shaped by this event, but our assumptions about the world in which we live, about the nature of the human subject and of the Divine, have been thrown into question, even negated. What does it mean to be human in a world that performed and passively witnessed such destruction? And how can we now imagine or conceive of a God who did not save under those circumstances? In what sort of language might we even frame these questions and to whom might we address them? Have not the very coherence of language and the continuity of tradition been broken, shattered by this event?

It is not only the meanings of particular words in particular languages that have been corrupted and, thus, broken by the event. It is the very coherence and meaning of language in general and God-language in particular that was negated. This rupture within language is the radical negation of our asssumptions and conceptions of the human subject that ground the very coherence of language. Furthermore, this rupture within discourse cannot be mended simply by appealing to an undisrupted, ever-available God-language, for our basic conceptions of a Just and Merciful God are themselves thrown into question by the event. Both discourse in general and God-language in particular are thus ruptured, their coherence shattered, their meaningfulness broken.

Three related experiences led to this double rupture of language. The first experience is the Holocaust victims' pervasive sense of having been abandoned by God. 'Theirs was the kingdom of night. Forgotten by God, forsaken by him, they lived alone, suffered alone, fought alone.' The second is the purposeful attempt by the Nazis to dehumanise their victims totally before exterminating them. The third experience was the Jews' virtually complete abandonment by the rest of the world to this fate. Alone. That is the key word, the haunting theme. Alone with no allies, no friends, totally, desperately alone. . . The world knew and kept silent. . . Mankind let them suffer and agonize and perish alone. And yet, and yet, they did not die alone, for something in all of us died with them. These three dimensions of the experience of the Holocaust ruptured not only the relation between God and humankind necessary for the intelligibility of language about or addressed to God. They ruptured as well those primary social relations and functions, such as friendship, family loyalty, and even the desire to live, that, as *sensus communis*, underlie and found coherent speech itself.

249

Not only did God hang on the gallows with the young boy in *Night*, but the very idea of humanity was incinerated in the Holocaust.

(Susan Shapiro, 'Hearing the Testimony of Radical Negation' in Elisabeth Schüssler Fiorenza and David Tracy (eds), *The Holocaust as Interruption*, Edinburgh, T. and T. Clark, 1984, 3–4)

Listening to Radical Negation

This being the case, we are all, Christian and Jew however differently, implicated within this rupture of and within discourse. It is, thus, this testimony of radical negation that we must learn to hear: Negation in language, negation of language. For what is at stake is our concept of God and our concept of humanness. 'Let us tell tales so as to remember how vulnerable man is when faced with overwhelming evil. Let us tell tales so as not to allow the executioner to have the last word. The last word belongs to the victim. It is up to the witness to capture it, shape it, and then communicate that secret to others. . . '[1]

The need to communicate, somehow, across the abyss and for the sake of the future, moved people to write about and in every circumstance of horror, despair, and courage. They wrote ceaselessly, passionately, despite the fact that the world was not listening and, for the most part, did not care. Despite this cultivated deafness on the part of most of the world, the victims wrote continuously and obsessively, even, and most often, at great personal risk. This compelling necessity to serve witness to the very horrors of history, this courageous will and risk to communicate to testify to every detail, to every aspect of the event, itself forms a testimony that demands our attention. . .

Are we today listening to this testimony? Have we not heard its claim? Sadly, tragically for us all, the answer to these questions seems to be clearly, no. Wiesel writes 'as one who has tried for some twenty-five years to speak on this subject, I feel I must confess to a sense of defeat. The witness was not heard. The world is world. . . our testimony has made no difference. . . '[2]

If part of the radically negative character of the event was the apparent abandonment by God and virtually all of the world of the victims of the Holocaust while it was occurring, then our failure today to hear the testimony of those victims is precisely to repeat that radical negativity. . .

Why is it that testimony has as yet not been heard, that so very little theological reflection on the event of the Holocaust, especially but not only in the Christian traditions, has been written? One possible reason is the failure on the part of some to recognise that the Holocaust was not a parochial event, but an event that shatters the coherence of all human discourse and of theological language in particular. To hear the claim that the Holocaust makes upon us is not to parochialise our attention. Rather, it is the hearing of its claim in its radical disruption of virtually all our assumptions about humanity and the Divine. It is, thus, in its radical particularity that the claim of the Holocaust can best be heard. For one cannot hear the claim of suffering in general. In fact, it is always particular individuals and groups who suffer, and it is their distinctive voices that we must both hear and respond to. Rather than deafening one to the voices of the suffering of others, then, the recognition of the uniqueness of the Holocaust radically opens one to the particular and distinctive voices and claims of the suffering of others.

(Susan Shapiro, 'Hearing the Testimony of Radical Negation' in Elisabeth Schüssler Fiorenza and David Tracy (eds), *The Holocaust as Interruption*, Edinburgh, T. and T. Clark, 1984, 4–5)

References

1. Elie Wiesel, 'Art and Culture after the Holocaust' in Eva Fleischner (ed.) *Auschwitz: Beginning of a New Era?*, New York, KTAV, 1977, 403
2. Ibid., 405

Discussion

1. Did the Holocaust shatter the coherence of all human discourse?
2. Does the Holocaust open one to the claims of the sufferings of others?

Harold Schulweis: The Holocaust and Evil

Harold Schulweis has served as a rabbi at Valley Beth Shalom Synagogue in Encino, California. In Evil and the Morality of God, *he argues that traditional theodicies are inadequate. In their place he proposes a predicative theology which focuses on actions which are godly rather than the nature of God.*

Predicate Theology

Is there an alternative to the inherited form of subject theology and subject theodicy? Can the moral ideal of divine perfection be conceptualized without its being devoured by an omnivorous subject? Is there another way to integrate the insights and values of metaphysical and personalisitc theology without violating the moral dimension. . .

The theological task changes accordingly. The aim is not to prove the existence of the subject but to demonstrate the reality of the predicates. For subject theology faith is belief in the subject and atheism is the denial of its existence. The critical question for predicate theology is not 'Do you believe that God is merciful, caring, peace-making?' but 'Do you believe that doing mercy, caring, making peace are godly?' The energy of theology would be directed not toward convincing men that a subject possesses certain qualities themselves. Following the inversionary proposal, the religious contention is not that a subject is in some sense good or loving or intelligent or creator but that the humanly comprehensible qualities of goodness, love, intelligence, and creativity are godly: that they themselves are worthy of adoration, cultivation, and emulation in the lives of the believer. . .

What is important to note here is that the qualities do not derive their meaning and their worth from another realm of being. They are experienced and valued for themselves. They are not valued as appendages attached to a supersensible subject but are discovered in the course of man's transactions with his environment, human and nonhuman. They are not cast down from above or projected from below but revealed in the areas between persons and between persons and things. . .

To see God or godliness through the eyes of the predicates focuses upon the complex processes which disclose godly qualities, the proper objects of adoration and emulation. The God-terms of subject theology, which have been reified, enwrapped in noun substantives and located in an occult Power, are unravelled and demystified. The transactions between the self, individual and collective, and the environment, human and non-human, are revelatory. Qualities are discovered in doing, feeling, thinking, willing, prizing and evaluating experience. . .

The predicates do not refer to preexistent hypostasized entities lodged in a mysterious subject and claimed as divine on the grounds that they are so declared by the subject. They are qualities discovered, not invented, tested, lived and sustained by human beings. These qualities are more suitably described by verbs or adverbs than by non-substantive locutions. Translating 'God is love' or 'God has wisdom' or 'God possesses compassion' or 'God makes peace' into 'acting lovingly, or acting wisely, or acting compassionately, or making peace is godly' emphasizes the significance of human interaction and responsibility.

By definition, no unknowable God can be known. Nothing can be said of that which in itself is beyond our comprehension. Whatever is claimed as knowledge of God must therefore be relational. God as revealed to human beings is not God-in-himself. Predicative theology openly acknowledges an anthropological constant in all our encounters and theological claims. Accordingly, 'God' is not a substantive noun which refers to things as they are in themselves, e.g., silver, stone, wood. 'God' is a functional noun which can be understood in terms of its relation to others. . .

Elie Wiesel is a traditionalist, but like many believers, he cannot endure theology as usual after Auschwitz. In his novel *The Accident*, he portrays the tormented spirit of Sarah, the prostitute, victim of the death camps. His hero has heard the story of her tortures and the terrible price she pays for her survival. Enraged, he cries out, 'Whoever listens to Sarah and doesn't change, whoever enters Sarah's world and does not invent new gods and new religions, deserves death and destruction.' This is not the voice of atheism. It is the sound of those who recognize that theological sameness is no compliment to authentic religious tradition. It is the sound which echoes the religious audacity of tradition and that calls for new ways to understand divinity. The proposal for predicate theology and predicate liturgy, despite the analytic character of its presentation, is offered in response to Wiesel's passionate challenge. It is not meant for everyone. It is for those who are embarrassed by the theological rationalizations which leave God morally defenseless or indifferent to suffering. Predicate theology and theodicy are for those who cannot go home again using old routes, but who choose not to remain homeless.

(Harold Schulweis, *Evil and the Morality of God*, Cincinnati, Hebrew Union College Press, 1984, 122–145)

Discussion

1. Is it possible to discover godly qualities independent of the Divine?
2. Does predicative theology resolve the dilemmas of the Holocaust?

Zachary Braiterman: Jewish Thought after Auschwitz

Zachary Braiterman has served as Assistant Professor of Religious Studies at Syracuse University. In (God) After Auschwitz, he discusses the writings of major Holocaust theologians. In his view, postmodernist theories illuminate post-Holocaust theology in a number of areas.

Holocaust Theology

The conditions that made for the emergence of Rubenstein, Berkovits, and Fackenheim's theological and textual revisions were semiotic. Each thinker manipulated a more or less fluid web, composed of 'signs' taken from more or less determinate historical strata. Those strata that have directly concerned this study are biblical, rabbinic, and modern. Rubenstein, Berkovits, and Fackenheim moved what had since become marginal outbursts of anger along with priestly, mystical and feminine figures into the centre of their discourse. They hardened tradition's central concern for the community of Israel into stubborn solidarity. They deactivated central tropes like retribution, the world-to-come, afflictions of love, and prophetic rebuke by moving them out into the margins of their thought. In the process, post-Holocaust religious thought came to constitute a unique, antitheodic loop in the semiotic loop in the semiotic web of Jewish tradition.

Such a conclusion contradicts those who argue that the murder of European Jewry has produced no new theological expression not already present in the pages of Bible, midrash, or modernist poetry and literature. It contradicts those who suggest that Auschwitz was just another, albeit extreme site of Jewish suffering. In terms of strict content, the antitheodic tropes used by Rubenstein, Berkovits and Fackenheim admittedly remain the same throughout time—but not their formal arrangement *vis-à-vis* previously hegemonic theodic patterns. . . the Holocaust and its memory have radically recast the theodic and antitheodic contours of Jewish theology. Antitheodic expression shifts from the margins of classical Jewish literature, moving from the literary horizons afforded by Yiddish and Hebrew literary modernism into the very centre of religious thought. This shift speaks to the changed face of catastrophe in the modern era. Antitheodicy (the refusal to justify, accept and value suffering) proves especially compelling in an age of extermination camps and nuclear weaponry.

(Zachary Braiterman, *(God) After Auschwitz*, Princeton, Princeton University Press, 1998, 166–167)

Divine Promise

Wyschogrod's thought works within the post-Holocaust parameters set by Rubenstein, Berkovits, and Fackenheim. On one point, however, Wyschogrod's book ends on a messianic hope that is a little too bright for the landscape that he himself describes. His messianism is maximalist, expecting that unexpected moment when a divine act will bring history to an apocalyptic climax. According to Wyschogrod, this act will redeem a broken cosmos by mending the spiritual and political ruptures that rend it. However, by his own accounts Wyschogrod has no right to conclude so confidently. Wyschogrod himself has argued that the future envisioned by Judaism is not assured by the nature of things but rather hinges upon a divine promise. Surely Wyschogrod must know how thin this promise appears in the twentieth century. Perhaps God has seen it proper to protect the Jewish people. But why should it be God who protects now when God did not protect then? And that God protects now does not ensure that God will continue to do so in the near or distant future. In my view, Rubenstein, Berkovits and Fackenheim better expressed the restless uncertainty that Wyschogrod himself shares throughout most of The Body of Faith.

(Zachary Braiterman, *(God) After Auschwitz*, Princeton, Princeton University Press, 1998, 177)

Postmodern Theory

One does not begrudge any attempt to find a good that might illuminate the second half of our post-Holocaust diptych. Rubenstein, Berkovits, and Fackenheim also recognized good after Auschwitz. However, the tentative goods they identified belong to this-world and its present, not to a still-uncertain future. The fragility of good represents a theme that runs throughout the post-Holocaust literature. Its authors pointed to the survival of the Jewish people, to its rebirth in the State of Israel, to Jewish life and ritual. These goods remain vulnerable, perpetually at risk, never taken for granted. They lack the power to transform the very order of our moral world. Wyschogrod might have made his messianic future-scape more subtle and less secure by adopting a similar circumspection. There is of course no ultimate way to adjudicate conflicting claims about this-worldly goods and apocalyptic good, except to say that verifying claims about the former involves a lot less waiting.

It should be obvious by now that the Holocaust has been left behind in the wake of its memory. Flight from Egypt already points to the future. Shulamite remains an imperfect memorial to the past. These and the theological landscapes that I have described. . . are post-Holocaust. They surround a lived past that I myself cannot imagine. Those of us untouched directly by the event (whether by geography or birth) have nothing more than the memories and memoirs of survivors, the emerging historical record, and documentary images and dialogues. When the last survivor dies, these will be as close as we get to the lived experience of the event itself. To be sure, the children of survivors carry their own traumas. However, even the best-informed attempts to remember and draw conclusions from the testimonies of this event will miss the mark. This includes my own study of theodicy and antitheodicy. For that I am sorry. I have tried my best to address insoluble theological problems created by the catastrophic suffering of other people.

(Zachary Braiterman, *(God) After Auschwitz*, Princeton, Princeton University Press, 1998, 177–178)

Discussion

1. Was Auschwitz simply another manifestation of Judeophobia?
2. What goods have emerged as a result of the Holocaust?

Steven Jacobs: The Holocaust and Jewish Faith

Steven Jacobs has served as a Reform rabbi at Temple B'nai Shalom in Huntsville, Alabama. In Rethinking Jewish Faith, *he outlines a number of central areas which need to be considered in light of the Nazi onslaught against the Jews. In his view, Jewish theology must be reformulated in a radically new fashion.*

Jewish Theology

Those Jewish writers who have directly confronted the Holocaust and

256

its religious and theological implications—Eliezer Berkovits, Arthur Cohen, Emil Fackenheim, Irving Greenberg, Bernard Maza, and, of course, Richard L. Rubenstein—have profoundly and eloquently presented their thoughts to the worldwide Jewish community. But, like the 'psychological school', they have not directly extended their thinking to the impact of the legacy of the Holocaust upon the very generation who have now grown to maturity as adults, marriage partners, and parents, deeply affected by the experiences of their parents, still connected to and committed to the Jewish people and faith, but no longer either comfortable with or contented with the historically traditional responses of Judaism. That Christian writers on the Holocaust have not addressed this particular audience should come as no surprise: The foci of their concerns have been twofold: (1) to build a bridge of reconciliation with the Jewish people, and (2) to make their own Christian communities more fully aware of the religious and philosophical, not to mention historical, implications of the Holocaust.

What follows, then, is a preliminary investigation and exploration of those topic areas central to the Jewish faith experience by one child of a survivor. . . with a primary concern being that of the concept of 'commander-commandment' continuum, a rethinking of the whole notion of *mitzvot* or religiously commanded obligation Jewishly understood. Only indirectly will the implications of this journey for contemporary Christianity be addressed.

(Steven Jacobs, *Rethinking Jewish Faith*, Albany, State University of New York Press, 1994, 118)

Theological Concerns

1. Both the Bible and postbiblical or rabbinic Judaism (not to mention Christianity) present their understanding of Deity as the God-who-acts-in-history, whose caring and concern for Jews was ultimately expressed at Sinai (and through Jesus the Christ for Christians at Calvary), for reasons largely unknown to his human children. No longer acceptable or comforting, when juxtaposed to the Holocaust, is the midrashic..understanding of a Deity, who, sadly, went with his children into exile in Egypt and rejoiced, gladly, with them when they celebrated their liberation from slavery and bondage. No amount of rationalization can overcome the enormity of the loss of 6 million. . . by asserting that Providence prevented the number from escalating higher. If truth now be told: not only did 6 million of our Jewish brothers and

sisters die at Auschwitz, as well as 5 million non-Jews, but the historically traditional notion of God also died, for some among us, in the concentration camps which puncture the landscape of Europe.

What is now demanded in the realm of theological integrity is a notion of a Deity compatible with the reality of radical evil at work and at play in our world, a notion which, also, admits of human freedom for good or evil because he or she could not act. To continue to affirm the historically traditional notions of faith in God as presented by both biblical and rabbinic traditions (as well as Christianity) is to ignore those who, like myself, continue to feel the pain of family loss, yet want to remain committed to Jewish survival, not because Deity wills it, but because without even this battered community, we are cut off from this most fragile of moorings.

2. Such a different understanding of Deity is, however, contingent upon accepting the Holocaust as a unique and radical departure from the 'normative' development and evolution of Jewish and world history. While the debate still rages in both scholarly and religious circles, for the child of survivors, armed with even a minimal knowledge of Jewish history and tragedy, the Holocaust is literally 'something else', and must be so regarded or ignored. How else to understand the shift from pre-Christian manifestations of antisemitism to and through theological and religious antisemitism to the 'modern' notion of biological antisemitism from which no Jew could escape, including the members of one's own family? How else to understand the very modernity of the Holocaust as the marriage of bureaucractic excellence and technological perfection which perceived *Die Endlösung*, the 'Final Solution', within the reality of human possibilities? How else to confront the pain of loss and, even haltingly, begin to make some sense of it?

3. Such an understanding is, likewise, contingent upon accepting a notion of God as other than historically and traditionally presented by both Judaism and Christianity. A possible source of divine affirmation, to the degree to which such affirmation is either desired or acknowledged as desired, lies in the concept of 'limited Deity' who could neither choose nor reject action during the dark years of 1933 (39)–1945, who could not have responded to those humanly created and crafted processes of destruction even if he or she had wanted to do so. Notions of omniscience and omnipotence quickly fall by the

wayside; the alternative possibilities are a Deity who was ignorant of the designs of his or her German children and their European cousins and impotent to act even when he or she learned of their plans, or a limited Deity whose own nonknowledge and limited power precluded both foreknowledge and interference. The very technology of Nazism forever shattered the easy appeal to a Deity who will, somehow, curb the limits of human intellect and action for evil or good, and, in the future, prevent a repetition or recurrence of the Holocaust. If anything, the reverse is now possible: Having let the genie of destructive forces out the bottle of human ignorance, our best hope for survival lies not in the heavens, but in our ability to educate the next generation to evince the same intellectual expertise to creative measures as has thus been evidence to destructive measures.

4. Of necessity, the notion of *brith* or covenant must now be redefined. A violated but never abrogated biblical understanding of covenant only makes sense in relation to the God-who-acts-in-history. Covenant with Deity whereby both divine and human partners agree to certain stipulations in order to maintain harmony and equilibrium is no longer logical nor desirable outside of such historically traditional ways of thinking. . .

5. Prayer, too, now stands in need of rethinking. Appeals to correct present situations or to dramatically alter future possibilities have. . . proven themselves of no avail. Having realized no response from on high to words spoken in earnestness and fervor during the long night of Nazism's all-too-successful reign of terror, to now expect God to respond on a less frightful level, to less critical pleas, is theological absurdity. . .

6. At the heart of the Jewish experience is the notion of *mitzvah* or 'commandment' as obligated act in response to the 'call' of the *mitzaveh* or commander. Having tentatively and painfully rethought such notions of God, covenant, and prayer, to continue to maintain such an historically traditional notion of *mitzvah* not only begs the question, but negates the historical realities of the Holocaust itself.

(Steven Jacobs, *Rethinking Jewish Faith*, Albany, State University of New York Press, 1994, 119–122)

Discussion

1. Is the notion of a limited God a solution to the theological problems posed by the Holocaust?
2. What are the implications for Judaism if God were conceived as limited?

Edward Feld: The Holocaust and Spirituality

Edward Feld has served as Chaplain to Smith College, Massachusetts and Religious Advisor at Amherst College, Massachusetts. In The Spirit of Renewal: Finding Faith after the Holocaust, *he rejects various traditional responses to the problem of evil. In his view, it is now necessary to formulate a new theology in which God is understood as manifest in human life.*

Theodicy

Nor is the appeal to an otherworldly reward helpful. Many of us had already been affected by the Enlightenment and its aftermath and had given up believing in an afterlife. Even for those who retained this belief, the rabbinic solution that the reward for the good is to be found in the next world is an unsatisfactory response to the mass death experienced in the Holocaust. Can the thought that 'now all who are dead are with their maker' really comfort us? Can an afterlife really make up for the terrible loss? Have all the dead, sinners and saints alike, now been given a dispensation?

While the past romantic notions could attach themselves to the martyr's death, to speak of the witnessing of the righteous in this context seems wholly inappropriate. So many of those who died in the Holocaust desperately wanted to live, so many were killed who could ascribe no content to the word 'Jew' for which they now suffered, and those who experienced malnutrition and typhus had no thought of the 'Sanctification of the Name'. These were not consciously chosen martyrs' deaths, and reward in the afterlife can not make up for their loss. Are all six million, believers and unbelievers, secularists and faithful, pietists and rascals, deniers of their Judaism, converts to Christianity and the defenders of the faith now to be considered martyrs? Are all those who longed to live rather than die, who did not want the afterlife but wanted the here and now, to be rewarded in the

260

world to come? Are they now to be judged, their lives weighed and their rewards and punishments meted out? Can we imagine that such accounting would mitigate the horror of what they experienced? Appeals to an afterlife hardly seem appropriate in this circumstance.

Nor can these events be justified as part of any divine plan, some mysterious unfolding that will only be revealed to us in its entirety in the end of days. Given the enormity of what has occurred that seems too facile a solution, too easy a bypassing of the terror we have experienced.

Some have argued that we cannot question God's power but that God has handed over the realm of history to the human, whatever the consequence. There is even the contention that classical Judaism never took seriously the formulation 'because of our sins were we exiled'— a curious reading of the tradition. If more is meant by the relationship with God than a simple Deistic one, based on the notion that God once having set the world in motion then stepped away from that creation, then it must be realized that in the tradition God's presence was to be realized in the afterlife, an idea that provided a sense of ultimate judgment and justice. But if one loses faith in a settling of accounts, then of what use is a God who once was active but is no longer? In what sense can we say God is present if the world is given over to the human? Why concern ourselves with God?

Even as they seek to justify God, these theologians agree that the pain we have suffered prevents us from believing literally and simplistically in a beneficent creator God who miraculously redeems us. The rent in the universe is too deep, the tragedy of existence too overwhelming for the goodness of God ever again to be clearly manifest to us. The destruction wrought without any divine intervention speaks of God's absence from the stage of human action.

(Edward Feld, *The Spirit of Renewal*, Woodstock, Vermont, Jewish Lights, 1994, 136–137)

God and Evil

We now realize that when theologians of earlier generations spoke of God's will and power, when we imagined God watching over creation and playing the games of history, our theological language said too much. Our understanding of God's relationship to history was false. We conceived of God as too much of a person when God is really spirit. Our images of God were idolatrous and are now shattered by the events we have witnessed.

We can no longer believe in a divine intervention that will come

261

from the outside, but we must learn that we can let holiness enter, that we can make a space for the divine, that which is most deeply nourishing, that which sparks the soul of each of us. When we listen to the silent calling of God, impelling us to reach out and shatter the hard reality constructed by evil, to affirm the humanity of our neighbour—that is divine intervention. . .

We have relinquished the God sitting 'up there', the all–powerful one guaranteeing a redemption in an unknown endtime. But we have not forsaken the process of redemption altogether.

We do not await a God who parts the seas or brings down plagues on our enemies, but we can still seek moments of holiness: a Judah approaching his brother filled with regret, the midwife who in Exodus refuses to destroy a new life (celebrated in tradition as the mother of Moses), a prophet who risks death by accusing a king of terrible misconduct, our resting on the seventh day, the washing of hands before we eat. The holy that can be encountered everywhere is as much at the heart of the universe as the darkness in which it is found. After the Holocaust we continue to testify that there is a sacred aspect to life, that the world is not simply the dwelling place of evil. Biblical religion understood that there was a fundamental distinction between God and what was life sustaining on the one hand, and death and impurity on the other. They were opposites, and if one entered the realm of death then one could not be a part of the world of the holy. The biblical emphasis on ritual purity was a way of physically expressing the separation between life and death. . .

We know the divine in a new way, yet we know so little. Our entry into the mystery is through the force of will that reaches deep within us and there finds a mournful tune shattering the emptiness, the silence around us. . .

We believe not in a God of strength but in a fragile light of the spirit that is always threatened by the power of night and that must always be fought for. A place can be made to let that spirit in, human beings can act in a way that affirms another world than that of the Nazis; it is for us to choose that world we want to enter. We believe not in an omnipotent God who will transform the reality closing in around us, which is the given of our lives, but in a God who in a delicate voice calls us from within that reality to break through its hardness and create a resting place for the Divine Presence.

(Edward Feld, *The Spirit of Renewal*, Woodstock, Vermont, Jewish Lights, 1994, 140–143)

Discussion

1. Is the afterlife an unsatisfactory consolation to mass death in the concentration camps?
2. Is the reformulation of belief in God as spirit an adequate response to the dilemmas posed by the *Shoah*?

Eliezer Schweid: The Holocaust and Jewish Thought

Eliezer Schweid has served as Professor in the Department of Jewish Philosophy at the Hebrew University, Israel. In Wrestling Until Day-Break, *he provides a critical evaluation of responses to the Holocaust from both radical and Orthodox thinkers. In his view, none of these theologies provide an adequate solution to the religious problems raised by the Nazi era.*

Jewish Theology and the Holocaust

The first published responses of religious writers, poets and thinkers who survived the Holocaust were generally based on this paradox—they expressed a traumatized belief, which, standing the trial of the Holocaust, was too profound to be pacified by any of the ready-made theological 'solutions'. One may even put it this way—the mere idea of a possible solution was anathema to their feeling of absolutely justified amazement. Precisely because they did believe in spite of what they had lived through, there could be no answer to their unjustifiable suffering, unless God himself could be described as a victim of Radical Evil together with his chosen people. Thus, they experienced their protest as an inner necessary dimension of belief after the Holocaust. This feeling, it seems, was the source of the varieties of 'Protest Theologies' or 'Revolt Theologies' which occupied the greatest part of Jewish theological literature published in the aftermath of the Holocaust...

But besides these main responses there were some contradictory responses of ultra-Orthodox and modern Orthodox theologians. These religious movements, of course, could not accept such attitudes of protest as an adequate basis for their religious education. Striving to protect the foundations of their religious world views they could not admit the extraordinary uniqueness of the Holocaust in this sense; therefore, they were looking back to the traditional argumentation in spite of the felt difficulties.

(Eliezer Schweid, *Wrestling Until Day-Break*, Lanham, Maryland, University Press of America, 1994, 332–333)

A New Theodicy

We tried to show that after World War II and the Holocaust the whole variety of traditional theodicies, by and large, lost their validity or their convincing weight. We do not and cannot claim that they were simply refuted, or disproved, but they appear actually to be insufficient. So much so, because even those who deny the uniqueness of the theological problem raised by the Holocaust, and pretend to return to former Orthodox arguments, actually misused or significantly changed the traditional argumentations, and thus contained, or incorporated, the unique challenge of the Holocaust in their argumentation without being able either to face its full impact or to solve it as it really is. On the other hand, we tried to show that during the war and the Holocaust, and within the experience of a spiritual crisis which was effected by the war and the Holocaust, and by the whole syndrome of modernity, there has been awakened a new need, a new demand, even a new will for return to religious belief and faith, and precisely to its fundamental existential core. The great paradox seems to be that, at one and the same time, the originative sources of religious belief and faith had lost the reliability of their empirical testimony yet were recharged with existential meaning, for which people desperately long. Moreover, we claim that the demand contained in the theologies of revolt and protest to confront the Holocaust as an absolutely unique event which keeps its actuality permanently, as if beyond and above history, has no moral justification and actually cannot be fulfilled. From this point of view, the modern Orthodox thinkers are right—we should examine the Holocaust by taking into account both the short perspective of the period that passed since the end of the war and the long perspective of Jewish history before the Holocaust, and looking for religious sustenance from all the sources which incorporate religious wisdom. The uniqueness of the crisis should be recognized, but historical continuity should persist.

But the main conclusion of this discussion seems to be the clear recognition of the fact that the crisis must remain a fixed central component of religious experience and, therefore, also of religious thought. We have no ground to hope for smooth and well-rounded systematic solutions, as in traditional and post-traditional religious philosophies of the past. Relying on the accumulated wisdom of religious experience and religious thought in our long history, we may follow, phase by phase and step by step, the story of an evergrowing enigma which confronts a believing man, and a believing Jew the more so. He must take upon himself an ever-growing share of responsibility for the evidence of his own ground for faith, namely, the evidence of divine presence in the world. His is the task of testifying by his own way of life, while only very rarely he may have the reassuring experience of achievement and response. The difficulties which this state of affairs raises on the believers' way of life, and especially on the way of religious education, is quite obvious. It seems, indeed, that these difficulties explain, and may even excuse the desperate efforts of responsible modern Orthodox theologians like Eliezer Berkovitz and Immanuel Jacobovits to overcome the crisis and offer a full and coherent intellectual solution. But this seems to be also the main source of their failure—they incorporated the crisis in their argumentation without an admitted recognition of the fact, thus claiming the achievement of what they did not really achieve. The failure must be overcome by a full philosophical recognition. When the believer must take upon himself, in full awareness, the greatest share of responsibility for his and his communities' religious orientation, the enigma of faith, and beyond it the enigma of the Jewish believer's loneliness before a hiding God, must remain a permanent challenge.

(Eliezer Schweid, *Wrestling Until Day-Break*, Lanham, Maryland, University Press of America, 1994, 362–364)

Discussion

1. Are traditional theodicies undermined by the Holocaust?
2. Is a new theology required by the events of the Nazi period?

Robert Reeve Brenner: Holocaust Survivors and Religious Belief

Robert Reeve Brenner has served as the Reform rabbi of Bethesda Jewish Congregation in Maryland. In a study of Holocaust survivors, The Faith and Doubt of Holocaust Survivors, *he explores the nature of their religious convictions.*

Holocaust and Afterlife

Throughout the course of the development of the Jewish system of thought, the suffering of the innocent has often been attributed to God's unchallenged prerogative of putting the pious to the supreme test of faith as in the biblical book of Job—regardless of the question of the justice of the evil unleashed.

Nearly always linked to God's test of man's faith in Jewish tradition is his wish to instruct and discipline man to follow his Toratic teachings. To the pious survivor, then, perhaps this reasoning may be attributable to God and provide for his bringing about or allowing the Holocaust to have happened.

Moreover, Jewish tradition has at various periods offered a way out of the dilemma of the innocent suffering in this world by positing a recompensing world-to-come, a solution conspicuously absent from the book of Job.

Significantly, among these 708 twentieth-century Jewish victims not one thought the world-to-come—whether as afterlife, heaven, messianic future, resurrection, or whatever a survivor may conceive— was sufficient alone to make sense out of the Holocaust.

(Robert Reeve Brenner, *The Faith and Doubt of Holocaust Survivors*, New York, Free Press, 1980, 206)

Rejection of Jewish Belief

Among the views not offered by survivors, and quite prominent in its absence, is that the evil of the Holocaust is illusory, an unreal manifestation, merely an opposite reflection of good. . . Another theological posture without representative survivor spokesmen is the Mishnaic dictum that the sufferings of the righteous are real enough but they are 'trials of divine love.'

Similarly, the Holocaust was too severe for any adherents of the Herman Cohen view of suffering: It is God's way of strengthening us and he inflicts some pains on man to refine his nature or to purify his moral character. . . Nor was there support from survivors of the view that God causes or permits suffering to reveal his enormous power to mortal man. For Holocaust survivors God could have found other ways of demonstrating his might. . .

(Robert Reeve Brenner, *The Faith and Doubt of Holocaust Survivors*, New York, Free Press, 1980, 210–211)

Resurrection

Turning to the theological views of the hereafter denied by survivors, the doctrine of the resurrection of the dead is undoubtedly the most prominent. In Jewish thought the doctrine of resurrection held so important a place that, although not taught explicitly in the Torah, it became expressed as one of Maimonides' Thirteen Principles or Articles of Faith. . .

If the survivors of Nazi terror in any way reflect the current status of contemporary Jewish theology, then it can be said that, except as an aspect of the coming of the Messiah for a small portion of ultra-observant survivors, the doctrine has now been abandoned with the same zest and alacrity as it had been championed by some in previous periods. Despite their experiences in this life, Holocaust survivors with near unanimity did not feel compelled to postulate a return to this world after their deaths when the iniquities would be released and divine justice made evident.

(Robert Reeve Brenner, *The Faith and Doubt of Holocaust Survivors*, New York, Free Press, 1980, 212–213)

Divine Responsibility

27 percent resolved the problem of God's whereabouts by contending that God had nothing to do with the destruction of the six million. . . It is inappropriate to blame God for the acts of man (man may decide to kill or not to kill). One survivor spoke movingly of the vision he had while in the camps, of God, in sorrow, weeping for his people and at man's inhumanity to man. These survivors were generally of one mind in their view except for the few. . . whose religious coloration suggests a modern deist as much as a pious Jew. . .

Of those preferring to stress man's role in the destruction, 84 percent were nonobservant survivors, and the remaining 16 percent observant survivors. Concentrating on the consistently observant survivors alone. . . fully 60 percent preferred not to judge God with regard to the death of the six million; 14 percent preferred to judge man. . . an answer well in conformity with traditional Judaism. And 16 percent. . . attributed the Holocaust to God's will.

(Robert Reeve Brenner, *The Faith and Doubt of Holocaust Survivors*, New York, Free Press, 1980, 217–218)

Divine Will

Our attention should be drawn to the fact that the second most frequently selected answer of survivors who remained observant was that the Holocaust was the will of God. That is, 30 percent of all Jews who remained observant throughout the years were divided between the view that man alone can be held responsible for the Holocaust since he is free to kill, and the view that the Holocaust was God's will, part of his divine plan for the Jewish people, with the latter group slightly larger.

These two apparently antithetical positions were reconciled with little difficulty in the minds of survivors by the contention that while the Holocaust was God's will, man himself must be held responsible for bringing it about. . . It is also undeniable that the attitudes that man must not judge God and that the Holocaust was God's will may be looked upon as not only eminently reconcilable but as sides of the same theological coin: We must not judge God for allowing the Holocaust or for bringing it about. The unwillingness to judge God is an aspect of pious resignation reflected in rabbinic Judaism's view that he, in his perfect wisdom and goodness, knows best. And his visitations and dispensations must be accepted without complaint and without murmuring.

(Robert Reeve Brenner, *The Faith and Doubt of Holocaust Survivors*, New York, Free Press, 1980, 218)

Omnipotence

A finite God-conception was thought to be far less radical and more admissible today after the Holocaust for some survivors. Still, asking survivors in an interview about a limited God was seen as rather vague; about an 'all-knowing' God as not especially pertinent; about a 'nonbenevolent' God. . . as almost entirely inadmissible for God-believers. Survivors were therefore surveyed concerning their belief in God's 'omnipotence' alone. And one of every twenty survivors responding to the question expressed the view that God is not omnipotent and could not have prevented the Holocaust.

(Robert Reeve Brenner, *The Faith and Doubt of Holocaust Survivors*, New York, Free Press, 1980, 223)

Religious Doubt

In the course of administering the questionnaire there emerged among certain survivors the attitude of indignation and rage directed at God for not having interceded to save the six million. Forgiveness of God's inadequacies was hardly the disposition of this final subgroup of survivors responding to the question. One of every four, far from forgiveness, convicted God for not having prevented the calamity. The formulation of the question accurately reflected their resentment and indignation: 'Nothing can excuse God for not having saved them.'. . . For the most part, however, these are survivors who in their indignation do not deny that God exists; rather they are determined to renounce him for not intervening in the Holocaust. Not denied but denounced is He.

(Robert Reeve Brenner, *The Faith and Doubt of Holocaust Survivors*, New York, Free Press, 1980, 233–234)

Discussion

1. Can the Holocaust be understood as the result of divine providence?
2. Does a finite God concept resolve the problems raised by the Holocaust?

PART IV

Jews, Christians and the Holocaust

Chapter 14: The Holocaust and Christian Responsibility   **273**

David A. Rausch: The Holocaust and the Church   273

Rolf Hochhuth: The Holocaust and Christian Indifference   276

Susannah Heschel: The Holocaust and German Theology   280

Michael D. Ryan: The Theology of Adolf Hitler   282

Ben Zion Bokser: Christianity and the Nazis   286

Eberhard Bethge: The Church Struggle   288

Leonore Siegele-Wenschkewitz: The Holocaust and Christian
Anti-Judaism   291

Edward Flannery: The Holocaust and Christian Anti-Semitism   294

Gordon C. Zahn: Catholic Resistance   297

Michael Marrus: The Holocaust and Catholicism   300

Hyam Maccoby: The Holocaust and Anti-Semitism   303

Franklin H. Littell: The Holocaust and Church Struggle   306

Stephen T. Davis: The Holocaust and Christian Evangelicals   309

Chapter 15: Re-evaluating Christian Theology   **313**

Rosemary Radford Ruether: Reinterpreting Christology   313

John Pawlikowski: The Holocaust and Christology   316

Gregory Baum: Reinterpreting Christianity   319

Mary Knutsen: The Holocaust and Truth   322

Michael McGarry: The Holocaust and Christology   327

Paul Tillich: Jewish History and the Holocaust   329

Stephen Haynes: Post-Holocaust Christian Theology   333

Alice Eckardt: Theology of the Holocaust   335

Roy Eckardt: The Holocaust and Christian Spirituality   338

Clark Williamson: Christian Theology and the Shoah   341

James F. Moore: Christianity after Auschwitz   344

Yosef Hayim Yerushalmi: Christianity and Nazi Anti-Semitism 347

Thomas J.J. Altizer: The Holocaust and God's Absence   350

William Hamilton: The Holocaust and Radical Theology   352

Chapter 16: Jewish–Christian Dialogue   **355**

Edward Kessler: The Holocaust and Jewish–Christian Dialogue 355

Katharine T. Hargrove: Contemporary Holocaust Theology   358

Isabel Wollaston: Christian Theology and the Holocaust   362

Randall Falk: The Holocaust, Jews and Christians   364

Walter Harrelson: The Holocaust and the Modern World   367

Johann Baptist Metz: Jews and Christians after the Holocaust   369

Frank Longford: The Holocaust and Forgiveness   372

Albert Friedlander: The Holocaust and Jewish–Christian
    Dialogue   376

Eugene Fisher: Catholics and Jews   379

CHAPTER FOURTEEN

The Holocaust and Christian Responsibility

David A. Rausch: The Holocaust and the Church

David A. Rausch has served as Professor of History at Ashland University, Ohio. In A Legacy of Hatred, *he discusses the failure of the Christian church to protest against the policies of the Nazi state. With few exceptions, church leaders did not live up to the moral ideals of the Christian faith.*

Evangelicals and Fascists

As the Nazis consolidated their power in the early months of 1933, German Protestants were active in furthering their own position with the new state. All of the forces of *Volk* and fatherland came to fruition as church representatives undertook the formation of a new national Evangelical church. On April 25, 1933, Hitler named Army District Chaplain Ludwig Mueller as his representative to the Evangelical church with the specific charge to establish a Reich Evangelical church. Mueller was the leader of the Faith Movement of German Christians (referred to as 'German Christians') in East Prussia, a movement launched in 1932 to support right-wing politics and economics. It espoused a 'positive Christianity' that rejected 'Christian cosmopolitanism' and believed that National Socialism and Christianity should complement one another. 'Christianity,' they held, 'should not lose its connection with the folk and national socialism should not become a movement without faith in God'. Compromising with Evangelical church leaders at every turn in order to obtain a working constitution for the new national church, Mueller was present when the German Evangelical Church Confederation approved such a constitution on May 27, 1933. In July 1933, Hitler informed President Hindenburg that the drafted document had been signed by representatives of German churches. Article I read: 'The inviolable foundation of the German Evangelical church is the gospel of Jesus Christ, as testified to us in the Holy Scriptures and brought to light again in the creeds of the Reformation. The full powers which the church needs for her mission are thereby determined and limited.'

Church elections were held on July 23. . . The 'German Christians' movement swept the offices, and a number of laws were soon enacted. One law discharged those who 'on the basis of their previous activity do not guarantee that they will at all times unreservedly support the national State, and the German Evangelical Church.' Another retired all pastors and officials of 'non-Aryan descent' or those 'married to a person of non-Aryan descent.'

(David A. Rausch, *A Legacy of Hatred*, Grand Rapids, Michigan, Baker Book House, 1990, 163–164)

Christian Protest

A storm of protest ensued as churchmen realized they were losing their freedom. On September 21, 1933, Martin Niemöller, pastor of Berlin's Dahlem Church, wrote to ministers inviting them to join a 'Pastors Emergency Alliance'. Concerned with the political power of the 'German Christians' movement, Niemöller's letter interpreted what had transpired in the preceding few months. . . Within a week, two thousand pastors responded by attending the Barmen Synod, the first synod of the Confessing Church. The Barmen Confession of May 1934, written under the guidance of Karl Barth, repudiated the false doctrine of the 'German Christians' and recalled the German Evangelical church to the central truths of Christianity. It also rejected undivided loyalty to the State and the State's attempt to usurp the role of the church.

Unfortunately, although Niemöller attacked the laws against non-Aryans in the ministry as a violation of the confessional stance of the church of Christ, and although many of these men fought for the rights of their Hebrew Christian pastors, the Confessing Church failed to cry out against the violation of the civil and religious rights of the Jewish people. Dietrich Bonhoeffer, who realized in 1933 that the critical issue was the Nazi treatment of the Jews, was an exception. . . It was not until May 1936, after the Confessing Church had split (moderates leaving) and the infamous Nuremberg Laws had been decreed, that the remaining 'radical' Confessing Christians issued a statement specifically

274

condemning the Nazis' hatred of the Jews.

(David A. Rausch, *A Legacy of Hatred*, Grand Rapids, Michigan, Baker Book House, 1990, 164–166)

Roman Catholics

The Roman Catholic church also compromised with Hitler. Because of its political party and labour union, the German Catholic church was very visible. Consequently, the Nazis prepared for a wholesale attack against priests. As soon as Hitler gained power Catholic clergymen were mistreated by the SA and arrested. Rectories were ransacked and parish schools intimidated. The laity of the Catholic church, caught up in the spirit of the New Germany, brought enormous pressure on the bishops. The Catholic church believed it had no choice but to negotiate for the best terms possible with Hitler. On July 29, 1933, the church signed an agreement with the German government. Cardinal Eugenio Pacelli was the Vatican representative who formally affixed his signature to the document. In the spring of 1939 he became Pope Pius XII, known as a master of the language of diplomatic ambiguity. Unlike a number of priests and bishops who opposed Hitler and helped Jewish people, he refused to denounce the Nazis throughout the war and restricted his public statements about murdered Jews to mild expressions of sympathy for 'victims of injustice' (declining to say 'Jew'). . .

And yet, with reference to the German church struggle, there were individual Catholics and Protestants who gave sacrificially of themselves (some giving their lives) to help the Jewish people and to stand steadfast against a powerful Nazi regime. Their struggle is a lesson to us, because standing for what is right is not easy. Pressures are brought to bear through our employment, our families, and our friends. Spiritually unhealthy attitudes toward other religions or races blind us to love and decency, while we rationalize that justice is occurring. Propaganda may lull us into compromise and complacency, postures from which we may never return. One of the greatest lessons of all is how wonderful words, even religious and biblical words, can be twisted into rationalizations for genocide—for the brutal murder of men, women and children. The struggle against all this is not easy.

(David A. Rausch, *A Legacy of Hatred*, Grand Rapids, Michigan, Baker Book House, 1990, 167–168)

Discussion

1. Were German Christians culpable for the Holocaust?
2. What distinguished those Christians who protested against the Nazis?

Rolf Hochhuth: The Holocaust and Christian Indifference

In The Deputy, *the German Protestant playwright Rolf Hochhuth portrays the Catholic Church as indifferent to the plight of Jewry during the Nazi era. In this stage play Riccardo, a young Catholic priest, attempts to persuade the church authorities to intervene on behalf of the Jews. Eventually he goes to Auschwitz where he is confronted by the camp doctor who challenges religion and God.*

The Death Camps

Doctor: Why should a man so close to God as you be afraid!

Riccardo (insistently): People are being burned here. . . .
The smell of burning flesh and hair—

Doctor (addressing him more as an equal): What foolish ideas you have.
What you see here is only industry.
The smell comes from lubricating oil and horsehair,
drugs and nitrates, rubber and sulphur.
A second Ruhr is growing up here.
I.G. Farben, Buna, have built branches here.
Krupp will be coming soon.
Air raids don't bother us.
Labour is cheap.

Riccardo: I've known for a year what this place is used for.
Only my imagination was too feeble.
And today, I no longer had the courage—to go along.

Doctor: Ah, then you know about it. Very well.
I understand your ambition to be crucified,
but in the name of God, the Father,
the Son and the Holy Ghost,
I intend to have a little sport

deflating your self-importance.
I have something quite different in mind for you. . .

Doctor (to the child): Uncle Doctor has some candy for you. Come
here!

He takes a bag from his pocket. The child reaches out eagerly.

The Girl (shyly): Thank you. . .

Doctor (scornfully): So affectionate! (Pleasantly to the child). What is
your name?

(The child does not answer.)

A pity the little girl has no twin brother.
Research on twins is my special hobby.
Other children here never live
more than six hours, even when we're rushed.
Nor their mothers either—we have enough workhorses
and we're sufficiently accommodating
To gas children under fifteen
together with their mothers.
It saves a lot of screaming. What's wrong. You did say you knew
what we do here.

Riccardo (hoarse from horror): Get it over with.

Doctor: Don't tell me you want to die right now!
You'd like that, wouldn't you:
inhaling for fifteen minutes, and then
sitting at God's right hand as saint! No!
I cannot give you such preferential treatment
while so many others go up in smoke without that consolation.
As long as you can believe, my dear priest,
dying is just a joke.

(Rolf Hochhuth, *The Deputy* in Albert Friedlander (ed.), *Out of the Whirlwind*, New
York, Schocken, 1976, 373–375)

God's Silence

Doctor: Not long ago the brutal idiots here
had their fun with a certain Polish priest
who said he wanted to die in place

of another prisoner—a man with a family.
A voluntary prisoner—a man with a family.
A voluntary offering, in short, like yours.
They kept him in a starvation cell ten days,
then even put a barbed wire crown on him.
Oh well, he had what he wanted, what your kind wants:
suffering in Christ—and Rome
will surely canonize him some day.
He died as an individual,
a fine, old-fashioned, personal death.
You my dear friend would be merely gassed.
Quite simply gassed, and no one,
no man, Pope or God, will ever find out.
At best you may be missed
like an enlisted man on the Volga,
or a U-boat sailor in the Atlantic.
If you insist on it, you'll die here
like a snail crushed under an auto tire—
die as the heroes of today do die, namelessly,
snuffed out by powers they have never known,
let alone can fight. In other words, meaninglessly.

Riccardo (scornfully): Do you think God would overlook a sacrifice,
merely because the killing is done
without pomp and circumstance?
Your ideas can't be as primitive as that!

Doctor: Aha, you think God does not overlook
the sacrifice! Really?
You know, at bottom all my work's concerned
entirely with this one question. Really, now,
I'm doing all I can.
Since July of '42, for fifteen months,
weekdays and Sabbath, I've been sending people to God.
Do thou think he's made the slightest acknowledgement?
He has not even directed
a bolt of lightning against me.
Can you understand that? You ought to know.
Nine thousand in one day a while back.

Riccardo (groans, says against his better knowledge): That isn't true,
it can't be. . .

(Rolf Hochhuth, *The Deputy* in Albert Friedlander (ed.), *Out of the Whirlwind*, New York, Schocken, 1976, 377–378)

Christian Disregard

Riccardo (haltingly): How could I tell the Pope anything new?
Details, of course. But that the Jews
are being gassed in Poland—the whole world
has known that for a year.

Doctor: Yes—but the Deputy of Christ
should speak out. Why is he silent?
(Eagerly). You couldn't yet have heard the news:
last week two or three bombs
which killed nobody, fell in the Vatican gardens.
For days that's been the great sensation
all over the world!
The Americans, the British, and the Germans
are all desperately trying to prove
that they could not have been the culprits.
There you have it again: the Pope is sacred
even to heretics. Make use of that.
Demand that he—what's wrong with you?
Sit down.
You're whiter than the walls of a gas chamber.

Riccardo: I have already asked the Pope to protest.
But he is playing politics.
My father stood by me—my father.

Doctor (with infernal laughter): Politics! Yes, that's what he's good for,
the windbag. . .

Kapo: Major!

Doctor (indicating Riccardo): This fellow goes along to the
crematorium.
No jokes with him, understand.
He is my personal patient. He's to work there.
(Ironically, to Riccardo) I will not forget you, Father.
You'll have plenty to eat,
and a normal workday of about nine hours.
You can engage in studies there,

theological studies. Find out about God.
In two weeks I'll take you into the laboratory,
as my assistant, if you wish.
I'm sure you will.

(Rolf Hochhuth, *The Deputy* in Albert Friedlander (ed.), *Out of the Whirlwind*, New York, Schocken, 1976, 388–389)

Discussion

1. Was the Pope guilty for not protesting about the Holocaust?
2. Why was the Catholic Church indifferent to the plight of the Jews during the War?

Susannah Heschel: The Holocaust and German Theology

Susannah Heschel has held the Eli Black Chair in Jewish Studies at Darmouth College, New Hampshire. In her view, German theologians were culpable for the plight of the Jews during the Holocaust. Today however there is the attempt on the part of some scholars to eradicate anti-Judaism from Christian theology.

German Theologians and the Holocaust

What do these statements of theologians have to do with the actual murder of Jews, I am sometimes asked. After all, Hitler's plans were conceived and carried out by soldiers, not ministers. The theology formulated by the Institute indicates, of course, the utter corruption of its members and of the hierarchy of the church, which not only failed to stop the propaganda, but actually supported it. Through the Institute for the Study of Jewish Influence on German Religious Life, the church attempted to create a niche for itself within a Nazi regime that had little use for theologians. To become important, the theologians exploited one of their self-proclaimed strengths: their expertise as scholars of Judaism. Rather than confine that expertise to the academic realm, the Institute became a vehicle to disseminate propaganda in support of the persecution of Jews. Certainly, an antisemitic sermon from a pastor, delivered each week from the chancel, carried a far greater impact on the moral vision of the public than the weekly newspaper, *Der Stürmer*, with its semipornographic offences to bourgeois values.

280

On the other hand, the Institute should not be seen solely in terms of the politics of the Third Reich. Rather, its roots lie deep in a German tradition of Protestant New Testament scholarship that presented Jesus in opposition to the Judaism of his day, rather than as representative of it, as Jewish historians such as Geiger had suggested. Geiger's depiction of Jesus as a Jew was unacceptable, because of the terrible dilemma it created in undermining Christian claims to originality. Christian theological anti-Judaism, in other words, is not only the product of negative attitudes toward Jews and Judaism, but the result of unresolved dilemmas within Christian theology. Dissatisfied with the implications of a Jewish Jesus preaching the standard rabbinic teachings of his day, Judaism was projected as the supposed barrier to the kind of Christian theology liberal Protestants longed for. Judaism was fetishized as a degenerate, legalistic religion to distract from the failure of Christian theology to maintain a coherent claim to originality and uniqueness. So long as Christianity, particularly in its liberal Protestant manifestation, is unable to decide upon an original message, or accept the unoriginality of the teachings of Jesus, it will rely upon anti-Jewish maneuvers to constitute its theological significance. Ultimately, if the content of Jesus' teachings were unavoidably recognized as Jewish, then he might be 'saved' for Christians by insisting that his actual identity was Aryan.

(Susannah Heschel, 'Post-Holocaust Jewish Reflections on German Theology' in Carol Rittner and John Roth (eds), *From the Unthinkable to the Unavoidable*, London and Westport, Connecticut, Greenwood Press, 1997, 65–66)

Post-War German Scholarship

The postwar years in the German theological community have brought two trends, one that continues the antisemitism of the past, even the theological tendencies of the *Deutsche Christen*, and one that makes the overcoming of antisemitism its central preoccupation. Both tendencies coexist. One of the great shocks I experienced came when I began reading the work of German feminist theologians. Not only did they perpetuate the same language of a Jewish 'legalism' in contrast to a Jesus of 'love', but many blamed Judaism—especially the Hebrew Bible and the Talmud—for patriarchy, war, violence, and sexual abuse of women. Worst of all were statements drawing analogies between the Nazis' demands for blind obedience to orders and the Jews' adherence to divine commandments; both, in the words of Christa Mulack, are ethics of 'obedience to authority' that typify patriarchy, of which Nazism is one manifestation.

On the other hand, Germany today has some of the best Protestant theologians working on eradicating anti-Judaism from Christian theology and creating a christology that also affirms Judaism. There is no one in the multicultural United States comparable to the great Friedrich Wilhelm Marquardt, of Berlin's Free University, and the multivolume systematic christology he has published. Nor are there as many New Testament scholars and students in the United States who make a positive relation between Jesus and first-century Judaism so central to their work. It is remarkable how many German students preparing to become ministers spend a year or two studying in Israel, and how many of them declare that the central issue of their lives is eradicating antisemitism.

Throughout my life I have fantasized about what my life might have been like if 'what happened' had not occurred. What if my father had remained as a professor in Berlin, and I had been born and raised there? Would I have studied at a German university, and would I have studied Second Temple Judaism or theology? Would the traditions of Wellhausen, Schürer, and Harnack have changed if Hitler had not come to power? What if the *Deutsche Christen* and their Aryan Jesus had been laughed into oblivion? Would today's Christian feminist theologians in Germany be speaking differently had they grown up side by side with Jewish women engaged in parallel feminist struggles?

(Susannah Heschel, 'Post-Holocaust Jewish Reflections on German Theology' in Carol Rittner and John Roth (eds), *From the Unthinkable to the Unavoidable*, London and Westport, Connecticut, Greenwood Press, 1997, 66–67)

Discussion

1. How were theologians corrupted by the Nazi regime?
2. In what respects is anti-Semitism the result of an unresolved dilemma within Christian thought?

Michael D. Ryan: The Theology of Adolf Hitler

Michael D. Ryan has served as Professor Emeritus of Historical Theology at Drew University, New Jersey. In 'Hitler's Challenge to the Churches: A Theological Political Analysis of Mein Kampf*, he argues that there is a* *theological underpinning of* Mein Kampf. *In his view, Hitler subscribed to a world-view in which eternal struggle was the key motif. This ideology is akin to a religious faith which condones any form of brutality for its realization. Such a vision has important implications for Christian faith in modern society.*

The Philosophy of *Mein Kampf*

The basic logic of *Mein Kampf* is one that, when reduced to a brief formulation, horrifies the beholder. Then it fascinates him with the question of how such a logic could have captured the minds of so many people and left most of Europe in shambles before it had run its course. It can be reduced to the following propositions:

1. In his *Kampf*, his struggle, Adolf Hitler learned the basic laws of life to which a people must adhere if they are not only to survive but also to be a truly great people in history.

2. In the course of his struggle through the dregs of society in Vienna he learned the right political implications of these basic laws of life while at the same time discerning a fundamental sickness at the heart of European, but especially Austrian and German, society.

3. These political lessons enabled him to discern with clarity the true fundamental causes for the capitulation of Kaiser Wilhelm's regime. It rotted from within.

4. By displaying in his work this basic insight into reality and into the real causes for Germany's collapse, Hitler commended himself as the physician qualified to correct the ills he had discerned and to formulate a political doctrine that would unite the German people on a genuinely national basis, and unleash their true creativity to deal with all their social and political problems in a manner that would allow them to rise to a heretofore unknown level of greatness.

5. Thus, properly understood, Hitler's personal struggle was really Germany's struggle for recovery, and so he was worthy to be the leader because he fought not for himself but for the whole people.

(Michael D. Ryan, 'Hitler's Challenge to the Churches: A Theological Political Analysis of *Mein Kampf*' in Franklin H. Littell and Hubert G. Locke (eds), *The German Church Struggle and the Holocaust*, Detroit, Wayne State University Press, 1974, 152–153)

Hitler's View of Society

By his own standard of validity, namely, that of visible success, Hitler's world view was true because he was able to create a mass movement by means of it. This cannot be lightly dismissed, if for no other reason than because it brought so many people to accept the principle of total war. . .

For him the basic law of nature is eternal struggle. It is ultimate wisdom to know that nature remains mistress of all things, especially of men and nations. Not to realize this meant according to Hitler to suffer delusion like those poor half-educated souls who believe that man is the master of nature. Because no special laws govern men, their highest realization and achievement must come about according to the law of eternal struggle. . .

From this basic view of nature as eternal struggle Hitler took two laws that governed his political faith from beginning to end—the law of heredity and the law of self-preservation. In his view nature operates with 'all means' to prevent the mixing of the separate species in reproduction and to preserve the strongest while elmininating the weakest. She is utterly ruthless in following the shortest, most efficient route to select the strongest for survival. . . Brutality, aggression, the idea of using 'all means' with a maximum of force were for Hitler self-evident principles that should be applied directly to all human institutions and especially to politics.

(Michael D. Ryan, 'Hitler's Challenge to the Churches: A Theological Political Analysis of *Mein Kampf* in Franklin H. Littell and Hubert G. Locke (eds), *The German Church Struggle and the Holocaust*, Detroit, Wayne State University Press, 1974, 154–155)

Hitler's Faith

Hitler's faith was a nature religion because its content was drawn from nature as interpreted by Hitler. But it was a religion because when he set out to express his world view as to its character and place in human subjectivity, he drew all of his analogies from religion—to repeat, religion—as he understood it.

For Hitler a world view takes shape in that place in human subjectivity above political compromises when awareness of human needs and weaknesses and the consciousness of human possibilities and strengths intersect. . . As for the propagation of the world view itself, Hitler was not ashamed to draw freely on the idea of religious dogma—

again as he understood it. For example, the concept of *völkisch* is patently vague and subject to many different interpretations, as are the religious ideas of the 'indestructability of the soul, of eternity and its existence, the existence of a higher being, etc.' But when they become formulated as part of a creed with apodictic force, which for Hitler means when the highest ideals of a man are acknowledged and bound to the deepest needs of his earthly life, then there is no disputing about, or questioning of them. So, too, must the ideas of a world view be accepted by his followers. . .

If there is one lesson for theologians and pastors to learn from the Nazi experience, it is, I believe, that the idea of an invulnerable area of theology, which became current with the publication of Martin Kahler's *The So-Called Historical Jesus and the Historic Biblical Christ* in the 1890s, has in the light of the Nazi persecution of the churches to be laid to rest. None were untouched by guilt, even as in their theologizing during the period, Kahler's attempt to separate theology from historical inquiry by the device of distinguishing between *Geschichte*, as the realm of historical significance and effectiveness, and *Historie*, as that which is subject to historical investigation has been rendered most dubious. The history of National Socialism shows that something may be highly significant in history, may have an enormous impact, and yet be poles away from the truth. . .

Because of the Holocaust and because we have been challenged in all seriousness by the example of a man like Richard Rubenstein in his work *After Auschwitz*, I believe that theologians of the church should come down out of the Barthian 'above' in theology and pursue with historians all along the way the truth question in regard to the whole history of the church, but especially the historical Jesus and the relationship of a chastened Christianity to Judaism. . . Let us talk about faith within the limits that make faith intelligible as faith, namely, the limited perspectives entailed by the fact of our finitude, of our acknowledged creature-hood before God.

(Michael D. Ryan, 'Hitler's Challenge to the Churches: A Theological Political Analysis of *Mein Kampf* in Franklin H. Littell and Hubert G. Locke (eds), *The German Church Struggle and the Holocaust*, Detroit, Wayne State University Press, 1974, 161–164)

Discussion

1. Was Hitler's ideology a religious view?
2. Should theologians and historians join together in a search for a

greater awareness of the relationship between Judaism and Christianity?

Ben Zion Bokser: Christianity and the Nazis

Ben Zion Bokser served as the rabbi of the Forest Hills Jewish Center, Queens, New York. In Judaism and the Christian Predicament, *he argues that Christianity had desensitized the German population from an awareness of the evils of the Nazi regime.*

Christians and Nazis

Throughout the Middle Ages Jewish expulsions, massacres and all kinds of discriminatory legislation were common. Church leaders, in most cases, felt no sense of outrage. On the contrary in many instances they even encouraged these actions. Jewish suffering did not trouble their conscience because they saw it in the light of their obsession with Jewish guilt. Even when they themselves instigated the suffering, they felt at peace with themselves instigating the suffering. . . for in their own eyes they were aiding a divinely ordained process of retribution to act against its intended victim.

The desensitizing of the Christian conscience enabled some Christians to face even the crimes of Nazism without a sense of outrage. The Protestant Federation of France interpreted the sufferings of the Jews under the Nazis as a divine reminder of their error, and an 'appeal to conversion and to turn from their unfaithfulness.' . . . While Hitler readied the ovens for the 'final solution' of the Jewish question, H. Frauenknecht, a leader of Evangelical Christianity in Germany, wrote contemptuously: 'The Messiah came, but his people cried "Crucify him". They were angered as much by his sharp rejection of pharisaic self-righteousness as by his human lowliness and they rejected as blasphemy his claim to be the son of God. Thus they called down the judgment of God upon themselves. "His blood be on us, and on our children". In this rather than in political or general human factors, lies the secret of the strange destiny of this people since then, a destiny characterized by blood and tears.' The Reichsbruderrat of the Evangelical Church in Germany, meeting at Darmstadt in 1948, declared: 'Christ was crucified and rose again, also for the Jews. . . The fate of the Jews is a silent sermon, reminding us that God will not allow himself to be mocked. It is a warning to us, and an admonition to the Jews to be converted to him, who is their sole hope of salvation.'

(Ben Zion Bokser, *Judaism and the Christian Predicament*, New York, Alfred Knopf, 1967, 346–347)

Nazis and the Christian Community

The most shattering event that has given many Christians a sense of urgency in revising the Christian attitude toward the Jew was the Nazi holocaust. Nazism exposed the ghastly possibilities in all anti-Semitism. The painful fact that Christian teaching, instead of preventing this bestiality, was in truth one of the causes that helped precipitate it proved a shattering realization to sensitive Christians. It was this disturbance that challenged the young German poet Rolf Hochhuth to write *The Deputy*, an impassioned protest against the failure of Pope Pius XII to speak out against Nazi atrocities.

Some of the defenders of Pope Pius have maintained that his protest would have been ineffectual, since it would have been in conflict with the overriding loyalties of the German people to their state and nation, but this only defines the full scope of the Christian predicament. In the words of Claire Huchet Bishop, in her introduction to Jules Isaac's *The Teaching of Contempt*: 'It must be shamefully confessed that it took nothing less than destruction of European Jewry to awaken the collective Christian conscience. How could Hitler's Germany have been possible, a country which had been Christian for fifteen hundred years? The terrifying responsibility for this unbelievable cruelty has been underlined by the Protestant scholar, Dr. Bernard E. Olson: "Hitler's programme was but the crown and pinnacle of a long history of hatred toward the Jew, participated in (if not initiated) by those whose duty it was to teach their children the truths of Christianity."'

The ethical failure of Christianity, exposed so glaringly by Nazism, seemed especially disturbing to those who had felt the impact of a growing Christian liberalism, with its profound social consciousness. Marxist criticism of religion as an 'opiate of the masses' that dulled them to the problems of society and the need for social change had stimulated a shift of emphasis in all religious communities. Doctrinal and ritual issues receded and the ethical loomed larger in importance. Religious and lay leaders in all religious denominations felt that religion had to concern itself with the problems of the social order, that it had to lead men as did the prophets of old toward social justice, racial equality, toward the freedom of the individual and the national community, and toward world peace. . .

The growing concern with the problems of the existential world automatically narrowed the rift between Judaism and Christianity. For this was the primary emphasis in Judaism, in contrast to Christianity, which has a strong tendency to otherworldliness. Christian liberals felt a new appreciation for biblical law, which had as one of its main objectives to establish a just order of human relationships. They felt a new reverence for the impassioned writings of the prophets in protest against oppression and in affirmation of the ideal of a good society, where men were free of material deprivation, of oppressive government, and the scourge of war.

(Ben Zion Bokser, *Judaism and the Christian Predicament*, New York, Alfred Knopf, 1967, 357–359)

Discussion

1. During the Nazi period was the Christian conscience desensitized?
2. Should Christianity concern itself with the social order?

Eberhard Bethge: The Church Struggle

Eberhard Bethge has served as Honorary Professor at the University of Bonn. In 'Troubled Self-Interpretation and Uncertain Reception in the Church Struggle', he explores the evolution of the German Church Struggle from 1933 to the post-1945 period. In his view, the true nature of the Church Struggle has been largely misrepresented. With few exceptions, those who engaged in the opposition to the Nazi regime were not political resisters. Such a re-evaluation of the nature of this movement has important implications for the church's self-understanding.

The Early Church Struggle

No doubt the Protestant opposition, which organized itself slowly in the Confessing Church of the Barmen and Dahlem synods, in the first years called its fight strictly a Church Struggle and nothing else. Certainly it was not conceived as a political struggle; as such it would have been understood as a betrayal, politically wrong and theologically weak, of the church cause. And, we should remember, adherents of the opposition considered the fight the struggle of a *Weltanschauung*, an escape from the real issue; they pointed at people who, stressing their general duty to carry on the *Weltanschauung*'s struggle, in the long run evaded every concrete and dangerous church allegiance and thereby avoided the real risks. The combatants of the Confessing Church emphasized their fight for the 'pure Word of God', for the confessions of the Reformation, and against the new heresies inside the church which destroyed pure doctrine and the uncorrupted preaching of the gospel. They were therefore anxious at all costs not to appear to be political reactionaries, internationalists, or degenerate Western democrats. . .

In this struggle against the attacks of 'German Christian' doctrines they experienced an amazing rediscovery of the Reformation Confessions. And in this act of confession an unexpected partnership with the so-called former liberals and orthodox positivists emerged. Under the pressure of the Führer principle in church government and synods they experienced a rediscovery of the unity of spiritual and organizational matters under the Kingship of Christ, and led the opposition church by means of Brethren Councils. And this purely confession- and church-oriented opposition in its totalitarian surroundings became not only a witness but even an organized stronghold of freedom.

(Eberhard Bethge, 'Troubled Self-Interpretation and Uncertain Reception in the Church Struggle' in Franklin H. Littell and Hubert G. Locke (eds), *The German Church Struggle and the Holocaust*, Detroit, Wayne State University Press, 1974, 168–171)

The Developing Struggle

The basis for this self-understanding of the Confessing Church suffered a decisive shock in 1935 when the Nazi regime changed its policy from indirect influence on or occasional interference in church matters to state legislation which openly and directly interfered with church administration and the freedom to proclaim the gospel. . .

From that point on, a noticeable and deep change took place, which speedily resulted in a remarkable decline in memberships in the Barmen–Dahlem opposition and in deep and fatal cracks inside the general Protestant front itself. . . As a result of this state legislation it became ever more clear that whoever continued to follow the line of the Barmen–Dahlem synods and continued to follow the emergency church government in the form of the Brethren Councils was openly disobeying the decrees and laws of the state. The claim to fight heretics inside the church and their distortion of the image of the church became difficult to maintain. . .

The self-interpretation of the Confessing Church in its struggle ran into its deepest crisis with the Crystal Night (*Kristallnacht*) of 1938 and the brutal preparations for and implications of the imminent war. . . The already difficult step from nonconformism to disobedience toward the government was not followed by the further, definitely harder, step of political resistance. . .

As for the strong wish of the Confessing Church to serve the nation in war: the hundreds of young confessing pastors who volunteer information today speak with sufficient clarity, and especially about the high rate of casualties among the men in their ranks. I have never talked to one of them who had not accepted his draft card as an experience of inner liberation from his guilt which arose from his severe embarrassment at being considered politically suspect just because he was a member of the Confessing Church; who had not accepted the draft card as the long-sought opportunity to prove his inner national conviction and to sacrifice himself for the nation as a soldier. . .

If there were some men in the Brethren Councils and in the ranks of the young pastors who knew that their reasoning was deceptive, they did not have the instruments, assistants, or doctrines—or the occasions—to express themselves. Karl Barth alone—soon after the war. . . showed them how a theological doctrine of political resistance and uprising could be thought out and verbalized. The earlier Confessing Church lacked all presuppositions for so acting. . .

John Conway has recently given a vivid account of how the confessors of faith, so long silent, had to tell their story after the war— of course along the line of their self-interpretation, of their having fought the Church Struggle. This story was now told by men who perhaps had been put back into the offices of a church which—on the whole—had just resumed the role and organizational structure it had prior to 1933; they called the church's 'time of disgrace' in those twelve years a passing episode instead of the new starting point which young utopians like Bonhoeffer had believed in. And this story was told by men who suddenly appeared as members of 'the resistance' without clearly defining what kind of resistance was meant. But the blame for this lack of clarity was not entirely theirs. When the Allies, not having beforehand the best information about the real character of the Church Struggle, sought out people whom they could trust, they made of us churchmen the kind of resisters we actually had not been. The time came when we were inclined to believe them, to believe that we had been political resisters.

(Eberhard Bethge, 'Troubled Self-Interpretation and Uncertain Reception in the Church Struggle' in Franklin H. Littell and Hubert G. Locke (eds), *The German Church Struggle and the Holocaust*, Detroit, Wayne State University Press, 1974, 172–179)

Discussion

1. Was the Church Struggle politically or religiously motivated?
2. Were members of the Confessing Church loyal to the Christian faith?

Leonore Siegele-Wenschkewitz: The Holocaust and Christian Anti-Judaism

Leonore Siegele-Wenschkewitz has served as Professor at the Johann Wolfgang Goethe University in Frankfurt. In 'The Contribution of Church History to a Post-Holocaust Theology: Christian Anti-Judaism as the Root of Anti-Semitism', she argues that even the Confessing Church was not free of anti-Jewish attitudes during the Second World War. In her view, this heritage of anti-Semitism served as the basis for the denigration of Judaism and the Jewish people during the Nazi period.

The Holocaust and the Christian Church

At the end of the Second World War the Confessing Church in Germany was recognized by the Allies as a resistance organization, and it was on this presupposition that the first studies were made of the history of the Evangelical Church in Nazi Germany. As a rule the historians described their own history in the sense that, despite persecution by the Nazi regime, the Confessing Church had succeeded in keeping God's word loyally and giving the Church's prophetic witness. . .

At the start of the 1960s young historians who had not been old enough to have played an active part in this struggle themselves turned their attention to groups within the Evangelical Church that had no ideological reservations about collaborating with Nazism and in practice did so. But against the background of German Christians who

291

collaborated with Nazism the Confessing Church remained the true Church of Jesus Christ which had known and seized the hour when it was put to the test.

The Church's relationship and attitude to the Jews was not a separate subject in these studies. People were aware that the German Christians had been prepared to make far reaching compromises with regard to the Nazi philosophy, especially with regard to racism. But the Confessing Church was regarded as a model of integrity in view of its standing up for the Jews.

At the end of the 1960s three dissertations were presented which had as their subject the attitude of the Evangelical Church to the Jewish question, as it was called, during the Weimar Republic and in the Third Reich. These studies brought to light how great the failure even of the Confessing Church had been with regard to the Jews, and the way in which traditional anti-Jewish and anti-Semitic ways of thought had prevented even the Christians of the Confessing Church from speaking out and acting without compromise and unequivocally on behalf of the persecuted Jews.

(Leonore Siegele-Wenschkewitz, 'The Contribution of Church History to a Post-Holocaust Theology: Christian Anti-Judaism as the Root of Anti-Semitism' in Elisabeth Schüssler Fiorenza and David Tracy (eds), *The Holocaust as Interruption*, Edinburgh, T. and T. Clark, 1984, 60–61)

Christian Theologians and Nazism

The form taken by this collaboration between professors of theology and Nazism can be described briefly. The task theologians set themselves in the context of the racial anti-Semitism of the Nazi regime was to 'de-Judaise' theology and the Church and indeed Christianity as a whole. Christianity should be separated from its Jewish roots; people tried to rid themselves of the joint Judaeo-Christian tradition handed down in the Bible by stressing the aspect of mutual struggle and Christianity's assertion of its own identity *vis-à-vis* Judaism.

For this intellectual annihilation of the Jewish heritage within Christianity there were various State and Church institutions in which well-known theologians collaborated; the Reich Institute for the History of the New Germany, which was founded in Munich in 1936 under the direction of the Nazi historian Walter Frank, in which two Protestant professors of theology from Tübingen tried to work out a concept of race for the history of ideas; the Bremen Bible School of the 'Church of the Future', which was set up by the city's German Christians and which wanted to produce a 'de-Judaised' Bible; and the Institute for the Investigation of Jewish Influence on German Church Life founded in Thuringia in 1939 on the Wartburg near Eisenach. These two Church institutions were able to include a large number of theologians in anti-Jewish study groups. There was hardly a single one of the eighteen state faculties of Protestant theology in Germany where at least one member of the staff, and usually several, were not involved in some State or Church programme of 'de-Judification'.

Because they regarded anti-Judaism as belonging essentially to Christianity, these theologians were not able to draw a boundary which would shut off racial anti-Semitism. The kinds of theological argument they used against Judaism took on an immediate political relevance in the conditions of the Third Reich: for example, their argument that the relationship of Christianity and Judaism was to be determined solely on the basis of the opposition between the two religions cut the Christian Churches off from the Jews; it released them from their responsibility for the Jews and indeed aimed at forging a coalition with the Nazis. It was asserted implicitly and explicitly that Nazism and Christianity were allied in the struggle against the Jews.

A further anti-Jewish argument that could easily merge into Nazi anti-Semitism was that Christianity went beyond Judaism and superseded it, that ethically it was the superior religion. This kind of theological thinking in terms of progress made Judaism inferior as a religion and, because it had been superseded by Christianity, superfluous. In Nazi propaganda the argument appeared as the superiority of the Aryan race over the inferior and immoral Jewish race.

The integration of anti-Jewish thinking and behaviour in anti-Semitic ideology and policies did not happen for the first time in Nazi Germany. On innumerable occasions in the history of the Church anti-Jewish theological arguments had led to pogroms. . . A theology that aids the intellectual and physical annihilation of the Jews and indeed of any supposed opponent betrays the Gospel of Jesus Christ. If Christians in Germany did not want to recognise this and could not recognise this before the Holocaust, after Auschwitz it has become an irrefutable insight.

(Leonore Siegele-Wenschkewitz, 'The Contribution of Church History to a Post-Holocaust Theology: Christian Anti-Judaism as the Root of Anti-Semitism' in Elisabeth Schüssler Fiorenza and David Tracy (eds), *The Holocaust as Interruption*, Edinburgh, T. and T. Clark, 1984, 63)

Discussion

1. Was the Confessing Church culpable during the Nazi era?
2. How could Christian theologians have participated in the Nazi crime against the Jewish people?

Edward Flannery: The Holocaust and Christian Anti-Semitism

Edward Flannery has served as Director of Catholic Relations for the Bishops Committee for Ecumenical and Interreligious Affairs. In The Anguish of the Jews, *he argues that while there is continuity between Christian anti-Semitism and the Nazi attitude toward the Jewish people, there are important distinctions. The Nazi assault against Jewry could not have been sanctioned by the Christian faith.*

The Origins of Anti-Semitism

Gentile reaction to the Jewish fact took many forms throughout the centuries and sprung from many motivations, to such a point that it is not possible to consider it a homogeneous development. This must not dispense us, however, from seeking to identify the principal cause, historical or psychological, that best explains the durability and power of this unending animus. Does such a cause stand out? The microscopic view of its history that we have taken permits an answer: The deicide accusation. It was this theological construct that provided the cornerstone of Christian antisemitism and laid the foundation upon which all subsequent antisemitism would in one way or another build: Slayers and rejectors of God in the person of his son, Jews were transformed in the Christian mind into an accursed people, hated of God and humankind, doomed to live miserably in expiation for their blasphemous deed. This horrendous accusation proved to be the deepest root of that 'powerful, millenary, and strongly rooted trunk' of which Jules Isaac spoke. Throughout Christian history it was the attribute of deicide imposed upon the Jew that tipped the scales and perpetuated the hatred against him regardless of whatever involvement he may have had in situations that ordinarily induce prejudice and persecution. Christian antisemitism thus has always remained in its core theological.

294

It remained theological, moreover, because Judaism, proclaimed as having been replaced by the Church, lived on as theological challenge to the Christian claim to be the new and true Israel. The discomfort, indeed the threat that this challenge represented can hardly be overestimated. And the persistent Judaizing among the faithful could only exacerbate the threat. In the minds of the Church Fathers the only solution to this appeal of the old Israel was a drastic one: discredit the Jewish theologically, depict him/her as rejected, even cursed, by God, diabolical—the slayer of God himself; thus only would both his claim and his appeal come to naught. A startling example of theological overkill! Christian antisemitism originated, in short, in an intense theological rivalry. In retrospect, it is permitted to wonder whether, humanly speaking, a certain inevitability did not affect this conflict between two faiths laying claim to election by the one true God and to a large extent using the same source of revelation to uphold their claim.

(Edward Flannery, *The Anguish of the Jews*, New York, Paulist Press, 1985, 288–289)

Christian and Nazi Anti-Semitism

Controversy continues to stir the question of the relationship of Christian and modern racist antisemitism. Scholars who have wrestled with the problem divide into two camps. In one, modern racist Jew-hatred is regarded as no more than an intensified phase of the age old demonry that found its sustenance in Christian teachings; in the other, both are sharply distinguished from one another, and the racist development is considered to be as anti-Christian as it is anti-Jewish. The first opinion sees a difference only of degree; the second, a difference of kind.

It is not impossible to mediate these conflicting positions. Each contains a partial truth. Ontologically considered (in essence), Christian and modern racist antisemitism are radically different and opposed; historically they form a continuum. Modern racist antisemitism, as exemplified in its purest culture by the Nazi regime, would not have been possible without centuries of anti-Judaic and antisemitic precedents. From the beginning of his programme, Hitler had his target, the Jews, already set up, defenseless, and discredited. Professor Raul Hilberg has been able graphically to document the historical connection by paralleling measures taken against Jews taken by the Church and those taken by the Nazi regime. It is an impressive comparison, and yet insofar as it may suggest an identity linking the Nazi and Christian types of antisemitism, it is deceptive. What does not show up in the parallelism is the fact that the measures taken by the Church were the limit-point of Christian antisemitism, most of them having been enacted during the Middle Ages when the Church and the Christian State had total control of the Jewish circumstance. The Nazi listing, on the other hand, is obviously just the starting point of the Nazi offensive that was relentlessly to pursue its inexorable logic to its conclusion: extermination. The Nazis, in short, took up at the point beyond which the Church could not go. Christians decreed that Jews, as reprobate unbelievers, must be converted and baptized, otherwise quarantined, exiled, humiliated, but they must not be killed. In the Nazi design, Jews, constitutionally corrupt and corrupting and unredeemable by conversion or baptism, must be oppressed, quarantined, and when possible, exterminated. In Christianity, baptism could turn a Jew into an honoured citizen; in Nazi racism it could not prolong his life a single day. Cognizant of this difference separating the two types of antisemitism, Professor Yosef Yerushalmi, commenting on oppressive Christian legislation against Jews in the Middle Ages, had this to say: 'Between this and Nazi Germany lies not merely a "transformation" but a leap into a different dimension. The slaughter of Jews by the State was not part of the medieval Christian world order. It became possible with the breakdown of that order.'[1]

(Edward Flannery, *The Anguish of the Jews*, New York, Paulist Press, 1985, 289–290)

References

1. Yosef Hayim Yerushalmi, 'Response to Rosemary Ruether' in Eve Fleishner (ed.), *Auschwitz: Beginning of a New Era?* New York, KTAV, 1977, 104

Discussion

1. Was Christian anti-Semitism the cause of the Holocaust?
2. Is Christian anti-Semitism different in nature from Nazi anti-Semitism?

Gordon C. Zahn: Catholic Resistance

Gordon Zahn has served as Professor of Sociology at the University of Massachusetts, Boston. In 'Catholic Resistance? A Yes and a No', he argues that a proper evaluation of Catholic resistance against the Third Reich can now be undertaken given the wealth of documentary evidence. What such an analysis reveals is that there was no uniform policy within the church. Rather, there was both acquiescence and active determination to expose the moral degeneracy of the Nazi state.

Catholic Resistance Against the Nazis

Few historians of merit today, I suspect, would endorse the enthusiastic and uncritical defence of the record of the churches under Hitler. Similarly, few would share the accusatory fervour which marked much of the work—and probably accounted for most of the motivation—of the destroyers of the myth. What we should be striving for today is an awareness of the balance between good marks and bad in the record of the major Christian communities for the Nazi years. Some, it is true, may have fewer of the latter than others; but where this is so, it is proper to question if this was due to the purity and courage of their commitment or if it is to be explained in terms of the regime's refusal to grant them the chance to become part of the National Socialist dream. On the other hand, if the final historical accounting, as I am inclined to believe, should show that religion in general and the Catholic church in particular contributed more in the way of effective support than in effective opposition and resistance. This will have to be seen in the context of the fact that the church was about the only social institution to offer any effective resistance at all. . .

To return to the formulation of religion as institution with the dual function of providing support for the existing social order and serving, when the situation seems to demand, as a potential source of dissent and disobedience, both can be amply demonstrated by the Catholic experience. Taking the support function first, one finds certain elements which all but assured the ineffectiveness of whatever resistance the church did attempt or might have attempted. Three are particularly crucial: the church's almost fanatical opposition to Communism or, as it was usually named, Bolshevism; the Concordat and its consequences; and, finally, church traditions and rhetoric which served to augment and reinforce the nationalistic excesses which proved to be its undoing. . .

Hitler came to power in February 1933; the Concordat was formally signed in July; and less than a year later the official Catholic resistance was under way. The June 1934 pastoral of the combined German hierarchy meeting at Fulda was a public and formal protest against the crippling structures already placed upon Catholic press and organizational activity at the same time that a 'new heathenism' was being given free rein to further its cause and win new adherents. . . .

The open battle, such as it was, was waged and lost in the first five years of Nazi rule. Though underground centres of Catholic resistance existed and may have grown in strength, World War II and the total mobilization of material and human resources virtually smothered all effective protest of a public or official nature. The great exception to this, of course, was the episcopal outcry against the euthanasia program as late as 1940 and 1941; not only was this protest official and public, it was successful. For the most part, however, as the struggle developed, the initiative lay with the Nazi rulers. They determined the areas of contest and the timing, and the leaders of the church responded as best they could. As the regime's power became ever more total and more efficiently consolidated, the resistance represented by formal episcopal protest became ever more hopeless. . .

From our vantage point in time it is easy to argue that the resistance mounted by the church was doomed to failure because the bishops and other official spokesmen did not 'give things their right name' in the fullest sense. . . Not only did they (bishops) refrain from making Hitler the direct object of their protest but they also persisted in maintaining the polite fiction that the fault lay with lesser officials and subordinates. Wherever possible they larded their protests with quotations from speeches and published statements to show that the disputed policies and programs were not in accord with the Führer's personal intentions and assurances. . .

(Gordon C. Zahn, 'Catholic Resistance? A Yes and a No' in Franklin H. Littell and Hubert G. Locke (eds), *The German Church Struggle and the Holocaust*, Detroit, Wayne State University Press, 1974, 205–215)

The Church and the Nazi State

What we have seen then. . . is that the official church did 'resist' the Nazi state by protesting what its spokesmen regarded as infringements upon the rights and freedom of religion and, in particular, as violations of the letter and spirit of the 1933 Concordat. For the period covered by the documents upon which this review has been based, the major areas of contention between the protesting church and the increasingly repressive state were the Rosenberg ideological challenge, the deconfessionalization of the schools, the progressive elimination of religious youth services, and, finally, an ever tightening noose of restrictions upon church facilities and activities coupled. . . with a smear campaign almost without parallel designed to discredit the church by discrediting the priesthood. . .

The one issue that, above all others, has troubled the conscience of mankind since the collapse of the Third Reich, the attempted extermination of European Jewry, finds virtually no mention at all in the group of documents. The absence seems significant even though the 'final solution' did not get under way until a later period than that covered by the data at my disposal. One might have expected some comment to be occasioned by Crystal Night and its aftermath in 1938, but none is recorded here. . .

It is a relatively simple matter to explain why the official Catholic resistance to Hitler was largely unsuccessful, at least as success would be measured by changes in Nazi policy. The national state will always have a broad array of controls and sanctions available to it that, from the individual's point of view, are more immediately threatening than those available to competing institutions of society. The totalitarian state, by definition, expands this normal advantage to an absolute monopoly of power so that any opposition to its purpose or programs carries serious risks indeed. That the creation of just such a state was the Nazi objective none can deny; that they came frighteningly close to reaching the objective is a matter of record.

(Gordon C. Zahn, 'Catholic Resistance? A Yes and a No' in Franklin H. Littell and Hubert G. Locke (eds), *The German Church Struggle and the Holocaust*, Detroit, Wayne State University Press, 1974, 225–227)

Discussion

1. To what extent were Christians culpable during the Holocaust?
2. Why did resistance against Hitler fail?

Michael Marrus: The Holocaust and Catholicism

Michael Marrus has served as Professor at the University of Toronto. In The Holocaust in History, *he explores the motives of the Vatican and Catholic leaders during the Third Reich. In his view, the Pope and others were guided by diplomatic considerations rather than humanitarian concerns. However there were Catholic officials who sought to ameliorate the condition of Jews during the war.*

The Vatican

For the first few years persecution seems to have caused few ripples at the Vatican and awakened no more interest or sympathy than in the 1930s. Church diplomats continued to speak in favour of 'justice and charity', but were largely unconcerned about the persecution of Jews by the Nazi or collaborationist governments. A striking illustration comes from the autum of 1941, when the French ambassador to the Holy See, Léon Bérard, sent an extensive report to Vichy on the Vatican's views. According to this diplomat the Holy See was not interested in the French antisemitic laws and worried only that they might undermine church jurisdiction or involve occasional breaches of 'justice and charity'. So far as the French were concerned, the Vatican essentially gave them a green light to legislate as they chose against Jews.

When mass killings began, the Vatican was extremely well informed through its own diplomatic channels and through a variety of other contacts. Church officials may have been the first to pass on to the Holy See sinister reports about the significance of deportation convoys in 1942, and they continued to receive the most detailed information about mass murder in the east. Despite numerous appeals, however, the pope refused to issue explicit denunciations of the murder of Jews or call upon the Nazis directly to stop the killing. Pius determinedly maintained his posture of neutrality and declined to associate himself with Allied declarations against Nazi war crimes. The most the pope would do was to encourage humanitarian aid by subordinates within the church, issue vague appeals against the oppression of unnamed racial and religious groups, and try to ease the lot of Catholics of Jewish origin, caught up in the Nazis' net of persecution. And with distinguished exceptions, the corps of Vatican diplomats did no better.

As Léon Papeleux makes clear, the Vatican's posture shifted during the course of the war, as did that of other neutrals: the Holy See gradually became more forthcoming in its demarches on behalf of Jews and more overt in its assistance to the persecuted. But the pope remained reluctant to speak out almost until the very end. In the autumn of 1943, with Rome under German occupation, the Nazis began roundups of Jews virtually on the doorstep of the papal palace. On a knife's edge, the pope seems to have balanced carefully, fearing at any moment that the SS might descend on the Vatican itself. In his signals to Berlin, the German ambassador to the Holy See Ernst von Weizsäcker portrayed a pro-German pope, alluding to his reluctance to protest the assault on the Jews. Was Weizsäcker delicately trying to subvert the intentions of the SS by suggesting the high price the Reich might have to pay for the persecutions? Was he trying to protect the pope from direct Nazi moves against him? Or was he accurately reporting the perspectives of the Holy See. Interpretations of this episode vary widely—from those who see Pius playing a delicate, complicated game with Nazi occupiers, expressing himself cryptically, to those who read the incident as further indication of church reluctance to take any risks on behalf of Jews.

(Michael Marrus, *The Holocaust in History*, London, Penguin, 1993, 180–181)

Catholics and Jewry

Our understanding of church policy now extends considerably beyond Hochhuth's accusations and related charges of pro-German and antisemitic pressures on the Vatican. It is true that Pacelli had served many years as papal nuncio in Germany and feared mightily during the war that the defeat of the Nazis would lead to the triumph of Bolshevism in Europe. But Vatican documents do not indicate a guarded pro-Nazism or a supreme priority of opposition to the Soviet Union. Nor do they reveal a particular indifference to the fate of Jews, let alone hostility toward them. Rather, the Vatican's communications, along with other evidence, suggest a resolute commitment to its traditional policy of reserve and conciliation.

The goal was to limit the global conflict where possible and above all to protect the influence and standing of the church as an independent voice. Continually apprehensive of schisms within the church, Pius strove to maintain the allegiance of Catholics in Germany, in Poland, and elsewhere. Fearful too of threats from the outside, the pope dared not confront the Nazis or the Italian Fascists directly. Notably, the papacy maintained its reserve not against Jewish appeals but in the face of others as well. The Holy See turned a deaf ear to anguished calls from Polish bishops to denounce the Nazis' atrocities in Poland; issued no explicit call to stop the so-called euthanasia campaign in the Reich; deeply offended many by receiving the Croatian dictator Ante Pavelic, whose men butchered an estimated 700,000 Orthodox Serbs; and refused to denounce Italian aggression against Greece. Beyond this, there is a widespread sense that, however misguided politically, Pius himself felt increasingly isolated, threatened, and verging on despair. With an exaggerated faith in the efficacy of his mediative diplomacy, Pius clung to the wreckage of his prewar policy—'a kind of anxiously preserved virginity in the the midst of torn souls and bodies', as one sympathetic observer puts it.

Individual churchmen, of course, reacted otherwise, and there is a long list of Catholic clergy who saw their Christian duty as requiring intervention on behalf of persecuted Jews. Often the deportation convoys galvanized priests to action. In some cases, as with the intervention of the apostolic delegate Giuseppe Burzio in Catholic Slovakia, such appeals may well have made a difference. In Bucharest Nuncio Andreia Cassulo pleaded with the Rumanian government for humane treatment for the Jews. . . In Budapest Nuncio Angelo Rotta intervened repeatedly with Admiral Horthy on behalf of Hungarian Jews and may have helped secure papal intervention in the summer of 1944. Angelo Roncalli, the apostolic delegate in Turkey and the future Pope John XXIII, was among the most sensitive to the Jewish tragedy and most vigorous in rescue efforts despite his reflection, at the time, of traditional Catholic attitudes towards Jews. Elsewhere, on the other hand, church leaders replicated the posture of the Vatican itself—or even deferred with greater or lesser sympathy to those directing the machinery of destruction.

(Michael Marrus, *The Holocaust in History*, London, Penguin, 1993, 181–182)

Discussion

1. Was the Pope responsible for human suffering during the Nazi regime?
2. How can one understand the Pope's reluctance to respond to the tragedy of the Holocaust?

Hyam Maccoby: The Holocaust and Anti-Semitism

Hyam Maccoby has served as Visiting Professor at the University of Leeds. In A Pariah People, *he argues that Christianity is responsible for laying the foundations for the Nazis' attitude toward the Jews. In his view, Hitler is the inheritor of a tradition of denunciation of the Jews as pariahs.*

Christians, Jews and the Nazis

In view of this continuity, it seems necessary to say that there was no mystery about the Holocaust. If a people has been subjected to constant vilification and demonisation over a period of centuries, so that a popular loathing has been instilled so deeply as to operate like an instinct, it is no surprise that eventually a movement will arise that has as its aim the extermination of this alleged pest and enemy of humanity. If a nation has suffered humiliating defeat in a general war, and is also suffering economic hardship, it is not in the least surprising that a scapegoat will be found in an unarmed minority group that, in the minds of the people, still bears pariah status deriving from profound religious salvation-bringing conceptions, or that a political movement capitalising on national distress will fail to utilize such a dynamic unifying political weapon as the loathing and distrust of the Jews. . .

I have stressed the fact that the Jews were a necessary element in the Christian religious economy of the Middle Ages, and that this explains the preservation of the Jews from the fate suffered by the Albigenses and other heretics. St Bernard of Clairvaux is the leading example of this Christian concern to save the Jews from annihilation; important here was not only 'the witness' borne by the Jews, but also the belief that the Second Coming could not take place without their conversion. It was because of this belief in the need for Jewish survival that the Jews became a caste in Christendom—a pariah caste, to be sure, but one that was needed, like the Untouchables of Hinduism, to complete the religious spectrum.

Hitler's decision to annihilate the Jews altogether may thus be seen as a departure from the traditional Christian policy towards the Jews. Yet in fact it was not a complete departure, for the scenario of 'the Final Solution' was also present in Christianity. It is found in the millenarian movements that arose from time to time, and which focused on the concept of the 'Antichrist', based chiefly on the exegesis of II Thessalonians 2:3–12. . . The Pauline passage was widely interpreted to mean that at the end of days a Jewish Antichrist would arise, who would be regarded by the Jews as the Messiah, and who would lead a powerful Jewish army against the forces of Christianity which would be led by Christ himself. It was also believed that the result of this conflict would be the total annihilation of the Jews, men, women and children, by the Christian forces. . . Thus Hitler did have a model in one strand of Christian tradition for his conception of the Final Solution. Indeed, the millenarian tradition was particularly strong in Germany, where Hitler's ringing phrase 'the Thousand-year Reich' had a millenarian resonance.

(Hyam Maccoby, *A Pariah People*, London, Constable, 1996, 200–201)

The Holocaust and Christianity

A number of factors have combined to prevent the obviousness of the antecedents of the Holocaust from being widely accepted. Most Jewish publicists and scholars have shrunk from attributing the Holocaust to Christian teaching and societal arrangements. Bernard Levin, for example, writes at intervals about the Holocaust in *The Times,* and his message is always the same: the Holocaust is an unfathomable mystery. At a higher level, Jewish thinkers such as Elie Wiesel and Emil Fackenheim have also made a mystery of the Holocaust, assigning as its cause some deep element of evil in the Universe. Fackenheim and others have even called for a modification of the theology of Judaism, giving greater metaphysical status to the existence of evil. This has been welcomed by Christian theologians, who see here a turning by Jews toward the theology of the Cross. Some Christian theologians, in their eagerness for Christian–Jewish rapprochement, have seen the sufferings of the Jews in the Holocaust as echoing the Crucifixion, and some statements of Elie Wiesel seem to support this interpretation. It was only a step from this to see the Holocaust as not a specifically Jewish experience, but as also part of the history and mission of Christianity. Some Christians, especially those of Jewish origin, but also including some who, despite general Christian indifference, attempted to support the Jews, died in the death camps. The death of these Christians, most of whom died as Jews not as Christians, was held to support the claim to Christian participation as victims in the Holocaust. In this spirit, a group of Carmelite nuns attempted to set up a convent on the site of Auschwitz, and were surprised to encounter Jewish opposition, which however nobody explained as deriving from the Jewish conviction that the Holocaust was an outcome of Christian teaching, rather than a proof of its truth.

The Holocaust is indeed part of the history of Christianity, but not in the sense intended by those Christians who seek to appropriate the Holocaust for Christian theology. The Holocaust is the greatest crisis that Christianity has ever faced, far greater, for example, than the Reformation. The Christian response to the Holocaust will decide the future of Christianity, or whether it has a future. Many Christians are aware of this, and are reformulating the doctrines of Christianity, especially those of Christology in the light of the appalling results of past doctrines. But there is still very little understanding of the role of the New Testament and the Early Fathers in the development of the demonisation of the Jews. Some Christian writers. . . do acknowledge now that the Gospels are antisemitic. . . The fashionable escape from the antisemitic vituperation of the Gospels is to attribute it to 'intra-Jewish rivalry'—one more attempt to blame antisemitism on the Jews! If the reformulation of Christian doctrine is left to a tiny minority of scholars, and has no effect on the Christian canon, it is hardly likely to produce much impact on the Church as a whole, especially as the vast majority of Christians. . . are still untouched by the modern critical approach.

(Hyam Maccoby, *A Pariah People*, London, Constable, 1996, 202–203)

Discussion

1. Did Hitler base his policy of annihilating the Jews on Christian attitudes toward the Jewish people?

2. Is the Holocaust the greatest threat facing Christianity today?

Franklin H. Littell: The Holocaust and Church Struggle

Franklin H. Littell has served as Professor of Holocaust and Genocide Studies at Richard Stockton College, New Jersey. In 'Church Struggle and the Holocaust', he argues that the actions of the Confessing Church are of critical importance in understanding the Christian message in opposition to a false form of Christian witness. In his view, National Socialism represents a total distortion of the Christian faith. According to Littell, the Holocaust challenges both Jews and Christians to consider the terrifying potential of contemporary barbarism.

A Theology of National Socialism

In theological terms, Nazism was the true—if legitimate—offspring of a false relationship between the Christian church and the ethnic bloc or nation. And it has its analogues today in places as distant from each other as Alabama and South Africa, Belfast and Beirut. When ethnic history is infused with spirituality, and a political programme is mounted on disciplined cadres to return a people to a mythical monism of the past, a frontal challenge to the True Church—on pilgrimage and supranational—is thrown down. The situation is confused, however, because most of the baptized will accommodate in church committees or apostatize, e.g., in White Citizens' Councils, rather than give the head of the Church the undivided loyalty they once promised him.

It was the glory of the Confessing Church to have perceived that a frontal confrontation was involved and not the mere issue of everyday politics in a disaster area. The fact that some saw the sweeping dimensions of the struggle sooner than others, and that even the Confessing Church did not immediately understand the meaning of hatred of the Jews as a hatred of the Jew, Jesus of Nazareth, does not detract one iota from the debt the whole church owes the men of Barmen and what they did. Karl Barth put it directly:

> National Socialism, according to its own revelation of what it is—a self-revelation to which it has devoted all the time and chance till now allowed—is as well without any doubt something quite different from a political experiment. It is, namely, a religious institution of salvation.
>
> It is impossible to understand National Socialism unless we see it in fact as a new Islam.[1]

And the men who presented the Memorandum of May 1936 to the Führer of the Third Reich rightly identified Nazism's offense to the True Church:

> When blood, race, nationality, and honour are regarded as eternal values the first commandment obliges the Christian to refuse this evaluation. When the Aryan is glorified, the Word of God teaches that all men are sinful. If the Christian is faced by the Anti-Semitism of the Nazi *Weltanschauung* to hate the Jews, he is, on the contrary, bidden by the Christian Commandment to love his neighbour.[2]

Dietrich Bonhoeffer, martyred as the war was ending, drew one concrete conclusion—but a conclusion on which there is still little guidance in Christian theological literature: 'If we claim to be Christians there is no room for expediency. Hitler is the Anti-Christ. Therefore we must go on with our work and eliminate him whether he is successful or not.'[3]

The problem of discerning and defining the Christian obligation and style to resist illegitimate authority, not to mention illegitimate action by legitimate authority, remains one of the most excruciating agonies of Christians today. The word Antichrist is the clue: for the Antichrist is not the honest and open adversary but the one who was once numbered within and has now gone over to the opposition. The misery of the Church Struggle is not first to battle with an open opposition: it is to face the apostasy of the baptized, the convulsion of Christendom.

(Franklin H. Littell, 'Church Struggle and the Holocaust' in Franklin H. Littell and Hubert G. Locke (eds), *The German Church Struggle and the Holocaust*, Detroit, Wayne State University Press, 1975, 14–15)

Love of Neighbour

The moral claims of religion-in-general died at Auschwitz and Theresienstadt. The pretensions of the Christian intellectuals to a love of humanity—quite divorced from love, even compassion, toward specific persons and groups—floundered on the mechanical precision of the Nazi extermination of European Jewry. The German liberal intellectual, overcome by a kind of spiritual vertigo as he contemplated the vast stretch of humanity, settled for national we-feeling, for ethnic (Teutonic) identity which automatically excluded the Jews. . .

We are so situated in our various national and racial contexts that we cannot in fact love humanity without loving concrete earthly, historical persons and groups. Under pressure, we shall either retrogress to a first love of the Gentile tribe or nation, or we shall love that Israel whose prophets and seers point us toward a day of universal justice and righteousness, mercy and peace. Hatred of the Jews is often the first seismographic reading of the covert emergence of a false particularism, and we must learn to recognize it as such. . .

For Christians—and not just for the Jewish people—the Holocaust is the most important event in recent church history. For working theologians, it has called into question the whole fabric of Christendom, indeed the very language of traditional religion, just as among youth and students it has rendered the churches incredible.

(Franklin H. Littell, 'Church Struggle and the Holocaust' in Franklin H. Littell and Hubert G. Locke (eds), *The German Church Struggle and the Holocaust*, Detroit, Wayne State University Press, 1975, 17–19)

Challenging the Church

We return to the original question: The relationship of the Church Struggle to the Holocaust. When an effort is made to cut Christianity from its essentially Jewish base, when an artificial effort is made to reestablish the myth of Christendom, when the culture-religion of a Gentile race or nation becomes infused with spirituality and historic destiny, we are face to face with the Adversary. . .

For me the problem is basically theological: it concerns the nature of man, his ultimate loyalty, his final identity, his end-time (eschaton). The nature of the historical process—as well as summation is itself at stake. . . As for the question whether Jews and Christians share a common future—which may move a theologian to read and think about the evidence—each of us may use his own vernacular. . . as we do that, we shall again begin to speak for man—and not continue to contribute to his fragmentation, alienation, and dehumanization at the hands of political and academic machines. We shall also perceive that the most awful figure of this century is the technically competent barbarian—especially when he claims the sanction of religion for his politics of pride.

(Franklin H. Littell, 'Church Struggle and the Holocaust' in Franklin H. Littell and Hubert G. Locke (eds), *The German Church Struggle and the Holocaust*, Detroit, Wayne State University Press, 1975, 28–29)

References

1. Karl Barth, *The Church and the Political Problem of our Day*, New York, Charles Scribner's Sons, 1939, 41–43
2. Hugh Martin et al., *Christian Counter-Attack*, New York, Charles Scribner's Sons, 1944, 135
3. Dietrich Bonhoeffer, *Gesammelte Schriften*, Munich, Chrs. Kaiser Verlag, 1958, 1:297–98

Discussion

1. What aspects of Christianity need to be altered in a post-Holocaust world?
2. What lessons can be learned from the Holocaust?

Stephen T. Davis: The Holocaust and Christian Evangelicals

Stephen T. Davis has served as Professor of Philosophy and Religion at Claremont McKenna College, California. In 'Evangelical Christians and Holocaust Theology', he argues that despite the terrors of the Holocaust, evangelical Christians hold fast to a series of central Christian doctrines. In answer to the question whether Christians were responsible for the Holocaust, he differentiates between cultural and committed Christians. In his view, it is impossible to reconcile the actions of the Nazis and the religious ideology of the Christian faith.

The Holocaust and Christian Theologians

A growing number of Christian theologians in the United States are being decisively influenced by Jewish thinking and by the Holocaust. They are convinced, as I am, that Christians ought to think long and hard about the theological and religious implications of that event. Some such theologians are proposing radical revisions in Christian thought. Some seem to regard the Holocaust as a kind of theological absolute, almost as if it were on a par with divine revelation as a basic datum of Christian theology. Others hold that the traditional God of Christianity died in the Holocaust or at least, less metaphorically, that given Auschwitz it is no longer rationally possible for Christians to believe that God is both all-powerful and perfectly good. Some even suggest that in the light of Antisemitism and the Holocaust Christians must give up Christian themes that are offensive to Jews, e.g., the

309

notion that Jesus is the messiah or the notion that Christians ought to engage in evangelism.

Although I am not a fundamentalist or a 'moral majority'-type, I am an evangelical Christian, and thus I am unwilling to accept any of the above suggested revisions in Christian thought. In the light of such a commitment, how should I, as an evangelical, think about the Holocaust? That is the question I shall consider here. I suspect my suggestions will seem unimpressive to the Christian thinkers who are pioneers in this field—what might be called Holocaust theology. Most of them seem to be rather liberal or even radical in their approach to Christianity, and they probably will not like what I am about to say. Doubtless I will be accused of 'not taking the Holocaust seriously enough'—that seems to be the charge such people level at those who find their proposals too extreme.

(Stephen T. Davis, 'Evangelical Christians and Holocaust Theology', *American Journal of Theology and Philosophy*, 2, 3, 1981, 121)

Successionism

Many theologians who reflect on the Holocaust single out for criticism the traditional Christian notion that it succeeds or supersedes or fulfils Judaism. Christian successionism comes in many forms, and some of them, I agree, are clearly unacceptable. However, as an evangelical Christian, I . . . am not prepared to give up the notions: (1) that Jews were once God's sole elect people and that Christians are now chosen too, and (2) that all people should believe in Jesus.

Do these propositions entail that Judaism is a religious relic, that it has been nullified, that it has no *raison d'être*, that Jews no longer have any standing before God and should have disappeared? Apparently Franklin H. Littell thinks so. In *The Crucifixion of the Jews*, he argues that 'the cornerstone of Christian Antisemitism is the superseding or displacement myth.' This myth, he says, 'already rings with a genocidal note', having 'murderous implications which murderers will in time spell out.'

Most evangelicals would find these remarks by Littell not only false but outrageous. In the first place, they do not think the notion that Christianity succeeded Judaism is a myth. In the second place, they will point out that there is no necessary connection whatsoever between believing in successionism and being an Antisemite, let alone a condoner of genocide. Antisemitism and genocide are both about as clearly contrary to the Christian ethic as anything is. It just is not true that successionism has murderous implications. In the third place, it does not follow from successionism, as I have defined it, that there is no longer any justification for the existence of Judaism. St. Paul argues in Romans 9–11 that Israel has a continued role to play in God's redemptive plan, and evangelical Christians follow Paul in affirming that it is so. Furthermore, as we all know, for very understandable reasons most Jews find it psychologically impossible to believe in Christianity. In the fourth place, we cannot hold Paul and the other 'successionist' biblical writers morally guilty of the later murder of Jews even if it is true (which certainly can be doubted) that theological successionism helped motivate the later murderers. The crucial point is that Paul and the others had no intention of supporting genocide, nor any reason to suspect their words might later be used to support genocide.

Jews should not expect Christians, even in their desire for good relations with Jews, to surrender crucial Christian notions. Some liberal Christians seem eager to do so, but evangelical Christians will not do so. What evangelical Christians must say to Jews, then, is I imagine something like this: 'We love you as Jews and not just as candidates for baptism; we affirm your freedom to believe and practice Judaism without any sort of coercive interference from us; we will cooperate with you and stand shoulder-to-shoulder with you in areas of agreement (e.g. opposition to Antisemitism), but we believe that Jesus is the messiah and Son of God and those who deny it are mistaken.'

(Stephen T. Davis, 'Evangelical Christians and Holocaust Theology', *American Journal of Theology and Philosophy*, 2, 3, 1981, 122–123)

The Holocaust and Christianity

Were Christians responsible for the horrors of the Holocaust? In the first sense of the word 'Christian'—what we might call a 'cultural Christian' as opposed to a 'committed Christian'—the answer is obviously yes. Does Christianity have anything to do with the fact that certain cultural Christians committed acts of murder and genocide? This is a complex question. The Hitler regime, as we all know, was a pagan regime, strongly opposed to Christianity, and its leaders were not committed Christians. A good many Christians died in the Holocaust. The Nazis, in fact, seemed bent on destroying all who confessed an absolute moral alternative to Hitler—God for Jews,

Christians, and Jehovah's Witnesses; history for Marxists.

Nevertheless, the main victims of the Holocaust were Jews, and it seems fair to conclude that historic attitudes towards Jews fostered in the church did play a role in the success of the Nazis in achieving their ends. Here, I believe, the church must plead guilty. These attitudes distort true Christian teachings, to be sure, but they were there, nonetheless. The culturally Christian Antisemites who did Hitler's work were able to do so with relative ease and impunity in part because of (l) Antisemitic attitudes sanctioned by the church, (2) idolatrous nationalism sanctioned by virtually all Western Christians, cultural and committed, and (3) the silence of many committed Christians in the face of genocide.

Were committed Christians responsible for the Holocaust? For the Antisemitic attitudes many of them had, yes. For the silence of many of the others, yes. But were any active and serious followers of Jesus Christ murderers? Here I must say no. . . It is impossible for any sane person to reconcile Christianity with genocide.

(Stephen T. Davis, 'Evangelical Christians and Holocaust Theology', *American Journal of Theology and Philosophy*, 2, 3, 1981)

Discussion

1. Does Christian theology need to be reformulated in the light of the Nazi era?
2. Does the belief in successionism give rise to hostility toward the Jewish nation?

CHAPTER FIFTEEN

Re-evaluating Christian Theology

Rosemary Radford Ruether: Reinterpreting Christology

Rosemary Radford Ruether has served as Georgia Harkness Professor of Applied Theology at the Garrett Theological Seminary, Illinois. In 'Anti-Semitism and Christian Theology', she argues that anti-Jewish attitudes within the Church are grounded in traditional Christology. Implicit in the doctrine of the Incarnation is a rejection of the Jewish faith. Because of this stance, Christian theologians developed an exegetical tradition which reinterpreted the Hebrew Bible in Christological terms. What is now required is for the Church to repudiate its previous conviction that the Christian faith is the sole way to salvation.

Anti-Semitism in the Church

The anti-Semitic legacy of Christian civilization cannot be dealt with as an accidental or peripheral element or as a product of purely sociological conflicts between the church and the synagogue. Neither can it be dismissed as a mere continuation of pagan anti-Jewishness or a transfer of ethnocentric attitudes from Judaism itself. Although elements from these two traditions feed into Christian anti-Judaic traditions, neither of these sources provides the main data or formative motivation for Christian anti-Judaism. The frequent efforts of Christian apologists to blame either or both of these sources, therefore, constitute an illicit refusal to examine the strictly Christian theological roots of anti-Semitism in Christianity.

At its root anti-Semitism in Christian civilization springs directly from Christian theological anti-Judaism. It was Christian theology which developed the thesis of the eternal reprobate status of the Jew in history, and laid the foundation for the demonic view of the Jews which fanned the flames of popular hatred. This hatred was not only inculcated by Christian preaching and biblical exegesis, but it became incorporated into the structure of Christian canon law and the civil law formed under Christendom and expressed as early as the Code of Theodosius (438 AD) and Justinian (6th century). The anti-Judaic laws of the church and the Christian state laid the basis for the inferiorization of the civic and personal status of Jews in Christian society from the time of Constantine until the emancipation of the Jews in the nineteenth century. . .

Anti-Judaism developed theologically in Christianity as the left hand of Christology. That is to say, anti-Judaism was the negative side of the Christian claim that Jesus was the Christ. Christianity saw itself as the heir of the Jewish Messianic hope, and believed that in Jesus that hope for the coming of the Messiah was fulfilled. But since the Jewish tradition rejected this claim, the church developed a polemic against the Jews and the Jewish religious tradition, to explain how the church could be the fulfillment of a Jewish religious tradition against Jewish rejection of this claim. At the root of this dispute lies a fundamentally different interpretation of the meaning of the word 'Messiah' (Christ) in Christianity, which gradually separated it so radically from the meaning of this word in the Old Testament and Jewish tradition that the two traditions became incapable of communicating with each other.

(Rosemary Radford Ruether, 'Anti-Semitism and Christian Theology' in Eva Fleischner (ed.), *Auschwitz: Beginning of a New Era?*, New York, KTAV, 1977, 79–80)

A New Christology

The politics of paranoia and displacement of judgment must be laid at the door, ultimately, of a psychology created by Christian theology itself. The Christian theological teaching that the Jew is reprobate in history until the end of time translated itself into a practice of social denigration, to demonstrate this state of divine reprobation through the outward evidence of dishonour and misery. This legal tradition of social inferiorization of the Jews, in turn, interacted with sociological and economic changes, until it became translated into what we must now recognize as a state of mass paranoia toward the Jewish community endemic to Christian popular culture. If the misery of the Jews is necessary to prove their reprobate status and the triumph of the church, then it tends to follow that any prospering of the Jews in Christian society, any power or success they gain among Christians will be regarded as an affront to Christian society and an implicit challenge to the superiority of the Christian faith. It was this mass paranoia that flourished in the pogroms which began with the Crusades and lasted through the age of the ghetto into the twentieth century. In secular form, this politics of paranoia and displacement of judgement from one's own internal flaws upon some outside 'insidious' enemy, typified by the Jews, has proven a potent instrument in modern social crises as well, ever revivable in new guises. The Jew, caught between the Christian ruling class and the impoverished masses, shuttling between the conservative politics of survival and the liberal politics of sympathy with the oppressed, becomes again and again the sacrifical victim for conflicts which he did not create and only marginally represents.

To bring this tragic history to an end will demand something like a massive repentant acceptance of responsibility by the Christian church, and a dramatic shift in the spirituality which it teaches. The Jewish community has traditionally taken evils that have befallen it upon its own shoulders. The Christian church, imbued with a self-image of infallible righteousness resulting from its doctrine of Messianic fulfilment, has typically displaced evil upon outside enemies, the unredeemed world and the godless forces without its walls, rather than take responsibility for its own sins. Displacement of fulfilment upon the Jews has been the special archetype of this refusal to internalize self-judgment for its own sins. A repentant church was demanded already by the Protestant Reformation; but only with the Second Vatican Council has Catholicism begun to fashion a theology that incorporates self-judgement and breaks with the tradition of ecclesiastical triumphalism.

Ultimately such a shift in spirituality demands a reexamination of Christology, for this is the original root of theological anti-Judaism. A repentant Christianity is a Christianity which has turned from the theology of Messianic triumphalism to the theology of hope. This is possible only if we recognize that Messianic hope is not primarily behind us, as a *fait accompli*, but is ahead of us, as a horizon of redemption that still eludes us both, Christian and Jew. Christians, like Jews, must take responsibility for their sins in the still sinful world of which we too are a part.

(Rosemary Radford Ruether, 'Anti-Semitism and Christian Theology' in Eva Fleischner (ed.), *Auschwitz: Beginning of a New Era?*, New York, KTAV, 1977, 91–92)

Discussion

1. Does anti-Semitism spring directly from Christian theological anti-Judaism?
2. Did anti-Judaism develop theologically in Christianity as the left hand of Christology?

John Pawlikowski: The Holocaust and Christology

John Pawlikowski has served as Professor of Social Ethics at the Catholic Theological Union, Illinois. In 'The Holocaust and Contemporary Christology', he argues that both Judaism and Christianity are currently wrestling with the religious issues raised by the events of the Nazi era. In his view, Christians must re-evaluate Christology in the light of the Holocaust.

The Holocaust and Christian Theology

Anyone even minimally acquainted with directions in contemporary Jewish thought will recognise that the Nazi Holocaust has come to play a central role in reflections on present-day Jewish religious identity. There certainly exist significant differences of interpretation among the principal commentators who include Irving Greenberg, Emil Fackenheim, Richard Rubenstein, Arthur Cohen and Elie Wiesel, to name but a few.

Most Orthodox Jewish writers such as Michael Wyschograd have not thought it possible to advance the theological discussion of the Holocaust beyond the traditional category of evil, admitting, however, that the monstrous nature of Auschwitz comes close to breaking the classical parameters of this category. Non-Orthodox theologians and some at the far edges of contemporary Jewish Orthodoxy such as Irving Greenberg have called for some measure of faith reformulation after the Holocaust. Recently some challenges to the theological centrality of the Holocaust have begun to emerge in non-Orthodox circles, principally in the writings of Eugene Borowitz. In his recent volume *Choices in Modern Jewish Thought: A Partisan Guide* Borowitz argues that the Holocaust must be re-integrated into a more primary discussion—the continued meaning of the commanding presence of the covenantal God and its relationship to personal autonomy in faith expression. It is the latter, personal autonomy, that he defines as the central reality of

Jewish theological reflection today.

The ferment about the religious significance of the Holocaust will no doubt continue for some time to come. It is a debate that Christian theologians will need to follow closely. I continue to stand by the thesis that the Holocaust is what Irving Greenberg has called an 'orienting event' for contemporary theology. The challenge to this claim by Borowitz and others, while raising some critical questions which need attention, fails to deal adequately with theology's relationship to history and to grasp the profound connection between 'personal autonomy' and Auschwitz.

Turning now to the Holocaust's significance for Christian theological reflection one reality seems clear. Given the centrality of Christology in Christian faith expression the Holocaust must have implications for this dimension of Christian faith or it can hardly be termed an 'orienting event.'

(John Pawlikowski, 'The Holocaust and Contemporary Christology' in Elisabeth Schüssler Fiorenza and David Tracy (eds), *The Holocaust as Interruption*, Edinburgh, T. and T. Clark, 1984, 43)

Christianity and Contemporary Christology

In the light of the Holocaust and related examples of the brutalisation of human power it is incumbent upon contemporary Christianity to devise ways to affirm the new sense of freedom that is continuing to dawn within mankind while channelling it into constructive outlets. Post-Holocaust Christian faith expression must fully recognise and welcome this development of a new sense of human freedom and elevation as a positive and central part of the process of human salvation. But the Nazi experience will of necessity mute any wild applause for this new sense of human freedom. The challenge facing Christianity is whether it can now provide an understanding and experience of the God–human person relationship which can guide this newly discovered power and freedom constructively and creatively. . .

What I am claiming is that the Holocaust represents at one and the same time the ultimate expression of human freedom and evil—the two are intimately linked. The initial divine act of creation constituted the liberation of humanity from its total encasement in the Godhead. The Creator God acknowledged that there is need to let go part of divine humanity as part of the development of the divine creative potential. But that part of God's humanity that now assumed an independent existence was faced with the task of establishing its own identity. At times there was a strong desire to supplant the Creator. Here lie the roots of human evil. But until the modern age fear of divine punishment kept such a desire in check. But the Enlightenment, Nietzsche and other contemporary movements of human liberation changed all that. People began to lose the fear of divine retribution that had controlled human behaviour in the past. The Nazis clearly believed they had become the final arbiters of right and wrong. This new sense of freedom, this growing Prometheus-Unbound experience, in Western society, coupled with unresolved identity problems within humanity, resulted in a catastrophic plan of human destruction in Nazi Germany. The ultimate assertion of human freedom from God in our time that the Holocaust represents may in fact prove the beginning of the final resolution of the conflict. When humanity finally recognises the destruction it can produce when it totally rejects its Creator, as it did in the Holocaust, when it recognises such rejection as a perversion not an affirmation of human freedom, a new stage in human consciousness may be dawning. We may finally be coming to grips with evil at its roots, the centuries-long struggle of the human community to work out its identity by overcoming God. The power of evil will wane only when humankind develops along with a sense of profound dignity because of its links with God through Christ, a corresponding sense of humility occasioned by a searching encounter with the devastation it is capable of producing when left to its own wits. A sense of profound humility evoked by the experience of the healing power present in the ultimate Creator of human power. . .

Only the integration of this awareness of humility into human consciousness will finally overcome evil and neutralise attempts such as the Holocaust in which humanity tries to 'elevate' itself above the Creator. This human self-realisation will come easier in light of the understanding of divine vulnerability that the Holocaust made manifest in such a dramatic fashion. It is no longer 'ungodly' to express dependence upon others—the Creator has done it. The full maturity vital for the humane exercise of human co-creatorship requires the assertion of this interdependence to which the Nazis were blind.

(John Pawlikowski, 'The Holocaust and Contemporary Christology' in Elisabeth Schüssler Fiorenza and David Tracy (eds), *The Holocaust as Interruption*, Edinburgh, T. and T. Clark, 1984, 45–48)

Discussion

1. Is the Holocaust an overwhelming event for contemporary theology?
2. Does the Holocaust provide humanity with a new sense of freedom?

Gregory Baum: Reinterpreting Christianity

Of German origin, Gregory Baum has served as Professor Emeritus at McGill University, Canada. In 'Rethinking the Church's Mission after Auschwitz', he discusses the question why most Christianity has not undergone a fundamental change given the events of the Holocaust. In his view, Christian symbols are so powerful that their significance persists even in a post-Holocaust age. Yet, Christians should now transcend previous triumphalist attitudes and view Jewish–Christian relations in terms of positive dialogue. Christian theology must be reinterpreted so that the Church's eschatological views can be recovered in modern society. In Christian Theology after Auschwitz *he formulates a doctrine of God which confronts the theological problems raised by the Holocaust.*

The Holocaust and the Church

After Auschwitz the Christian churches no longer wish to convert the Jews. While they may not be sure of the theological grounds that dispense them from this mission, the churches have become aware that asking the Jews to become Christians is a spiritual way of blotting them out of existence and thus only reinforces the effects of the Holocaust. The churches, moreover, realize the deadly irony implicit in a Christian plea for the conversion of the Jews; for after Auschwitz and the participation of the nations, it is the Christian world that is in need of conversion. The major churches have come to repudiate mission to the Jews, even if they have not justified this by adequate doctrinal explanations. We have here a case, frequently found in church history, where a practical decision on the part of the churches, in response to a significant event, precedes dogmatic reflection and in fact becomes the guide to future doctrinal development. Moved by a sense of shame over the doctrinal formulations that negate Jewish existence, the churches have come to recognize Judaism as an authentic religion before God, with independent value and meaning, not as a stage on the way to Christianity.

(Gregory Baum, 'Rethinking the Church's Mission after Auschwitz' in Eva Fleischner (ed.), *Auschwitz: Beginning of a New Era?*, New York, KTAV, 1977, 113)

Reinterpreting Mission

The last two views of mission—mission as dialogue and mission as service—go together very well. They are based on a common trinitarian faith in the presence of the spirit in the human family, in the Word summoning all people to new life, and in the ultimate horizon of love and reconciliation to which broken and divided humanity is destined. These two views of mission are based on the church's solidarity with the entire human family. It is not easy, however, to reconcile this new understanding of mission with the more traditional understanding of evangelization. We acknowledge, of course, that if the church were deeply involved in missionary activity in terms of dialogue and service, the image of Christian life would become so attractive and Christian witness so powerful that many people would become Christians and join the community of believers. In other words, the new understanding of mission does not neglect the church's continuity, extension, and vitality.

The new openness to Jewish faith and the emergence of a new understanding of mission reflect the response of the Christian conscience to the voice of the Holocaust and, less directly, to the protest of the Third World. The churches believe that they have been addressed by God's Word through these events: they have placed themselves under God's judgment. Even without elaborating an adequate dogmatic basis, they have made significant public declarations and changed their public policy in remarkable ways. Christian theologians have reflected on the new trends and tried to establish their doctrinal foundation. Christian educators have begun to rewrite catechisms and schoolbooks. Many missionary congregations and Christian-action groups have abandoned their former ideal of evangelization and adopted a new policy, according to which missionaries enter into solidarity with the people in whose midst they serve, bear the burdens of life with them, and promote the self-discovery and humanization taking place in their midst. In particular the churches have renounced the desire to convert the Jews; they have begun to call them brothers and sisters.

(Gregory Baum, 'Rethinking the Church's Mission after Auschwitz' in Eva Fleischner (ed.), *Auschwitz: Beginning of a New Era?*, New York, KTAV, 1977, 116–117)

Reconstructing Christian Eschatology

Only as the church recovers the eschatological tension in which it was created is it able to reconcile Christian dogma with the recognition of religious pluralism as part of divine dispensation. This means that whatever the future of the church, Christians are meant to be a restless people, never totally at home in the world, never fully identified with their culture, always eager for the reform of life and the deliverance from the structures of domination. Christianity has inherited an ardent Messianic hope for the future. Every day Christians call upon God that his kingdom come and that his will, which is justice and love, be done on earth, i.e., in human history. This eschatological turn will affect the church's reading of Christology. In Jesus Christ, humanity's ultimate future has taken visible shape. In his suffering and exaltation the church holds the assurance of God's victory over all the enemies of life. When the church prays, 'Come Lord Jesus, come!', it acknowledges the fragmentary and unfinished character of present redemption and confesses its eager hope in the approaching liberation. The church's absolutes are valid only in this eschatologic perspective.

(Gregory Baum, 'Rethinking the Church's Mission after Auschwitz' in Eva Fleischner (ed.), *Auschwitz: Beginning of a New Era?*, New York, KTAV, 1977, 128)

Christian Theology

The theology I have turned to when examining the religious nature of 'troubled theism' may also help to deal with the important question posed to believers by the Holocaust. After witnessing the awful event, it becomes almost impossible to believe in a Divinity endowed with infinite wisdom and power, capable of stopping the machinery of destruction that led to the Holocaust but choosing not to do so. This is the God whom we cannot accept. But what does Divine Rule mean when God is imagined not above the world but in-and-through the world as its forward movement? Here God rules simply as summons. . . in people's lives. Here God does not rule from above, but from within—and this rule from within is not necessarily sovereign power. In this perspective God cannot, at will, stop all movements of human sin and destruction. In this new perspective, God's omnipotence and omniscience have quite different meanings. To call God 'omnipotent' does not mean that God could do in the world whatever he wants; it means, rather, that despite human sin and human evil, God remains the forward movement operative in people's lives enabling them to enter more deeply into authentic humanity. And to call God 'omniscient' in this perspective does not mean that God knows beforehand what will happen in history; it means, rather, that despite the darkness which sin and evil create in the world, God continues to call people to insight and understanding. . .

I do not claim that the doctrine of God with stress on divine imminence, which has emerged when we examined troubled theism, is able to solve the problem of faith created by the Holocaust. Not at all. Theism remains troubled. Still, to my mind at least, a religious imagination which pictures God as ground, orientation and horizon of human life makes a significant difference. . . For here God does not appear as the heavenly super-person whom we seek to address, but as the mystery of life that undergirds and directs us in the self-construction of our lives and whose summons we hear in our being. In this perspective, God is not so much lord and master (with all the attendant doubts about the permission granted for Auschwitz); rather, God is reviver.

(Gregory Baum, *Christian Theology after Auschwitz*, London, Council of Christians and Jews, 1976, 20–21)

Discussion

1. Is the desire to convert Jews a way of insuring the annihilation of the Jewish people?
2. Can God stop all sin and destruction?

Mary Knutsen: The Holocaust and Truth

Mary Knutsen has taught at St John's University in Collegeville, Minnesota. In 'The Holocaust in Theology and Philosophy', she stresses the challenge to Christian theology and philosophy posed by the events of the Nazi era. In her view, Auschwitz calls for a revolution in Christian orientation and a renewed conception of suffering in relation to God's will.

The Challenge of the Holocaust

In an important article entitled 'Christians and Jews After Auschwitz', J.B. Metz addresses a clear imperative to contemporary Christian theologians: 'Never again to do theology in such a way that its construction remains unaffected, or could remain unaffected, by Auschwitz.'[1] And in the course of his own reflections on the implications of this imperative for contemporary Christian theology and Jewish–Christian dialogue, he issues the following warning about the question of truth: 'Everything has to be measured by Auschwitz', he writes.

> This includes our Christian way of bringing into play the question of truth. . . But confronting the truth means first of all not avoiding the truth about Auschwitz, and ruthlessly unmasking the myths of self-exculpation and the mechanisms of trivialisation which have been so long disseminated among Christians. . . Too often, in fact, has truth—or rather what Christians all too triumphantly and uncompassionately portrayed as truth—been used as a weapon, an instrument of torture and persecution against Jews.[2]

(Mary Knutsen, 'The Holocaust in Theology and Philosophy: The Question of Truth' in Elisabeth Schüssler Fiorenza and David Tracy (eds), *The Holocaust as Interruption*, Edinburgh, T. and T. Clark, 1984, 67)

The Situation

'Never again to do theology in such a way that its construction remains unaffected, or could remain unaffected, by Auschwitz.' Already within this simple but extremely demanding imperative, it is possible to discern a certain sequence. First, and most importantly, there lies at the heart of this imperative an indicative, a statement of fact: Auschwitz has happened. Yet immediately this event is more than an event among other historical events, for it must divide theologies into a before and after; it is an event that divides epochs. At least part of the meaning of this imperative, then, is that Christian theologies acknowledge this and be affected by it. At the same time, however, it is a demand that Christian theological thinking be such that it can, in principle, recognise this and be open to alteration by this event; ruled out is not only any contemporary Christian theology that remains unaffected by Auschwitz but also any that 'could remain unaffected.' What kind of thinking need this be? What happens when it encounters the unalterable actuality of Auschwitz? It is this sequence and these questions which guide our reflection here. . .

323

The numbers, the geography of this death, stun. Yet with them we only begin our descent into the concrete actuality symbolised in the word Auschwitz. Mind and imagination reel before the sheer scope of this machinery of dehumanisation and death, the horrifying numbers of those murdered and of those millions more, still silent, who actively or inactively acceded to its course; stagger at the bottomless depths of the hatred which is disclosed there, the unutterable evil for evil's sake of a human machinery which, superseding and even undermining military and political objectives, had as its sole purpose not only the imposition of death but also the extremest degradation and suffering prior to death; finally fall and shatter upon the unfathomable horror of the actuality.

(Mary Knutsen, 'The Holocaust in Theology and Philosophy: The Question of Truth' in Elisabeth Schüssler Fiorenza and David Tracy (eds), *The Holocaust as Interruption*, Edinburgh, T. and T. Clark, 1984, 67–68)

Revolution in Theology

What happens when a Christian theological thinking that understands itself in this way finds itself confronted with the actuality of Auschwitz? To put it more specifically: What happens to philosophical and theological reflection when history and society are understood not just as objects for but as constitutive of the reflective self? What new problems emerge at the interior of thought, challenging the very possibility of understanding or thinking at all? For my own part, these problems are at least two, and both emerge from an encounter with the actuality of Auschwitz: on the one hand, the irruptive force of historical events, and especially historical events of such enormity—of such radically unacceptable human suffering—that they shatter the traditional genres and even the very rhetoric of our historical (and religious) self-understanding; on the other hand the release of the (self-involving) question of ideological distortion in the traditions, texts and institutions in which one's own self-understanding has been formed—the systematic distortion in Christian traditions, teachings and texts which is Christian anti-semitism. . .

Metz's theology has I think great power and importance as a critical powerful retrieval of the apocalyptic within Christian texts and traditions, and as an even more powerful expression of a response to human suffering and death which is at once deeply Christian, moral and rhetorical. First, it is a recovery, in contrast to what too often is a

Christian complacency before the suffering of others, of a fundamental moral sensibility and principle. Within the framework of (personal) compassion for and (personal, political, and religious) solidarity with victims, there is also the necessity for the recognition of a double alterity: the otherness of the victim, whose experience of suffering and death may never be appropriated by another and whose testimony of that experience bears an inviolable authority; and the otherness of that suffering and death from what should be. . .

Here then is I think a recovery of possibility for an authentically Christian response to the horror of Auschwitz which avoids the temptation both of Christian appropriationism and Christian complacency. That such a theology does not, and need not, replace but rather include a religious and theological understanding of such realities as the sheer giftedness of existence and the presence of grace to and in the world and in human life is I hope evident. To believe, as I do, that we also need speak of the gracious, redeeming presence of God in history is not, here, the statement of an objection; after Auschwitz it can only be the statement of a question, a question which I cannot answer and which in no wise is intended to lessen the importance of this response. In a post-Holocaust world, the recognition of the radical unacceptability of such suffering and of that radical not-yet might be an index not only of our Christianity but of our humanity as well. . .

No Christian theology, teaching, or symbol can be true which has the effect of systematically devaluing and denying the existence, authenticity, and rights to interpretation of others. Put more positively, it involves I think an important shift in the understanding of the character of religious and theological truth reflective of a recognition of the communicative construction of self and world: objectivity and truth are not a function of a monological correspondence of facts and theories but of a linguistically mediated intersubjectivity. What is at stake in a critique of the systematic distortion in Christian traditions, institutions and history which is anti-Semitism is not just the question of justice—the legitimation of oppression; what is also at stake as well is the question of truth.

(Mary Knutsen, 'The Holocaust in Theology and Philosophy: The Question of Truth' in Elisabeth Schüssler Fiorenza and David Tracy (eds), *The Holocaust as Interruption*, Edinburgh, T. and T. Clark, 1984, 70–73)

References

1. J.B. Metz, *The Emerging Church*, New York, 1981, 28
2. Ibid., 21–22

Discussion

1. Can one do theology in the same way as in the past given the tragedy of the Holocaust?
2. Has the concept of truth changed as a result of the Holocaust?

Michael McGarry: The Holocaust and Christology

In Christology After Auschwitz *the Catholic theologian Michael McGarry explores the development of Christian attitudes to Judaism in the post-Holocaust era. In his view it is necessary for the Christian community to reinterpret previous Christian doctrines concerning the Jewish religion.*

Christians and Jews

In the last thirty-five years, a host of factors have pushed Christians into a rethinking of their portrayal of Jews in their catechetics and popular preaching. Similarly, Christians have examined anew how Christianity is related to Judaism and reflected about the abiding validity of Judaism, and about how Christian theology leaves room for, or encroaches upon, that validity. It is primarily within the last decade that these latter themes have received focused and conscious attention from Christian denominations and thinkers. . .

We have tried to refrain from a 'running' evaluation of these Christologies, although value-laden adjectives like 'progressive', 'contradictory', 'absolutist', etc., have crept into our primarily descriptive analysis. Sometimes, too, our categorizing a theologian within a particular group has obscured the nuances which properly accrue to a full, worked out Christology, but such associating may be as unavoidable as it is misleading in such a study. We have striven for comprehensiveness perhaps at the expense of incisiveness, yet the many ways this issue may be treated—through notions of election, covenant, Christology, ecclesiology, missiology, soteriology—justifies, we think, this course of action. It is now time to make some general observations.

Initial Christological proposals can only be provisional because of the incipient character of the Jewish–Christian dialogue. There has not yet been time for theologians to assess one another's work on this topic, or even to narrow the issue enough to reflect thematically upon it. Indeed it is as if the starting gate were thrown open, and each person/Church has raced down the track without opportunity yet to look at, and assess, the track performance of the other contestants. Perhaps our study has thrown light on common themes which will integrate and sharpen Christological reflection in the future. From our viewpoint, some of these reflections might go in the following direction.

Eva Marie Fleischner notes that a pluralism of Christologies exists already within the New Testament to say nothing of within the Christological development after apostolic times. Doctrinal pluralism is a relatively new thematic consideration for the Christian Church, but its importance and ramifications are being noted more and more. A properly worked-out theology of pluralism may provide the most fruitful method of approaching our problem. Admittedly this complicates an already crowded theological agenda, but the importance of theological pluralism lies in the fact that Judaism, like Christianity, is a complex, multi-faceted reality, affected too by its own theological pluralism. Christians have as often as not oversimplified their position *vis-à-vis* Judaism when they have made sweeping assertions that Judaism believes this or that.

(Michael McGarry, *Christology After Auschwitz*, New York, Paulist Press, 1977, 99–101)

Christology in a Post-Holocaust World

Religious pluralism is a fact that Christians must explain to themselves in the light of their belief in the universal efficacy of Christ. But pluralism is not a good in itself. If it were, then it would be incumbent upon Christians to spread it by encouraging a multiplication of religions. Confronted by the fact of pluralism, then, some form of *logos*-Christology may prove most fruitful as a way for Christians to recognize the validity of other religions (and, *a fortiori*, of Judaism). Karl Rahner employs *logos*-Christology as a way of working out a Christology in the face of the plurality of religions, and the success of this effort with regard to leaving theological room for Judaism has been noted by Eugene Borowitz. Interestingly enough, recent, but very different, Christological studies by John Cobb and David Tracy have noted the usefulness and compatibility of the *logos* tradition for constructing a

Christology which respects, and accounts for, pluralism in religion from a Christian point of view. Our study cannot evaluate these recent attempts, nor, much less, outline in more detail a Christology fully worked out in the context of the Jewish–Christian dialogue. This would require another full study. But it can at least be said that *logos*-Christology, properly understood, does not see Judaism as only preparatory to Christianity, as destined to disappear from the earth. Rather it sees Judaism as one of God's ways of speaking to his world through his continued election of the Jewish people in terms which Christians can understand. *Logos*-Christology does not dictate a Christian self-understanding to Jews. . .

The Christian does claim, however, a vision of truth. It is a vision he is committed to talk about, one that he treasures, and one that he may share. This vision, more and more Christians are coming to see, includes the validity and value of the Jewish faith in itself and of the Hebrew Scriptures in themselves and as preparatory to Christian faith in Christ. For the Christian to eliminate the preparatory character as a valid way to understand the Hebrew Scriptures would be to remove the anchor which gives Christianity any validity and would open it to the ahistorical temptations of Gnosticism and Docetism. The Christian debt to Judaism is not only for their sacred books and for their interpretation, but also for the Christian saviour and for the Christian interpretation of that saviour.

A theological pluralism, fleshed out by a *logos*-Christology which would grant and account for a Christ who is Messiah for Christians and for the abiding validity of the Jewish tradition for Jews, may, in the end, bring about a new rapprochement between Jew and Christian. This theological pluralism would reflect more accurately, too, the many and varied ways that God has spoken and does speak to his people. . .

Christology, as Christianity itself, is open to, and in need of, constant revision. Because revelation stands before us as well as behind us, Christian insight into its own mystery stands within an ever widening horizon. The fear of tampering with doctrines and viewpoints that have been handed down through the ages may be somewhat calmed when it is realized that the God of Abraham, who is the God of Jesus, is the same faithful God who speaks to his people and draws them forward to that final day. And it may just turn out that the rethinking of Christian belief in Jesus, in the face of the abiding validity of Judaism, will turn into an ever-deepening, rather than a shallow, expression of their faith.

(Michael McGarry, *Christology after Auschwitz*, New York, Paulist Press, 1977, 101–107)

Discussion

1. After Auschwitz should Christians re-evaluate their conception of Judaism and the Jewish people?
2. Does a *logos* tradition provide a new framework for understanding other religions?

Paul Tillich: Jewish History and the Holocaust

In 'A Final Conversation with Paul Tillich', the Reform rabbi Albert Friedlander describes a conversation he had with Paul Tillich, the former Professor at Union Theological Seminary, New York. According to Tillich, Nazism was opposed to the values of the Jewish tradition. In assessing God's role in this tragedy, Tillich argues that it is a mistake to expect him to have prevented the atrocities of this period.

The *Shoah* and Jewish History

'*Shoah*—a fascinating word,' said Dr. Tillich. 'I did not realize that there is already a technical vocabulary about what happened in those days: holocaust and *Shoah*. It is a Biblical word, of course: "a devastating storm". But you know it is only one storm in the whole history of Jewish life. You must teach it as part of the other persecutions: the Inquisition, the Middle Ages—they are part of the story'. . .

'But why is this all part of the Jewish story?' I asked Dr. Tillich. 'When our high school students turn to you as a friend—and as a Christian theologian viewing Jewish history—how will you answer their question: why did it happen to us?'

We sat quietly for a while, pondering the question. Then, Tillich broke the silence.

'I've been asked that question before,' he said, 'One of the judges in the Eichmann trial came to me when it was all over. He spent the whole day with me, asking questions in countless different ways. Week after week, he had been plowing through the material dealing with the destruction of European Jewry. And he felt the need for an answer that was not really mine to give.'

'You see,' said Paul Tillich, 'you cannot just ask: why did it happen to us? It happens to all, and it is still taking place. We do not have particular questions about the nature of the world in which we live.

And philosophy helps us analyse the structures of being which we encounter in every meeting with reality. But you asked an ultimate question. You asked about the meaning of this reality for us; and that is a question for theology. Now, there is the revelation in Judaism that gives you an answer; and there is the revelation in Christianity that helps me in understanding what happened. But we each have to reach our own answers; and while they will agree, your students must discover the answer of Judaism. Nevertheless, there are some answers that I can give, and that I have given before. They deal with the fact that Hitler represented everything to which Judaism was opposed, that Judaism simply had to be the opponent of the false nationalism which we find in National Socialism.'

('A Final Conversation with Paul Tillich' in Albert Friedlander (ed.), *Out of the Whirlwind*, New York, Schocken, 1976, 516–517)

God and the Holocaust

'So many people', said Paul Tillich, 'talk about "*der Liebe Gott*" as though he were just a super-human figure who could do everything possible or impossible. There is so much primitive, perverted thinking about God by people who insist on seeing Him in man's image. God is not a kindly father-figure. He is the ground of all being, and His imprint is upon everything. "*Der liebe Gott*" who is all powerful does not exist; man's freedom is a limitation here that must be recognized if man is to assert himself and is to gain his victory over space. We should not ask: why does God permit suffering? Instead, we should recognize that there is that in the depth of our being which will enable us to challenge evil, to overcome suffering, to work for the fulfilment of the ultimate goal which is the goal of history. And part of Jewish suffering, and part of Jewish greatness, is that the Jew has historically aligned himself with universal justice, and has been the great opponent of evil.'

('A Final Conversation with Paul Tillich' in Albert Friedlander (ed.), *Out of the Whirlwind*, New York, Schocken, 1976, 519)

Jewish Heroism

And so we talked about the prophets; about the greatness of Jewish history; about Jewish life in every age. But always, we came back to the history of the holocaust, to the *Shoah*. And once more, I had a question for Dr. Tillich: 'How can we evaluate the details of that history? How can we judge what happened in the concentration camps?'

'We cannot fully judge what happened there,' said Tillich. 'We were not inside the camps. And so I cannot accept some scholars' indictment of Jewish leaders. Of course there were some who faltered. But when I think of the greatness that was revealed there. . . '

We talked about the great Jews of our time whom he had met. Tillich had known Leo Baeck. He had been in Frankfurt in time to know and to appreciate Martin Buber; and he deeply regretted that Franz Rosenzweig was already dying at that time, and was not accessible to him. Rosenzweig's friend Rosenstock-Heussy had been also a close friend of Tillich's. But there were differences:

'He believed in converting the Jews; and this is something that I cannot accept. I have never tried to convert Jews; we have a common task, and synagogue and church can and must work together.'

Talking about Leo Baeck, Tillich expressed his conviction that Baeck's actions were always examples of true goodness in action: the greatness of his ministry to the Jewish community, his heroism in staying when he could have left—these were 'true testimony'.

'There is one point where I might have disagreed with Baeck,' said Tillich, 'if I had been in his place, in the concentration camp. But I was not there. I might have shared the last iota of information, the fact that the way of those railroad tracks to Auschwitz led to certain death. The full existential truth should always be made available. But the concentration camp was a special place, outside our knowledge; and nothing could be done inside that place to change the fate of those imprisoned there. It's hard to judge.'

('A Final Conversation with Paul Tillich' in Albert Friedlander (ed.), *Out of the Whirlwind*, New York, Schocken, 1976, 519–520)

Discussion

1. Is it a mistake to ask why God permits suffering?
2. Were Jewish leaders culpable for not revealing the horrors of the death camps to those who were destined to perish?

Stephen R. Haynes: Post-Holocaust Christian Theology

Stephen R. Haynes has served as Albert B. Curry Chair of Religious Studies at Rhodes College in Memphis, Tennessee. In Prospects for Post-Holocaust Theology, *he argues that post-Holocaust Christian theology should undergo a fundamental change. Drawing on the writings of Barth, Jürgen Moltmann and Paul van Buren, he outlines a new conception of the relationship between the Christian community and Israel.*

Post-Holocaust Theology

1. In the past, theology could be 'wrong about the Jews'. . . and still be 'good theology'. This is no longer possible for post-Holocaust theology. For the Holocaust itself teaches us that theology which is wrong about the Jews may lead to evils so great that they overwhelm any other advantages of such a theology and render it nearly useless. For this reason, the effective history of texts (both biblical and theological) becomes as crucial to their understanding and their classification as their authorial intent or their official interpretation.

2. The problems and issues we have outlined. . . should not lead the church to silence with regard to Israel. Karl Barth once expressed the paradoxical situation of the theologian in this way: 'as theologians we ought to speak of God; we are human, however, and so cannot speak of God'.[1] We might well adapt his words to describe the situation of the Christian theologian after the Holocaust: as a theologian one ought to speak of Israel; as a Christian, however, one cannot speak of Israel. This version of the statement would appear to capture the dilemma of the post-Holocaust Christian theologian. This person is simultaneously aware of the duty and problems associated with Christian reflection on Israel. Taking both aspects of this paradoxical situation to heart should not lead to silence, however, but to fresh ways of speaking which take the past and the future with equal seriousness.

3. Post-Holocaust Christian theology must not ignore the Jewish people as they exist in contemporary society. This focus on the Jewish people can be lost either in an emphasis on biblical Israel, or on a preoccupation with Jews who were lost in the Holocaust. It is true that it is only possible to go beyond Auschwitz with its victims in mind. But since all Jews (and indirectly, all non-Jews) are victims of

Auschwitz in one sense or another, the church would do well to adopt Paul van Buren's maxim that live, not dead, Jews should serve as the focus for its theological inquiries.

4. The Protestant churches need to insure perpetual recognition of two important facts. First: some Christian theologians, clergy and lay persons resisted Hitler and his anti-Jewish policies. The stories of these persons should be recounted in the community of faith, and the theological rationale for their stances of opposition studied and critiqued. Second: in most cases the resistance offered by these theologians and other Christians was insufficient and ineffective in deterring the Nazis' slaughter of the Jews. The first of these recognitions has led many Protestant churches to celebrate the 'Barmen Declaration' of 1934. The second recognition should result in the churches taking more seriously the 'Stuttgart Declaration' of 1945, where leaders of the German Church confessed that, 'unending suffering has been brought by us to many peoples and countries. . . we accuse ourselves that we did not witness more courageously, pray more faithfully, believe more joyously, love more ardently.'

5. Post-Holocaust Christian theology must not sacrifice either its identity (and thus, its connection with the Christian tradition) or its relevance (and thus, its ability to hear and speak to Jews). All theology which is to remain relevant after the Holocaust must either be post-Holocaust theology, or theology which is subjected to a thorough post-Holocaust critique. If it is to be theology for the church, however, it must retain its distinctive Christian identity, no matter how radically it reinterprets the church's traditions. What aspects of the church's theology are absolutely necessary to this identity is unclear, but they certainly include the life, death and resurrection of Jesus Christ as attested in Scripture.

6. The Protestant churches must encourage significant contacts with Judaism and Jews if theological visions of complementary existence are to become reality. The church must also envision new ways of overcoming the actual separation between Christians and Jews, which remain nearly as common in institutions of theological study as in places of worship in society in general.

7. A single 'Christian' understanding of the significance of the Holocaust and the founding of the state of Israel is probably not possible or desirable as long as there is so much disagreement among Jews. Post-

Holocaust Christian theology, however, cannot afford to ignore these matters, and must arrive at some guidelines for Christian thinking about them. In each case, Christian opinion is broad: the Holocaust is seen as 'revelation' on one hand, and as one more example of humanity's inhumanity on the other. The state of Israel is perceived as a 'sign', as a realization of God's kingdom within history, or as another secular state. While arrival at a single 'Christian' view of either the Holocaust or the state of Israel is not likely, post-Holocaust theology must continue to pursue theological clarity in its understanding of these elements of what Paul van Buren calls 'Jewish history'.

8. Despite the difficulties outlined earlier concerning the doctrine of election and Christian–Jewish relations, post-Holocaust theology, especially in the Reformed tradition, must not abandon the notion of Israel's divine election, since it is the theological foundation of the church's calling and existence. The task of establishing Israel's unconditional election without adopting an understanding of Jewish existence which is open to 'mythological' interpretation in the Christian imagination is still before Christian post-Holocaust theology, however.

9. Post-Holocaust Christian theology must find its way and establish its position between the Christian Zionism popular among premillennialists, biblical literalists and some Holocaust theologians and the forms of hostile anti-Zionism which can often influence the churches. In doing so, any 'Christian philosemitism' or 'Christian Zionism' which it adopts must be motivated by a positive response to the church's awakening perception of its unique relationship with Israel, by the church's coming to terms with its history *vis-à-vis* the Jewish people, and by the church's responsibility for encouraging peace and righteousness among all parties in the Middle East.

Many Jews and Christians doubt that Christian theology has come far enough to provide a basis for genuine dialogue and mutual acceptance between 'average' Christians and Jews. Jürgen Moltmann and Paul van Buren would no doubt agree with such a verdict. Our analysis of Barth, Moltmann and van Buren has allowed us to observe the extent to which theologians living in the post-war era have advanced in affirming 'Israel' in its many dimensions, and in overcoming traditional forms of anti-Judaism. Although it appears that the weaknesses to which Barth was blind in his own work are in the process of being corrected by followers of the second generation, much is left to be done. We have argued in this essay that the work of Moltmann and van Buren contains a variety of prospects for post-Holocaust theology, not that the church has succeeded in creating such a theology, and certainly not that all or even most Christians perceive the need for it. If such prospects for post-Holocaust theology are to become an effective part of the history of the church–Israel relationship which has been so poisoned in the past, courage and imagination will be required in the future, as well as the grace of the God whom Jews and Christians serve.

(Stephen Haynes, *Prospects for Post-Holocaust Theology*, Atlanta, Scholars Press, 1991, 285–287)

References

1. Karl Barth, 'The Word of God and the Task of Ministry' in Eberhard Jüngel, *Karl Barth: A Theological Legacy*, Philadelphia, Westminster, 1986, 69

Discussion

1. Should all Christian theology be post-Holocaust theology?
2. Was the Holocaust a form of revelation?

Alice Eckardt: Theology of the Holocaust

Alice Eckardt has served as Emeritus Professor of Religious Studies at Lehigh University, Pennsylvania. In 'The Shoah *Road to a Revised/Revived Christianity', she calls for a Christian theology of the Holocaust. In her view, Christians must recognize the need to re-evaluate Christian teaching in the light of the events of the Nazi period.*

Christianity after the Holocaust

Can there be a theology of the Holocaust? No. There can only be a theology before the Holocaust, and one after the Holocaust. . .

Today many more Christian scholars, clergy, and church governing bodies have some awareness of the history of Christian mistreatment of Jews, the churches' negative teachings about Judaism, and the very serious challenge these factors pose to their proclaimed gospel. Even so, the worldwide Christian community in particular, as well as large portions of American and European Christianity, remain either largely ignorant of that history or disinterested in its pertinence to the Church's message, and this is the main challenge for Christian faith. Indeed, some Christians are so incensed at any challenge to the absolute primacy of the Christian faith and its obligations to convert all other peoples that they will not consider the fundamental challenges of this long history. Moreover, *pre-Shoah*, anti-Jewish preaching can still be heard from some clergy in all branches of the Church.

Even those who are aware of the problem remain largely baffled about how to purify the 'good news of Christ Jesus' of its built-in anti-Jewish aspect and how to deal with some of the New Testament's texts. And the task of rethinking and revising Christian theology from the ground up has still not received major attention, especially from those considered 'leading' theologians, that is, those holding prestigious appointments and writing most of the books used in the field. . . Why did it require the Nazis' 'Final Solution of the Jewish Question' for Christians to begin to look at and question their centuries-long 'teaching of contempt' toward the Jewish people and Judaism? And why do we find Christians still refusing to concede that there is a problem for their faith community? Is it mere stubbornness? Or is it a too deeply inculcated hatred of, or conviction about, the evil they believe Jews and Judaism represent? Is it fear of the loss of security their traditional faith has provided them and therefore resistance to any change in it, the yearning for an absolute that holds all the answers and does not require difficult decision making? Whatever the reasons may be, unremitting work is required to overcome the resistance they engender. And unless that resistance is overcome, Christian society and persons may continue to contribute to harming those outside their own community. That would hardly be a future to look forward to. Having gazed into the abyss of the *shoah*, I am compelled to try to alert and arouse fellow Christians to the life-and-death issue of so much of our inherited teaching.

(Alice Eckardt, 'The *Shoah*-Road to a Revised/Revived Christianity' in Carol Rittner and John Roth (eds), *From the Unthinkable to the Unavoidable*, London and Westport, Connecticut, Greenwood Press, 1997, 140–142)

Christian Theology in a New Era

In addition to the danger of an *adversus Judaeos* continuum, I gradually came to discern two foundational issues that required attention: the need to rediscover God in a radically new understanding, and to apprehend more fundamentally the essential role of humankind in history. These issues require a good deal of rethinking and have led me to tackle some difficult and troubling issues facing us, both apart from the *Shoah per se* and yet given a demanding prominence by the events of that deadly twelve-year period.

Suffering and evil have always challenged the thinking of any system of ethical thought or of believers in a good creator, and hence any number of explanations or justifications have been constructed to meet the problem. Usually the victims are said to be at fault, even though no one but God may have known what wrongdoing they have committed. Alternatively, the sufferers are told they must endure their pains and sorrows because it somehow fits into the divine scheme.

Suffering of the worst sort, both psychologically and physically, is epitomized in the Nazis' Final Solution program. Inevitably it raises questions about God's 'goodness' or God's action in history, for if that evil did not call forth divine response, what would? Neither the long-held Jewish view that God expects them to bear the role of 'suffering servant' until the world accepts and lives by God's *Torah*, nor the traditional Christian view that Jesus' suffering was God's way of offering humankind salvation from 'original sin' helps us when we see such vast and useless suffering. We are convinced that God would not wish any people to have to endure this. And we begin to wonder whether we have misunderstood. Has God deprived herself/himself of absolute power and made Godself vulnerable to powerlessness, suffering, even possibly death? If so, what are the ramifications of that action?

Having pondered over these interrelated questions for quite some years, and having given them and various attempted answers lengthy attention, I came out where I began, convinced that suffering is not part of God's will or wish for the creation. I reached much the same conclusion (however tenuous it may be) as did Hans Jonas: that God cares about all those in the creation and wishes only good for all its creatures; but that God has left the future in the hands of those she/he created and consequently God is indeed vulnerable and subject to being hurt and diminished. However, when God suffers, the world shares that pain until it relieves the divine agony by relieving the agony of fellow humans and other living creatures.

(Alice Eckardt, 'The *Shoah*-Road to a Revised/Revived Christianity' in Carol Rittner and John Roth (eds), *From the Unthinkable to the Unavoidable*, London and Westport, Connecticut, Greenwood Press, 1997, 142–143)

Discussion

1. In what ways has the Christian teaching of contempt corrupted history?
2. After the Holocaust is it possible to believe that God cares for all creation?

Roy Eckardt: The Holocaust and Christian Spirituality

Roy Eckardt has served as Emeritus Professor of Religious Studies at Lehigh University, Pennyslvania. In his view, the Holocaust should give rise to a new spirituality. What is now required, he states, is for Christians to come to terms with the devastation of the Holocaust and its implications for Christian thinking.

Anti-Semitism

My initial publication appeared in 1946. The short piece declaimed against 'the religion of Nazism' as a 'pagan absolutism of blood, nation and soil', and hence as perforce annihilative of the Jewish people and Judaism, whose God and ethos transcend and fight all such sacrilege. My first book, grounded in a doctoral dissertation in the Department of Philosophy, Columbia University (1947), began: 'Before a British military court at Lueneburg, Germany, on October 1, 1945, a Rumanian Jew testified that eighty thousand Jews, the entire population of the ghetto of Lodz, Poland, had been killed and burned in a single night' at the Oswiecim death camp.

Do such historical declaration and like materials within these and subsequent writings of mine serve to label me a 'philosopher of the Holocaust'? That phrasing is not happy. Any Christian thinker who desires to be identified via such language is met by a massive obstacle, at once analytic and substantive: The *Shoah* is unable to comprise the ultimately decisive event, prompting, or concern upon the Christian side of the relation—simply because, for all its salience and horror and fatefully determinist power, the *Shoah* is no more than/no less than the logical, moral (immoral) climax of some nineteen hundred years of Christian antisemitism. It is assuredly a fact—long a truism—that the Holocaust is unqualifiedly 'unprecedented' (Emil Fackenheim) as a world-historical and world-decisive concatenation of events. Accordingly, we are impelled to classify the *Shoah*—I speak with full

338

scientific objectivity—as a unique event. . .

Nevertheless, Christian *Judenfeindschaft*, objectively construed, cannot be assimilated to the Holocaust: the Holocaust has to be assimilated to Christian anti-semitism. We are forbidden to appeal the sentence that history has passed upon us. Robert A. Everett reminds us how James Parkes did not need the *Shoah* in order to wage his lifelong war against Christian antisemitism. Parkes' battles well preceded Nazism. So, too, the single and singular motivation of my own poor endeavours inside the Christian Jewish *Begegnung* was always and remains now the struggle against antisemitism.

(Roy Eckardt, 'Once and Not Future Partisan: A Plea for History' in Carol Rittner and John Roth (eds), *From the Unthinkable to the Unavoidable*, London and Westport, Connecticut, Greenwood Press, 1997, 112–113)

Spirituality in a New Age

In *New Theology Review*, editor (and friend) John T. Pawlikowski writes tellingly: 'The Holocaust has shattered all simplistic notions of a "commanding" God. Such a "commanding" God can no longer be the touchstone of ethical behaviour.'[1] The contemporary crisis of Jewish, Christian and (why not?) Muslim theological ethics centres in the moral issue of whether God any longer deserves (or even deserved?) to be obeyed. . . Human beings need salvation because of the evils they responsibly commit. God needs salvation because God is culpable for allowing radical evil in a world where the creatures of God have no say whatsoever in being born. . . .In *The Trial of God*. . .Elie Wiesel uncovers for us that the only figure in the entire crude courtroom who will volunteer to defend God for the divine crimes is—the Devil. (Thus takes place the funeral of all theodicy.) The 'trial of God' emerged relatively early in my thinking, but for some time it remained inchoate. It was Jewish spokespersons and friends alone who brought me to assert this truth unreservedly.

The moral question of today's existential cosmos/chaos is: Who, if anyone, is left to speak for God?. . . Who will stand, if only in silence, with the God who has individually decreed (performed?) many capital crimes but who is alone now, who is forlorn, who is friendless, who must pass endless days and endless nights (days and nights that once were the very sovereign workplace of God) consigned to death row?

Perhaps nobody. Or perhaps one single soul or even two (in simple iteration of their (infinitely innocent) archetype Jesus.) In standing with

God, this one/these two plunge inside a *mysterium tremendum* that exceeds, for intensity and terror, though also in opportunity (Revelations 21:5 'See, I make everything new'), one or other *mysterium tremendum* of the past, of the present, of the future. For this one/these two take upon themselves an accountability that is utterly gratuitous, terrifyingly 'wrong' (it accepts the unacceptable).

Yet, were the Devil, Evil of Evil, to rise to defend God, while the people of God were at that very moment failing, refusing to do so, would there not come into being the worst, the saddest irony of all? But will a defence of God by the people of God only shipwreck them upon the lost island of the Devil? Of course, the Devil's defence of God only shrieks out of diabolic unfaithfulness. The Devil's proposal to defend God is a consummate joke: It is on *Purim* that he makes his offer! When the people of God (this one/these two) speak for God it is not that they are 'defending someone'. It is not that they are falling into an *apologia*. Rather do they merely speak the truth—and fast!— the truth that holiness is proved by righteousness (Isaiah 5:16). The power of love, of *agape*, enters the scene. It is posssible—indeed, is it not morally determinate (grace-full?)—that the child will speak out for the parent who lies tied up and forsaken at the final hour, bone of the child's bone, flesh of the child's flesh, blood of the child's blood: 'You made me without my consent, yet you are my mother, you are my father.'

This standing in solidarity with the finally guilty one may comprise, in truth, all that is left of faith and for faith amidst the ashes, amidst the 'secrets of European responsibility', amidst the unforgiving aftermath of Europe's fall. From out of the abyss a kind of consolation may be aborning, a kind of spirituality beyond spirituality, the start of a condition in which God and humankind, having been made as one in their crimes, may now become one as forgiving and forgiven lovers: a comedy that is divine.

(Roy Eckardt, 'Once and Not Future Partisan: A Plea for History' in Carol Rittner and John Roth (eds), *From the Unthinkable to the Unavoidable*, London and Westport, Connecticut, Greenwood Press, 1997, 116–121)

References

1. John T. Pawlikowski, 'Reclaiming a Compelling God', *Theology Review*, 8:3, 1955, 3

Discussion

1. Was the Holocaust the result of nineteen centuries of anti-Semitism?
2. Has the Holocaust shattered the concept of a commanding God?

Clark Williamson: Christian Theology and the Shoah

Clark Williamson has served as Indiana Professor of Christian Thought at the Christian Theological Seminary, Indiana. In A Guest in the House of Israel: Post-Holocaust Church Theology, *he argues that Christian theology must be conducted in the light of the events of the Holocaust. In his view, Christians should acknowledge the anti-Jewish legacy of the Church and seek to overcome such teachings in the formulation of a new theology for modern society.*

Christian Anti-Semitism

Much theology has been done since the *Shoah*, but not much by theologians who are critically aware that they do their thinking 'after Auschwitz'. . . We cannot simply adopt one of these theologies and apply its approach to the subject of Christian theology after Auschwitz. Rather, we must heed the warning given us by the Roman Catholic theologian Johann-Baptist Metz: 'Ask yourselves if the theology you are learning is such that it could remain unchanged before and after Auschwitz. If this is the case, be on your guard.' (Metz is not proposing an absolute ban on every theological statement made before the *Shoah*, but is suggesting that we test them to determine if they express a supersessionist ideology *vis-à-vis* Jews and Judaism.) Metz's rule is to be taken seriously because of two features of traditional Christian theology. First, its claim that the church displaced the Israel of God in the covenant with God also signified that Jews were religiously out of business, that they should cease being Jews and become Christians. Second, this supersessionist ideology, which inspired and reinforced an anti-Jewish practice embodied in preaching, teaching, and identity-formation, was expressed in both legislation and acts of violence.

As Rosemary Ruether analyses the anti-Jewish ideology of the church, it turns upon two major themes: rejection/election and inferiority/superiority. According to the first, in rejecting Jesus Christ the Jews are rejected by God, and in accepting Jesus Christ the Gentiles are elected. The price of the election of the Gentiles is the rejection of the Jews. Gentile believers displace them in the economy of salvation and in God's favour. This motif pays a lot of attention to the 'two peoples' allegory, the elder/younger brother stories in the Bible, and the claim that Jewish history is a 'trail of crimes' culminating in deicide.

According to the second theme, everything about Jewish faith and life is inferior to Christian faith and life, which is, in all respects, better. Christian ethics, worship, and biblical interpretation improve upon Jewish 'law', worship, and exegesis. The Christian way of doing things 'fulfils' biblical promises, which Jews, being blind to the meaning of their own scriptures, misunderstand. Only Christians can rightly interpret the Hebrew Bible, which they make over into an 'Old Testament'. Jews fail to recognize that their covenant has been superseded and continue to pursue patently invalid modes of commitment to it.

David P. Efroymson's somewhat different analysis looks upon anti-Judaism as a double-edged model, a model of and a model for. First, it is a model of Judaism, on which Judaism is a system and Jews a people 'rejected by God, unfaithful to God, opposed to Christianity, and caught up in the crimes appropriate to their carnality, hardness, blindness and *vetustas* (obdurate commitment to what is past and gone, oldness).' Jews are a people of oldness, Judaism a religion of oldness. On the same model, Christians, by contrast, are 'a people and a system of newness, of fidelity, of spirituality, of moral vigour, and of universality'. . . If we ask what Christianity is, the anti-Jewish answer is: everything new, good, spiritual, and universal that the old, bad, carnal, and ethnocentric Jews can never be.

Every Christian doctrine can be and was interpreted through the lens of this anti-Jewish hermeneutic. God is the God who displaces Jews and replaces them with Christians. Christ is the mediator on behalf of Christians who cut a displacement deal with God. The church is the replacement people who displace Jews in the covenant. The covenant is a new covenant, replacing the old.

(Clark Williamson, *A Guest in the House of Israel: Post-Holocaust Church Theology*, Louisville, Kentucky, Westminster/John Knox Press, 1993, 3–5)

Post-*Shoah* Theology

Post-*Shoah* Theology takes as its task critical reflection on the historical anti-Jewish praxis of the church, and to liberate the church's witness and theology from its inherited *adversus Judaeos* ideology. Post-*Shoah* theology is a form of liberation theology in two senses: it criticizes the church's supersessionist ideology toward Jews and Judaism, an ideology that has sanctioned oppression, and it does so in solidarity with the victims of that oppression, namely, with Jews. It expresses this solidarity by the simple means of speaking up, within the church, on behalf of those who have no voice in the church. . .

Metz alerts us to a danger facing Christian theology: if we are not mindful of what we are doing, we may repeat after the *Shoah* the very theological attitudes that preceded it and made it possible. Like every hermeneutic of suspicion, a critique of the anti-Judaism of the Christian tradition has a negative and a constructive pole. If we accept Metz's warning, we will remove Christian anti-Judaism from our theology. But with what shall we replace it? The constructive pole of the hermeneutic comes into play in answer to this question. . .

First, we must finally learn a lesson that we neglected as long ago as the latter part of the first century—that Christians cannot give theological shape to their self-understanding as Christians without engaging in conversation with Jews. . . Second. . . we will accept Irving Greenberg's working principle: 'No statement, theological or otherwise, should be made that would not be credible in the presence of the burning children'[1]. . . Third, a Christian theology developed in conversation with Jews will lay heavy stress on faith as discipleship, as a way of life. The primary lesson we can learn from Jews and Judaism is the importance of faith as a way given us by God to walk in the world and through history and, paradoxically, as a way that we are responsible for determining while we walk it. . .

Christian theology has to go beyond the emphasis on historical consciousness and historicity as those were stressed in the Liberal and Neo-Reformation eras. It must move into the actual history of suffering and oppression, which it cannot do without facing the awful ways in which it has contributed to that history, particularly in the case of the praxis of the teaching and contempt for Jews and Judaism and the reality of the *Shoah*.

(Clark Williamson, *A Guest in the House of Israel: Post-Holocaust Church Theology*, Louisville, Kentucky, Westminster/John Knox Press, 1993, 7–14)

References

1. Irving Greenberg, 'Cloud of Smoke, Pillar of Fire' in Eva Fleischner (ed.), *Auschwitz: Beginning of a New Era?*, New York, KTAV, 1977, 25

Discussion

1. Should Christians liberate themselves from supersessionism?

2. Can anti-Judaism be removed from Christian theology without distorting the Christian past?

James F. Moore: Christianity after Auschwitz

James F. Moore has served as Professor of Theology at Luther Theological Seminary at the University of Chicago. In 'A Spectrum of Views: Traditional Christian Responses to the Holocaust', he provides a survey of Christian reactions to the challenges posed by the Nazi onslaught against the Jewish people. In his view, the task of reformulating Christian theology is an ongoing process.

The Challenge of the Holocaust

A group of Jews and Christians gathered June 3–6 1974 at the Cathedral of St. John the Divine in New York City, for the International Symposium on the Holocaust, on the theme 'Auschwitz: Beginning of a New Era?' During that meeting Irving Greenberg issued a challenge to both Christians and Jews, but especially to Christians: 'To put it another way: if the Holocaust challenges the fundamental religious claims of Christianity (and Judaism), then the penumbra of Christian complicity may challenge the credibility of Christianity to make these claims.'[1] Of course, this challenge was made at a time when dialogue between Christians and Jews had only begun to produce real fruit, so it could be accepted with both seriousness and the hope that together both Christians and Jews could find ways to respond adequately to such a challenge. Nevertheless, Greenberg's challenge is directed at Christians in such a way as to emphasize the obvious: that the Holocaust is an event that threatens the very core of Christian belief and life just as it threatened and continues to threaten the existence of world Jewry.

(James F. Moore, 'A Spectrum of Views: Traditional Christian Responses to the Holocaust', *Journal of Ecumenical Studies*, 25, 2, Spring, 1988, 212–213)

Christian Reactions

The fact is that Christians have responded to this challenge not in a single direction but with a full spectrum of proposals that focus not only on different issues of concern but also on different ways to understand the impact of Auschwitz upon Christian theology and

344

action. . . One quite common response is to conserve the tradition intact as a means for responding to the Holocaust. Those who hold such views are by no means merely conservative. Many who would otherwise be critical of tradition have proposed an approach like that of traditional conservatives, claiming that the complicity of Christians has come not from deficiencies in the tradition itself but from deficient understanding of the tradition or deficient Christian action. One of the most surprising traditional conservatives with respect to the Holocaust is Dorothee Sölle, the German liberation theologian, who otherwise seems quite liberal in her views. . .

Sölle's vision of the Christian tradition is one that has been untapped by those who use 'only the oppressive traditions of Christianity and not the liberating ones.' She clearly believes that the tradition holds the key for overcoming the great difficulties that our modern, post-Christian, secularized culture faces. Even if Sölle finds the miracles to be those that arise out of radical action, she is still ready to associate those radical changes with the action of Christ. This way of universalizing the place of Christ is a clue to her approach to any pressing theological problem, including how Christians deal with the impact of the Holocaust. . .

Another kind of response to the Holocaust is reflected in the work of Paul van Buren. He borrows the two-covenant approach to understand the relationship between Judaism and Christianity and, thus, aims to conserve two covenant traditions that are obviously closely related. He can speak of the people of God or, more often, the Israel of God, and he can speak of God's gentile church. He can fully recognize the covenant of God with Israel through Sinai, and he can speak of the new revelation that the covenant be extended to the gentiles. Though this position is hardly new, van Buren is clearly proposing a different approach than mere orthodoxy. The relationship between Judaism and Christianity, for van Buren, is unbreakable; therefore, any reading of Christianity that would break the relationship and, thereby, discount the validity of Judaism would be a distortion of Christianity. . .

A third response to the Holocaust is represented by the work of David Tracy. His position stands in respectful relation to the view offered by Arthur A. Cohen; he wrote:

Arthur Cohen's expression for that event—the *tremendum*—seems to me to capture the religious and theological dimensions of that event itself. The event is tremendous in the original meaning of that word—earthshaking and frightening. The event is tremendous in the religious meaning of the word—awesome, incomprehensible, frightening, and world shattering. The Holocaust, in Catholic theological terms, discloses the classic countersign of our age. That negative countersign changes the optimistic, secure, consoling signs of the times in our age into signs of radical ambiguity. . . [2]

This unavoidable ambiguity leads thinkers like Tracy to a revisionist theology that means at least two things. First, no theology that calls itself Christian in a post-Holocaust world can make confident truth-claims in the same way as they were made previously. That is, Christians cannot be genuine to their own tradition if they continue to make exclusive claims about the truth they confess. Second, no genuine Christian theology can be constructed post-Holocaust that is not constructed from within the Jewish–Christian conversation. . .

There are some who build from a position like Tracy's but aim to go much further in their revising. Rosemary Radford Ruether has consistently suggested a theological response to the Holocaust that provides a blueprint not only for revising Christian theology but also for restructuring that theology. . . In *Faith and Fratricide*, she wrote: 'Our theological critique of Christian anti-Judaism, therefore, must turn to what was also the other side of anti-Judaism, namely Christology.'[3] In other words a critique of pre-Holocaust Christian theology starts at the centre with the very heart of that theology. . . Ruether's position clearly differs from that of Tracy in that she moves beyond the claim of ambiguity to the claim that there is error in the tradition. A genuine Christian post-Holocaust theology, then, must both face the errors and eliminate them. . .

Two thinkers stand out as primary examples of such an effort to take Greenberg seriously—A. Roy Eckardt and Franklin H. Littell. . . Littell has written of the need for Christians to take more seriously the presence of the State of Israel as an important part of contemporary Judaism's effort to respond to the Holocaust. Above all, he wishes to encourage Christians to recognize the biblical legitimacy of a Jewish claim to the land. . . Christians must find a place for a post-Christian claim to the land of Israel for Jews, and this place must be theologically grounded as a part of God's past promises and future messianic plan. . .

Like Littell, Eckardt develops a post-Holocaust theology that maintains the use of some traditional Christian language but fills that language with irony. The language can no longer be univocal in meaning but is responsible theological language only when both Jews and Christians, in their quite distinct ways, can be held together by the language. . . Eckardt's resolution is far more radical that that of Littell. While he approaches traditional language in much the same way as Littell (and Tracy, for that matter), Eckardt is ready to follow Ruether's style in restructing Christian theology and theological terms.

(James F. Moore, 'A Spectrum of Views: Traditional Christian Responses to the Holocaust', *Journal of Ecumenical Studies*, 25, 2, Spring, 1988, 214–223)

References

1. Irving Greenberg, 'Cloud of Smoke, Pillar of Fire: Judaism, Christianity and Modernity after the Holocaust' in Eva Fleischner (ed.), *Auschwitz: Beginning of a New Era?*, New York, KTAV, 1977, 13
2. David Tracy, 'Religious Values after the Holocaust: A Catholic View', in Abraham J. Peck (ed.), *Jews and Christians after the Holocaust*, Philadelphia, Fortress, 1982, 92
3. Rosemary Radford Ruether, *Faith and Fratricide*, New York, Seabury Press, 1974, 246

Discussion

1. Should Christian theology be constructed from within the Jewish–Christian conversation?
2. Are Christians under an obligation to find a place for the Jewish post-Holocaust claim to the land of Israel?

Yosef Hayim Yerushalmi: Christianity and Nazi Anti-Semitism

Yosef Hayim Yerushalmi has served as Salo Wittmayer Baron Professor of Jewish History, Culture and Society at Columbia University, New York City. In 'Response to Rosemary Radford Ruether' in Auschwitz: Beginning of a New Era?, *he disputes Ruether's view that Nazi anti-Semitism is a modern transformation of Christian contempt for Jews and Judaism. Despite the church's hostility toward Jewry, it never sought to eradicate the entire Jewish community. Further, Yerushalmi argues that a reformation of Christian theology is not necessary for a positive Jewish–Christian encounter.*

Modern Anti-Semitism

Coming to modern times, Rosemary Ruether states that modern anti-

Semitism is both a continuation and a transformation of the medieval theological and economic scapegoating of the Jews. Few, I think, would deny that medieval anti-Semitism survives into the modern age both in its original and in certain secularized forms, and that there is a continuum between the two. The crucial word is 'transformation,' and it is this which raises more complex questions.

Is modern anti-Semitism merely a metamorphosed medieval Christian anti-Semitism? Through what conduits and channels did the transformation occur? If, as been proposed by some, it was through the French Enlightenment, then one must obviously take into account its non-Christian sources as well. But this is not the time to discuss such purely historical matters. More important, what is the nature of the transformation itself, and what are the consequences thereof? What happens along the way in the shift from religious to secular, theological to racial, anti-Semitism? Here, it seems to me, Ruether's formulation explains little and glosses over much.

The issue is physical extermination. Not reprobation, discrimination, or any variety of opprobrium, but—genocide. From Rosemary Ruether we gather that genocide against the Jews was an inexorable consequence of Christian theological teaching. I do not think that is quite the case. If it were, genocide should have come upon the Jews in the Middle Ages. By this I do not in any way intend to exonerate the church of its real and palpable guilt. There is no question but that Christian anti-Semitism through the ages helped create the climate and mentality in which genocide, once conceived, could be achieved with little or no opposition. But even if we grant that Christian teaching was a necessary cause leading to the Holocaust, it was surely not a sufficient one. The crucial problem in the shift from medieval to modern anti-Semitism is that while the Christian tradition of 'reprobation' continued into the modern era, the Christian tradition of 'preservation' fell by the wayside and was no longer operative. To state only that modern anti-Semitism is a 'transformed' medieval anti-Semitism is to skirt this central issue. Surely there must be some significance in the fact that the Holocaust took place in our secular century, and not in the Middle Ages. Moreover, medieval anti-Jewish massacres were the work of the mob and the rabble. State-inspired pogroms of the type that took place in Czarist Russia, state-instigated genocide of the Nazi type—these are entirely modern phenomena.

(Yosef Hayim Yerushalmi, 'Response to Rosemary Radford Ruether' in Eva Fleischner (ed.), *Auschwitz: Beginning of a New Era?*, New York, KTAV, 1977, 102–103)

Jewish–Christian Encounter

If the entire theological and historical tradition forged by Christianity is one of anti-Semitism, then the only hope lies in the radical erosion of Christianity itself. It would mean that in order to achieve a more positive relationship to Jews and Judaism Christians must, in effect, repudiate their entire heritage. But that, in turn, does not impress me as a very realistic expectation. It is partly for that reason that I have felt it important to argue that the historical record is more varied and complex than can be anticipated from this account.

Rosemary Ruether calls. . . for a 'massive repentance.' I am not certain that this is what is required. There is something about the phrase that worries me. Knowledge and acknowledgement of what has been done to the Jews in the name of the crucified Messiah, yes. But no more. I do not welcome a collective *mea culpa* from Christendom. It tends toward a kind of masochism, behind which may lurk an eventual sadism. I do not want Christians to brood on the guilt of their forebears and to keep apologizing for it. I do not want to encounter Christians as confessor and penitent. . .

To Christians generally I should like to say: I hope that the condition for our dialogue is not our mutual secularization (though at times it certainly seems so). You do not have to repudiate everything in the Christian past concerning the Jews. Much of the record is dark. There were also some patches of light. There was 'reprobation' and there was 'preservation', and each has to be understood in its historical context. It is up to you to choose that with which you will identify.

(Yosef Hayim Yerushalmi, 'Response to Rosemary Radford Ruether' in Eva Fleischner (ed.), *Auschwitz: Beginning of a New Era?*, New York, KTAV, 1977, 106–107)

Discussion

1. Did Christian teaching about the Jews provide the basis for Nazi anti-Semitism?
2. Should the Holocaust compel Christians to repudiate the Christian heritage?

Thomas J.J. Altizer: The Holocaust and God's Absence

Thomas J.J. Altizer has served as Professor at Emory University, Georgia and at the State University of New York. In 'The Death of God and the Holocaust', he argues that Christian thought must undergo a major change in light of the tragedy of the Holocaust.

The Impact of the Holocaust

Theologically, it would appear to be impossible to deny that the Holocaust is an apocalyptic event, so that a theological acceptance of the Holocaust would appear to demand an apocalyptic theology. But Christian theology has been an apocalyptic theology only in its beginning in Paul and in its expressions in the most radical or sectarian forms of Christianity. The great body of Christian theology has not only been non-apocalyptic but anti-apocalyptic, and never more so than in the twentieth century, despite the fact that our world is so clearly an apocalyptic world, as above all manifest in the Holocaust itself. So it is that the Holocaust was a cataclysmic even for Christian theology, not only assaulting the doctrine of providence, but more deeply, assaulting the deepest grounds of all established theology. This was a crisis far deeper than the crisis known by the 'crisis theology' following World War I; for it was a deep negation of theology itself, and many of its most astute critics understood the death of God theology as a consequence of the end of society and culture as a whole, and if the death of God theology generated a public attention and furore unknown in our theological past, this simply astounds our younger religious scholars.

(Thomas J.J. Altizer, 'The Holocaust and the Theology of the Death of God' in Stephen R. Haynes and John K. Roth (eds), *The Death of God Movement and the Holocaust*, Westport, Connecticut, Greenwood Press, 1999, 20)

Radical Theology and the Holocaust

A death of God theology first openly appears in America, and while the deepest thinking about the death of God and the deepest imaginative enactments of the death of God have occurred in Europe, it is only in America that theology itself has affirmed the death of God. But this theology was the first Christian theology that was not only a response to the Holocaust but grounded itself in the ultimacy of a Holocaust that had ended every trace of a just or beneficent providence. While it is true that there are few references to the Holocaust in the Christian death of God theological writing in the 1960s, there are also few references here to any historical events, and whereas an earlier Christian theological writing could know history as the arena of revelation and salvation itself, now this becomes impossible, and impossible because history now first appears to the modern theologian as an arena of darkness and horror, and of ultimate and final horror and darkness. Although this may well not be due to the Holocaust alone, it is the Holocaust alone that openly embodies such horror, and we may presume that the Holocaust was a generating cause of the death of God theologies, as it certainly was so for this theologian.

It is not insignificant that it was then Richard Rubenstein who called for the most passionate theological response, and perhaps most so in his reversal or inversion of the doctrine of providence, which he passionately insisted was inevitable as a consequence of the Holocaust. Subsequently many or most theologians have simply bracketed or erased the doctrine of providence, but that is clearly simply a failure of theological thinking, or only a rhetorical retreat with no substantial theological meaning. The simple truth is that it is no longer possible to affirm a providential God unless one affirms that God wills or effects ultimate evil, and this is clearly a consequence of the Holocaust.

(Thomas J.J. Altizer, 'The Holocaust and the Theology of the Death of God' in Stephen R. Haynes and John K. Roth (eds), *The Death of God Movement and the Holocaust*, Westport, Connecticut, Greenwood Press, 1999, 19)

Contemporary Theology

Is a theology possible that is not at bottom an erasure of the Holocaust? Perhaps so, if a theology without God is a genuine possibility, or a theology wholly and finally distant from everything that our history has known and affirmed as God. The deep resurgence of Gnosticism in our world is not divorced from this situation, and just as the original advent of Gnosticism was a consequence of the ending of the ancient world, a new advent of Gnosticism may well be a consequence of the ending of the modern world. But Christianity itself was made possible by the ending of the ancient world, and if ancient Gnosticism itself was an expression of Christianity, our new Gnosticism may well be an expression of Christianity, and one even present in a newly orthodox and ultimately sectarian Christianity. This is the only Christianity that is manifestly or openly present today, and if it is a consequence of a postmodernity inaugurated by the Holocaust itself, then the Holocaust may well be the germinating origin of our world, but one before which we will be nameless if we cannot name the Holocaust. And if we must name the Holocaust, then we must name it theologically, and name it theologically by speaking of God and by speaking of that dead and alien God who is the God of the Holocaust, or the only God who can be named in the wake of the Holocaust.

(Thomas J.J. Altizer, 'The Holocaust and the Theology of the Death of God' in Stephen R. Haynes and John K. Roth (eds), *The Death of God Movement and the Holocaust*, Westport, Connecticut, Greenwood Press, 1999, 22)

Discussion

1. Does the Holocaust require Christians to abandon the traditional view of God?
2. Do the events of the Nazi era call for a radical reformulation of Christian theology?

William Hamilton: The Holocaust and Radical Theology

In 'Genocide and the Death of God', William Hamilton, who has served as Chairman of Historical Theology at Colgate Rochester Divinity School, argues that radical theology has an immeasurably important task in confronting the religious issues raised by the Nazi regime.

Christian Theology and the Holocaust

The Holocaust was a genocide committed by pagans, non-Christians, and Christians against Jews (and others) on soil fertilized by Christianity. One effect of Daniel Goldhagen's study is surely to Christianize even more indelibly the perpetrators. His 'ordinary Germans' are ordinary Christian Germans. Wiesel has noted that obvious fact: 'All the killers were Christians. . . The Nazi system. . . had its roots deep in a tradition that prophesied it, prepared for it, and brought it to maturity. That tradition was inseparable from the past of Christian, civilized Europe'. . .

It will not be easy for Americans to admit that monotheism has become a great danger. It was only yesterday. . . that we managed to relinquish the idea that we were the redeemer nation, chosen or almost chosen on God's side and therefore invulnerable... and innocent... What is there about the claim to possess one God that makes men and women dangerous? Perhaps the cry of Nietzsche suggests the beginning of an answer: 'If there were gods, how could I endure not to be a god!' To claim to possess one of the gods of monotheism is more a moral than an intellectual defect. Possession entails a claim to uniqueness, conferring inferiority on all who do not similarly possess. Saying 'yes' to your God not only distinguishes you from those who say 'no', it requires you to say 'no' to the 'no-sayers'. Those I negate I am bound to deny, to deny their right to deny my affirmation, and finally, to deny their right to be. To possess God is to possess the most powerful instrument of self-aproval our times have devised, and this mirror can turn quickly into a sword of judgment. The Christian God appears to be turning his advocates into self-righteous and dangerous sinners and, ultimately, into killers...

The bridge between monotheism and killing is a long, twisting, and largely unexplored one. It cannot be negotiated in a day. Perhaps it can only be studied in monographic bits and pieces. I propose to conclude my meditation on radical theology and genocide by a brief exegetical... exercise...

19. Surely thou wilt slay the wicked, O God!
Depart from me, therefore, ye bloody men!
20. For they speak against thee wickedly,
And thine enemies take thy name in vain.
21. Do I not hate them, O Yahweh, that hate thee?
And am I not grieved with those that rise up against thee?
22. I hate them with perfect hatred;
I count them mine own enemies. . . .

When you believe that you possess God and deserve to, when you believe that God has an infinite number of very kindly thoughts about you, then this is the kind of thing you may find yourself saying. The wicked, the enemies are those who take God's name in vain, or who have a different god, or none. God is asked to slay such dissenters, and the psalmist proudly boasts about the splendid greatness of his hatred of the haters of God. And in that hatred, he clearly believes he is doing God's work.

Traditional exegetes have sometimes tried to escape from the problems that verses 19 through 22 (Psalm 139) present. Perhaps they were a late scribal addition, or perhaps they dropped into this place from another psalm. But we have no textual grounds for excision. They belong and they need to be explained.

In the psalm's final verses:

> 23. Search me, O God, and know my heart;
> Try me, and know my doubts;
> 24. And see if there be any wicked way in me,
> And lead me in the way everlasting!

we get a slight sense that the psalmist may be a little ashamed of his outburst just before. 'See if there be any wicked way'! Indeed. He seems almost to admit it, and to be sorry. It makes a modestly hopeful conclusion to a breathtaking and tormented poem.

(William Hamilton, 'Genocide and the Death of God' in Stephen R. Haynes and John K. Roth (eds), *The Death of God Movement and the Holocaust*, Westport, Connecticut, Greenwood Press, 1999, 25–30)

Discussion

1. Is there a connection between Christianity and the murder of innocent victims?
2. Does the belief in absolute truth lead to intolerance of others?

CHAPTER SIXTEEN

Jewish–Christian Dialogue

Edward Kessler: The Holocaust and Jewish–Christian Dialogue

Edward Kessler has served as Executive Director of the Centre for Jewish–Christian Relations at Cambridge. In 'The Future of Jewish–Christian Relations', he addresses the question of whether the Holocaust on its own can serve as the basis for Jewish–Christian dialogue. Although he recognizes the significance of the Shoah in the life of the Jewish nation, he argues that neither the destruction of six million Jews under the Nazis nor the emergence of the Jewish state can alone provide a basis for a fruitful encounter between Christians and Jews.

The *Shoah* and Jewish–Christian Relations

Although it is true that a small number of outstanding Jews and Christians, such as Montefiore and Parkes in the UK, paved the way in the first half of the twentieth century, these figures were the exception to the rule. It was the *Shoah*, first and foremost, which spurred an intense desire amongst many Christians and Jews to learn about the history, theology, and other aspects of Jewish–Christian relations.

For Christians, the *Shoah* resulted in an awareness of the immensity of the burden of guilt which the Church carried not only for its general silence, with some noble exceptions, during 1933–45, but also because of the 'teaching of contempt' towards Jews and Judaism which it carried on for so many centuries. As Jules Isaac showed immediately after the war, it was this that sowed the seeds of hatred and made it so easy for Hitler to use anti-Semitism as a political weapon. Although no-one would deny that Nazism was opposed to Christianity, it is well known that Hitler often justified his his anti-Semitism with reference to the Church and Christian attitudes towards Judaism.

As a result of the soul-searching which took place after 1945, many Christians began the painful process of re-examining the sources of the teaching of contempt and repudiating them. Consequently, many Christian institutions, most notably the Vatican, the World Council of Churches, and certain Protestant denominations have issued declarations against the perpetuation of this teaching.

The Holocaust not only caused Christianity to reassess its relationship with Judaism but also stirred greater Jewish interest in Christianity. As Jonathan Sacks explained, 'today we meet and talk together because we must; because we have considered the alternative and seen where it ends and we are shocked to the core by what we have seen.'[1] Many Jews agreed with Fackenheim's famous declaration that the *Shoah* resulted in a new commandment, the 614th, which stressed that it was incumbent upon Jews to survive after the *Shoah*. One remained a Jew so as not to provide Hitler a posthumous victory. As a result, Jewish identity became *Shoah*-centred.

Indeed, such was the centrality of the *Shoah* to Jewish life that a new commemoration entered the Jewish calendar on 27th Nissan—*Yom ha-Shoah*. It is worth noting that a religious commemoration was initially rejected by many Jews, not least Israeli Jews such as Ben Gurion to whom the *Shoah* was a negative model. Nevertheless, by the late 1950s *Yom ha-Shoah* had become an accepted part of the Jewish calendar to all but a very small group of ultra-orthodox Jews.

As a result of the centrality of the *Shoah* in Judaism and Christianity, Jewish–Christian dialogue itself became *Shoah*-centred. Dialogue often consisted of an attempt to educate Christians about Judaism in order to prevent or, at the very least, to reduce Christian anti-Semitism. Thus, both Jews and Christians became involved in Jewish–Christian dialogue on account of defensive factors: to stop the possibility of anti-Semitism from breaking out in churches in the future.

Consequently, many of the studies which were published on Jewish–Christian relations examined, in particular, Christian anti-Semitism. A perusal of any recommended reading list in the field of Jewish–Christian relations would reveal a majority of works which focus on anti-Semitism. This tendency was reinforced by the publication of a number of key works which placed as their focus of study Christian anti-Semitism. These works included institutional publications such as *Nostra Aetate* and individual studies such as Ruether's *Faith and Fratricide*. The agenda of Jewish–Christian dialogue was influenced by such works.

(Edward Kessler, 'The Future of Jewish–Christian Relations' in Dan Cohn-Sherbok (ed.), *The Future of Jewish–Christian Dialogue*, Lewiston, New York, Edwin Mellen, 1999, 150–152)

The *Shoah*, Israel, and Jewish–Christian Relations

The question I would now like to consider is what is 'the meaning of our relationship in the future.' To be sure, for many people, the *Shoah* will continue to provide an adequate justification for dialogue. No-one can deny the importance of fighting ignorance and prejudice, wherever it is found. However, will the *Shoah* alone provide the basis for Jewish–Christian dialogue in the future? Is it possible that the *Shoah* will suffer the same fate as World War I, i.e. remain a pivotal event to those who suffered during the years of war, as well as to their children, but for some of the grandchildren and the following generations, became one more terrible incident of history which will be studied in books and viewed in newsreels? In sum, will the *Shoah*, on its own, provide the cornerstone for Jewish–Christian relations.

What about the State of Israel? After fifty years of perilous existence, Israel is no longer a recent creation. After the large *aliyah* from the former Soviet Union, Israel no longer attracts significant numbers of Jewish immigrants. In addition, its own inter-faith activities are directed more toward the Arab Islamic communities than the Christian. As the actions of the State of Israel cause more friction within the Jewish communities of the world (as well as being the subject of differing views within Christianity), will Israel remain the justification for Jewish–Christian dialogue? Clearly, the State of Israel by its very geographical location, as well as its contribution over the last fifty years, will remain a significant factor in Jewish–Christian dialogue. However, whether on its own, Israel can provide the cornerstone for Jewish–Christian relations in the future is open to doubt. I would suggest that although both the *Shoah* and the State of Israel will continue to be pillars of Jewish–Christian dialogue in the future, new subjects will need to be explored.

(Edward Kessler, 'The Future of Jewish–Christian Relations' in Dan Cohn-Sherbok (ed.), *The Future of Jewish-Christian Dialogue*, Lewiston, New York, Edwin Mellen, 1999, 153–154)

References

1. Helen Fry (ed.), *Jewish–Christian Dialogue: A Reader*, Exeter, University of Exeter Press, 1996, xi

Discussion

1. Should Jewish-Christian dialogue be *Shoah*-centred?
2. Is Israel the justification for Jewish–Christian dialogue?

Katharine T. Hargrove: Contemporary Holocaust Theology

Katharine T. Hargrove has served as Professor of Theology at Manhattan College in Purchase, New York. In Seeds of Reconciliation, *she argues that Christians today must seriously contemplate the conclusions reached by Jewish Holocaust theologians if they are to engage in fruitful Jewish–Christian dialogue.*

Christians, Jews and the Holocaust

Facing Auschwitz some years ago, a good many Christians would have been content to discuss the facts of the Hitlerian outrage in the clinical atmosphere of the academicians. Not so today. The pressures of the current situation with its renewed threats of genocide preclude this kind of escapism. That is why we are listening so intently to 'The Holocaust Theologians', trying to find in them viable answers to what is happening on the contemporary scene.

Even though Jacob Neusner holds that 'Judaic theologians ill-serve the faithful' when they claim Auschwitz marks a 'turning' as in Rubenstein's case, or a 'new beginning' as in Fackenheim's, it is imperative for the *goyim* today to grasp their message. Keyword or not, Auschwitz does conjure up the lurid hatred that is anti-Semitism. For those of us who stand outside the Jewish tradition, the shock of even a vicarious insight into human decadence can be therapeutic. Whatever Neusner regards as harmful in the teaching of these men as they present the religious dimensions of the Final Solution, it is necessary to heed what they have to tell us. Otherwise, it will be impossible for us on our part to make the changes called for in our tradition which permitted the spawning of such evil.

From personal knowledge of Hitlerian depravity, Emil Fackenheim makes his response to Auschwitz problematic. While he recoils from the memory of the horrors he witnessed, the tragedies through which he lived, he emphasizes the truth as he sees it now, that 'the survivor is gradually becoming the paradigm of the entire Jewish people.'[1] If we read him correctly, then we have to come to grips with the connection he makes between the destruction of European Jewry and the consequent collective, enduring witness of the State of Israel. '*Am Yisrael Chai*', he assures us; yes, the people of Israel live because the model of Israel's heroism was forged in the fires of the death camps.

As a survivor, Fackenheim pleads with every human being to confront the future with unswerving trust in the abiding faithfulness of God. . . Given the religious posture of American Jewry before and after World War II, Neusner may unwittingly be agreeing with Fackenheim that one of the many outcomes of the massacre of Jewish innocents has been a new beginning. . . One example among many of this newness can be found in a sermon by Eugene Borowitz entitled 'Auschwitz and the Death of God'. Almost as if reacting to Fackenheim's 'Voice of Auschwitz', he asks:

> The Jews have known God from their history but what shall we say of his presence in Jewish history in recent years? Where was he when Hitler did what no man should ever do? Why did he not reveal himself to a supplicating, forsaken people who might have died in triumph if only they could have been certain that they died in his name?[2]

These are not the timeworn echoes of a disillusioned Elie Wiesel or the corroding bitterness of an afflicted Wdowinski. They are rather the pregnant beauty of faith that matures into hope because:

> The Jewish people knows that history is more than the house of bondage. We came into being as a people in Egypt and pledged ourselves to God at Sinai so that the message of redemption, dim and obscure as it may be in one era and another, will never be forgotten among men. As long as we are in history, faithful to him, men cannot ignore God.[3]

(Katharine T. Hargrove (ed.) *Seeds of Reconciliation*, North Richland Hills, Texas, Bibal Press, 1996, 193–196)

Reconstructing the Jewish Tradition

Rubenstein sounds a totally different note from either Fackenheim or Borowitz. For him, there is no commanding voice issuing from the gas chambers. Neither apparently is there any upsurge of prayer like that with which Borowitz ends his exhortation: 'Forgive us, Lord, for having failed thee again and again, and grant us the courage to testify of thee in all our ways, Amen.' Nevertheless, despite charges levelled against him as a negativist, a nihilist, he has his own prophetic thrust:

> Traditional Jewish theology maintains that God is the ultimate, omnipotent actor in the historical drama. It has interpreted every major catastrophe in Jewish history as God's punishment of a sinful Israel. I fail to see how this position can be maintained without regarding Hitler and the SS as instruments of God's will. The agony of European Jewry cannot be likened to the testing of Job. To see any purpose in the death camps, the traditional believer is forced to regard the most demonic, inhuman explosion in all history as a meaningful expression of God's purposes. The idea is simply too obscene for me to accept. . . [4]

Given a basic difference in theological rationale, Fackenheim takes Rubenstein to task on the grounds that the latter's rejection of divine providence is undermining Jewish unity at this critical juncture of its development. Rubenstein, for his part, contends that nowhere in Fackenheim's works can he discover any effectual attempt to cope with the implications in the truism that 'six million dead cannot simply be shoved under a rug'.

(Katharine T. Hargrove (ed.) *Seeds of Reconciliation*, North Richland Hills, Texas, Bibal Press, 1996, 196–197)

Jews and Christians

Michael Wyschogrod vigorously endorses this approach to the Judeao-Christian dialogue today. Whatever the charges against the Church for her silence and her non-involvement, he makes it clear that he feels safer in a Christian than in a pagan world. Enduring like all of us the syndrome of secularization in our decade, he has no illusions about the possibility of nuclear warfare. But convinced that 'the voice of the prophet is stronger than the voice of the concentration camp'; he wants us all, no matter what our tradition, to relearn the truth about Israel's suffering.

His argument is that throughout the millennia of her existence, although agony has often been the lot of his people, this has never touched the heart of Judaism. Sorrow, in the *siddur*, is relegated to 'minor feast days'. The core of Jewish belief has always been and must remain, despite the Holocaust, the gladsome proclamation of Passover, *Hanukkah, Purim*. . .

The Holocaust is peripheral to Judaism? Accustomed as we have been to the enormity of Hitler's hatred, maybe this insistence of Wyschogrod's will recall two fundamental points of clarification. The first is that the Holocaust was 'a sacrifice which is burnt completely and therefore considered of particular holiness.[5] The second is that 'the burnt offering was the only offering accepted from non-Jews.' Here indeed is a strange consolation for us, an unequivocal confirmation that Wyschogrod is, in his own way, taking his place in the classical tradition of biblical Judaism. . .

Neusner reveals the all-embracing quality of that loving kindness which resembles a seed of eternity in the human heart. While he envisages Christianity today as

> entering a time of exile, it need not fear greatly, if Christians are prepared to affirm their faith through faith. . . As Christianity enters the Jewish situation, it need not, therefore, worry for its future. *Golah* is not a situation to be chosen, but to be accepted at the hand of God as a test of faith and an opportunity for regeneration and purification. We did not choose to go into exile, any more than the Christian would choose to abandon the world. Having gone into exile, having lost the world, Jew and Christian alike may uncover new resources of conviction, new potentialities for sanctity, than they knew they had.[6]

(Katharine T. Hargrove (ed.) *Seeds of Reconciliation*, North Richland Hills, Texas, Bibal Press, 1996, 199–200)

References

1. Emil Fackenheim in Jacob Neusner (ed.), *Understanding Jewish Theology*, New York, KTAV, 1973, 172
2. Eugene Borowitz, *How Can a Jew Speak of Faith Today?*, Philadelphia, Westminster Press, 1969, 33
3. Ibid., 34
4. Richard Rubenstein in Jacob Neusner, op. cit., 185
5. Neusner, op. cit., 190
6. Neusner, op. cit., 264

Discussion

1. Does Auschwitz inaugurate a new beginning?
2. Is the Holocaust peripheral to Judaism?

Isabel Wollaston: Christian Theology and the Holocaust

Isabel Wollaston has served as a lecturer in theology at the University of Birmingham. In 'Responses to Anti-Judaism and Anti-Semitism in Contemporary Christian-Jewish relations', she discusses a range of Christian responses to the the Holocaust. In her view, there are serious dangers confronting those theologians who feel overwhelming guilt over Christian responsibility for the horrors of the Nazi regime. In particular, she maintains that such attitudes can stifle legitimate criticism of Israeli policy.

The Holocaust and Christian Theology

Holocaust theologians agree that there is a need for a thoroughgoing critique of Christian theology. They differ over whether the problem lies with the Christian gospel *per se* or with institutional and dogmatic embodiments of it. Thus, on the one hand, Rosemary Radford Ruether argues that 'the antisemitic heritage of Christian civilization is neither accidental nor a peripheral element. . . Anti-Judaism in Western civilization springs, at its root, from Christian anti-Judaism.'[1] This theological anti-Judaism is rooted in the core dogmatic claims of classical Christianity, primarily christology: 'theologically, anti-Judaism developed as the left hand of christology. Anti-Judaism was the negative side of the Christian affirmation that Jesus was the Christ.' Thus, it can only be removed if we revise and relativize core Christian teachings, particularly those concerning the absolute nature of the Christ event. For Ruether, it is impossible to combine absolute claims concerning Christ with a repudiation of Christian anti-Judaism. She suggests that such absolute claims inevitably give rise to supersessionism and triumphalism. On the other hand, Franklin Littell adopts a slightly different approach. He agrees with Ruether to a considerable extent in referring to 'the red thread that ties a Justin Martyr or a Chrysostom to Auschwitz and Treblinka.'[2] In addition, he argues that 'the cornerstone of Christian Anti-Semitism is the superseding or displacement myth, which already rings with the genocidal note.' However, he differs from Ruether in defining supersessionism as 'false teaching' and 'wholesale apostasy.' Such 'false teaching' characterized the actions and theology of the empowered church, from the time of Constantine onwards, and is rooted in the success of the mission to the Gentiles. However, contra Ruether, Littell does not believe that anti-

Judaism and anti-Semitism *per se* are to be found in the New Testament: 'to construct a theological Anti-Semitism, it has been necessary to wrench the proof texts and to write into them something not there.'

Despite such variations, Christian Holocaust theology is characterized by broad common concerns, both negative and positive, destructive and constructive. It is destructive in its determination to critique Christianity and purge Christianity. Most Holocaust theologians identify this purged Christianity with the values embodied in the teaching of Jesus and some strands of the early Church (as in Littell). It is countercultural and prophetic, egalitarian and non-oppressive. From many, it takes the form of a rediscovery of the 'Jewish roots' of Christianity. Johann Baptist Metz talks of messianic Christianity (as opposed to bourgeois, Constantinian Christianity). Rosemary Radford Ruether identifies a 'prophetic liberating tradition.' Elisabeth Schüssler Fiorenza speaks of a 'discipleship of equals', and so on. According to such analyses, these forms of Christianity were in constant tension with a rapidly emerging Constantinian Christianity, and were soon marginalized and repressed. . . .We are assured that such a purged, reconstructed Christianity will look and act very differently from its Constantinian rival, particularly in its understanding of christology, authority, scripture, and canon, and the relationship of church and state.

(Isabel Wollaston, 'Responses to Anti-Judaism and Anti-Semitism in Contemporary Christian–Jewish Relations' in Dan Cohn-Sherbok (ed.), *The Future of Jewish–Christian Dialogue*, Lewiston, New York, Edwin Mellen, 1999, 33–35)

Christian Guilt and the Holocaust

In the context of Christian–Jewish dialogue and Holocaust theology, much emphasis has been placed, particularly in Christian discourse, on the need for repentance and forgiveness. However, can such an emphasis upon Christian guilt serve to silence the Christian partner in dialogue, save for expressions of guilt, remorse and intra-Christian discussions about post-Holocaust theology? Is this preoccupation with guilt healthy? Yerushalmi acknowledges that 'a forthright repudiation of anti-Jewish teachings, both in theory and in school curricula, would certainly help clear the air.'[3] However, he then suggests that this is all that can—and should—be required: 'Knowledge and acknowledgement of what has been done to the Jews in the name of a crucified Messiah, yes. But no more. I do not welcome a collective *mea culpa* from Christendom. It tends towards a kind of masochism, behind which may lurk an eventual sadism. I do not want Christians to brood on the guilt of their forebearers and to keep apologizing for it.'. . . There is a growing concern over the ideological uses to which the Holocaust can be put. In this context, our concern is with the ways in which Christian guilt can be utilized. In certain circumstances, it can serve to undermine the legitimacy of any Christian critiques of the policies of the State of Israel.

(Isabel Wollaston, 'Responses to Anti-Judaism and Anti-Semitism in Contemporary Christian–Jewish Relations' in Dan Cohn-Sherbok (ed.), *The Future of Jewish–Christian Dialogue*, Lewiston, New York, Edwin Mellen, 1999, 36)

References

1. Rosemary Radford Ruether, *To Change the World*, London, SCM Press, 1981, 31
2. Franklin Littell, *The Crucifixion of the Jews*, Mercer University Press, 1986, 1–2
3. Yosef Yerushalmi, 'Response to Rosemary Radford Ruether', in Eva Fleischner (ed.), *Auschwitz: Beginning of a New Era?*, New York, KTAV, 1977, 105

Discussion

1. Is Holocaust theology destructive or constructive with regard to Christian teaching?
2. Is Christian guilt a constructive or destructive element in Jewish–Christian discussion?

Randall Falk: The Holocaust, Jews and Christians

Randall Falk has served as Rabbi Emeritus of Congregation Ohabei Shalom in Nashville. In Jews and Christians, *he discusses Hitler's attitude toward the Jews. In his view, despite the heroic actions of some Christians during the war, the Christian community is culpable for the crimes inflicted against the Jewish people.*

Hitler and the Jews

The most horrendous of all crimes against the Jews, however, was perpetrated by the Nazi Party under the leadership of Adolf Hitler, and with the support of some prominent Christian theologians and clergymen in Germany in the third decade of the twentieth century.

One of the major issues on which Hitler rode to power was his assertion that Jews were responsible for the economic collapse of Germany at the end of the First World War. His solution to the financial bankruptcy of Germany was to confiscate Jewish property and then to make Germany '*Judenrein*'. The German people, with a long history of anti-Semitism, responded with great enthusiasm to Hitler's campaign against the Jews. Almost immediately, upon his ascension to power, Hitler deprived the Jews of basic civil and human rights. Jews were deprived of their means of a livelihood, educational opportunities for Jewish children were limited and finally eliminated, and even respected professionals in every field found their activities severely curtailed. These economic and political disabilities were followed by the infamous *Kristallnacht*, when synagogues throughout Germany were looted and destroyed. Then came the concentration camps and finally gas chambers in Germany and Poland. Six million Jews lost their lives in these bestial places of torture and mass murder. Six million other human beings—Catholics, Protestant protesters, gypsies, labour leaders, and other dissidents—also were murdered. It was only the Jews, however, who were singled out for annihilation for no other reason than that they were Jews. No age in human history has ever experienced such massive genocide. . .

How could this happen in civilized, cultured nations in the twentieth century? Many sociologists, psychologists, and historians have sought to find an answer. In the play *The Deputy*, Rolf Hochhuth's thesis is that Pope Pius XII could have thwarted Hitler's war against the Jews by exerting his influence and using his good efforts on their behalf. Certainly the pope could have been a more positive force in opposing fascism. And though we shall always be grateful for the hundreds of Jews, especially children, who did survive, hidden in convents and monasteries at great risk to the host priests and nuns, historians will not let us forget that had not the official Catholic Church equivocated at crucial moments they might have saved thousands more.

(Walter Harrelson and Randall Falk, *Jews and Christians*, Nashville, Abingdon, 1990, 130–132)

The Holocaust and Christian Protest

Over against such figures as Kittel, Althaus, and Hirsch, were Protestant theologians and leaders like Paul Tillich, Dietrich Bonhoeffer, and Martin Niemöller, who vehemently opposed every aspect of Nazism.

With great personal sacrifice and at risk of their very lives, they spoke out courageously in defence of Jews and of Christian principles that were diametrically opposed to the ugly racism and nationalism that dominated Germany under Hitler. And we do not wish to minimize the contributions of more than seven hundred Christians of at least fourteen nationalities including Germans and Poles for whom trees have been planted on the 'Avenue of the Righteous', the sloping path that leads to *Yad Vashem*, the memorial in Jerusalem to the victims of the Holocaust. Undoubtedly there were many more Christians who saved Jews and provided food and shelter at great personal risk. Unfortunately, though, most Catholic and Protestant leaders, clerical and lay, were stonily silent in the face of the atrocities that were being committed in support of German nationalism.

If blame is to be assessed for the tragedy of fascism in Germany, Poland, Italy, and Austria, it is not only the political and church leaders who must bear the responsibility for the horrors that were perpetrated by Hitler and his cohorts. It was the silent 'good' people who lived in the shadow of the concentration camps and the gas chambers and pretended, perhaps even to themselves, not to know what was occurring in their cities and villages. Unfortunately, this was also true in the United States. We did not want to believe that such bestiality was rampant. By our silence and inaction, we, too, were guilty of permitting six million human beings to become victims of the worst instance of anti-Semitism that the world has ever known. . .

Our greatest hope for successfully combating the challenges that still confront us from the hatemongers of this generation is the fact that genuine progress in Christian–Jewish relations has been made since Vatican Council II, and because of the stands taken against anti-Semitism by most major Protestant denominations. We can never afford complacency, though, nor can we cease building bridges of understanding and mutual respect, which must be the foundation for true brotherhood and sisterhood.

(Walter Harrelson and Randall Falk, *Jews and Christians*, Nashville, Abingdon, 1990, 133–134)

Discussion

1. Why did Christians fail to protest against the evils of the Nazi era?
2. In a post-Holocaust world how can Jews and Christians overcome feelings of mistrust?

Walter Harrelson: The Holocaust and the Modern World

Walter Harrelson has served as Professor Emeritus at Vanderbilt University, Tennessee. In Jews and Christians, *he confronts the tragedy of the Holocaust. In his view, despite the horrors of the Nazi period there have been positive developments which have occurred as a result of this terrible period of history.*

The Holocaust in Contemporary Society

It is remarkable to see just how deeply implanted into the consciousness of a large part of the world the Holocaust has become within the several decades since the end of the Second World War. It did not happen easily. The Nuremberg trials in the late 1940s began the process of laying out the monstrous story, in the actual words of victims, onlookers, collaborators, and oppressors, as well as in the testimony of some of the chief architects of the plan to eradicate the Jewish people from Europe. Slow, painstaking work continued to document the actual events, to collect names, to secure testimony from survivors, to track down perpetrators who had escaped. Much of the world wished to forget, to leave the affair alone, but many Jews and Christians and others recognized that with the Holocaust a turning point in human affairs had been reached. Vividly before the world was an increasingly clear and inescapable picture of the depths to which human evil could go. What were the roots of this evil? Was there any logic in it at all? Or was the whole affair the irrational outcome of a deranged mind?

Holocaust studies on university campuses, state memorial acts and structures (the most notable being *Yad Vashem* in Israel), collections of Holocaust art, and regular commemorations of the event have established the depth of the evil, an evil that opens up an abyss for the human spirit. Studies have also revealed a kind of dreadful logic in the events that led up to the Holocaust and in its carrying through. A sufficient number of people believed in the 'rightness' of this plan to destroy the Jewish people to make the plan workable. That is an unmistakable fact that cannot be denied.

It is therefore essential that the Holocaust be remembered, not only by the Jewish people, not only by the Christian communities of the world, but by all people. Hatred has led to violence in the dealings of peoples and nations throughout human history. Occasionally there have been acts of wholesale slaughter of peoples (the Armenians in

Turkey in 1915; the Native Americans during the nineteenth century in the United States; tribal groups in many lands of Africa, Asia, and Latin America; the slaughter of whole communities by Stalin; and so on). Never, however, in the history of the world has there been an instance in which the systematic mistreatment and persecution of a people has persisted over centuries, preparing the ground for the introduction of an extermination plan that very nearly succeeded. The Holocaust had many causes, but one contributing factor is undeniable: Christian misunderstanding of Judaism and mistreatment of Jews over the centuries.

(Walter Harrelson and Randall Falk, *Jews and Christians*, Nashville, Abingdon, 1990, 138–139)

The Aftermath of the Holocaust

Good sometimes follows evil, though it is hardly right to say that evil ever produces good. The State of Israel would have come into existence apart from the Holocaust, in all likelihood, but a shamed world was certainly ready, after the Holocaust and the struggles of Jews from Europe to get to Israel, to support the Partition Plan that led to the establishment of the state. The very existence of the State of Israel has served to keep alive the memory of the Holocaust. The continuing conflicts between Israel and the Arab states have been reminders of how precarious is the life of this small state, a fact that immediately calls to mind Hitler's effort to exterminate the Jews and the acquiescence and indeed collusion of many in the effort. Arabs rightly point out that it was not they who planned and executed the Holocaust; that atrocity was the responsibility of the 'Christian' West. Even so, Arab Christians and Muslims have done their part in perpetuating the Christian and Islamic ways of reading the story of the Jews. There is blame enough to go around.

Many other valuable things have happened in response to the Holocaust. The testimony of survivors has been collected. The sheer record of the names of the victims and the survivors, the collaborators and the resistors, the helpers and the martyrs, is being painstakingly collected and studied. Research centres exist on a number of campuses and in other localities, supported by state and private funds. Lecture series are planned by Christians and Jews working together, in some instances drawn together as never before as they address this turning point in world history.

It also seems clear that the issuance of *Nostra Aetate*, the Vatican encyclical that did so much to change the relations of the Roman Catholic Church and the Jewish community, followed in response to the Holocaust, as did the changed attitude that was already present at the Second Vatican Council (1962–65). The Christian community should never have had in its liturgical life maledictions against the Jews for their participation in Jesus' death—but it did. The public renunciation of that way of thinking and speaking on the part of the highest authority in the Roman Catholic Church was a step of major significance.

This step had behind it the careful and patient labours of many Christians and Jews over many years. Local, national, and international committees and groups have been meeting for decades to seek better and deeper understanding of one another. Some Jews have studied Christian history, theology and ethics, and liturgy with great care in order to be better able to engage in dialogue and confrontation of the sort that has brought about this changed outlook within the Christian community. Some Christians have also studied Jewish history and literature and religious thought, including *Mishnah* and *Gemara* and Jewish mystical texts, in order to be better informed and more discerning partners in the debate.

(Walter Harrelson and Randall Falk, *Jews and Christians*, Nashville, Abingdon, 1990, 139–140)

Discussion

1. Is the Holocaust the result of Christian misunderstanding of the Jewish people?
2. Has good come out of the events of the Nazi era?

Johann Baptist Metz: Jews and Christians after the Holocaust

In The Emergent Church: The Future of Christianity in a Postbourgeois World, *the Catholic theologian Johann Baptist Metz, who has served as Professor of Fundamental Theology at the University of Muenster, argues that Auschwitz serves as a turning point in the relationship between the Jewish and Christian faiths. In his view, the dialogue between Judaism and Christianity has profoundly changed in the light of the Nazi assault upon the Jewish nation.*

JEWS, CHRISTIANS AND THE HOLOCAUST

Auschwitz as a Turning Point in Jewish–Christian Relations

The question whether there will be a reformation and a radical conversion in the relations between Christians and Jews will ultimately be decided, at least in Germany, by the attitude we Christians adopt toward Auschwitz and the value it really has for ourselves. Will we actually allow it to be the end point, the disruption which it really was, the catastrophe of our history, out of which we can find a way only through a radical change of direction achieved via new standards of action? Or will we see it only as a monstrous accident within this history but not affecting history's course. . .

We Christians can never again go back behind Auschwitz: to go beyond Auschwitz, if we see clearly, is impossible for us of ourselves. It is possible only together with the victims of Auschwitz. This, in my eyes, is the root of Jewish–Christian ecumenism. The turning point in relations between Jews and Christians corresponds to the radical character of the end point which befell us in Auschwitz. Only when we confront this end point will we recognize what this 'new' relationship between Jews and Christians is, or at least could become.

To confront Auschwitz is in no way to comprehend it. Anyone wishing to comprehend in this area will have comprehended nothing. As it gazes towards us incomprehensibly out of our most recent history, it eludes our every attempt at some kind of amicable reconciliation which would allow us to dismiss it from our consciousness. The only thing 'objective' about Auschwitz are the victims, the mourners, and those who do penance. Faced with Auschwitz, there can be no abstention, no inability to relate. To attempt such a thing would be yet another case of secret complicity with the unfathomed horror. Yet how are we Christians to come to terms with Auschwitz? We will in any case forgo the temptation to interpret the suffering of the Jewish people from our standpoint, in terms of saving history. Under no circumstances is it our task to mystify this suffering! We encounter in this suffering first of all only the riddle of our own lack of feeling, the mystery of our own apathy, not, however, the traces of God.

Faced with Auschwitz, I consider as blasphemy every Christian theodicy (i.e., every attempt at a so-called 'justification of God') and all language about 'meaning' when these are initiated outside this catastrophe or on some level above it. Meaning, even divine meaning, can be invoked by us only to the extent that such meaning was not also abandoned in Auschwitz itself. But this means that we Christians for our very own sakes are from now on assigned to the victims of Auschwitz—assigned, in fact, in an alliance belonging to the heart of saving history, provided the word 'history' in this Christian expression is to have a definite meaning and not just serve as a screen for a triumphalist metaphysic of salvation which never learns from catastrophes nor finds in them a cause for conversion, since in its view such catastrophes of meaning do not in fact exist at all.

(Johann Baptist Metz, *The Emergent Church: The Future of Christianity in a Postbourgeois World*, London, SCM, 1981, 18–20)

The Holocaust and Jewish–Christian Encounter

When these connections are seen, the question becomes obsolete as to whether Christians in their relations to Jews are now finally moving on from missionizing to dialogue. Dialogue itself seems, in fact, a weak and inappropriate description of this connection. For, after all, what does dialogue between Jews and Christians mean in remembrance of Auschwitz? It seems to me important to ask this question even though—or rather because—Christian–Jewish dialogue is booming at the present time and numerous organizations and institutions exist to support it.

1. Jewish–Christian dialogue in remembrance of Auschwitz means for us Christians first: It is not we who have the opening word, nor do we begin the dialogue. Victims are not offered a dialogue. We can only come into a dialogue when the victims themselves begin to speak. And then it is our primary duty as Christians to listen—for once to begin really listening—to what Jews are saying of themselves and about themselves. . .

2. No prepared patterns exist for this dialogue between Jews and Christians, patterns which could somehow be taken over from the familiar repertoire of inner-Christian ecumenism. Everything has to be measured by Auschwitz. This includes our Christian way of bringing into play the question of truth. Ecumenism, we often hear, can never succeed if it evades the question of truth: it must therefore continually derive from this its authentic direction. No one would deny this. But confronting the truth means first of all not avoiding the truth about Auschwitz, and ruthlessly unmasking the myths of self-exculpation and the mechanisms of trivialization which have been long since

disseminated among Christians. . .

When we engage in this Christian–Jewish dialogue, we Christians should be more cautious about the titles we give ourselves and the sweeping comparisons we make. Faced with Auschwitz, who would dare to call our Christianity the 'true' religion of the suffering, of the persecuted, of the dispersed? The caution and discretion I am recommending here, the theological principle of economy, do not imply any kind of defeatism regarding the question of truth. They are rather expressions of mistrust in relation to any ecumenism separated from concrete situations and devoid of memory, that so-called purely doctrinal ecumenism. . .

3. There is yet another reason why the Jewish–Christian dialogue after Auschwitz eludes every stereotyped pattern of ecumenism. The Jewish partner in this sought-after new relationship would not only be the religious Jew, in the confessional sense of the term, but, in a universal sense, every Jew threatened by Auschwitz. Jean Amery expressed it thus, shortly before his death: 'In the inferno (of Auschwitz) the differences now became more than ever tangible and burned themselves into our skin like the tattooed numbers with which they branded us.'

(Johann Baptist Metz, *The Emergent Church: The Future of Christianity in a Postbourgeois World*, London, SCM, 1981, 20–23)

Discussion

1. Is it possible to comprehend the Holocaust?
2. In a post-Holocaust age, can Christians claim to know the truth about divine suffering?

Frank Longford: The Holocaust and Forgiveness

Frank Longford was the Earl of Packenham and has written various books dealing with Christianity. In Forgiveness of Man by Man, *he compares the Jewish and Christian attitudes toward forgiveness. In analysing the positions of two eminent writers, he suggests that Jews are misguided in not adopting an attitude of forgiveness for those who perpetuated the most heinous crimes against the Jewish people during the Holocaust.*

372

Jews and the Holocaust

The contrast between Christian and Jewish attitudes in regard to forgiveness was thrashed out in *The Times* with clarity and charity in 1985 and 1986. The controversy was set off by the visit of President Reagan to the Nazi S.S. graves in May 1985. Dr. Friedlander, editor of *European Judaism*, then and later played a leading part in the public discussion. As a child of eleven in 1939 he was arrested in Berlin, his home city. He escaped with his family to Cuba and later to the United States. He is now Dean of Leo Baeck College and minister of the Westminster Synagogue.

His striking contribution to *The Times* on 4 May 1985 begins with the affirmation: 'the holocaust must not be forgotten'. He admits that, 'let us forgive and forget is a central thought within our society'. But he says that, 'it is addressed mainly to the Jews' and he refuses to agree for a moment that the Jews can now forgive their persecutors. 'Can we forgive?', he asks. 'Who are we to usurp God's rule?' He then tells a striking anecdote, which many Christians will find disturbing:

> Some years ago speaking at a Church Conference at Nuremberg I talked about the anguish of Auschwitz. An elderly man approached me: 'Rabbi', he said, 'I was a guard at a concentration camp. Can you forgive me?' I looked at him. 'No', I said, 'I cannot forgive. It is not the function of rabbis to give absolution, to be pardoners. In Judaism there is a ten-day period of Penitence, between the New Year and the Day of Atonement, where we try to go to any person whom we have wronged, and ask for forgiveness. But you cannot speak for them. Nor can I speak for God. But you are here at a church conference. God's forgiving grace may touch you; but I am not a mediator, pardoner, or spokesman for God'. . . [1]

(Frank Longford, *Forgiveness of Man by Man*, Northamptonshire, Buchebroc Press, 1989, 15–16)

Christians and the Nazis

The Christian standpoint was powerfully expressed by Canon Phillips, Chaplain of St John's College, Oxford, under the heading 'Why the Jews Should Forgive'. The concluding passage which aroused a good deal of resentment among Jewish contributors ran as follows: 'To remember and not to forgive can only invite further bloodshed, as the history of Ulster confirms. A theology unwilling to come to terms with the oppressors, however heinous their crimes, imprisons itself in its own past, jeopardizing the very future it would ensure. Without forgiveness there can be no healing within the community, no wholeness, holiness. The failure to forgive is not a neutral act: it adds to the sum total of evil in the world and dehumanizes the victims in a way the oppressors could never on their own achieve. In remembering the Holocaust, Jews hope to prevent its recurrence; by declining to forgive, I fear that they unwittingly invite it.'

To return to Dr. Friedlander and his article, 'Judaism and the Concept of Forgiving'. He writes, 'In the Jewish tradition we begin by asking: what does God require of the sinner? How can the sinner achieve forgiveness? Let him bring a sin offering, and his guilt will be atoned! Sin is an uncleanness which adheres to the malefactor; and the vocabulary of forgiveness is replete with such verbs as *either* (purify), *machah* (wipe), *kibbesk* (wash), *kipper* (purge) and God removes that sin from the guilty party'.[2]

Tremendous emphasis is laid from the beginning on the need for the sinner to put himself right with God. The Rabbi stresses the fact that Judaism, unlike Christianity, is opposed to original sin. But I cannot feel that this difference in itself is responsible for the main divergence in regard to forgiveness. Here is one of the cardinal passages in Dr. Friedlander's article:

> The winning of forgiveness depends upon the action of the sinner. The wrong done must be acknowledged and confessed. It must have become abhorrent to the sinner. The sinner must change before receiving forgiveness and public acts of fasting and self-abasement must be followed by actions demonstrating a change of heart and a new way of life. The sinner and the one who has suffered from the sin cannot come back to each other until the sinner has turned in repentance in total sincerity.[3]

Later in the same essay Rabbi Friedlander insists that the Jewish world is not consumed with hate and feelings of revenge. He cannot, however, resist indicating the scale of the atrocities undergone...He concludes: 'Gently but firmly we have to point out that the actions needed to secure pardon for these crimes must initially come from the perpetrators—and they must be placed before the altar of God. Then and only then and as individuals rather than one collective might we begin to say words of comfort to our neighbours. But not yet...not yet.'[4]

On this analysis how can the Jews ever forgive the present Germans whatever acts of redemption the latter perform?

The main perpetrators of the crimes are either dead or so old that they are in no position to make effective atonement. When the concentration camp guard approached Rabbi Friedlander he must be thought to have repented. His presence at a church conference suggested that his acts were corresponding to his good intentions. But still the rabbi told him, and feels sure that he was right to tell him, that only God could forgive him. If this is to be the last word on the subject it would, on the face of it, make nonsense of all community attempts to forgive one another. . . .

In Dr. Friedlander's view, which I am taking as representative of Judaism, in the Bible only God has judged a people guilty, and only God has forgiven a people. Can humans usurp that role?

This leads him on to repeat his refusal to agree that Israel could or should forgive Germany for its collective guilt. What collective guilt?, he asks. 'We are not God to make our judgment.' He would now appear to be saying that the Jews can neither condemn the Germans as a whole nor forgive them. . .

The deepest difference between Dr. Friedlander and myself, a representative Jew and a far from representative Christian, is his insistence that 'repentance precedes forgiving'. He puts in the thought-provoking coment 'We say repentance precedes forgiving; you start from the other side. One of the many flaws I find in the Christian position here is that the unrepentant sinner neither wants nor needs forgiveness'. . . [5]

Christians will surely say that the act of love involved in forgiving the sinner, repentant or unrepentant, is itself an instrument for good, of benefit to oneself, to the sinner, and who knows to how many others.

(Frank Longford, *Forgiveness of Man by Man*, Northamptonshire, Buchebroc Press, 1989, 17–20)

References

1. Albert Friedlander, *The Times*, 4 May, 1985
2. Albert Friedlander, 'Judaism and the Concept of Forgiving', *Christian–Jewish Relations*, 1986
3. Ibid.
4. Ibid.
5. Ibid.

Discussion

1. Should Jews forgive the Nazis?
2. Is the Jewish or Christian attitude toward forgiveness preferable?

Albert Friedlander: The Holocaust and Jewish–Christian Dialogue

Albert Friedlander is a Reform rabbi and has served as Dean of Leo Baeck College, England. In 'The Shoah *and Contemporary Religious Thinking', he discusses the nature of Jewish and Christian dialogue in contemporary society. In his view, Christians must now re-evaluate their relationship to the Jewish people in the light of the horrors of the Holocaust, and such reflection should embrace prayer as well. Turning to theology, Friedlander contends that theodicy is an inappropriate response to the terrors of the Nazi era.*

Jews and Christians

We move into the area of dialogue between Judaism and Christianity under the shadow of the Holocaust at this point. It is not the old 'forgive and forget' demand made of the Jews a half-century after the Holocaust. That discussion (also important) deals with the nature of repentance and the function of forgiveness within the divine sphere of justice. Here, we are at an earlier stage: what type of self-examination is needed for Jews and Christians after the Holocaust which will permit us to come together in order to begin rebuilding our broken community? How can we speak to one another? To whom are we speaking? And what do we have to say to one another?

Much depends upon what we have said to ourselves before such an encounter. To some extent, the Christian self-examination will resemble the Jewish quest for identity. Christians were also victims, are represented by the priests and confessing Christians in the death camps, by resistance fighters in occupied countries and even in Germany, yet their primary suffering may well be one which they refuse to acknowledge for themselves because it appears to be more a cause and encouragement for evil, a crime rather than a consequence: they suffered from apathy and became passive onlookers! Self flagellation for this aspect of their past is not necessarily incorrect, but it must not obscure the fact that this was also a consequence of that time, a maiming of their character, a grievous wound inflicted upon them by the evil of the time. A key word for our dialogue emerges now: compassion. We must have compassion for the Christian who lost his or her true Christianity, either as an onlooker or as a participant in acts of evil, just as Christians try to bind up the wounds of their Jewish neighbours.

Christians—those professing Christianity as well as those who had shaken off the name—Christians did evil at that time. That must be acknowledged and dealt with, by the community as well as by the individual. It must be dealt with from within. . . For Christians, this inner healing must involve various levels of action: the inner confession and repentance of the individual and the Christian community. That process will be judged by them and by God, not by neighbours. It must also result in visible actions which we can understand, removing the anti-Jewish teaching from the textbooks; exhibiting greater under-standing for the suffering of the survivors who can still meet their torturers on the streets after their prison term has been commuted or when it seems safe to emerge from their hiding places.

(Albert Friedlander, 'The *Shoah* and Contemporary Religious Thinking' in Katharine T. Hargrove (ed.), *Seeds of Reconciliation*, North Richland Hills, Texas, Bibal Press, 1996, 183–184)

Public Prayer

When might we pray together? *Yom Ha-Shoah*, the Holocaust Remembrance Day in the Jewish community, varies from year to year according to the lunar calendar. It is observed by many Jewish communities. More often than not, concerned Christian laity and clergy join us in these prayers. Nevertheless, the thought that fills me continually is that Christians must pray in their own churches, within their own liturgies, in their response to the Holocaust which changed the world. In Germany, Professor Metz once said that there can be no theology today in which the knowledge of and the wrestling with Auschwitz is not present. There is no theology without Auschwitz. And there should be no liturgy without Auschwitz. The questions of guilt, of compassion, of repentance, and of reconciliation belong to the prayers of Christianity—and can any one of them avoid or circumvent the Holocaust. . .

What can and what will happen within the structure of Christian prayer cannot be predicted by an outsider, particularly when such prayers can only be the end-product of a period of self-examination.

It may well be that no words can be found, or that the ancient prayers of penitence and confession can be enlarged or simply come to contain the new experience of anguish. Within the Jewish liturgy, this has happened—at least, it has happened for Orthodoxy. That is why Lord Jakobovits can look at a history of suffering reaching through the millennia, point to the times of fasting and penitence, of confession and grief, and can declare quite firmly that no liturgy is to be written to reflect the immediate past: all is contained in the old prayers.

(Albert Friedlander, 'The *Shoah* and Contemporary Religious Thinking' in Katharine T. Hargrove (ed.), *Seeds of Reconciliation*, North Richland Hills, Texas, Bibal Press, 1996, 188–189)

Sharing Together

Is there other comfort, is there other knowledge which Judaism and Christianity can share with each other in the darkness of the holocaust? It is so hard to speak to one another when we do not have the words. What can we even call that darkness, that terror? We say 'Holocaust' because that is the accepted current word, even though the biblical notion of a burnt offering does not suit that terrible event. We say '*Shoah*' because that is the term used in Israel, a whirlwind of destruction sweeping through a world of darkness and fear. Some Jews prefer the term '*Churban*', a destruction which is likened to the *churban*, the destruction of the First and the Second Temple. The late, gifted American theologian and writer Arthur A. Cohen gave that event the name '*Tremendum*', following Rudolf Otto's use: a word describing that which is in the end beyond our understanding, whether it is the Holy or absolute evil. The Nazi terms must drop out of our language and terms used generally: genocide, mass murder, etc. do not begin to say anything significant in this event. Perhaps we go back to prayer here: to silent prayer. . .

One last word on a topic that has no end: if historians should not use the term 'genocide', theologians should be wary of the word 'theodicy'. First, because it is an attempt to file away the horror and the evil by handing it back to God in a critical fashion: 'How could you permit it?' But the problem is not solved or even filed correctly. What we heard during that long period of darkness was a mob of humans, murdering and destroying. What we also heard was 'not the silence of God', but the silence of humankind. Moreover, theodicy means putting God on trial. Elie Wiesel does this in a profoundly moving play: God is tried in the concentration camp—and found guilty. Then the jury adjourns: it is time to pray.

In the time after the Holocaust, it may well be that we can only speak to one another if we speak to God. And perhaps we can only speak to God if we speak to each other.

(Albert Friedlander, 'The *Shoah* and Contemporary Religious Thinking' in Katharine T. Hargrove (ed.), *Seeds of Reconciliation*, North Richland Hills, Texas, Bibal Press, 1996, 189–191)

Discussion

1. In what way can Christians exhibit their desire for forgiveness from the Jewish community for the sins of the Holocaust?
2. After Auschwitz should theologians be wary of theodicy?

Eugene Fisher: Catholics and Jews

Eugene Fisher has served as Executive Secretary of the Secretariat for Catholic–Jewish Relations of the National Conference of Catholic Bishops. In 'Being Catholic, Learning Jewish', he discusses the view that Christian antipathy to Judaism led to the Holocaust. In his view, this is too simple a theory which does not take account of other factors which influenced the Nazis. Nonetheless, Christians must be sensitive to past conflict between Christianity and Judaism in their current activities dealing with the Holocaust.

Christian Antipathy to Jews

Another paper that redirected my thinking as a Christian was Harvard historian Yosef Hayim Yerushalmi's response to Rosemary Ruether's summary of her book. I think until that time I had just assumed in a general sort of way that since Christians had perpetrated genocide, traditional Christian teaching (although arguably not the Gospels themselves) must have supplied an underlying rationale for it. What Ruether's book had done was to sharpen that general sort of acknowledgment and make it very pointed. But after Yerushalmi's paper I had a new set of questions.

Here is how Eva Fleischner, I believe quite accurately, summarizes the Ruetherian thesis: 'Anti-Semitism in the West is a direct outgrowth of Christian theological anti-Judaism. . . Anti-Judaism (is) the claim

379

that Jesus is the Christ. This claim inevitably pitted the Church against the synagogue. . . This is the meaning of her statement that anti-Judaism is endemic to Christianity, an inevitable consequence of the Christian kerygma.'

This is an enticing definition of the question. If the problem is that Christian kerygma as such, one has only to change the kerygma to solve it. Two problems intrude on this comfortable solution, however, one theological and the other historical. Theologically, if Ruether is correct that 'anti-Judaism' (and therefore antisemitism, which she sees as simply an extension of anti-Judaism) is 'inevitable' and 'endemic', that is, as essential to the kerygma of the New Testament itself, then we Christians are stuck with the harsh choice between abandoning our Christian faith or simply learning to live with being endemically and inevitably antisemitic.

We will return to what I see as a false, forced choice. In the meantime Yerushalmi asks the basic historical question that proponents of the straight line method from gospel to Auschwitz still have trouble with. If genocide is endemic to Christianity and its inevitable consequence, why did it take almost two millennia for the inevitable to manifest itself?. . . One need not agree with Yerushalmi's own historical conclusion that 'the Holocaust was the work of a thoroughly modern, neo-pagan state' to realize the significance of his question for theories of Holocaust causality. . .

From Leon Poliakov to Gavin Langmuir, the scholarship in the field that has most influenced my thinking has fallen within the flexible boundaries of the Yerushalmi paradigm. There exists continuity between ancient church teaching and modern antisemitism that cannot be denied if one is to understand what happened in the twentieth century. There also exists discontinuity and newness, from age to age and place to place, if one is to understand why it did not happen until the twentieth century and the widely different reactions among Christians to it.

(Eugene Fischer, 'Being Catholic, Learning Jewish' in Carol Rittner and John Roth (eds), *From the Unthinkable to the Unavoidable*, London and Westport, Connecticut, Greenwood Press, 1997, 46–48)

Catholic and Jewish Conflict

The past decade has been marked by a series of crises between Catholics and Jews over issues related to the Holocaust. These have naturally formed a consuming portion of my professional and personal life. In 1988 I began to put together a chronicle of these events along with a commentary on their significance for Catholic teaching and theology. This chronicle dealt with the crises between Catholics and Jews that had been, ironically, bracketed by two of the most positive events in the history of the dialogue: the pope's visit to the Great Synagogue in Rome, April 13, 1986, and his meeting with four hundred leaders of the world's largest Jewish community in Miami on September 11, 1987. After the Hebrew *gematria* for life (chai=eighteen), I entitled the article 'Eighteen Months in Catholic–Jewish Relations.' The crises that intervened between the first event in Rome to threaten the second event in the United States were Holocaust related: the beatification of Edith Stein, the Auschwitz convent, and the meeting between the pope and Kurt Waldheim, then-president of Austria.

A case can be made that, viewed dispassionately, none of these events, or even all three taken together, should have raised anywhere near the level of emotion and controversy that spilled over into the public forum. Edith Stein was by no means the only Jewish convert to Christianity to be murdered by the Nazis for the crime of being Jewish. The convent, objectively, was not so placed as to be noticeable by visitors to Auschwitz-Birkenau. One could reasonably have presumed that its cloistered nuns would cause no more discomfort to visitors than had been caused by the presence of a similarly humbly placed Carmelite convent and chapel at Dachau over the previous decades. Mr. Waldheim, while having hidden his unsavoury past, was by no means the most immoral or evil person with whom popes have met in pursuing state relations as head of the Roman Catholic Church.

What was at stake, I believe, was not so much the incidents themselves but what underlay the specifics of all three controversies. The real issue was (and is) memory, the memory of the victims, the memory of whether perpetrators and onlookers might, in history's eye, pass themselves off as victims. Rabbi A. James Rudin of the American Jewish Committee, for one, sensed this immediately concerning the Auschwitz convent. 'You know, Gene,' he told me during a phone conversation shortly after we had heard of the flap in far-off Belgium over a fund-raising campaign for the convent, 'this molehill may well become a mountain to trip us all.' That Rabbi Rudin was correct is an understatement.

In 1988 Rabbi Daniel Polish received an award from the Catholic Press Association for an article explaining to Catholics just what concerned the Jewish community reacting to such Catholic initiatives as the beatification of Edith Stein and the Auschwitz convent. There were fears stemming from a history of forced conversions and a specific *Shoah*-related fear that the Catholic Church, whether consciously or not, was engaged in a series of actions that would, in effect, absorb the Holocaust into itself, making it a Catholic event, just as the church has made part of its own history the pre-New Testament history of Israel as recorded in the Hebrew Bible, redefining that history, including the Exodus and the prophets, as a promise fulfilled in Christianity.

(Eugene Fischer, 'Being Catholic, Learning Jewish' in Carol Rittner and John Roth (eds), *From the Unthinkable to the Unavoidable*, London and Westport, Connecticut, Greenwood Press, 1997, 50–51)

Discussion

1. Was the Holocaust a consequence of Christian teaching?
2. Should the Christian community refrain from involvement in commemorating the events of the Nazi era?

Epilogue

The Future of Holocaust Theology

In my previous book, *Holocaust Theology*, published over ten years ago, I argued that the varied theologies of the Holocaust which I explored— the writings of Bernard Maza, Ignaz Maybaum, Emil Fackenheim, Eliezer Berkovits, Arthur Cohen, Richard Rubenstein, Elie Wiesel and Marc Ellis—all suffer from numerous defects. In particular I emphasized that one element was absent from all these justifications of Jewish suffering: there was no appeal to the Hereafter. On the basis of the belief in eternal salvation which sustained the Jewish people through centuries of persecution, it might have been expected that Holocaust theologians would attempt to explain the events of the Nazi period in the context of a future life. Yet, this did not occur. Instead, these writers set doctrines concerning messianic redemption, resurrection and final judgement. This, I contended, was a mistake. I wrote:

> It is not surprising that Jewish Holocaust theologians have refrained from appealing to the traditional belief in other-worldly reward and punishment in formulating their responses to the horrors of the death camps. Yet without this belief, it is simply impossible to make sense of the world as the creation of an all-good and all-powerful God. Without eventual vindication of the righteous in Paradise, there is no way to sustain the belief in a providential God who watches over his chosen people. The essence of the Jewish understanding of God is that he loves his chosen people. If death means extinction, there is no way to make sense of the claim that he loves and cherishes all those who died in the concentration camps, for suffering and death would ultimately triumph over each of those who perished. But if there is eternal life in a World to Come, then there is hope that the righteous will share in a divine life. Moreover, the divine attribute of justice demands that the righteous of Israel who met their death as innocent victims of the Nazis will reap an everlasting reward.[1]

383

As we have seen, few of the Jewish and Christian writers surveyed in this volume seek to provide an answer to the religious perplexities of the Holocaust by appealing to the promise of immortality. Instead they stress the faith of those who perished in the Holocaust, seek to demonstrate that God exercised his providential will in bringing about this event, focus on God's suffering, emphasize that God granted human beings free will, concentrate on human responsibility for the terrors that occurred, or discuss the role of the Church during this tragic period. In only a few cases has there been any consideration of the hope of eternal reward for the righteous.

Nonetheless on reflection, I now believe that a different direction should be taken in considering the horrors of the Holocaust. Rather than develop a modern eschatological Jewish theology based on the experience of the Jewish people over the centuries, the time has come for a radical revision of Jewish theology. As we have seen, a number of thinkers in this volume have attempted to pave the way for such a reconstruction of Jewish thought.

In Chapter 13 of this book, I included a range of Jewish writers who argue along these lines. In 'Despair and Hope in Post-Shoah Jewish life', Professor David Blumenthal, for example, maintains that the religious implications of the Holocaust must now be faced. What is required, he states, is a theology of protest. Undeniably, human beings were responsible for the Holocaust; nonetheless, if one accepts the doctrine of divine providence, then God is ultimately responsible for this human calamity. In his view, we must not piously avoid this challenge. According to Blumenthal, God is present and responsible even in moments of great evil. This leaves us, he writes, with a God who is not perfect, not even always good, but who is still our God and the God of our ancestors.

The Conservative rabbi Arthur A. Cohen adopts a different approach in seeking to reconstruct Jewish theology after the Nazi era. In *Tremendum*, he contends that it is a mistake to long for an interruptive God who can intervene magically in the course of human history. If there were such a God, he states, then the created order would be an extension of his will rather than an independent domain brought about by God's creative love. Thus he writes: 'God is not the strategist of our particularities or of our historical condition, but rather the mystery of our futurity, always our *posse*, never our acts.'

For Dr Melissa Raphael in 'When God Beheld God', the Holocaust demands a revision of traditional Jewish theology. In her view, the patriarchal models of God must be transcended in confronting the religious dilemmas posed by the Holocaust. The patriarchal model of God was the God who failed Israel during the Nazi regime. Drawing on women's experiences in the camps, she seeks to develop a reconstructed conception of God's presence.

For Rabbi Harold Shulweis in *Evil and the Morality of God*, traditional theodicies are inadequate in a post-Holocaust world. What is now required is a radical reconsideration of Jewish belief. Here he argues for what he calls 'predicate theology' in which divine predicates do not refer to pre-existent hypostasized entities lodged in a mysterious subject and claimed as divine. They are instead qualities discovered, not invented, tested, lived and sustained by human beings. Hence he writes: 'Translating "God is love" or "God has wisdom" or "God possesses compassion" or "God makes peace" into "acting lovingly, or acting wisely, or acting compassionately, or making peace is godly" emphasizes the significance of human interaction and responsibility'.

According to Rabbi Steven Jacobs, in *Rethinking the Jewish Faith* the Holocaust demands a new theology for the modern Jew. In his view, it is an error to believe that God acts in history. What is now required, he writes: 'is a notion of a Deity compatible with the reality of radical evil at work and at play in our world, a notion which, also, admits of human freedom for good or evil because he or she could not act'. Such theological revision is contingent, he writes, upon accepting a notion of God as other than historically and traditionally presented by both Judaism and Christianity.

These and other writers in this volume have paved the way for a radically new theological approach. Arguably in our post-Holocaust world, we can no longer accept that traditional doctrines of God are valid. Instead, we must reconsider traditional theological belief in the light of the tragedies of the modern age. Hence, rather than endorsing the traditional understanding of God and the unfolding of a future life in which the righteous will be rewarded as I did in *Holocaust Theology*, I would now advocate a very different approach to the perplexities of the Holocaust. In my view, such theological reconstruction is now necessary given the inadequacies of the various theodicies outlined in this study.

Throughout this volume both Jewish and Christian thinkers have wrestled with the religious problems of the Holocaust due to their acceptance of the traditional understanding of God. Yet, arguably what is required today is a complete reorientation in theological reflection—

in a post-Holocaust world what is needed is a theological structure consonant with a contemporary understanding of Divine Reality as conceived in the world's faiths.

Arguably, such a revised theology should be based on the distinction between the world-as-it-is and the world-as-perceived. Following this differentiation, the Real *an sich* (in itself) should be distinguished from the Real as conceived in human thought and experience. Such a contrast is a central feature of many of the world's faiths: thus in Judaism God the transcendental Infinite is conceived as *En Sof*, as distinct from the *Shekhinah* (God's Presence) which is manifest in the terrestrial plane; in Hindu thought the *nirguna Brahman*, the Ultimate in itself, beyond all human categories, is distinguished from the *saguna Brahman*, the Ultimate as known to finite consciousness as a personal deity, in Isvara; in Taoist thought 'the *tao* that can be expressed is not the eternal *Tao*'; in Mahayana Buddhism there is a contrast between the eternal cosmic Buddha-nature, which is also the infinite void, and on the other hand the realm of the heavenly Buddha figures in their incarnations in the earthly Buddhas.

In attempting to represent Ultimate Reality, the different religions have conceptualized the Divine in two distinct modes: the Real personalized and the Real as absolute. In Judaism, God is understood as Lord; in the Christian faith as Father; in Islam as Allah; in the Indian traditions as Shiva or Vishnu, or Parameter. In each case these personal deities are conceived as acting within the history of the various communities.

The concept of the Absolute is alternatively schematized to form a range of divine conceptualizations in the world's religions such as *Brahman*, the *Dharma*, the *Tao*, *Nirvana* and *Sunyata* in Eastern traditions. Unlike divine *personae* which are concrete and often visualized, divine *impersonae* constitute a variety of concepts such as the infinite being-consciousness-bliss of *Brahman*, the beginningless and endless cosmic change of Buddhist teachings, the ineffable further shore of *Nirvana*, the eternal Buddha-nature or the ultimate Emptiness which is also the fullness of the world, and the eternal principle of the *Tao*. These non-personal representations of the Divine inform modes of consciousness ranging from the experience of becoming one with the Infinite to the finding of total reality in a concrete historical moment of existence.

Given the diversity of images of the Real among the various religious systems that have emerged throughout history, it is not surprising that there are innumerable conflicts between the teachings of the world's faiths—in all cases believers have maintained that the doctrines of their respective traditions are true and superior to competing claims. Thus Jews contend that they are God's chosen people and partners in a special covenant—their mission is to be a light to the nations. In this sense the Jewish people stand in a unique relationship with God. This does not lead to the quest to convert others to Judaism, but it does give rise to a sense of pride in having been born into the Jewish fold.

Within Islam, Muslims are convinced that Muhammad was the seal of the prophets and that through the Quran God revealed himself decisively to the world. This implies that while Muslims are obligated to recognize the veracity of the other Abrahmaic traditions—and in some cases extend the Quranic concept of the People of the Book to other faiths as well, they nonetheless assert that the Quran has a unique status as God's final, decisive word. On the basis of this central dogma, they view themselves as the heirs of the one and only true religion. Convinced that only those who belong to the true faith can be saved, the Christian community has similarly throughout history sought to convert all human beings to the Gospel.

Hindus, on the other hand, believe that it is possible to have access to eternal truth as incarnated in human language in the Vedas. Although Hindus are tolerant of other faiths, it is assumed that in this life or in the life to come, all will come to the fullness of Vedic understanding. Further, in *advaitic* philosophy it is maintained that the theistic forms of religion embody an inferior conception of ultimate Reality. Thus, Hindus believe that their faith is uniquely superior to other religious conceptions. Likewise, in the Buddhist tradition it is assumed that the true understanding in the human condition is presented in the teachings of Gautama Buddha. The *Dharma*, Buddhists stress, contains the full saving truth for all humanity.

Each of these religious traditions then affirms its own superiority— all rival claims are regarded as misapprehensions of Ultimate Reality. From a pluralistic perspective, however, there is no way to ascertain which, if any, of these spiritual paths accurately reflects the nature of the Real *an sich*. In the end, the varied truth claims of the world's faiths must be regarded as human images which are constructed from within particular social and cultural contexts. Hence from a pluralistic perspective it is impossible to make judgements about the veracity of the various conceptions of the Divine within the world's religions.

Neither Jew, Muslim, Christian, Hindu nor Buddhist has any justification for believing that his or her respective tradition embodies the uniquely true and superior religious path. Instead the adherents of all the world's faiths must recognize the inevitable human subjectivity of religious conceptualization.

This recognition calls for a complete reorientation of religious apprehension. What is now required is for Jews and Christians to acknowledge that their conceptual system, form of worship, lifestyle and scriptures are in the end nothing more than lenses through which Reality is perceived, but the Divine as it is in itself is beyond human understanding. Within this new theological framework, the absolute claims about God in the Jewish and Christian faiths should be understood as human conceptions stemming from the religious experience of Jews and Christians through the centuries. In all cases pious believers and thinkers have expressed their understanding of God's activity on the basis of their own personal as well as communal encounter with the Divine. Yet given that the Real *an sich* is beyond human comprehension, the Jewish and Christian understanding of God cannot be viewed as definitive and final. In this respect, it makes no sense for either Jews or Christians to believe that they possess the unique truth about God and his action in the world; on the contrary, universalistic truth-claims about divine Reality must give way to a recognition of the inevitable subjectivity of beliefs about the Real.

The implications of this shift from the absolutism of the past to a new vision of Jewish and Christian Holocaust theology are radical and far-reaching. As we have seen, throughout this book Jewish and Christian theologians have formulated a wide range of interpretations of the events of the Nazi era based on traditional conceptions of God's nature and activity. Yet, an acknowledgement of the inevitable subjectivity of religious belief can liberate Jewish and Christian theology from such a struggle. The Holocaust is an overwheming religious perplexity precisely because Jews and Christians perceive God as an omnipotent and benevolent Deity, a loving Father of all humanity. However, if the Divine lies beyond human comprehension, then the puzzle of God's providence during the Holocaust ceases to be an insoluble problem. Instead, it is an unfathomable mystery.

References

1. Dan Cohn-Sherbok, *Holocaust Theology*, London, Lamp, 1991, 128–129

Bibliography

Abel, Theodor, *Why Hitler Came to Power*, Cambridge, Massachusetts, Harvard University Press, 1986

Altizer, Thomas J.J., 'The Holocaust and the Theology of the Death of God' in Stephen R. Haynes and John K. Roth (eds), *The Death of God Movement and the Holocaust*, Westport, Connecticut, Greenwood Press, 1999

Arad, Yitzhak, *The Pictorial History of the Holocaust*, New York, Praeger, 1990

Arendt, Hannah, *Eichmann in Jerusalem*, Harmondsworth, Penguin, 1979

Ariel, David, *What Do Jews Believe?*, London, Rider, 1996

Baeck, Leo, 'In Memory of Two of Our Dead' and 'This People Israel' in Albert Friedlander (ed.), *Out of the Whirlwind*, New York, Schocken, 1976

Baird, J.W., *The Mythical World of Nazi Propaganda 1939–1945*, Minneapolis, University of Minnesota Press, 1974

Baum, Gregory, *Christian Theology after Auschwitz*, London, Council of Christians and Jews, 1976

Baum, Gregory, 'Rethinking the Church's Mission after Auschwitz' in Eva Fleischner (ed.), *Auschwitz: Beginning of a New Era?*, New York, KTAV, 1977

Baumont, Maurice, *The Third Reich*, New York, Praeger, 1955

Bayfield, Tony and Braybrooke, Marcus (eds), *Dialogue with a Difference*, London, SCM, 1992

Bemporad, Jack, 'The Concept of Man after Auschwitz' in Albert Friedlander (ed.), *Out of the Whirlwind*, New York, Schocken, 1976

Berenbaum, Michael, *The Vision of the Void: Theology Reflections on the Works of Elie Wiesel*, Middletown, Connecticut, Wesleyan University Press, 1979

Berkovits, Eliezer, *Faith after the Holocaust*, New York, KTAV, 1973

Berkovits, Eliezer, *With God in Hell*, New York, Sanhedrin Press, 1979

Bethge, Eberhard, 'Troubled Self-Interpretation and Uncertain Reception in the Church Struggle' in Franklin H. Littell and Hubert G. Locke (eds), *The German Church Struggle and the Holocaust*, Detroit, Wayne State University

Press, 1975

Birnbaum, David, *God and Evil,* Hoboken, New Jersey, KTAV, 1989

Blumenthal, David, 'Despair and Hope in Post-*Shoah* Jewish Life', *Bridges,* Fall/Winter, 1999

Blumenthal, David R., *The Banality of Good and Evil: Moral Lessons from the Shoah and Jewish Tradition,* Washington DC, Georgetown University Press, 1999

Bokser, Ben Zion, *Judaism and the Christian Predicament,* New York, Alfred Knopf, 1967

Borowitz, Eugene, *Choices in Modern Jewish Thought,* New York, Behrman House, 1983

Botwinick, R., *A History of the Holocaust,* London, Prentice Hall, 1996

Braiterman, Zachary, *(God) After Auschwitz,* Princeton, Princeton University Press, 1998

Braybrooke, Marcus, 'The Power of Suffering Love' in Tony Bayfield and Marcus Braybrooke (eds), *Dialogue with a Difference,* London, SCM, 1992

Brenner, Robert Reeve, *The Faith and Doubt of Holocaust Survivors,* New York, Free Press, 1980

Brockway, Allan R., 'Religious Values after the Holocaust: A Protestant View' in Abraham J. Peck (ed.), *Jews and Christians after the Holocaust,* Philadelphia, Fortress Press, 1982

Broszat, Martin, *The Hitler State,* New York, Longman, 1981

Browning, Christopher, *Ordinary Men,* New York, Aaron Asher Books, 1992

Bullock, Alan, *Hitler: A Study in Tyranny,* New York, Harper and Row, 1962

Buren, Paul van, *Discerning the Way: A Theology of the Jewish–Christian Reality,* New York, Seabury Press, 1980

Burleigh, Michael and Wippermann, Wolfgang, *The Racial State: Germany 1933–1945,* Cambridge, Cambridge University Press, 1991

Cargas, Harry James, 'Interview with Dorothee Sölle', *Encounter,* 49/2

Cargas, Harry James, *Reflections of a Post-Holocaust Christian,* Detroit, Wayne State University Press, 1989

Cargas, Harry James, *Shadows of Auschwitz: A Christian Response to the Holocaust,* New York, Crossroad, 1990

Childers, Thomas and Caplan, Jane (eds), *Re-evaluating the Third Reich,* New York, Holmes and Meier, 1993

Cohen, Arthur A., *Tremendum: A Theological Interpretation of the Holocaust,* New York, Crossroad, 1981

Cohen, Sha'ar Yashuv, '*Hester Panim* in the Holocaust versus the Manifest

Miracles in our Generation' in Yehezkel Fogel (ed.), *I Will be Sanctified*, Northvale, New Jersey, Jason Aronson, 1998

Cohn-Sherbok, Dan, *The Future of Jewish–Christian Dialogue*, Lewiston, New York, Edwin Mellen, 1999

Cohn-Sherbok, Dan, *Holocaust Theology*, London, Lamp, 1991

Colijn, G. Jan and Littell, Marcia Sachs (eds), *Confronting the Holocaust*, Lanham, Maryland, University Press of America, 1997

Davies, Alan T., 'Response to Irving Greenberg' in Eva Fleischner (ed.), *Auschwitz: Beginning of a New Era?*, New York, KTAV, 1977

Davis, Stephen T., 'Evangelical Christians and Holocaust Theology', *American Journal of Theology and Philosophy*, 2, 3, 1981

Dawidowicz, Lucy S., *The War Against the Jews*, New York, Rinehart and Winston, 1975

Donat, Alexander, 'The Holocaust Kingdom' in Albert Friedlander (ed.), *Out of the Whirlwind*, New York, Schocken, 1976

Dubois, Marcel Jacques, 'Christian Reflection on the Holocaust' in Katharine T. Hargrove (ed.), *Seeds of Reconciliation*, North Richland Hills, Texas, Bibal Press, 1996

Ecclestone, Alan, *The Night Sky of the Lord*, New York, Schocken, 1982

Eckardt, Alice, 'The *Shoah*-Road to a Revised/Revived Christianity' in Carol Rittner and John Roth (eds), *From the Unthinkable to the Unavoidable*, London and Westport, Connecticut, Greenwood Press, 1997

Eckardt, Alice L. and Eckardt, A. Roy, *Long Night's Journey into Day: A Revised Retrospective on the Holocaust*, Detroit, Wayne State University Press, 1982

Eckardt, Roy, 'Once and Not Future Partisan: A Plea for History' in Carol Rittner and John Roth (eds), *From the Unthinkable to the Unavoidable*, London and Westport, Connecticut, Greenwood Press, 1997

Eimer, Colin, 'Suffering: A Point of Meeting' in Tony Bayfield and Marcus Braybrooke (eds), *Dialogue with a Difference*, London, SCM, 1992

Eliach, Yaffa, *Hasidic Tales of the Holocaust*, New York, Oxford University Press, 1982

Ellis, Marc, *Beyond Innocence and Redemption*, San Francisco, Harper and Row, 1990

Ellis, Marc, *Toward a Jewish Theology of Liberation*, New York, Orbis, 1986

Ellis, Marc, *Unholy Alliance*, London, SCM, 1997

Fackenheim, Emil, *God's Presence in History: Jewish Affirmations and Philosophical Reflections*, New York, Harper and Row, 1972

Fackenheim, Emil, 'Jewish Faith and the Holocaust' and 'The Jewish Return into History' in Michael Morgan (ed.), *The Jewish Thought of Emil Fackenheim*, Detroit, Wayne State University Press, 1987

Fackenheim, Emil, *To Mend the World: Foundations of Future Jewish Thought,* New York, Schocken, 1982

Feld, Edward, *The Spirit of Renewal: Finding Faith after the Holocaust,* Woodstock, Vermont, Jewish Lights, 1994

Feuerlicht, Roberta Strauss, *The Fate of the Jews,* London, Quartet Books, 1984

Fiddes, Paul, *The Creative Suffering of God,* Oxford, Clarendon Press, 1988

Fiorenza, Elisabeth Schüssler and Tracy, David (eds), *The Holocaust as Interruption,* Edinburgh, T. and T. Clark, 1984

Fischer, Klaus P., *The History of an Obsession,* London, Constable, 1998

Fischer, Klaus P., *Nazi Germany,* London, Constable, 1995

Fisher, Eugene, 'Being Catholic, Learning Jewish' in Carol Rittner and John Roth (eds), *From the Unthinkable to the Unavoidable,* London and Westport, Connecticut, Greenwood Press, 1997

Flannery, Edward, *The Anguish of the Jews,* New York, Paulist Press, 1985

Fleischner, Eva (ed.), *Auschwitz: Beginning of a New Era?,* New York, KTAV, 1977

Fogel, Yehezkel (ed.), *I Will be Sanctified,* Northvale, New Jersey, Jason Aronson, 1998

Frei, Norbert, *National Socialist Rule in Germany: The Führer State 1933–1945,* trans. Simon B. Steyne, Oxford, Blackwell, 1993

Friedlander, Albert, 'A Final Conversation with Paul Tillich' in Albert Friedlander (ed.), *Out of the Whirlwind,* New York, Schocken, 1976

Friedlander, Albert (ed.), *Out of the Whirlwind,* New York, Schocken, 1976

Friedlander, Albert, 'The *Shoah* and Contemporary Religious Thinking' in Katharine T. Hargrove (ed.), *Seeds of Reconciliation,* North Richland Hills, Texas, Bibal Press, 1996

Friedlander, Saul, *Nazi Germany and the Jews,* London, Weidenfeld and Nicolson, 1987

Gilbert, Martin, *Atlas of the Holocaust,* London, Macmillan, 1982

Gilbert, Martin, *The Holocaust,* London, Macmillan, 1984

Gillman, Neil, *Sacred Fragments,* Philadelphia, Jewish Publication Society, 1990

Goldberg, Hillel, 'Holocaust Theology: The Survivor's Statement – Part II', *Tradition,* Winter, 1982

Goldberg, Michael, *Why Should Jews Survive?,* Oxford, Oxford University Press, 1995

Goldhagen, Daniel, *Hitler's Willing Executioners,* London, Abacus, 1997

Greenberg, Irving, 'Cloud of Smoke, Pillar of Fire: Judaism, Christianity and Modernity after the Holocaust' in Eva Fleischner (ed.), *Auschwitz:*

Beginning of a New Era?, New York, KTAV, 1977

Haas, Peter J., *Morality after Auschwitz: The Radical Challenge of the Nazi Ethic*, Philadelphia, Fortress Press, 1988

Hamilton, William, 'Genocide and the Death of God' in Stephen R. Haynes and John K. Roth (eds), *The Death of God Movement and the Holocaust*, Westport, Connecticut, Greenwood Press, 1999

Hargrove, Katharine T. (ed.), *Seeds of Reconciliation*, North Richland Hills, Texas, Bibal Press, 1996

Harrelson, Walter and Falk, Randall, *Jews and Christians*, Nashville, Abingdon, 1990

Harries, Richard, 'Theodicy Will Not Go Away' in Tony Bayfield and Marcus Braybrooke (eds), *Dialogue with a Difference*, London, SCM, 1992

Haynes, Stephen R., *Prospects for Post-Holocaust Theology*, Atlanta, Scholars Press, 1991

Haynes, Stephen R. and Roth, John K. (eds), *The Death of God Movement and the Holocaust*, Westport, Connecticut, Greenwood Press, 1999

Heschel, Abraham Joshua, 'The Meaning of This Hour' in Albert Friedlander (ed.), *Out of the Whirlwind*, New York, Schocken, 1976

Heschel, Susannah, 'Post-Holocaust Jewish Reflections on German Theology' in Carol Rittner and John Roth (eds), *From the Unthinkable to the Unavoidable*, London and Westport, Connecticut, Greenwood Press, 1997

Hilberg, Raul, *The Destruction of European Jews*, 3 vols, New York, Holmes and Meier, 1985

Hirsch, David H., 'Camp Music and Camp Songs' in G. Jan Colijn and Marcia Sachs Littell (eds), *Confronting the Holocaust*, Lanham, Maryland, University Press of America, 1997

Hochhuth, Rolf, *The Deputy* in Albert Friedlander (ed.), *Out of the Whirlwind*, New York, Schocken, 1976

Jacobs, Louis, *A Jewish Theology*, London, Darton, Longman and Todd, 1973

Jacobs, Steven, *Contemporary Christian Responses to the Shoah*, Lanham, Maryland, University Press of America, 1993

Jacobs, Steven, *Rethinking Jewish Faith*, Albany, State University of New York Press, 1994

Jakobovits, Immanuel, 'Where Was Man at Auschwitz?' in Helen Fry (ed.), *Christian–Jewish Dialogue*, Exeter, University of Exeter Press, 1996

Jocz, Jakob, 'Israel after Auschwitz' in David W. Torrance (ed.), *The Witness of the Jews to God,* Edinburgh, Hansel Press, 1982

Jocz, Jakob, *The Jewish People and Jesus Christ after Auschwitz*, Lanham, Maryland, University Press of America, 1991

Jonas, Hans, 'The Concept of God after Auschwitz' in Albert Friedlander (ed.), *Out of the Whirlwind*, New York, Schocken, 1976

Kanfo, Hayyim, 'Manifestation of Divine Providence in the Gloom of the Holocaust' in Yehezkel Fogel (ed.), *I Will Be Sanctified*, Northvale, New Jersey, Jason Aronson, 1998

Katz, Stephen T., *Post-Holocaust Dialogues*, New York, New York University Press, 1983

Keith, Graham, *Hated Without a Cause: A Survey of Anti-Semitism*, Carlisle, Paternoster Press, 1997

Kershaw, Ian, *The 'Hitler Myth': Image and Reality in the Third Reich*, New York, Oxford University Press, 1972

Kershaw, Ian, *The Nazi Dictatorship: Problems and Perspectives of Interpretation*, Baltimore, Edward Arnold, 1985

Kessler, Edward, 'The Future of Jewish–Christian Relations' in Dan Cohn-Sherbok (ed.), *The Future of Jewish–Christian Dialogue*, Lewiston, New York, Edwin Mellen, 1999

Kirschner, Robert (ed.), *Rabbinic Responses of the Holocaust Era*, New York, Schocken, 1985

Knutsen, Mary, 'The Holocaust in Theology and Philosophy: The Question of Truth' in Elisabeth Schüssler Fiorenza and David Tracy (eds), *The Holocaust as Interruption*, Edinburgh, T. and T. Clark, 1984

Kolitz, Zvi, 'Yossel Rakover's Appeal to God' in Albert Friedlander (ed.), *Out of the Whirlwind*, New York, Schocken, 1976

Lamm, Norman, 'The Ideology of the Neturei Karta—According to the Satmarer Version', *Tradition*, Fall, 1971

Landau, R., *The Nazi Holocaust*, London, I.B. Taurus, 1992

Lange, Nicholas de, 'Jesus Christ and Auschwitz' in Dan Cohn-Sherbok (ed.), *The Future of Jewish–Christian Dialogue*, Lewiston, New York, Edwin Mellen, 1999

Leaman, Oliver, *Evil and Suffering in Jewish Philosophy*, Cambridge, Cambridge University Press, 1995

Levi, Primo, 'If This is a Man' in Albert Friedlander (ed.), *Out of the Whirlwind*, New York, Schocken, 1976

Lifton, Robert J., *The Nazi Doctors: Medical Killing and the Psychology of Genocide*, New York, Basic Books, 1986

Lipstadt, Deborah, *Denying the Holocaust: The Growing Assault on Truth and Memory*, New York, Free Press, 1993

Littell, Franklin H., 'Christendom, Holocaust and Israel: The Importance for Christians of Recent Major Events in Jewish History', *Journal of Ecumenical Studies*, 10, 1973

Littell, Franklin H., 'Church Struggle and the Holocaust' in Franklin H. Littell and Hubert G. Locke (eds), *The German Church Struggle and the*

Holocaust, Detroit, Wayne State University Press, 1975

Littell, Franklin H. and Locke, Hubert G. (eds), *The German Church Struggle and the Holocaust*, Detroit, Wayne State University Press, 1975 (reprinted Edwin Mellen Press, 1990)

Littell, Marcia Sachs (ed.), *Liturgies on the Holocaust*, Lewiston, New York, Edwin Mellen, 1986

Longford, Frank, *Forgiveness of Man by Man*, Northamptonshire, Buchebroc Press, 1989

Maccoby, Hyam, *A Pariah People*, London, Constable, 1996

McGarry, Michael, *Christology After Auschwitz*, New York, Paulist Press, 1977

McGarry, Michael, 'The Holocaust' in Michael Shermis and Arthur Zannoni (eds), *Introduction to Jewish–Christian Relations*, New Jersey, Paulist Press, 1991

Maduro, Otto (ed.), *Judaism, Christianity and Liberation*, New York, Orbis, 1991

Marrus, Michael, *The Holocaust in History*, London, Penguin, 1993

Maybaum, Ignaz, *The Face of God after Auschwitz*, Amsterdam, Polak and Van Gennep, 1965

Maza, Bernard, *With Fury Poured Out*, New York, KTAV, 1986

Metz, Johann Baptist, *The Emergent Church: The Future of Christianity in a Postbourgeois World*, London, SCM, 1981

Montefiore, Hugh, *On Being a Jewish Christian*, London, Hodder and Stoughton, 1998

Moore, James F., 'A Spectrum of Views: Traditional Christian Responses to the Holocaust', *Journal of Ecumenical Studies*, 25, 2, Spring, 1988

Morgan, Michael, *The Jewish Thought of Emil Fackenheim*, Detroit, Wayne State University Press, 1987

Nadav, Nissim, 'The Lights of Faith and Heroism in the Darkness of the Holocaust' in Yehezkel Fogel (ed.), *I Will Be Sanctified*, Northvale, New Jersey, Jason Aronson, 1998

Neher, André, 'The Exile of the Word: From the Silence of the Bible to the Silence of Auschwitz' in John K. Roth and Michael Berenbaum (eds), *Holocaust: Religious and Philosophical Implications*, New York, Paragon House, 1989

Neusner, Jacob, *Introduction to American Judaism*, Minneapolis, Fortress Press, 1994

Noakes, J. and Pridham, G. (eds), *Nazism 1919–1945*, 4 vols, Exeter, University of Exeter Press: Volume 1 *The Rise to Power 1919–1934* (new edition with index) 1998; Volume 2 *State, Economy and Society 1933–1939* (new edition with index) 2000; Volume 3 *Foreign Policy, War and Racial*

Extermination (revised chapters on the Holocaust and with index) 2001; Volume 4 *The German Home Front in World War II*, 1998

Oppenheim, Michael, *Speaking/Writing of God*, Albany, State University of New York Press, 1997

Opsahl, Paul D. and Tanenbaum, Marc H. (eds), *Speaking of God Today*, Philadelphia, Fortress Press, 1974

Oshry, Efraim, *Responsa from the Holocaust*, New York, Judaica Press, 1983

Patterson, David, *Sun Turned to Darkness*, Syracuse, Syracuse University Press, 1998

Pawlikowski, John, 'The Holocaust and Contemporary Christology' in Elisabeth Schüssler Fiorenza and David Tracy (eds), *The Holocaust as Interruption*, Edinburgh, T. and T. Clark, 1984

Peck, Abraham J., (ed.), *Jews and Christians after the Holocaust*, Philadelphia, Fortress Press, 1982

Pollefyt, Didier, 'Auschwitz or How Good People Can Do Evil' in G. Jan Colijn and Marcia Sachs Littell (eds), *Confronting the Holocaust*, Lanham, Maryland, University Press of America, 1997

Raphael, Melissa, 'When God Beheld God', *Feminist Theology*, 21, 1999

Rausch, David A., *A Legacy of Hatred*, Grand Rapids, Michigan, Baker Book House, 1990

Reitlinger, Gerald, *The Final Solution: The Attempt to Exterminate the Jews of Europe*, London, Vallentine Mitchell, 1953

Rittner, Carol and Roth, John (eds), *From the Unthinkable to the Unavoidable*, London and Westport, Connecticut, Greenwood Press, 1997

Rosenbaum, Irving, *The Holocaust and Halakhah*, New York, KTAV, 1976

Rosenberg, Bernard H. and Heuman, Fred, *Theological and Halkhic Reflections on the Holocaust*, New York, KTAV, 1982

Roth, John, 'It Started with Tears' in Carol Rittner and John Roth (eds), *From the Unthinkable to the Unavoidable*, London and Westport, Connecticut, Greenwood Press, 1997

Roth, John K. and Berenbaum, Michael (eds), *Holocaust: Religious and Philosophical Implications*, New York, Paragon House, 1989

Roth, Yosef, 'The Jewish Fate and the Holocaust' in Yehezkel Fogel (ed.), *I Will Be Sanctified*, Northvale, New Jersey, Jason Aronson, 1998

Rubenstein, Richard, *After Auschwitz*, Indianapolis, Bobbs Merrill, 1966

Rubenstein, Richard and Roth, John, *Approaches to Auschwitz*, London, SCM, 1987

Rubenstein, W.D., *The Myth of Rescue: Why the Democracies Could Not Save More Jews from the Nazis*, London, Routledge, 1997

Rubinoff, Lionel, 'Auschwitz and the Theology of the Holocaust' in Paul D. Opsahl and Marc H. Tanenbaum (eds), *Speaking of God Today*,

Philadelphia, Fortress Press, 1974

Ruether, Rosemary Radford, 'Anti-Semitism and Christian Theology' in Eva Fleischner (ed.), *Auschwitz: Beginning of a New Era?*, New York, KTAV, 1977

Ryan, Michael D., 'Hitler's Challenge to the Churches: A Theological Political Analysis of *Mein Kampf* in Franklin H. Littell and Hubert G. Locke (eds), *The German Church Struggle and the Holocaust*, Detroit, Wayne State University Press, 1975

Sacks, Jonathan, *Tradition in an Untraditional Age*, London, Vallentine Mitchell, 1990

Santa Ana, Julio de, 'The Holocaust and Liberation' in Otto Maduro (ed.), *Judaism, Christianity, and Liberation*, New York, Orbis, 1991

Schindler, Pesach, *Hasidic Responses to the Holocaust in the Light of Hasidic Thought*, Hoboken, New Jersey, KTAV, 1990

Schulweis, Harold, *Evil and the Morality of God*, Cincinnati, Hebrew Union College Press, 1984

Schwartz, Dror, 'The Heroism of Masada and the Martyrs of the Holocaust' in Yehezkel Fogel (ed.), *I Will Be Sanctified*, Northvale, New Jersey, Jason Aronson, 1998

Schweid, Eliezer, *Wrestling Until Day-Break*, Lanham, Maryland, University Press of America, 1994

Shapira, Kalonymus Kalman, *The Holy Fire: The Teachings of Rabbi Kalonymus Kalman Shapira, the Rebbe of the Warsaw Ghetto*, ed. Nehemiah Polen, Northvale, New Jersey, Jason Aronson, 1994

Shapiro, Susan, 'Hearing the Testimony of Radical Negation' in Elisabeth Schüssler Fiorenza and David Tracy (eds), *The Holocaust as Interruption*, Edinburgh, T. and T. Clark, 1984

Sherman, Franklin, 'Speaking of God after Auschwitz' in Paul D. Opsahl and Marc H. Tanenbaum (eds), *Speaking of God Today*, Philadelphia, Fortress Press, 1974

Shermis, Michael and Zannoni, Arthur (eds), *Introduction to Jewish–Christian Relations*, New Jersey, Paulist Press, 1991

Sherwin, Byron, *Toward a Jewish Theology*, Lewiston, New York, Edwin Mellen, 1991

Shirer, William, *The Rise and Fall of the Third Reich*, New York, Simon and Schuster, 1959

Siegel, Seymour, 'Response to Emil Fackenheim' in Eva Fleischner (ed.), *Auschwitz: Beginning of a New Era?*, New York, KTAV, 1977

Siegele-Wenschkewitz, Leonore, 'The Contribution of Church History to a Post-Holocaust Theology: Christian Anti-Judaism as the Root of Anti-Semitism' in Elisabeth Schüssler Fiorenza and David Tracy (eds), *The Holocaust as Interruption*, Edinburgh, T. and T. Clark, 1984

Simon, Ulrich, *A Theology of Auschwitz*, London, SPCK, 1978

Sofsky, W., *The Order of Terror: The Concentration Camp*, Princeton, Princeton University Press, 1997

Sölle, Dorothee, 'God's Pain and Our Pain' in Otto Maduro (ed.), *Judaism, Christianity and Liberation*, New York, Orbis, 1991

Solomon, Norman, *Judaism and World Religion*, London, Macmillan, 1991

Stern, David, *Messianic Jewish Manifesto*, Clarkesville, Maryland, Jewish New Testament Publications, 1997

Tillich, Paul, 'A Final Conversation with Paul Tillich' in Albert Friedlander (ed.), *Out of the Whirlwind*, New York, Schocken, 1976

Torrance, David W. (ed.), *The Witness of the Jews to God*, Edinburgh, Hansel Press, 1982

Tracy, David, 'Religious Values after the Holocaust: A Catholic View' in Abraham J. Peck (ed.), *Jews and Christians after the Holocaust*, Philadelphia, Fortress Press, 1982

Trevor-Roper, H.R., *The Last Days of Adolf Hitler*, New York, Macmillan, 1947

Tusa, A. and J., *The Nuremberg Trial*, London, Macmillan, 1983

Weiss, David, 'The Holocaust and the New Covenant' in John K. Roth and Michael Berenbaum (eds), *Holocaust: Religious and Philosophical Implications*, New York, Paragon House, 1989

Weltsch, Robert, 'Wear the Yellow Badge with Pride' in Albert Friedlander (ed.), *Out of the Whirlwind*, New York, Schocken, 1976

Wiesel, Elie, *Night*, New York, Bantam Books, 1982

Williamson, Clark, *A Guest in the House of Israel: Post-Holocaust Church Theology*, Louisville, Kentucky, Westminster/John Knox Press, 1993

Wine, Sherwin, *Judaism Beyond God*, Farmington Hills, Michigan, Society for Humanistic Judaism, 1985

Wistrich, R., *Who's Who in Nazi Germany*, London, Routledge, 1995

Wollaston, Isabel, 'Responses to Anti-Judaism and Anti-Semitism in Contemporary Christian–Jewish Relations' in Dan Cohn-Sherbok (ed.), *The Future of Jewish–Christian Dialogue*, Lewiston, New York, Edwin Mellen, 1999

Wyschogrod, Michael, 'Faith in the Holocaust' *Judaism*, Summer, 1971

Yahil, Leni, *The Holcaust: The Fate of European Jews*, New York, 1990

Yerushalmi, Yosef Hayim, 'Response to Rosemary Radford Ruether' in Eva Fleischner (ed.), *Auschwitz: Beginning of a New Era?*, New York, KTAV, 1977

Zahn, Gordon C., 'Catholic Resistance? A Yes and a No' in Franklin H. Littell and Hubert G. Locke (eds), *The German Church Struggle and the Holocaust*, Detroit, Wayne State University Press, 1975

Acknowledgements

I would like to thank the following publishers for allowing me to quote copyright material from their publications:

New York University Press (Stephen T. Katz, *Post-Holocaust Dialogues*); State University of New York Press (Michael Oppenheim, *Speaking/Writing of God*; Steven Jacobs, *Rethinking Jewish Faith*); Cambridge University Press (Oliver Leaman, *Evil and Suffering in Jewish Philosophy*); Greenwood Press (Carol Rittner and John Roth (eds), *From the Unthinkable to the Unavoidable*; Stephen R. Haynes and John K. Roth (eds), *The Death of God Movement and the Holocaust*); Crossroad (Harry James Cargas, *Shadows of Auschwitz: A Christian Response to the Holocaust*; Arthur A. Cohen, *Tremendum: A Theological Interpretation of the Holocaust*); Jason Aronson (Yehezkel Fogel (ed.) *I Will Be Sanctified*); Hodder and Stoughton (Hugh Montefiore, *On Being a Jewish Christian*); Bibal Press (Katharine T. Hargrove (ed.), *Seeds of Reconciliation*); KTAV (Eva Fleischner (ed.), *Auschwitz: Beginning of a New Era?*; Eliezer Berkovits, *Faith after the Holocaust*; David Birnbaum, *God and Evil*; Bernard Maza, *With Fury Poured Out*; Irving Rosenbaum, *The Holocaust and Halakhah*; Pesach Schindler, *Hasidic Responses to the Holocaust in the Light of Hasidic Thought*); Fortress Press (Paul D. Opsahl and Marc H. Tanenbaum (eds), *Speaking of God Today*; Abraham J. Peck (ed.), *Jews and Christians after the Holocaust*); Palgrave (Norman Solomon, *Judaism and World Religion*); Orbis (Otto Maduro (ed.), *Judaism, Christianity and Liberation*); Schocken (Albert Friedlander (ed.), *Out of the Whirlwind*); Oxford University Press (Michael Goldberg, *Why Should Jews Survive?*; Paul Fiddes, *The Creative Suffering of God*; Yaffa Eliach, *Hasidic Tales of the Holocaust*); Paulist Press (Edward Flannery, *The Anguish of the Jews*; Michael McGarry, *Christology After Auschwitz*); University Press of America (G. Jan Colijn and Marcia Sachs Littell (eds), *Confronting the Holocaust*); Abingdon (Walter Harrelson and Randall Falk, *Jews and Christians*); SCM Press (Tony Bayfield and Marcus Braybrooke (eds), *Dialogue with a Difference*); T. and T. Clark (Elisabeth Schüssler Fiorenza and

David Tracy (eds), *The Holocaust as Interruption*); Wayne State University Press (Michael Morgan, *The Jewish Thought of Emil Fackenheim*); Princeton University Press (Zachary Braiterman, *(God) After Auschwitz*); Edwin Mellen Press (Franklin H. Littell and Hubert G . Locke (eds), *The German Church Struggle and the Holocaust*); Syracuse University Press (David Patterson, *Sun Turned to Darkness*).

I should note that I have attempted to contact publishers for permissions to use extracts from other sources; apologies are due if there are any omissions in the listing. The publishers would be interested to hear from any copyright holders not acknowledged above.

I would also like to thank Simon Baker, Anna Henderson and Genevieve Davey for their encouragement and help with this book.

Dan Cohn-Sherbok
December 2001

Index of Authors

Altizer, Thomas J.J., The Holocaust and God's Absence 350
Ariel, David, Divine Mystery 106
Baeck, Leo, The Holocaust and Faithfulness 80
Baum, Gregory, Reinterpreting Christianity 319
Bemporad, Jack, The Holocaust and Human Nature 199
Berkovits, Eliezer, The Holocaust and Human Free Will 153
Bethge, Eberhard, The Church Struggle 288
Birnbaum, David, The Holocaust and Freedom 162
Blumenthal, David, Theology and Protest 240
Bokser, Ben Zion, Christianity and the Nazis 286
Borowitz, Eugene, Covenant and Holocaust 186
Braiterman, Zachary, Jewish Thought after Auschwitz 254
Braybrooke, Marcus, Suffering Love 132
Brenner, Robert Reeve, Holocaust Survivors and Religious Belief 265
Brockway, Allan R., Religion and Faith 204
Buren, Paul van, Auschwitz and Moral Responsibility 195
Cargas, Harry James, The Holocaust and Christian Responsibility 64
Cohen, Arthur A., A Detached God 242
Cohen, Sha'ar Yashuv, The Holocaust and the Messiah 98
Cohn-Sherbok, Dan, The Holocaust and the Hereafter 183
Davies, Alan T., Overcoming Nihilism 192
Davis, Stephen T., The Holocaust and Christian Evangelicals 309
Donat, Alexander, The Holocaust and Human Perplexity 50
Dubois, Marcel Jacques, The Holocaust and the Cross 144
Eckardt, Alice, Theology of the Holocaust 335
Eckardt, Roy, The Holocaust and Christian Spirituality 338
Eimer, Colin, Jewish and Christian Suffering 135
Eliach, Yaffa, Faith among the Hasidim 73
Ellis, Marc, The Holocaust and Atrocity 212
Fackenheim, Emil, The Holocaust and the Commanding Voice 218
Falk, Randall, The Holocaust, Jews and Christians 364

Feld, Edward, The Holocaust and Spirituality — 260

Feuerlicht, Roberta Strauss, The Holocaust and Israel — 229

Fiddes, Paul, The Holocaust and Divine Suffering — 127

Fisher, Eugene, Catholics and Jews — 379

Flannery, Edward, The Holocaust and Christian Anti-Semitism — 294

Friedlander, Albert, The Holocaust and Jewish-Christian Dialogue — 376

Gillman, Neil, The Holocaust and Transcendence — 109

Goldberg, Michael, The Holocaust and Survival — 225

Greenberg, Irving, The Dialectic of Faith — 89

Hamilton, William, The Holocaust and Radical Theology — 352

Hargrove, Katharine T., Contemporary Holocaust Theology — 358

Harrelson, Walter, The Holocaust and the Modern World — 367

Harries, Richard, The Holocaust and the Kingdom of God — 178

Haynes, Stephen R., Post-Holocaust Christian Theology — 332

Heschel, Abraham Joshua, The Holocaust and Sin — 202

Heschel, Susannah, The Holocaust and German Theology — 280

Hirsch, David H., The Holocaust and Camp Songs — 47

Hochhuth, Rolf, The Holocaust and Christian Indifference — 276

Jacobs, Steven, The Holocaust and Jewish Faith — 256

Jakobovits, Immanuel, The Holocaust and Human Responsibility — 198

Jocz, Jakob, Judaism after the Holocaust — 61

Jonas, Hans, God after Auschwitz — 138

Kanfo, Hayyim, The Holocaust and Redemption — 101

Katz, Steven T., The Uniqueness of the Holocaust — 58

Keith, Graham, The Holocaust and Jewish Christianity — 170

Kessler, Edward, The Holocaust and Jewish-Christian Dialogue — 355

Knutsen, Mary, The Holocaust and Truth — 322

Kolitz, Zvi, Faith in the Ghetto — 78

Lange, Nicholas de, The Holocaust and Human Sin — 206

Leaman, Oliver, The Holocaust and Evil — 237

Levi, Primo, The Holocaust, the Doomed and the Saved — 232

Littell, Franklin H., The Holocaust and Church Struggle — 306

Longford, Frank, The Holocaust and Forgiveness — 372

Maccoby, Hyam, The Holocaust and Anti-Semitism — 303

McGarry, Michael, The Holocaust and Christology — 326

Marrus, Michael, The Holocaust and Catholicism — 300

Maybaum, Ignaz, The Holocaust and Modernity — 96

Maza, Bernard, The Holocaust and the Torah — 93

Metz, Johann Baptist, Jews and Christians after the Holocaust — 369

Montefiore, Hugh, The Holocaust and the Cross — 173

Moore, James F., Christianity after Auschwitz   344
Nadav, Nissim, The Holocaust and Jewish Heroism   83
Neher, André, The Holocaust and Human Free Will   160
Neusner, Jacob, The Holocaust and Redemption   234
Oppenheim, Michael, The Holocaust and Religious Language   55
Patterson, David, The Holocaust and Recovery   117
Pawlikowski, John, The Holocaust and Christology   316
Pollefyt, Didier, The Holocaust and Evil   166
Raphael, Melissa, The Holocaust and Jewish Feminism   245
Rausch, David A., The Holocaust and the Church   273
Rosenbaum, Irving, The Holocaust and Law   112
Roth, John, The Holocaust and Religious Perplexity   67
Roth, Yosef, The Holocaust and Providence   103
Rubenstein, Richard, The Death of God   41
Rubinoff, Lionel, The Holocaust and God's Presence   221
Ruether, Rosemary Radford, Reinterpreting Christology   313
Ryan, Michael D., The Theology of Adolf Hitler   282
Sacks, Jonathan, Evil, Free Will and Jewish History   157
Santa Ana, Julio de, The Holocaust and Liberation   209
Schindler, Pesach, Hasidim and the Holocaust   75
Schulweis, Harold, The Holocaust and Evil   251
Schwartz, Dror, The Holocaust and Sanctification of Life   86
Schweid, Eliezer, The Holocaust and Jewish Thought   263
Shapira, Kalonymus Kalman, The Holocaust and Divine Suffering   150
Shapiro, Susan, The Holocaust and Negation   248
Sherman, Franklin, Theodicy and Suffering   140
Sherwin, Byron, Jewish Survival and the Holocaust   223
Siegel, Seymour, The Holocaust and Messianism   180
Siegele-Wenschkewitz, Leonore, The Holocaust and Christian
    Anti-Judaism   291
Simon, Ulrich, The Holocaust and Sacrifice   120
Sölle, Dorothee, Divine Pain   129
Solomon, Norman, The Holocaust and the Jewish Tradition   115
Stern, David, The Holocaust and Evangelism   176
Tillich, Paul, Jewish History and the Holocaust   329
Tracy, David, Theology of Suspicion   147
Weiss, David, Holocaust and Covenant   189
Weltsch, Robert, Zionism and Jewish Survival   216
Wiesel, Elie, The Holocaust and Religious Protest   43
Williamson, Clark, Christian Theology and the Shoah   341

Wine, Sherwin, The Rejection of God   52
Wollaston, Isabel, Christian Theology and the Holocaust   362
Yerushalmi, Yosef Hayim, Christianity and Nazi Anti-Semitism   347
Zahn, Gordon C., Catholic Resistance   297

General Index

Authors' Readings appearing in this book are listed separately in the **Index of Authors** on page 401.

Abraham 66, 145, 164
absence of God 2, 3, 8, 41, 47, 61, 63, 153, 187, 238–239, 261, 359
adversus Judaeos 336, 342 (*see also* anti-Judaism)
afterlife 12, 18, 183–185, 260, 263, 266–267, 383
Akiva, rabbi 224
Altizer, Thomas J.J. 23, 153–154
American Jewry 15, 16, 223–225, 227, 230–231, 236, 359
Amery, Jean 372
Anielewicz, Mordecai 33
anti-Jewish decrees 27, 85
anti-Jewish teaching *see* anti-Judaism
anti-Judaism 20, 23, 25, 66, 133, 147, 148, 173, 281–182, 291–296, 313–315, 324, 334, 335, 336, 341–343, 346, 362, 363, 377, 379–380
anti-Semitism 13, 15, 19, 20, 23, 26, 147, 170–173, 176, 194, 209, 217, 227, 258, 281, 291, 292, 293, 294–296, 301, 305, 311, 313, 325, 338–340, 347–349, 355, 358, 363, 365, 366, 379
anti-Semitism, Christian 3, 20, 23, 148, 170–171, 194, 294, 295, 310, 312, 324, 338, 339, 348, 349, 356 (*see also* anti-Judaism)
anti-Zionism 100, 104, 229–231, 334
apocalyptic 24, 324, 350
Arabs 181, 231, 357, 368
Ariel, David 7
Armenians 367
atonement 98, 121, 375
Augustine 193
Auschwitz, the camp 13, 28, 29, 45, 67, 115, 141, 211, 307, 362, 381
Austria 26

Ba'al Shem Tov, Israel 76, 202
Baeck, Leo 4–5, 331
Barmen Synod 274, 288, 289, 333
Barth, Karl 204, 274, 290, 306, 332, 334
Baum, Gregory 22, 66
Belzec 28, 30
Bemporad, Jack 13, 14
Bérard, Leon 300
Bergen-Belsen 115, 141, 166
Berkovits, Eliezer 1, 10, 59, 61, 104, 158, 192, 194, 254–255, 257, 265, 327, 383
Berlin 51, 301
Bernard of Clairvaux, St 303
Bethge, Eberhard 20
Bible 53, 66, 97, 111, 113, 116, 120, 134, 281, 292, 313, 341, 375, 382

Birkenau 2, 28, 35, 36, 45, 47–49, 69, 381
Birnbaum, David 11
Bishop, Claire Huchet 287
blessing(s) 73, 93
Blumenthal, David 16, 384
Bluzhov, rabbi 74
Bokser, Ben Zion 19
Bolshevik revolution 26
Bonhoeffer, Dietrich 131, 149, 196, 204, 274, 290, 307, 365
Borowitz, Eugene 12, 316, 317, 359
Bosnia 214
Braiterman, Zachary 17
Brandeis, Louis 230
Braybrooke, Marcus 8
Bremen Bible School of the Church of the Future 293
Brenner, Robert Reeve 18
Brethren Councils 289, 290
Brockway, Allan R. 14
Brodsky, Leibele 93–94
Buber, Martin 42, 55, 144, 219, 220, 331
Buna 45
Buren, Paul van 13, 22, 332, 333, 334, 335, 345
Burzio, Giuseppe 302
bystanders 108

Cain, the mark of 202
camp songs 47–49
Cargas, Harry James 3, 132
Carmelite convent 304, 381–382
Cassulo, Andreia 302
Catholic Church see Roman Catholic Church
Chaim, Reb 93–94
Chelmno 28
children 30, 31, 35, 37, 51, 88, 90, 94, 107, 120, 132, 134, 141, 158, 192, 240, 256, 275, 343
chosen people 9, 10, 13, 61, 99, 174, 181, 184, 185, 387
Christ 8, 9, 11, 12, 14, 20, 22, 66, 120–122, 127–129, 145–147, 177, 179, 207, 286, 304, 314, 327, 343, 362, 380 (see also Christology)
Christian faith 11–12
Christian responsibility 18–21
Christian teaching 12, 21, 25, 295, 304, 305
Christology 21, 207, 282, 305, 313–319, 321, 326–329, 346, 362, 363 (see also logos-christology)
Chrysostom, John 147, 362
churban 96, 208, 209, 378
cleaving to God (devekut) 77
Cobb, John 327
Code of Theodosius 314
Cohen, Arthur A. 1, 17, 55, 56, 257, 316, 345, 378, 383, 384
Cohen, Herman 266
Cohen, Sha'ar Yashuv 6
Cohn-Sherbok, Dan 12
collaboration 20
commandment, 614th 218–220, 222, 356
commandments 7, 13, 15, 79, 88, 99, 104, 112, 114, 117, 259
commemoration 25
Communism 26
Concordat 297, 298, 299
Confessing Church 20, 21, 274, 289, 290, 291–293, 294, 306
Constantine, emperor 362
conversion 62, 133, 177, 331, 336
conversionary activity 23, 319 (see also evangelism, mission)
Conway, John 290
covenant 8, 12–13, 56, 82, 90, 118, 129, 135, 162, 165, 186–191, 215, 225, 259, 326, 341, 342, 345
Cracow 47

Cracow ghetto 28, 32
creation 10, 21, 23, 98, 138, 139, 180, 185, 196, 197, 317
Cross, the 8, 9, 13, 121, 128–129, 135, 136, 143, 144–147, 170, 179, 192–194, 304
crucifixion 21, 64, 134, 138, 141, 184, 304

Dachau 36, 381
Dahlem Synod 288, 289
Davies, Alan T. 13
Davis, Stephen T. 21
Day of Atonement 4, 34, 36, 46, 54, 235
death camps 28–37
death of God 2, 41–43, 107, 153, 350, 359
deicide 133, 294, 341
de-Judaising 20, 292, 293
devil see satan
dialogue 22, 25, 210, 320, 349, 355, 369, 371–372 (see also Jewish-Christian dialogue)
diaspora 14, 96, 99, 100, 101, 102, 196, 226
divine providence see providence
Donat, Alexander 2
double covenant theology 345
Dubois, Marcel Jacques 9

Easter 89
Eastern Europe 13, 26, 85, 94, 113
Eckardt, Alice 23
Eckardt, Roy 23, 346, 347
education 83, 141, 320, 356, 363
Efroymson, David 342
Eichmann, Adolf 89, 213
Eimer, Colin 9
election 326, 334, 341 (see also chosen people)
Eliach, Yaffa 4
Ellis, Marc 1, 4, 210, 383
Enlightenment 83, 260, 318

eschatology 22, 102, 111, 120, 147, 214–215, 308, 321, 384
eternal life 4, 43, 184 (see also afterlife)
ethical life 15, 139–140, 339
ethics 70, 282, 342, 369
European Jewry 6, 16, 27, 41, 65, 234, 287, 299, 307, 359
Evangelical Christians 21, 273–274, 286, 309–312
Evangelical Church 273, 286, 291, 292
evangelism 176–177, 310, 320 (see also conversion, mission)
Everett, Robert A. 339
evil 7, 8, 9, 10, 12, 18, 22, 60, 63, 90, 95, 108, 109, 110, 116, 134, 140, 144, 158, 163, 178, 187–188, 192–215, 220, 221, 251–253, 261–263, 304, 316–318, 324, 336, 337, 367, 374, 378, 384
exegesis 314, 342, 353
exile 6, 76, 86, 95, 103, 104, 246, 361
existentialism 42, 59, 60
exodus 89, 157, 193, 382
Ezekiel 95

Fackenheim, Emil 1, 12, 15, 55, 59, 158, 180, 221, 222, 254–255, 257, 304, 316, 338, 356, 358, 359, 360, 383
faith 4, 5, 7, 9, 14, 36, 73–92, 105, 142, 144, 155–156, 183, 194, 204–206, 225, 317, 341, 343
Faith Movement of German Christians 273
faithfulness 80–82
Falk, Randall 24
Feld, Edward 18
feminist theologians 17, 133, 281, 282
feminist theology 17, 131,

245–248, 282
Feuerlicht, Roberta Strauss 16
Fiddes, Paul 8
Fiorenza, Elisabeth Schüssler 363
Fisher, Eugene 25
Flannery, Edward 20
Fleischner, Eva 327, 379
forgiveness 25, 177, 208, 269, 359,
    363, 373–375
Frank, Walter 292
Frankfurter, Felix 230
Frauenknecht, H. 286
freewill 10–11, 17, 18, 22, 82, 104,
    105, 109, 111, 153–169, 317
Friedlander, Albert 22, 25, 329,
    373, 374–375
Fry, Helen P. 199, 357
fulfilment theology 172, 315, 342
future, the 14, 15, 219, 383–388

Gaon, Saadya 224
genocide 11, 23, 58, 70, 166, 173,
    199, 211, 310, 311, 348, 352,
    353, 358, 365, 378, 379
Gentiles 66, 96, 341, 345
German Church 19, 20, 288–291,
    333
German Evangelical Church
    Confederation 273
German Jewry 15, 20, 62
ghetto(s) 78, 87, 88, 156 (see also
    Warsaw ghetto, Lodz ghetto)
Gillman, Neil 7
gnosticism 328, 351
Goldberg, Michael 15
Goldhagen, Daniel 352
Great Depression 26, 27
Greenberg, Irving 5, 13, 56, 194,
    257, 316, 317, 343, 344
guilt 24, 107, 230, 312, 349, 355,
    362–364
Gurion, Ben 356
gypsies 91, 166, 244, 365

Halakah 7, 112–115, 164, 196, 197
Hamilton, William 24
Hargrove, Katharine T. 24
Harrelson, Walter 25
Harries, Richard 12
Hasidic tales 73–78
Hasidim 4, 73–78, 85, 107, 159,
    163
Haynes, Stephen R. 22
heaven 74, 228, 266
Hebrew Christians 274
hell 2, 29, 47, 49, 51
heroism 84–86, 108, 330–331, 359
Herzl, Theodor 216, 217
Heschel, Abraham Joshua 14, 55,
    111, 131
Heschel, Susannah 19
Hick, John 141
hidden face of God 18, 95,
    99–101, 104–105, 107, 136,
    153–154
High Holy Days 2
Hilberg, Paul 68, 295
Himmler, Heinrich 27
Hindenberg, Paul von 26
Hiroshima 160
Hirsch, David H. 2
history 8, 13, 66, 82, 90, 95,
    97–98, 105, 128, 157–159, 180,
    193, 196, 227, 244–245, 249,
    329–331, 337, 351, 359, 360,
    370–371, 384
Hitler, Adolf 5, 6, 15, 19, 20, 21,
    26–28, 41, 87, 96, 97, 98, 132,
    163, 167, 176, 181, 196, 205,
    218, 220, 275, 282–285, 286,
    295, 298, 303, 304, 307, 330,
    333, 355, 356, 360, 361,
    364–366, 368
Hochhuth, Rolf 19, 287, 301, 365
Holocaust, historical background
    26–37
Holocaust, retribution for sin 76,
    83, 93–93, 107, 108, 109

Holocaust, uniqueness of 104–105, 109, 112, 158–160, 207, 213, 238–239, 243–251, 258, 263, 264

Holocaust Day 3, 56, 110, 159, 226, 356, 377

humanism 52–54, 62, 214

humanity 3, 14, 15, 16

Hutner, Isaac, rabbi 100

identity 172, 333

Imago Dei (image of God) 62, 92, 108

Incarnation 9, 21, 138, 154, 178, 313

Institute for the Study of Jewish Influence on German Religious Life, The 19, 280, 293

Isaac, Jules 287, 355

Islam 357, 368, 386–387

Israel, the land 12, 14, 16, 24, 25, 55, 56, 76, 95, 99, 105, 181, 357 (*see also* State of Israel)

Israel, the people 4, 14, 41, 66, 76, 81, 85, 86, 146–147, 156, 172, 186–188, 311, 332, 334, 382

Israel Independence Day 3, 56

Israeli Jewry 15, 223–225, 356

Italy 198

Jacobs, Steven 18, 385

Jakobovits, Immanuel 13, 265, 378

Janowska 33, 74

Jehovah Witnesses 302

Jerusalem 90, 96, 97, 141, 181, 235

Jerusalem Day 3, 56

Jesus 9, 11, 19, 64, 65, 121, 128, 133, 134, 146–147, 170–173, 174–175, 180, 197, 205, 207–209, 274, 281, 282, 306, 310, 321, 341, 369

Jewish-Christian dialogue 24–25, 134, 135, 323, 327, 328, 355–382

Jewish-Christian relations 24, 25, 292, 304, 334, 349, 355, 356, 370–372

Jewish Fighting Organisation 32

Job 5, 7, 41, 62, 91, 97, 106, 111, 113, 142, 145, 155–156, 266, 360

Jocz, Jakob 3

John XXIII, Pope 148, 302

John's Gospel 171

Jonas, Hans 9, 131, 337

judgement 98, 142, 143, 184

justice 75, 113, 300, 325, 330, 376

Justinian Code 314

kabbalah 76, 77, 248

kaddish 16, 45, 111, 227, 228

Kahler, Martin 285

Kaluszyn 31

Kanfo, Hayyim 6

Katz, Steven T. 3

Keith, Graham 11

Kessler, Edward 24

kiddush ha-Hayyim see sanctification of life

kiddush ha-Shem see martyrdom *and* sanctification of the divine name

Kingdom of God 2, 12, 13, 49, 95, 179–180, 219, 334, 365

Knutsen, Mary 22

Kol Nidre 35, 36, 80, 93

Kolitz, Zvi 4

Kook, rabbi 99, 103

Korzec 31

Kovno ghetto 115

Kristallnacht 27, 290, 299, 365

Kruszyna 32

Kulisiewicz, Aleksander 2, 47–49

Lambeth Conference (1988) 179–180

Lange, Nicholas de 14

language, religious 56–57,

249–251, 347
Latin America 211–212
Leaman, Oliver 16
Levi, Primo 16
Levin, Bernard 304
Levinas, Emmanuel 57, 117–119
liberation theology 131, 141,
    209–212
Littell, Franklin H. 21, 65, 193,
    310, 346, 347, 362, 363
liturgy 56, 110, 148, 253, 369,
    377, 378 (*see also* worship)
Lodz ghetto 35, 115, 338
logos-christology 22, 327–329
Longford, Frank 25
Lublin 32
Lukow 31
Luther 142
Lutheran Church 141, 142, 201

Maccoby, Hyam 20
McGarry, Michael 22
Maimonides 162, 267
Majdanek 28
Malthausen 115
Marcinkance 32
Marquardt, F.W. 282
Marrus, Michael 20
Martyr, Justin 362
martyrdom 15, 51, 77, 117, 143,
    185
martyrs 5, 8, 98, 155, 183, 194,
    203, 224, 234, 260
Masada 87, 89, 224
Maybaum, Ignaz 1, 6, 59, 208, 383
Maza, Bernard 1, 6, 257, 383
Mein Kampf 19, 283
memory 15, 17, 118, 221, 381
Messiah 4, 6, 12, 22, 65, 76,
    98–101, 104, 105, 137, 141,
    150–151, 171, 174, 176, 177,
    196, 267, 286, 304, 310, 311,
    314, 328, 349, 363

messianic expectations 12, 76–77,
    97, 98–101, 163, 180–183, 184,
    266, 314, 321, 346
Messianic Jews 11, 171–173,
    176–177
Metz, Johann Baptist 25, 322, 324,
    341, 343, 363, 377
Middle Ages 96, 286, 296, 303,
    329, 348
midrash 55, 57, 101, 113, 135, 221,
    234
Mishnah 234, 369
mission 17, 25, 104, 171, 319,
    320–362, 371 (*see also*
    evangelism)
mitzvot see commandments
modernity 57, 96–98
Moltmann, Jürgen 22, 332, 334,
    335
Montefiore, Claude 355
Montefiore, Hugh 11
Moore, James F. 23
morality 13
Moses 114, 190, 195, 203
Mueller, Ludwig 273
Mulack, Christa 281
Munich 26, 27
music 47–49, 166, 175
Muslims *see* Islam
mysticism 17, 42, 73, 75, 179,
    247–248

Nachman, rabbi 74, 77, 95
Nadav, Nissim 5
National Conference of Catholic
    Bishops 65
National Council of Churches 65
National Socialism 21, 26, 216,
    229, 273, 285, 297, 306, 330
Neher, André 11, 118
Neusner, Jacob 16, 358, 359, 361
New Testament 133, 147, 148,
    171, 176, 305, 327, 336, 363,
    380, 382

New Testament, scholarship 19, 281
Nicaea, Council of 193
Niemöller, Martin 274, 365
Nietzsche 42, 318, 353
Nissenbaum, Yitzhak 5, 87
Nostra Aetate 356, 369
Nuremberg Laws 274
Nuremberg trials 30, 166, 367

Old Testament 314, 342
Olson, Bernard 287
omnipotence 8, 9, 10, 41, 61, 129–135, 164, 174, 268, 321, 388
omniscience 321
Oppenheim, Michael 2
original sin 200, 337, 374
Orthodox Serbs 302
Oswiecim camp 338
Otto, Rudolf 378

Pacelli, Eugenio (Cardinal) 275, 301
Palestine 15, 76, 230
Palestinians 14, 210, 213–215
Papeleux, Léon 301
Paris 29
Parkes, James 339, 355
Passover 54, 110, 121–122, 360
patriarchy 17, 245–248, 281–282, 384
Patterson, David 8
Paul, apostle 311, 350
Pavelic, Ante 302
Pawlikowski, John 21, 339
persecution, of Jews 7, 19
Pharisees 66, 133
philosophy 22, 55, 68, 69–70, 83, 130, 160, 175, 224, 238, 330
piety 4, 9
Pitzkova, Eva 88
plays 276–280, 287
poems 88

Poland 27, 47, 236, 301, 302
Polish bishops 302
Polish, Daniel 381
Polkehn, Klaus 229
Pollefyt, Didier 11
Pope 20, 279, 280, 301 (see also Pius XII, John XXIII)
prayer 68, 74, 80–81, 114, 134, 161, 164, 217, 228, 259, 377–378
prophecy 12, 83, 120
prophets 14, 94, 97, 288, 330, 360
Protestant Federation of France 286
Protestants 273, 275, 281, 282, 288–291, 333–334, 356
providence 5, 6, 8, 17, 22, 56, 66, 83, 93–105, 155, 173, 193, 240, 351, 360, 384, 388
Puis XII, Pope 275, 287, 300, 301, 302, 365
punishment 6, 78, 83, 91, 94, 95, 98, 100, 107, 109, 111

Rahner, Karl 22, 66, 327
Rakover, Yassel 4
Raphael, Melissa 17, 384
Rausch, David A. 19
reconciliation 377
redemption 6, 12, 13, 16, 76–77, 90, 95, 98–103, 120, 151, 163, 171, 181, 182, 184, 197, 225, 228, 230, 234–236, 262, 321
Reformation, the 274, 289, 305, 315
Reich Institute for the History of the New Germany 292
religious practice 18
remembrance 15, 25, 56
repentance 62, 97, 99, 375, 376, 377
resistance 15, 20, 31–33, 51, 52, 288–291, 297–299, 307, 333
responsibility, Christian 18–21,

64–67, 273–312, 315
restitution 177
restoration 76, 103, 247
resurrection (of Jesus) 13, 64, 121, 128, 135, 136, 179, 192–193, 333
revelation 89, 101, 117, 151, 194, 196, 197, 221, 222, 330, 334, 345, 351
Righteous, the 99–100, 184, 185, 366
Roman Catholic Church 10, 19, 24, 205, 275, 365, 369, 380–382
Roncalli, Angelo 302
Rosenbaum, Irving 7
Rosenzweig, Franz 57, 331
Roth, John 3
Roth, Yosef 6
Rotta, Angelo 302
Rubenstein, Richard 1, 2, 55, 56, 59, 61, 62, 69, 70, 107, 108, 144, 239, 255, 257, 285, 316, 351, 358, 359, 360, 383
Rubinoff, Lionel 15
Rudin, A. James 381
Ruether, Rosemary Radford 21, 23, 66, 341, 346, 347, 348, 349, 356, 362, 363, 379, 380
Russia 27, 198
Russian Jewry 28, 166
Ryan, Michael D. 19

Sachsenhausen 47
Sacks, Jonathan 10, 179, 356
sacrament 9
sacrifice 8, 97, 98, 99, 103, 105, 120–122, 360
sacrificial devotion (*mesirat nefesh*) 77
salvation 351, 370, 371, 383
sanctification of God's name (*kiddush ha-Shem*) 4, 52, 77, 79, 84, 86, 88, 159, 183–185, 260
sanctification of life 5, 77, 84,

86–88
Santa Ana, Julio de 14
Satan 11, 130, 170, 339–340
Schindler, Pesach 4
Schulweis, Harold 17, 385
Schwartz, Dror 5
Schweid, Eliezer 18
science 52, 53, 199, 200
Scriptures, Christian 66, 149, 170
Scriptures, Jewish 149, 190, 328, 342
Second Coming (of Christ) 303
Second Vatican Council (*see* Vatican II)
Secretariat for Catholic–Jewish Relations 65
secularism 56, 57
Shahak, Professor Israel 229
Shamir, Yitzhak 229
Shapira, Kalonymus Kalman 10
Shapiro, Susan 17
Shekhinah 76, 135, 151, 190, 246, 247, 386
Sherman, Franklin 9
Sherwin, Bryon 15
Shoah 3, 13, 16, 17, 24, 25, 116, 117, 132, 133, 134, 136, 137, 173–175, 178–179, 207, 240, 241, 329, 330, 336, 337, 338, 341, 343, 355, 356, 357, 378, 382
Siegel, Seymour 12
Siegele-Wenschkewitz, Leonore 20
silence, of the Church 19, 176, 332, 355, 360, 366
silence, of God 2, 43–46, 106, 107, 155, 160, 277–278
Simon, Ulrich 8
sin 6, 14, 25, 62, 76, 78, 94, 100, 107, 121, 150, 182, 184, 189, 200, 206, 215, 223, 287, 337, 339, 341
Sobibor 28

Sölle, Dorothee 8, 345
Solomon, Norman 7
Spira, Israel 74
State of Israel 85, 90, 91, 92, 100,
    104, 159, 181, 196, 209–215,
    222, 224, 225, 333, 334, 346,
    357, 359, 363, 368
Stein, Edith 381–382
Stern, David 11
Stuttgart Declaration 333
suffering God 8–10, 76, 127–152,
    337, 384
suffering, human 2, 8, 11, 22, 23,
    91, 106, 107, 116, 132, 134,
    246–248, 324
suffering, Jewish 2, 5, 7, 10, 75,
    76, 91, 100, 134, 141, 185, 207,
    330, 337, 360, 370
Suffering Servant 97, 120, 147,
    174, 207, 337
supercessionism 133, 175, 293,
    341, 343, 362
survival, Jewish 5, 15–16, 73, 87,
    88, 90, 97, 158–159, 213,
    216–236, 258, 359
survivors 18, 50, 87, 90, 184, 189,
    213, 231, 233–234, 256, 266,
    267, 268, 358, 359, 377
survivors, testimony of 28–31, 84,
    127, 156, 183–184, 256, 367,
    368

Talmud 53, 113, 134, 151, 183,
    281
teaching of contempt 23, 147, 148,
    287, 336, 338, 347, 355, 356
Teichthal, rabbi 76
Temple 96, 135, 189, 208, 219,
    235
teshuvah see repentance
testimonies see survivors
theodicy 5, 7, 18, 61, 104,
    109–111, 116, 130–143,
    178–180, 239, 251–253, 256,

    260–265, 370, 378, 385
Theresienstadt 88, 307
Third Reich 4, 14, 19, 20, 21, 51,
    80, 165, 281, 292, 293, 299
Tillich, Paul 22, 365
Torah 16, 57, 83, 84, 85, 88,
    93–94, 99, 104, 112, 152,
    187–188, 195, 210, 224, 225,
    227, 234, 235–236, 267, 337
Tracy, David 10, 327, 345, 346,
    347
Tradition 15, 16
Treblinka 28, 30, 32, 33, 90, 211,
    362

unbelief, Jewish 11
United Jewish Appeal 235

Vatican 20, 181, 275, 300–302,
    315, 356
Vatican II 141, 148, 366, 369
Vienna 26

Waldheim, Kurt 381
Warsaw ghetto 2, 4, 32, 33, 50,
    78, 115
Weimar, assembly 26
Weiss, David 13
Weizsäcker, Ernst von 301
Weltsch, Robert 15
whirlwind 5, 91, 194, 378
Wiesel, Elie 1, 2, 55, 61, 62, 63,
    64–65, 67, 68, 107, 108, 118,
    127, 130, 131, 174, 194, 222,
    253, 254–255, 304, 316, 339,
    352, 359, 378, 383
Wiesenthal, Simon 119
Williamson, Clark 23
Wine, Sherwin 2
Wisliceny, Dieter 89
Wollaston, Isabel 24
women 17, 246–248, 281, 385
World Council of Churches 356
World Religions 386–388

World To Come 12, 183–185 (*see also* afterlife, eternal life)
World War I 26, 357, 365
worship 10, 18, 25, 79, 96, 134, 135, 226, 235, 342, 388
Wyschogrod, Michael 255, 316, 360, 361

Yad Vashem 62, 366, 367
yellow badge 194, 217
Yerushalmi, Yosef Hayim 23, 296, 363, 379, 380

Yom Ha-Atzmaut see Israel Independence Day
Yom Kippur see Day of Atonement
Yom Ha-Soah see Holocaust Day
Yom Yerushalayim see Jerusalem Day

zaddik 73
Zahn, Gordon C. 20
Zion 102, 103, 183
Zionism 12, 76, 94, 100, 107, 180–183, 216, 218, 224–225, 229–231, 334